The Essential Child

Oxford Series in Cognitive Development

SERIES EDITORS
Paul Bloom and Susan A. Gelman

The Essential Child
Susan A. Gelman

The Essential Child

Origins of Essentialism in Everyday Thought

Susan A. Gelman

OXFORD
UNIVERSITY PRESS
2003

OXFORD
UNIVERSITY PRESS

Oxford   New York
Auckland   Bangkok   Buenos Aires   Cape Town   Chennai
Dar es Salaam   Delhi   Hong Kong   Istanbul   Karachi   Kolkata
Kuala Lumpur   Madrid   Melbourne   Mexico City   Mumbai   Nairobi
São Paulo   Shanghai   Taipei   Tokyo   Toronto

Copyright © 2003 by Oxford University Press, Inc.

Published by Oxford University Press, Inc.
198 Madison Avenue, New York, New York 10016

www.oup.com

Oxford is a registered trademark of Oxford University Press

Library of Congress Cataloging-in-Publication Data
Gelman, Susan A.
The essential child : origins of essentialism in everyday thought/
Susan A. Gelman.
p. cm.—(Oxford series in cognitive development)
Includes bibliographical references and index.
ISBN 0-19-515406-1
1. Categorization (Psychology) in children. 2. Cognition in children.
3. Children—Language. I. Title. II. Series.
BF723.C27   G45   2003
155.4'1323—dc21   20022008635

9   8   7   6   5   4   3   2   1

Printed in the United States of America
on acid-free paper

For my parents, Jane and Robert Gelman

Acknowledgments

I have been working on the problem of essentialism, in one form or another, for the past twenty years. Over this time I have had the rare good fortune to collaborate with wonderful colleagues and students whose ideas have shaped my thinking in profound ways. Foremost among these is Ellen Markman, my Ph.D. adviser, who first sparked my interest in essentialism in a graduate seminar she taught while I was in my second year of graduate school. In the seminar we read widely about concepts and natural kinds, from Bruner to Kripke, from Macnamara to Quine. My term paper for this seminar was a research proposal to study children's natural kind concepts. Out of that grew our collaborative work on category-based induction, and ultimately this book. Ellen has been the best mentor and collaborator imaginable.

While at the University of Michigan, I have been especially grateful to Larry Hirshfeld, Marilyn Shatz, Twila Tardif, and Henry Wellman for their wisdom and insights. I am also indebted to all my collaborators on the research reported here, especially Woo-kyoung Ahn, Paul Bloom, Eve Clark, John Coley, Gil Diesendruck, Karen Ebeling, Jonathan Flukes, Gail Gottfried, Grant Gutheil, Erin Hartman, Gail Heyman, Anne Hickling, Michelle Hollander, Jen Jipson, Chuck Kalish, Melissa Koenig, Kathy Kremer, David Lizotte, Ellen Markman, Doug Medin, Melanie Nyhof, John Opfer, Tina Pappas, Lakshmi Raman, Karl Rosengren, Jon Star, and Marianne Taylor. Throughout the years I have been guided and encouraged by members of the University of Michigan Language Lab, who have given me outstanding critical advice on this research. Tom Rodriguez gave expert help in setting up the CHILDES database for the generics study reported in chapter 8.

For reading and commenting on an earlier draft of the ms., my thanks go to Paul Bloom, Gil Diesendruck, Andrew Gelman, Alison Gopnik, Gail Heyman, Larry Hirschfeld, Bruce Mannheim, Ellen Markman, Marjorie Taylor, and Henry Wellman. I am particularly grateful to Paul Bloom, whose enormously detailed and trenchant reviews made me rethink major portions of the book. All problems, gaps, and inconsistencies that remain are my own. Rita Astuti, Gillian Feeley-Harnik, Alan Gelman, Andrew Gelman, Toby Jayaratne, Chuck Kalish, Greg Murphy, Lou Moses, and Harriet Whitehead provided useful help in answering questions. I thank Paul Bloom for suggesting the main title of the book, and Nancy Gelman, Larry Hirschfeld, Laura Novick, Barbara Sarnecka, and Marjorie Taylor for helpful feedback on cover ideas.

My research has been sponsored by the National Institute of Child Health and Human Development, the National Science Foundation, the Spencer Foundation, and the Guggenheim Foundation. I gratefully acknowledge their support. In writing this book, I have drawn from other published work, including Ahn, Kalish, Gelman, Medin, Luhmann, Atran, Coley, and Shafto (2001); S. Gelman (1996); S. Gelman (2000); S. Gelman (in press); S. Gelman and Coley (1991); S. Gelman, Coley, and Gottfried (1994); S. Gelman, Coley, Rosengren, Hartman, and Pappas (1998); S. Gelman and Diesendruck (1999); S. Gelman and Heyman (1999); S. Gelman and Hirschfeld (1999); S. Gelman, Hollander, Star, and Heyman (2000); S. Gelman and Kalish (1993); S. Gelman and Koenig (in press); S. Gelman and Opfer (2002); S. Gelman and Tardif (1998); S. Gelman and Taylor (2000); and Morris, Taplin, and Gelman (2000).

This book could not have been written without the generous assistance of the children, parents, and teachers who have participated in my research studies over the years. I am particularly indebted to the University of Michigan Children's Center and the University of Michigan Center for Working Families for their enthusiastic participation.

I have received much encouragement, help, and editorial advice from Catharine Carlin and John Rauschenberg of Oxford University Press. They have been both graceful and patient in working with me on this project.

And most of all, I am indebted to Bruce and our own essential children: Stephanie, Adam, and Ben. Adam (now age nine) asked me to add a final anecdote to this book, which as far as he can tell is about funny things that children say. Here it is: when Adam was about two and a half years old and taking a bath, I said, "I'm going to get the shampoo" (reaching for the bottle of shampoo, which had a cap in the form of Winnie-the-Pooh's head). He replied, without missing a beat, "I want sham-Piglet" (pointing at the bottle of bath bubbles, which had a cap in the form of Piglet's head). This example says nothing about essentialism, but I include it nonetheless as a reminder that young children are ingenious and charming as they go about the serious business of figuring out their world.

Contents

PART III. IMPLICATIONS AND SPECULATIONS

The Essential Child

Chapter 1

Introduction

> [Essence is] the very being of anything, whereby it is what it is. And thus the real internal, but generally . . . unknown constitution of things, whereon their discoverable qualities depend, may be called their essence.
>
> John Locke, *An Essay Concerning Human Understanding*

I begin this book with a confession: I was a child essentialist.

When I was no more than four or five years old, I asked my mother how boys and girls were different. I already knew the obvious answers—different bodies, different clothes, different hairstyles, different roles (this was, after all, the prefeminist, early 1960s). What I was searching for was some explanation of all of these apparent differences. I am not sure exactly what answer I expected to hear, but the answer I did get from my very practical mother ("boys have penises, girls don't") struck me as entirely unsatisfying. "Is that all??" I remember asking with disbelief. It seemed to me that there had to be a more profound basis for sex differences than that.

My early intuitions about intelligence were similar. I was in elementary school, maybe third grade. My classmates and I were waiting to take a standardized IQ test. As we sat, with our number 2 pencils sharpened and ready, I was awed by the power of this test. As I understood it, the IQ score would reveal my intellectual capacity—immutable, fixed, and unchanging. It was hidden and nonobvious, accessible to our teachers, but not something I would ever be allowed to know. The number would not change—it would stay in our permanent records, but more important, it would tell us who we were, and who we could become.

Both of these examples illustrate essentialist assumptions about categories (gender and intelligence, respectively). The present book concerns essentialism in everyday thought. Roughly, essentialism is the view that categories have an underlying reality or true nature that one cannot observe directly but that gives an object its identity. In other words, according to essentialism, categories (such as "boy," "girl," or "intelligence") are real, in several senses: they are discovered (rather than invented), they are natural (rather than artificial), they predict other properties, and they point to natural discontinuities in the world. Essentialist accounts have been around, in one form or another, for thousands of years, extending back at least to Plato's cave allegory in *The Republic.* Numerous fields—biology, philosophy, linguistics, literary criticism, and psychology—stake claims about essentialism.

The question of whether children are essentialists is not to be taken lightly, because it runs directly against a powerful portrait of children's concepts as perceptually driven, concrete, and atheoretical. I will be making an argument that children's concepts are not merely perceptually based, concrete, or built up from specifics, but rather reflect folk theories and a powerful capacity to look beyond the obvious. To many readers, this viewpoint will sound familiar, as the zeitgeist in cognitive development for the past twenty-five years or so has been to acknowledge that children exhibit greater competence and conceptual sophistication than has been attributed to them in the past. As any student of developmental psychology knows, Jean Piaget's vastly influential stage theory posited qualitative shifts in cognitive capacity over the course of development (Piaget, 1970). On his view, children in the preoperational stage (from two years of age to about age six or seven years) are characterized more by what they lack intellectually than by what they have achieved. In contrast, critics of Piaget have been arguing, at least since the 1970s, that children have greater cognitive competence and potential than Piaget allowed (R. Gelman, 1978). This "early competence" view has received wide support since the 1970s and is amply supported by research topics as varied as numerical reasoning, theory of mind, language learning, and physical reasoning (among others; see Wellman and Gelman, 1998, for review). Even the popular press has taken note of the amazing capacities of babies and young children.

Nonetheless, the issue is far from resolved, for two reasons. First, even the most ardent early-competence theorist cannot deny that children's categories look truly aberrant on many tasks. Two-year-olds overextend familiar words to unrelated objects (e.g., calling the moon "a ball"; Clark, 1973). On experimental tasks, three- to five-year-olds extend novel words to items matching in shape rather than taxonomic kind (e.g., extending "zav" from a birthday cake to a top hat, rather than to a pie; Imai, Gentner, and Uchida, 1994; see Figure 1.1). Children three years of age fail to incorporate function when learning words for which adults find function crucial (L. Smith, Jones, and Landau, 1996). Preschool and even early-elementary-school children define ordinary words, such as "island," in terms of characteristic features (a place that is sunny, with palm trees) rather than defining features (a land mass surrounded by water; Keil, 1989). In brief, children seem captivated by surface appearances during their first few years of life.

Children's well-documented focus on object appearances, even on categorization tasks, means that children provide a strong test of psychological essentialism. Children below age six or seven are most often characterized as not looking beyond the surface of things. To the extent that children's categories can be characterized as essentialist, this is newsworthy. At the same time, such a finding would demand an explanation. I cannot simply conclude that children are more sophisticated than previously thought; I will also need to reconcile children's apparent sophistication with their many errorful ways.

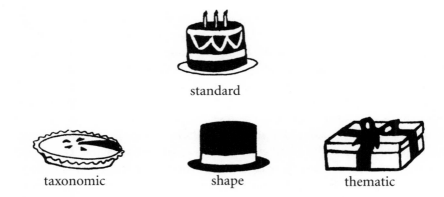

standard

taxonomic   shape   thematic

Figure 1.1.   Sample item set. *Source*: Imai et al. (1994). Reprinted with the permission of Elsevier Science.

A second reason for reexamining an early-competence view is the recent resurgence of interest in explanatory accounts that attribute less cognitive sophistication to the child (e.g., Cohen and Oakes, 1993; Rakison, 2000; L. Smith, Jones, and Landau, 1996). Even when young children's behavior seems mature, their competence is argued to be illusory, as children are relying on simple strategies for processing information. In the words of one group of researchers, children make use of "dumb attentional mechanisms" to learn words (L. Smith, Jones, and Landau, 1996). It is no accident that this proposal is characterized by such a pejorative phrase; the aim is to convey unambiguously that children are truly *un*sophisticated word learners. Instead, it is suggested, children rely on automatic, associative learning that operates independently of reflective thought. In contrast, one aim of the present book is to show how and why "dumb" learning mechanisms mischaracterize young children. (See especially chapter 9.)

ESSENTIALIST CONTROVERSIES

In any discussion of essentialism, controversies rage. Is essentialism in the world or in the mind? Is essentialism innate in the infant (Atran, 1998) or "a late and sophisticated achievement" (Fodor, 1998, p. 159)? Is essentialism a universal "habit of the mind" (Atran, 1998, p. 551) or limited to certain points in history (Fodor, 1998)? Do we essentialize all concepts (Carey, 1996) or most readily just biological species (Atran, 1998)? Does essentialism reflect the logic of nouns (Benveniste, 1971; Carey, 1996; Mayr, 1991), or is it independent of language? Debates about essentialism sit astride debates about the very nature of human cognition.

It is startling, and more than a little daunting, to recognize that all these competing claims have been argued in the literature—and argued with passion. As I step into these minefields, I will lay claim to a position that views essentialism from both a psychological perspective and a developmental (child) perspective. My colleagues and I, along with a growing number of other researchers in the fields of developmental and cognitive psychology, have examined essentialism as an empirical phenomenon, amenable to scientific study. Methods are diverse and converging: experimental studies of categorization, inductive inferences, and semantic interpretations; thought experiments with children and adults; and natural observation and analysis of ordinary language. The research participants are primarily middle-class, U.S., English-speaking children and adults, but we are beginning to see some much-needed cross-cultural and cross-linguistic investigations, too. This book is a progress report on the state of what we know about essentialism, in light of these results. It does not claim to be—and cannot be—the final word. For example, I cannot systematically address the metaphysical question of whether essentialism exists in the world, though I will briefly consider a few cases in order to see how essentialism misleads and assists us. But there are, I suggest, interesting and surprising findings to be discussed at this point.

I contend that essentialism is a pervasive, persistent reasoning bias that affects human categorization in profound ways. It is deeply ingrained in our conceptual systems, emerging at a very young age across highly varied cultural contexts. Our essentializing bias is not directly taught, nor does it simply reduce to a direct reading of cues that are "out there" in the world. Most decidedly, it is neither a late achievement nor a sophisticated one. The question of which categories we essentialize is a tricky one. In a nutshell, I argue that essentialism is the result of several converging psychological capacities, each of which is domain-general yet invoked differently in different domains. Collectively, when these capacities come together to form essentialism, they apply most powerfully to natural kinds[1] (including animal and plant species, and natural substances such as water or gold) and social kinds (including race and gender), but not artifacts made by people (such as tables and socks). This proposal rejects two alternative positions: the suggestion that we essentialize all concepts, and the suggestion that we essentialize only biological species. A final issue concerns how essentialized concepts are related to language. I suggest that essentialism does not require language, but language is one important cue children use when trying to figure out when and what to essentialize.

These proposals may seem simple enough, yet they contradict several fundamental assumptions about concepts, children, and language: that concepts are all structured alike, that children are limited to considering superficial perceptual features of the world, and that words simply reflect preexisting concepts. My primary purpose in writing this book is to trace the developmental roots of essentialism. In the course of doing so, I will also explore the broader lessons that these results imply concerning human concepts, children's thinking, and ways in which language influences thought.

In this chapter, I first go through some preliminaries: what is essentialism, and why is it important? I then lay preliminary groundwork for the three themes that weave through the book:

- As proposed earlier, essentialism is an early cognitive bias. It is not, as some have maintained, an historical accident. Essentialism has its source in the cognitive requirements of categorization in certain domains— particularly as they affect the young learner.
- Children's concepts are embedded in folk theories. They are not learned by means of simple associative learning strategies. They do not proceed from perceptual to conceptual, but incorporate both levels at once. More generally, developmental dichotomies (e.g., concrete to abstract, simple to complex, surface to deep, etc.) mischaracterize the nature of cognitive development.
- Although essentialism is foremost a cognitive bias, it is also supported and shaped by language. In particular, I will argue that two forms of language (count nouns and generic noun phrases) promote essentialist reasoning.

At the end of the chapter, I sketch out the structure and organization of the book.

PRELIMINARIES REGARDING ESSENTIALISM

What Is Essentialism?

Defining "essence" or "essentialism" is not an easy task, as the terms are used broadly by different scholars to mean different things. Nonetheless, I start with a brief intuitive characterization of what I take essentialism to mean. To begin, I am concerned with people's beliefs about the world (not metaphysical claims about the world per se). There are three components to psychological essentialism as an intuitive folk belief:

- First, people believe that certain categories are natural kinds: they are real (not fabricated by humans), discovered (not invented), and rooted in nature. (For this and each of the other components, the claims about what people "believe" refer to nonconscious, intuitive beliefs or assumptions, not metacognitive or explicit beliefs.)
- Second, people believe that there is some unobservable property (be it a part, substance, or ineffable quality)—the essence—that causes things to be the way they are. The essence gives rise to the observable similarities shared by members of a category.
- Third, people believe that everyday words reflect this real-world structure. Words such as *dog, tree, gold*, or *schizophrenic* are often believed to map directly onto the natural kinds of the world. Not all words do so, but at least words referring to basic-level categories of natural kinds, as well as many words for social categories.[2]

To summarize, roughly speaking, what I mean by an "essence" is an underlying reality or true nature, shared by members of a category, that one cannot observe directly but that gives an object its identity and is responsible for other similarities that category members share (James, 1890/1983; Locke, 1671/1959; Medin, 1989). This is not a metaphysical claim about the structure of the world but rather a psychological claim about people's implicit assumptions. In the domain of biology, an essence would be whatever quality is thought to remain unchanging as an organism grows, reproduces, and undergoes morphological transformations (baby to adult human; caterpillar to butterfly). In the domain of chemistry, an essence would be whatever quality is thought to remain unchanging as a substance changes shape, size, or state (e.g., from solid to liquid to gas).

However, what I mean by essence is not what all scholars mean by essence. Even among those who would agree with my characterization, there are subtle distinctions that must be made explicit. Lawrence Hirschfeld and I proposed that three factors jointly serve to map out the various types of essentialism (S. Gelman and Hirschfeld, 1999).

1. Where is essence located? Is it in the world (*metaphysical essentialism*) or in human representations (*representational essentialism*)?
2. What is the ontological type of an essence? Is it *sortal* (serving to define categories), *causal* (having consequences for category structure), or *ideal* (having no real-world instantiation)?
3. What degree of specificity is entailed? Are essences *specific* (their particulars known and identified) or *placeholder* (their particulars unknown and perhaps unknowable)?

I discuss these factors below, then clarify which sense of "essence" is assumed in this book.

METAPHYSICAL VERSUS REPRESENTATIONAL (PSYCHOLOGICAL, NOMINAL, CULTURAL).   I distinguish between essentialism as a philosophical position and essentialism as a folk belief. The former addresses the nature of objective reality and is concerned with whether or not essences are located in the world (a metaphysical question); the latter addresses the nature of people's representations of the world and so largely sidesteps the metaphysical question. Representational essentialism could be manifested in ordinary belief systems (psychological essentialism), language (nominal essentialism), and/or cultural practices (cultural essentialism).

SORTAL, CAUSAL, AND IDEAL ESSENCES.   The sortal essence is the set of defining characteristics that all and only members of a category share. This notion of essence is captured in Aristotle's (1924) distinction between essential and accidental properties (see also Keil's (1989) defining versus characteristic properties): the essential properties constitute the essence. For example, on this view the essence of a grandmother would be the property of being the mother of a person's parent (rather than the accidental or characteristic properties of wearing glasses and having gray hair; see Landau, 1982). In effect, this characterization is a restatement of the classical view of concepts: meaning (or identity) is supplied by a set of necessary and sufficient features that determine whether an entity does or does not belong in a category (E. Smith and Medin, 1981). Specific essentialist accounts, then, provide arguments concerning which sorts of features are essential. The viability of this account has been called into question by more-recent models of concepts that stress the importance of probabilistic features, exemplars, and theories in concepts (e.g., Murphy and Medin, 1985; Nosofsky, Kruschke, and McKinley, 1992; Rosch and Mervis, 1975).

In contrast, the causal essence is the substance, power, quality, process, relationship, or entity that causes other category-typical properties to emerge and be sustained, and that confers identity. The quote from Locke that began the chapter depicts this view. The causal essence is used to explain the observable properties of category members. Whereas the sortal essence could apply to any entity (pencils, wastebaskets, and tigers are all categories for which certain properties may be "essential," i.e., crucial for determining category membership), the causal essence applied only to entities for which hidden inherent properties determine observable qualities. For example, the causal essence of water may be something like H_2O, which is responsible for various observable properties that water has (but see Malt, 1994). The cluster of properties "odorless, tasteless, and colorless" is not a causal essence of water, despite being true of all members of the category "water," because the properties lack causal force.

The ideal essence is assumed to have no actual instantiation in the world. For example, on this view the essence of "goodness" is some pure, abstract quality that is imperfectly realized in real-world instances of people performing good deeds. None of these good deeds perfectly embodies "the good," but each reflects some aspect of it. Plato's cave allegory, in which what we see of the world are mere shadows of what is real and true, exemplifies this view. The ideal essence contrasts with both the sortal and the causal essences, which concern qualities of real-world entities.

SPECIFIC VERSUS PLACEHOLDER NOTION.   Specific essentialist construals can be found in concepts as divergent as "soul" and "DNA," though essentialism may also be sketchy and implicit—a belief that a category has a core, without knowing what that core is. (See also R. Gelman, 1990; Keil, 1989; Wellman, 1990; and Wellman and Gelman, 1988, for arguments concerning skeletal or framework concepts.) Medin proposes that people have an "essence placeholder" (Medin, 1989). For example, a child might believe, before ever learning about chromosomes or human physiology, that girls have some inner, nonobvious quality that distinguishes them from boys and that generates the many observable differences in appearance and behavior between boys and girls. Those who are scientifically informed may come to have quite detailed beliefs about an essence (e.g., for gold, that it has the atomic number of 79), but such conceptions are rare in everyday thought. Instead, the placeholder claim is that people hold an intuitive belief that an essence exists, even if its details have not yet been revealed. One consequence of this point is that an essence typically could not be part of the semantic core of a word, nor could it determine word extensions. Nonetheless, it has implications for people's beliefs regarding the depth and stability of a concept (Rothbart and Taylor, 1990).

SO WHAT DO I MEAN BY ESSENTIALISM?   Having made all these distinctions, what do I mean by essentialism? There are at least twelve different senses of "essence" (see Table 1.1), some of which have potentially either a specific or a placeholder version. (Placeholder notions make sense only for representational essentialism. It is not clear what a placeholder version of metaphysical essentialism could be.) I will be focusing on causal, representational, placeholder essentialism (marked in the table with asterisks). There are other distinctions one could make as well (e.g., is essentialism of a kind or of an individual? domain-specific or domain-general?), but I take these up in the course of the book.

Metaphysical essentialism is beyond the scope of this book, primarily because psychological methods cannot shed light on these issues. The empirical studies presented in the following chapters focus on beliefs about turtles, for example, not on turtles themselves. Thus, the claim that children are essentialist is not a claim that essentialism is accurate. Biologists and philosophers of science have seriously questioned whether essentialism can characterize biological kinds (Dupré, 1993; Mayr, 1982, 1991; Sober, 1994; see chapter 11 for more detailed discussion). When essentialism extends beyond the realm of the sciences to attach to social categories such as race and gender, there is little doubt that it woefully misrepresents reality (Templeton, 1998).

I also decline to consider sortal essences, primarily because they seem implausible from both a psychological and a linguistic perspective. Given decades of research on categorization, it is extremely unlikely that people represent features that can identify all and only members of a category (Rosch and Mervis, 1975), regardless of how confident they are that such features exist (Malt, 1994; McNamara and Sternberg, 1983).

Table 1.1.   Varieties of essentialism

	Sortal	Causal	Ideal
Metaphysical	•	•	•
Representational			
Psychological	•	*	•
Nominal	•	*	•
Cultural	•	*	•

Ideal essences have until recently been virtually ignored in studies of concept representation (but see Sperber, 1975). If anything, people's representations of most object concepts seem to be based on the structure and variability of what they encounter rather than nonrealized idealizations. When people are asked to rate the typicality of various instances of a category, for instance, their ratings usually reflect central tendencies (Rosch and Mervis, 1975). Interestingly, though, other kinds of categories do elicit ideals rather than central tendencies—for example, the prototype of a rich person is fabulously rich and not "average" rich (Barsalou, 1985), suggesting that it may be fruitful to examine ideal concepts in some content domains (see also Atran, 1999; Lynch, Coley, and Medin, 2000).

How does causal, representational essentialism manifest itself? For one, it is a doggedly realist view of the world, presupposing a reality beyond the phenomenal. A nonobvious essence is assumed to provide a "truer" representation of reality than can be observed, and the world is organized into densely complex and predictive clusters of correlated features. For example: when we classify an animal as a turtle, we are interested in much more than its outward appearance. We typically assume that this classification may have a nonobvious basis (e.g., though the presence of a shell or particular markings may be useful to classifying a turtle, these features can be overridden by other, more "biological" properties), that it fosters many novel inferences (e.g., regarding body temperature, number of offspring typically produced, and means of gathering food), and that it is open to revision. We presume there may be turtles that look like rocks (but are not), and rocks that look like turtles (but are not), or that one could discover new species of turtles that are unusually tiny or unusually large or that do not even have distinct shells. Table 1.2 summarizes some of these (overlapping) manifestations of essentialism.

How Essences Relate to Categories and Kinds

At this point, some readers may wonder if the claim of psychological essentialism is just a fancy way of saying that people form categories. The answer to this question is a resounding no. Causal essentialism is related to—but distinct from—categorization. A *category* is any grouping together of two or more discriminably different things (Bruner, Goodnow, and Austin, 1956). All organisms form categories: even mealworms have category-based preferences, and higher-order animals such as pigeons or octopi can display quite sophisticated categorical judgments (e.g., Herrnstein and de Villiers, 1980). But there are differences in the scope and variety of categories and category systems employed by different species (Markman and Callanan, 1983). I would certainly not wish to attribute essentialism to a mealworm, or even an octopus. More controversially, I would not attribute essentialism to a monkey or ape (see chapter 10).

Even considering only those categories used by humans, it is apparent that they are remarkably varied and diverse (Markman, 1989; Waxman, 1991). At one extreme, they include groupings that are encoded in language, that incorporate dense clusters of highly correlated features, and that display rich inductive potential

Table 1.2.   Essentialist versus nonessentialist positions regarding the nature of categories

Essentialist	Nonessentialist
Discovered	Invented
Intrinsic to individual category members	Product of external forces
Unalterable	Easily changed
Stable over transformations	Transient
High inductive potential	Low inductive potential
Nonobvious basis	Superficial basis
Mutually exclusive traits	Overlapping traits
Absolute category membership	Graded category membership

(such as "cat"); at the other extreme, they include groupings that are arbitrarily constructed, with but a single featural basis, and with little inductive potential (such as "white things"; Markman, 1989; Mill, 1843). There are also many categories intermediate between the two, such as simple artifacts (e.g., "cup," "chair"), which capture correlated feature clusters but have more-limited inductive potential than found in species of living things.

From these examples, it is clear that not all categories are essentialized. The richly structured types are often referred to as "natural kinds" (Lakoff, 1987; Schwartz, 1977, 1979), and these are the sorts of categories that I propose are most likely to be essentialized. Categories at the other extreme (such as "white things") do not have essences except in the most trivial sortal sense. Markman (1989) refers to this latter type of category as "arbitrary categories"; Shipley (1993) refers to them as "classes." A *natural kind* is a category that is treated by those who use it as being based in nature, discovered rather than invented, and capturing many deep regularities. In contrast, a category such as "white things" is treated as arbitrary, invented rather than discovered, and capturing little information beyond the basis of the original grouping. "Tigers" is a natural kind; the set of "striped things" (including tigers, striped shirts, and barbershop poles) is not, because it captures only a single, superficial property (stripedness); it does not capture nonobvious similarities, nor does it serve as a basis of induction. Similarly, ad hoc categories, such as "things to take on a camping trip," do not form natural kinds (Barsalou, 1991). Beyond these obvious examples, which categories are essentialized kinds (e.g., artifact categories? social categories?) is an open empirical question that I consider at various points throughout the book. I will be arguing that essentialism in the sense I mean is found in people's categories of natural kinds (both living and nonliving) and many social kinds (including races, ethnicities, and traits), but not artifact categories.[3]

There is a second sense, too, in which essentialism requires a notion of kind. Specifically, the essence of a category is attached not to an *individual object* but rather to the *kind* in which it is classified. We cannot meaningfully interpret the question "What is the essence of *that*?" (with the speaker pointing to a dog) without knowing more about what "that" is. The question is ambiguous: does "that" refer to Fido? poodles? dogs? animals? white things? The essence of dogs presumably differs from the essence of animals or the essence of white things. Even when one contrasts two distinct kind categories (such as dogs and poodles), the hypothesized essence presumably varies. In order to determine the relevant essence, we need to know which kind is under consideration. It is helpful here to review briefly Macnamara's (1986) argument regarding the logic of sortals. (Unfortunately the terminology here is confusing. "Sortals" here are not to be confused with "sortal essences," which are entirely separate.) Sortals are simply those categories to which common nouns refer (e.g., dog, cat, chair, pencil). Macnamara notes that sortals are required for individuating entities. For example, the question "How many?" makes no sense without supplying the sortal—how many *what* (e.g., dogs? legs? molecules?). Likewise, sortals are required for making judgments of identity. "Are these two things the same?" makes no sense without supplying the sortal—the same what (see also Carey and Xu, 1999, for discussion). I suggest that sortals are likewise required for determining essence. One cannot answer the question "What is the essence of this?" without supplying the sortal—of this "what."

Why Is Childhood Essentialism Important to Study?

Essentialism in children is important to study for several reasons. First, it is remarkably pervasive. It is pervasive over time (discussed at least over the past two thousand years), across radically different philosophical traditions (e.g., embraced by both Plato and Locke), and perhaps across cultures (e.g., Atran, 1998; Diesendruck, 2001). It is important to lay bare this set of persistent assumptions and to examine its origins and implications (good and bad) for human reasoning.

Second, the framework has revealed previously unsuspected abilities in young children, thereby contradicting a widely accepted view that children's concepts are limited to concrete, perceptual, and obvious qualities. As I will detail in the chapters that follow, children incorporate a variety of nonobvious features into their concepts, including internal parts, functions, causes, and ontological distinctions. By extension, this portrait suggests a shift in views of knowledge development— what is most basic, what is derived, and how knowledge develops. If unobservable constructs are present from the start, then observable surface features cannot be privileged, simpler, or more basic. These are the "good implications" of essentialism for human reasoning.

Third, essentialism seems to motivate and underlie stereotyping. These are the "bad implications" of essentialism for human reasoning. To put it bluntly: stereotyping borrows the language and conceptual framework of essentializing. Different groups of people are treated as distinct in deep, nonobvious ways, and social group differences are assumed to be innately determined and fixed. To the extent that people buy into this way of thinking, they will have a basis for treating social group differences as central to an individual's identity, for drawing inferences about an individual based on the group to which the individual belongs, and for attributing different motivations and explanations to those from different social groups. The stereotyping individual treats social groups as natural kinds (Rothbart and Taylor, 1990).

Fourth, the study of essentialism calls into question several core assumptions that guide how cognitive scientists think about and study word meaning and concepts. These assumptions include a focus on known (especially perceptual) properties, the belief that a single model suffices for all concepts, the notion that categorization is a single, unitary process, and implicit segregation of categorization from other high-level cognitive processes. Questions of essentialism have also inspired researchers to use a broader range of tasks to study categorization: not just identification and naming, but also induction and causal reasoning. These new tasks enrich our understanding of category functioning over development and suggest ways in which a wide range of distinct phenomena result from essentialist presumptions.

Finally, studies of essentialism have educational and social implications. Some scholars suggest that essentialist assumptions impede attempts to teach evolutionary theory (Evans, 2000, 2001; Mayr, 1982). More generally, much of our knowledge of the world is arrived at by means of inferences rather than being directly taught. Thus, any full account of knowledge acquisition must consider the conditions that promote or discourage inferential reasoning in children. I will argue that an essentialist assumption about categories, and essentialist language about categories, strongly influence children's inferences.

BACKGROUND CONTEXT FOR THE THEMES OF THE BOOK

I turn now to sketch out a bit of the theoretical context for the three themes of the book: essentialism as an early, domain-specific cognitive bias; children's concepts as embedded in theories; and language as an influence on cognitive development. Each of these themes will receive more detailed discussion throughout the volume. My modest aim here is simply to point out some of the theoretical controversies that exist, as background for the more extensive treatment that follows.

Essentialism as an Early, Domain-Specific Conceptual Bias

Essentialism is pervasive, but why? I will be arguing that essentialism is a cognitive predisposition that emerges early in childhood, particularly for understanding the natural world. This position is at odds with two alternative accounts, which I call "historical accident" and "inherent consequence of naming." On the historical accident position, essentialism is the by-product of modern Western philosophy, cultural and political traditions, or technology (Fuss, 1989; Guillaumin, 1980). For example, some have argued that we are essentialists at this point in history because we can view the scientific enterprise fairly close-up and know about unobservable entities such as DNA and molecules (Fodor, 1998). However, attributing essentialism to historical accident does not easily explain why preschool children essentialize.

The contrasting argument says that essentialism is an inherent consequence of naming (specifically, a consequence of count nouns). By giving distinct entities the same name, we imply there is some unchanging, underlying sameness that they share. On this view, essentialism is a logical consequence of language use (Carey, 1996; Hallett, 1991; Mayr, 1991). The problem with this position is the domain-specific application of essentialism. It cannot explain why we essentialize more in some domains than others.

My view is distinct from both the alternatives just sketched out. Unlike the historical accident account, essentialism is a universal habit of the mind. People are deep-down essentialists even without the benefit of science or Plato's *Republic*. However, unlike the inherent-consequence-of-naming account, essentialism applies more to some domains than others. Naming in and of itself does not lead children to essentialize.

My view is closest to an evolutionary adaptation position, which posits that humans evolved a universal essentializing tendency, because it is beneficial for interactions with the world (Atran, 1998; P. Bloom, 2000; Gil-White, 2001; Pinker, 1994, 2002). This position is appealing in accounting for the recurrence of essentialism across cultures, epochs, and developmental ages. However, I underscore three caveats.

1. I will argue that essentialism is not a *single* adaptation, but the result of several distinct cognitive biases that emerged for varying purposes. In other words, essentialism per se was not specifically selected, but components of essentialism were. I will have more to say about that in chapter 11.

2. Whereas evolutionary positions tend to emphasize adaptive benefits, I am equally struck by the costs—most notably with categories that are socially constructed, such as race. How do we understand the errors and perils of essentialism? Are they simply to be expected, because any adaptation is only approximate (i.e., useful but not wholly prescient)? Or do they suggest that what evolved was not essentialism per se, but rather other capacities that result in essentialism as a side effect? I will be arguing for the latter.

3. The view I lay out supplies an important role for language (see the following section). Language guides children to notice and essentialize some categories more than others. As such, essentialism is not a distinct, encapsulated module that gets triggered by perceptual inputs alone. Although an adaptationist position does not specifically exclude language from playing a role, neither does it easily explain how it would do so.

It is difficult to obtain evidence on these issues by studying adults, because with adults the effects of schooling and scientific training cannot easily be factored out.

Children, however, provide a more compelling test case, because they have scant knowledge of either Western philosophy or scientific theories. In this respect, the younger the child under investigation, the more powerful the test case.

The Role of Language in Essentialism

One reason for suspecting essentialism is that the meanings of certain words seem to depend on something other than known, superficial properties. Kripke (1971) and Putnam (1970, 1973) argue that meanings of proper nouns (Kripke) and natural kind terms (Putnam) are based not on a list of known properties, but rather on "deeper" properties—what we could call theory-laden properties—including those that might not even yet be known. For example, the name "Harry Potter" is not defined by a set of features such as "wears glasses, flies on a broom, and has two best friends named Ron and Hermione." If Harry Potter had died at birth, he would have none of these features, so they cannot be determinative of being Harry Potter. The only feature that seems *necessarily* linked to the name "Harry Potter" is that he was born of certain parents. According to Kripke, proper names refer but do not describe. Any description associated with a name merely helps us pick out the referent; it does not define the referent (see also Schwartz, 1977, 1979).

Kripke (1971, 1972) and especially Putnam (1970, 1973) extended this analysis of proper names to natural kind terms. They argue that, although a set of known features may be used to identify members of a natural kind category, the features do not serve as necessary and sufficient criteria. For example, whales are shaped like fish and live and swim in water as fish do, but they are not fish. Likewise, to use Putnam's example, most of us cannot distinguish an elm from a beech, yet nonetheless maintain that the words "elm" and "beech" differ in meaning. We seem to assume that elms and beeches are different kinds of things, that the differences are there in the world for us to discover, and that experts could tell us which is which (again signaling that the distinction is real). Putnam thus forcefully argues for a sociolinguistic division of labor, according to which the average speaker need not know how to recognize whether or not something is an "elm" (for example), but experts in the community have the ability to make such a determination. As Putnam famously insists, "'meanings' just ain't in the *head!*" (1975, p. 227). Meanings may not be in the head, but the conceptual underpinnings to such a system imply a kind of essentialism (in the head).

This brief review illustrates that language works in accordance with certain essentialist assumptions. However, it still leaves open the question of whether language per se contributes to essentialist thinking. It could be, instead, that essentialist reasoning contributes to how words are used.

Extant theories regarding the role of language on thought are wildly polarized, ranging from the claim that language is the lens through which we organize reality, leading different languages to adopt different worldviews (Hill and Mannheim, 1992; Lucy, 1997; Whorf, 1956), to the claim that language has no substantive effect whatsoever on human cognition (aside from very local influences, e.g., memories can be encoded in a verbal format) (Pinker, 1994). After years of rejection of language as an influence on thought, there is renewed interest, particularly from a developmental perspective. Important work on these issues is now emerging from scholars including Bowerman (1996, 2000); Danziger (2001); Gopnik and Choi (1990); Gopnik, Choi, and Baumberger (1996); Gumperz and Levinson (1996); Imai and Gentner (1997); Levinson (1996); Martinez and Shatz (1996); Naigles and Terrazas (1998); Sera, Rettinger, and Castillo-Pintado (1991); Shatz (1991); Tardif and Wellman (2000); and Waxman, Senghas, and Benveniste (1997). At the very least, the suggestion of linguistic influences on thought is respectable.

I will take a middle position. I do not think that language drives the basic phenomenon of essentializing. It does not, on my view, create the urge to essentialize. Nor do I think that different languages essentialize to radically different degrees (though there may be subtle differences; see Nisbett, Peng, et al., 2001). Nonetheless, the extent to which a *particular* category is essentialized (or even essentialized at all) is open to linguistic influence. In other words, language helps determine when essentialism is used. Specifically, I will propose that two linguistic forms (common nouns and generic noun phrases) subtly convey to children an essentialist perspective on categories. This position will be presented in chapter 8.

ORGANIZATION OF THIS BOOK

The remainder of this book is organized into three main parts. In part I, I review the empirical basis for arguing that essentialism is an early-emerging reasoning bias in children. Chapter 2 reports children's category-based inductive inferences. Chapter 3 reports a variety of studies reflecting the importance of nonobvious properties in children's categories. In chapter 4, I consider how children reason about nature/nurture conflicts, and particularly their intuitive belief that category members share an innate potential. Chapter 5 examines the role of causation in children's categories. Chapter 6 summarizes and integrates the findings from the previous four chapters, and considers (and refutes) some alternative interpretations of these results. Altogether, the five chapters of this section review a wealth of evidence that jointly undermines the view of children's concepts as perceptually driven, concrete, or atheoretical.

In part II, I turn to the question that naturally arises if one accepts the conclusions of part I: namely, how do essentialist beliefs emerge, and by what mechanisms are they acquired or transmitted? Chapter 7 reports a detailed study of maternal input to young children and argues that parents say very little that is explicit or concrete to endorse or promote essentialism. Nonetheless, I argue that essentialist assumptions are implicitly conveyed to young children by means of certain linguistic forms of maternal speech (namely, generic noun phrases). The forms of language that are and are not argued to promote essentialism are detailed in chapter 8, along with evidence from children's language interpretation. In chapter 9, I directly take up the question of what sort of developmental account best explains the acquisition of essentialized kinds in young children. To what extent do children rely on simple associative learning strategies as opposed to theories?

In part III, I address more speculatively the implications of parts I and II. In chapter 10, I raise and discuss unanswered questions that arose throughout the book, including essentialism across cultures, developmental change, individual variation, and how to disconfirm essentialism experimentally. Chapter 11 tackles several issues related to why children essentialize, including the scope of children's essentialist reasoning and how essentialism relates to other phenomena involving potent, nonobvious properties (including contagion, contamination, authenticity, and fetishes). Altogether, childhood essentialism has important lessons for our understanding of concepts, cognitive development, and language and thought.

PART I

THE PHENOMENA

Introduction to Part I:
Notes on Research Methods

In order to make a convincing study of essentialism as a fundamental folk notion, it is obviously crucial to provide evidence regarding the beliefs of ordinary folk. (Here I distinguish between "ordinary folk" and such luminaries as Aristotle, Plato, and Locke.) The notions sketched in chapter 1 may seem at first arcane and counter to common sense. What is commonsensical about invisible qualities that one can never know completely? Here it is important not to confuse the direct observability of the central construct with its status as common sense. Religious concepts provide an apt analogue: God is a mysterious concept, yet one that is readily embraced in folk theories (Boyer, 1994a, 1994b).

Direct evidence of essentialism is difficult to obtain. As I mentioned earlier, essentialism does not entail that people know what the essence of a given category is. Instead, it can be placeholder notion (Medin and Ortony, 1989). People may implicitly assume, for example, that there is some quality that bears have in common that confers category identity and causes their identifiable surface features, and they may use this belief to guide inductive inferences and produce explanations—without being able to identify any feature or trait as the bear essence. This belief can be considered an unarticulated heuristic rather than a detailed, well-worked-out theory.

Furthermore, an essence would rarely be consulted to determine category membership, for the simple reason that people often do not know (or cannot readily access) the relevant information (S. Gelman and Medin, 1993). In such instances, people use other features instead. Gender provides a useful example: although we typically assess someone's gender based on outward (clothed) appearance and voice, even young children acknowledge that genital information is more diagnostic (Bem, 1989), and in our technological society we even use chromosomal information in certain contexts (e.g., amniocentesis and Olympic Games committees). (My arguments here are backed up by the Kansas Supreme Court, which on March 15, 2002, ruled that chromosomal information determines not only biological gender ["a post-operative male-to-female transsexual is not a woman"], but also ordinary language use ["The words 'sex,' 'male' and 'female' in everyday understanding do not encompass transsexuals"]! See report in the *New York Times,* March 16, 2002.) This means that people's use of salient observable features cannot be taken as evidence against essentialism.

These initial points of clarification imply that essences are difficult (perhaps impossible) to access directly. Psychological essentialism entails that people believe in the existence of essences, not that people have detailed knowledge regarding the content of essences, nor that essences exist. Accordingly, some results that might at first appear to contradict essentialism (as when people classify instances based on nonessential features, or cannot specify an essence, or have concepts that conflict with scientific concepts, e.g., Dupré, 1993) are not evidence against psychological essentialism. They are valuable for examining what kinds of information are used in certain tasks, but they do not constitute tests of psychological essentialism as a folk theory of concepts.

As a result, we have relied on indirect, converging methods. These are sketched out in Figure 1.2. At times the evidence focuses on realist assumptions about categories, and other times on underlying essences. These shifting criteria may frustrate some readers; I will at least do my part to try to keep clear which sense of essentialism I am addressing. The evidence in chapters 2 through 6 comes from several related lines of research: inductive potential, incorporation of nonobvious properties, stability over transformations, sharp category boundaries, beliefs about the relative role of nature versus nurture, and incorporation of causal features into categories. Together, these studies show that young children's categories are richly structured and extend beyond surface features (chapters 2 and 3), incorporating nonvisible properties (chapter 3), beliefs about innateness (chapter 4), and causality (chapter 5). In chapter 10, I return to the question of to what extent these features jointly constitute an essentialist framework.

CATEGORY DOMAINS

I assume that categories differ substantially from one another in structure, that not all categories are essentialized, and that serious confusion will result from positing a theory of "concepts" without specifying the type of concept under consideration. To render this assumption intuitively plausible, contrast the animal kind "bird" with the artifact category "tchotchke" (Yiddish for knickknack or inexpensive trinket) (see also Markman, 1989, for an incisive discussion of Mill's example of the category of "white things"). Most laypeople reading these words would probably agree to most or all of the following essentialist propositions about birds (placed in quotes to indicate that these are folk beliefs rather than metaphysical certainties):

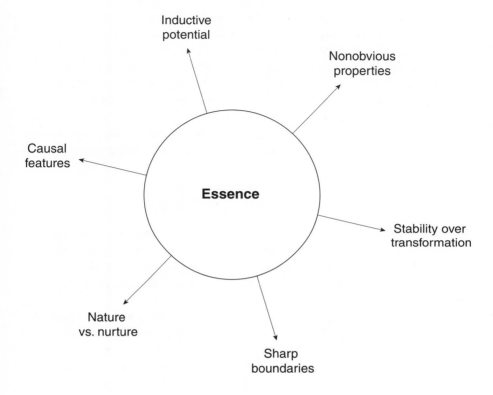

Figure 1.2.   Implications of essentialism.

1. "The category of 'birds' is not an artificial grouping invented simply for the convenience of humans. Rather, birds belong together in some natural sense. We *discovered* the category of birds."
2. "There are many nonobvious properties that birds have in common with one another, including properties that people haven't yet discovered but will discover in the future"
3. "There is some underlying property (maybe genetic code? maybe evolutionary history?) that causes birds to be alike."
4. "Many commonalities that birds share are biologically determined."
5. "Throughout its existence, an entity that is once a bird is *always* a bird—it cannot be turned into some other kind of thing."
6. "Something either is or is not a bird—it can't be 'kind of' a bird or 'partly' a bird."

Now try replacing "birds" with "tchotchkes" in each of these statements, and the differences between these two sorts of categories become quite clear.

It is interesting that much past work on categorization, continuing to the present, has focused on categories structured more like "tchotchkes" than like "birds" (Johnson-Laird and Wason, 1977). In contrast, most of the work I will review focuses on basic-level natural kind categories, as these are particularly likely to reveal essentialism (Markman, 1989; Keil, 1989). Artifact categories (including vehicles, furniture, and tools) and social categories (including gender, race, and psychological traits) are also occasionally included, to test the boundaries of essentialist thought. I will have more to say about the mapping of essentialism onto domains in chapters 6 and 11.

RESEARCH PARTICIPANTS AND DEVELOPMENTAL ISSUES

The research participants in these studies are, for the most part, preschool children of middle-class families in the United States. The choice of middle-class English-speaking children is one of convenience only, and in chapters 7, 8, and 11 I take up the complex and important issues of cultural variability. The choice of preschoolers, however, is quite deliberate, and I say a few words here to explain that choice.

As noted in chapter 1, preschool children seem to rely on different bases for classification than adults. Two- to five-years-olds make errors that an older child would find laughable. They tend to be captivated by salient appearances, as Piaget's conservation errors demonstrate. So preschool children provide either an especially apt choice for studying essentialism (because a demonstration of an essentialist bias in children would provide particularly strong evidence), or a decidedly foolish choice (because we might not find essentialism in children so young). Quine (1977), for example, has suggested that children are at first limited to "intuitive kinds" that reflect our innate sense of similarity and only gradually move beyond them to form theory-based categories. Neisser likewise assumed that similarity-based categories and theory-based categories "correspond to points on a developmental continuum" (1987, p. 6).

The analysis one adopts here depends on how one accounts for children's categorization errors. Let us consider three main candidate explanations (not that these exhaust the range of possibilities): lack of knowledge or expertise, tendency to focus on salient features of a task, and general limitations in logical capacity. I agree that children's categorization errors are due at least in part to a relative lack of knowledge about most domains (Gobbo and Chi, 1986; Bedard and Chi, 1992; K. Johnson and Eilers, 1998; Keil, 1987), and to a general tendency to focus on the most salient aspects of a task or event (Inhelder and Piaget, 1964). As Chi has demonstrated so strikingly in the domains of chess and dinosaurs, even a preschooler can become expert in a domain and shift to using less obvious, more casually central features (Chi and Koeske, 1983; see also Chi, Hutchinson, and Robin, 1989). Where I disagree is with the further claim that preschool children lack the logical structures that older children and adults use to form concepts (Inhelder and Piaget, 1964).

Young children pose particular challenges to designing a task to study essentialism. If we ask children to sort objects into categories of their own accord, chances are they will sort objects into categories that do not look anything like essentialized natural kinds. A hat and a birthday cake, for example, share little in the way of nonobvious commonalities. Likewise, on Inhelder and Piaget's free-form classification task (where a child is given an array of toys to group as they wish), children tend to be guided by the spatial configuration of objects in the array and "allow themselves to be guided by what they can perceive" (1964, p. 45) rather than making use of a coherent concept. For instance, they might group together a square and a triangle to make a house, rather than grouping a square with other squares, or a triangle with other triangles.

I agree that the focus on *what* is in a child's category yields a misleading portrait. What is critical instead is an examination of *how* the category functions. The studies that I report in chapters 2–6 typically supply children with a classification and then examine what sorts of inferences they make from the classification. These studies contrast with the standard sorting task, which requires children to form categories on their own. I will elaborate on this methodological issue at various points throughout the book.

In brief, by focusing on young children, I have placed my theoretical bets on a certain optimistic position regarding children's early concepts. I suggest that children are not limited to intuitive kinds, that they can look beyond similarity-based categories, and that they can form theory-based categories. I describe these capacities in the following chapters.

Chapter 2
The Inductive Potential of Categories

> Classifications are theories about the basis of natural order, not dull cata-
> logues compiled only to avoid chaos.
>
> Stephen Jay Gould, *Wonderful Life*

Preschool children are not scientists, but they would (implicitly) agree with Gould's assessment of categories, at least in certain domains. With their classifica-tions, children too are attempting to discover the "natural order" in the world. My goal in chapters 2 through 5 is to lay out the evidence for this claim. In this chapter I focus on children's capacity to use categories as the basis for novel inferences about the world. Children's category-based inferences are essentialist in two im-portant respects: they involve reasoning about nonobvious properties (including internal parts, novel behaviors, and causal effects) and an appreciation that ap-pearances can be deceiving when it comes to category membership.

To illustrate the centrality of categories in induction, consider the following real-world example. According to National Public Radio's *Morning Edition* news program (November 21, 2000), a large number of Magellan penguins were wash-ing up on the beaches of Rio de Janeiro. Many of the people who found them took them home and put them in their freezers to keep them cool. However, this species of penguins lives only a few hundred miles south, in year-round above-freezing temperatures. As a result, when the Brazilians eventually asked for help from the staff at the local zoo, many of the penguins were on the verge of dying from hy-pothermia. (Thanks to Nicola Knight for providing this example.)

The Brazilian caregivers were basing their actions on their understanding of pen-guins as a category. Other than that these creatures were penguins, there was no rea-son to assume that they should live in a freezer. After all, other creatures that wash up on the beaches of Rio presumably prefer warmer climates. The Brazilians apparently assumed (falsely, as it turned out) that knowing that a bird is a penguin allows you to infer that its habitat and body temperature are equivalent to those of other pen-guins. They relied on what they already knew about a subset of the category to make inferences about novel category members. Unfortunately, the category of penguins does not cohere as tightly as the Brazilians' naive theories led them to believe.

If we try to model the implicit reasoning involved in this example, we find that three plausible strategies may be involved:

1. All penguins live in cold climates.
   Beaky is a penguin.
   Therefore, Beaky lives in cold climates.

2. Waddles is a penguin.
   Waddles lives in cold climates.
   Therefore, all penguins live in cold climates.

3. Waddles and Beaky are penguins.
   Waddles lives in cold climates.
   Therefore, Beaky lives in cold climates.

The first is a straightforward deductive inference. It is rare, however, that people explicitly learn category statements in the form of universal quantifiers (for example, explicitly learning that all penguins live in cold climates; see chapter 7), and so deductive inferences are not the usual means of learning about the world. The other two kinds of inference are both inductive inferences, because they extend beyond what is already known or what could be known with logical certainty (as opposed to deductive inferences).[1] The reasoning processes in examples 2 and 3 may differ from one another in interesting ways, but both entail reasoning from the known to the unknown, and both rely (in one case more explicitly than the other) on categorical reasoning. The studies I detail below have (implicitly) the logic of example 3 above.

THE BASIC FINDING: CATEGORIES PROMOTE INFERENCES CONCERNING NONOBVIOUS PROPERTIES

For a number of years, my collaborators and I have examined category-based induction, or the inferences people make from one category member to another, especially for hidden, unobservable properties. In this section I will describe in some detail our original basic finding. This work sets the stage for more-recent studies examining the scope and development of children's inferences.

Carey's Induction Task

Carey (1985) pioneered the use of inductive inferences as a tool for examining the nature of children's concepts. In an ingenious set of experiments, children learned new, unfamiliar facts about certain categories (e.g., that a dog has a spleen inside), then were given opportunities to report whether or not these facts generalized to other instances that were more or less similar to the target category (e.g., does a person have a spleen inside? does a flower have a spleen inside?). The focus of

Carey's work was not essentialism, but rather conceptual change in children's bio-logical concepts. Nonetheless, two of her early findings nicely set the stage for the present discussion. Specifically, even the youngest children in her work (age four years) showed violations of similarity-based induction.

One finding was that children (especially four-year-olds, her youngest subjects) displayed a striking tendency to draw more inferences from properties taught about people than from properties taught about other animals. As a result, their patterns of inference conflicted with perceptual similarity. So, for example, four-year-olds more often projected properties from people to aardvarks (76%) than from dogs to aardvarks (29%), despite the greater similarity between dogs and aardvarks. Likewise, four-year-olds more often projected properties from people to stink-bugs (52%) than from bees to stinkbugs (12%), despite the greater similarity between bees and stinkbugs. The second finding was an asymmetry in inductive projections, with more inferences from people (e.g., people to dogs) than to people (e.g., dogs to people).

Carey provided a detailed theoretical explanation for these findings in terms of children's developing understanding of the animal domain. Most important for our purposes, preschool children's inductive inferences were constrained by their knowledge of categories, and did not follow a strict similarity-based pattern. The task revealed conceptual links that could not be accounted for strictly in terms of outward object appearance.

Gelman and Markman Triad Task

Ellen Markman and I conducted a series of studies using a task similar in basic structure to that used by Carey: in each of several picture sets, a child was taught a new fact and then tested on how she generalized the fact to other instances (S. Gel-man and Markman, 1986). Because of our interest in the relative power of category membership in guiding children's inferences, each picture set constituted a triad in which the third picture closely resembled one of the first two pictures but was from the same category as the other (see Figure 2.1). In other words, each item pitted perceptual similarity and category membership against one another. Adult simi-larity ratings confirmed that the picture sets conformed to this principle. Of inter-est was whether children would draw inferences from one picture to another on the basis of outward appearance or natural kind category membership.

Figure 2.1 shows one of the sets we used. However, it is important to keep in mind: that participants viewed twenty different triads, including a wide range of animal and natural-substance categories (see Table 2.1); that the properties used also ranged broadly, including such things as internal parts ("has little eggs in-side"), behavior ("eats grass"), physical transformations ("melts in an oven"), func-tion ("helps make snow melt"), and origins ("comes from inside a sea animal"); and that the results I report held up generally across the various item sets.

In one set, the pictures were a colorful tropical fish, a gray dolphin, and a gray

Figure 2.1.   Sample item set, S. Gelman and Markman (1986). *Source*: S. Gelman and Markman (1986). Reprinted with the permission of Elsevier Science.

shark (fish). The shark was similar in appearance to the dolphin and dissimilar from the tropical fish, but shared category membership with the tropical fish, not the dolphin. The procedure began with the researcher naming the target pictures ("fish" and "dolphin"), after which children learned an unfamiliar nonobvious property about each. (Pretesting as well as a control condition confirmed that four-year-olds did not previously know which property applied to each animal, on any of the twenty item sets.) In this example, the children were told, "This fish [i.e., tropical fish] stays underwater to breathe" and "This dolphin pops above the water to breathe." After being shown the picture of the shark and told that it was a fish, the participants were asked whether it stayed underwater to breathe like the fish or popped above the water to breathe like the dolphin.

To determine whether our analysis of category-based induction was sound for adults, we first gave the task to Stanford undergraduates. The task was a paper-and-pencil version of what children saw. The only substantive change was that we used less familiar properties such as "teeth have enamel" versus "teeth do not have enamel" for the tropical fish and dolphin, respectively. This change was needed in order to ensure that the adult participants had minimal preexisting beliefs or knowledge about the properties being tested (a point that was confirmed in a

Table 2.1.   Test items from S. Gelman and Markman (1986)

Same category	Same appearance	Test item
Living Kinds		
squirrel	rabbit	squirrel (long-eared kaibab)
fish (tropical)	dolphin	fish (gray shark)
dinosaur (brontosaurus)	rhinoceros	dinosaur (gray triceratops)
bird (flamingo)	bat	bird (blackbird)
lizard (red)	snake	lizard (legless)
flower (yellow tulip)	sea anemone (red & green)	flower (red & green)
snake (cobra)	worm	snake (small, brown)
coral ("brain" coral)	plant (fern)	coral (green, fernlike)
bug (beetle)	leaf	bug (leaf insect)
starfish (red, 5-legged)	pinecone	starfish (brown, 13-legged)
Nonliving Natural Kinds		
oil (brown)	honey (yellow)	oil (yellow)
metal (lump)	chalk (flat-surfaced)	metal (flat-surfaced)
shell (conch)	stone (oval)	shell (clam)
cotton (ball)	silk (cloth swatch)	cotton (cloth swatch)
wool (unspun)	string (ball)	wool (spun)
gold (brick)	clay (lump)	gold (lump)
diamond (ball)	glass (cut)	diamond (cut)
salt (granulated, pile)	rock (single piece)	salt (single large piece)
pearl (seed pearl, flat oval)	marble(spherical)	pearl (spherical)
sugar (cubes)	sand (brown, pile)	sugar (yellow-brown, pile)

Note: Descriptions in parentheses were not stated aloud in the experiments.

pretest with a separate group of adults). In the study proper, our undergraduate subjects inferred that pictures from the same category shared novel nonobvious properties on 86% of trials. This performance significantly exceeds what one would expect if they had simply been guessing (50%). Furthermore, the adult participants were highly confident of their answers, giving a mean confidence rating of 5.8 on a scale of 1 ("very unsure") to 7 ("very sure"). In their justifications, adults provided explicitly essentialist accounts, such as "Birds are structured internally alike," "Usually animals of the same species have similar characteristics," and "Gold is gold."

Given the excellent performance of adults, the performance of the preschool group was of particular interest. The results were strikingly similar to those of adults. Four-year-olds based 68% of their inferences on category membership, despite the lack of perceptual support. This figure was significantly above chance and significantly higher than the results of a control condition in which children were shown the labeled test pictures only (e.g., shark) and were asked the test questions (e.g., whether it breathed underwater or above the water). (Control studies were also included to rule out the possibility that children were simply responding to the superficial feature of whether or not identical labels were used. These are described at greater length later. To preview those findings, identical labels are neither necessary nor sufficient for children to draw inferences from one category member to another of the same kind.) When considering the response patterns of each child considered individually, over one-third of the children consistently based their inferences on category membership across items, whereas none of the children consistently based their answers on appearances. Children's justifications of their category-based choices were lucid, often appealing to category membership (see Table 2.2).

The results of this study are clear: children drew many novel inferences from one member of a category to another, even when the instances appeared very different on the surface and even when only the label told children that they were the same kind of thing. These inferences were nonobvious in two respects: the predicates concerned nonobvious properties, and the category membership was not obvious from outward appearances. My collaborators and I have replicated this finding with hundreds of preschool children, and the effect is very robust (Davidson and Gelman, 1990; S. Gelman, 1988; S. Gelman and Coley, 1990; S. Gelman, Collman, and Maccoby, 1986; S. Gelman and Markman, 1987; S. Gelman and O'Reilly, 1988).

Extensions to Younger Children

John Coley and I found that children as young as age two and a half are likewise sensitive to the rich inferential power of natural kind categories (S. Gelman and Coley, 1990). Children ranging in age from two years, one month (2;1) to three years, one month (3;1, mean age 2;8) were tested on a simplified version of the inference task already described. For each of nine items, children were shown a target picture from a familiar category (e.g., a bluebird) and reminded of a familiar property that described it (e.g., "This bird lives in a nest"). This target picture was then set aside and not referred to again, but was left in view. Each participant was then shown four test pictures, one at a time. These included a typical instance of the target category (another bluebird), an atypical instance of the target category (a dodo), a typical instance of a contrasting category (a stegosaurus), and an atypical instance of the same contrasting category (a pterodactyl) (see Figure 2.2 for a sample set). The atypical instance of the contrasting category was perceptually quite similar to the target picture, whereas the atypical instance of the target category was not. For example, the pterodactyl looked like the target bluebird, but the dodo did not. Perceptual similarity was confirmed by adult ratings. Finally, for half the subjects, category membership was conveyed via verbal labels (e.g., "This is a bird"); the other half heard no labels.

As expected, our young participants performed well on the typical items in

Table 2.2.   Sample of preschoolers' justifications of category-based choices; from
S. Gelman and Coley (1991)

A squirrel eats bugs, "because it's a squirrel."
A fish stays underwater to breathe, "because he's a fish."
A gold nugget melts like a gold bar, "because they're both the same thing."
A chunk of salt helps make snow melt, "because it's the same kind as this [fine-grained] salt."
A bug breathes air in, "because some bugs work like that."
A flower has tubes for water inside, because "every flower has tubes inside, so it does have tubes
     inside!"
The coral has to catch food, "because all corals do that."
A bug breathes air in, "because every bug breathes in and every leaf breathes out."
A dinosaur has cold blood, "'cause every dinosaur has cold blood, even when it's frozen."

Source: S. Gelman and Coley (1991). Reprinted with the permission of Cambridge University Press.

both conditions (75% correct overall). For example, they reported that the bluebird lived in a nest and the stegosaurus did not, whether or not these pictures were
labeled. For the atypical items, however, the participants who heard the labels drew
correct inferences at a level significantly above chance (69% correct), whereas
those who did not hear a label performed significantly below chance (42% correct). For example, the children inferred that a dodo, labeled "bird," lived in a nest
like the target bird, but that a pterodactyl, labeled "dinosaur," did not. When pic-

Figure 2.2.   Sample item set. *Source*: S. Gelman and Coley (1990). Reprinted with the
permission of the American Psychological Association.

tures were not labeled, two-year-olds were more likely to infer that the pterodactyl lived in a nest and that the dodo did not. These results extended to the perform-ance of children considered individually, not just when averaging across children. In the label condition, over half the children consistently based their inferences on category membership (answering on the basis of category membership for twenty-six or more of the thirty-six trials); none based their inferences consistently on ap-pearances. In the no-label condition, one child consistently responded on the basis of category membership, whereas over half consistently answered on the basis of appearances. (The remaining children showed no consistent response pattern.)

To sum up so far: for children as young as age two and a half, category member-ship promotes important inferences. This finding is remarkable, given the age of the participants, their lack of formal scientific training, and their persistent atten-tion to salient perceptual features on other tasks.

What of even younger children? Here the predictions are more contentious, especially given children's well-known (though variously interpreted) tendency to overextend their early words—for example, calling all round objects "ball." (See, for example, Naigles and Gelman [1995] for competing interpretations of what children's overextensions imply about their semantic representations and concepts.) Overextensions are especially common below age two and a half. Do overextensions mean that young children do not yet grasp the inductive potential of ordinary names? If a child truly believes that the word "ball" applies to apples, marbles, and lightbulbs, this belief would contradict the idea that words have deep inductive potential. I will have more to say about overextensions in chapter 9. For now, I focus on category-based induction in children below age two and a half.

Jaswal and Markman (2002) elegantly demonstrate category-based induction in twenty-four-month-olds, using an imitation task with familiar animal cate-gories (dogs, cats, horses, cows, bears, pigs, squirrels, and rabbits). Children saw pairs of items on which a researcher demonstrated two properties (such as a cat playing with a ball of yarn and a dog playing with a stick), then were given an op-portunity to act out these properties on new instances. Of greatest interest were those instances that were misleading in appearance (such as a dog with a catlike face and an unusually long tail). The instances were either labeled by the researcher (e.g., "Can you show me what this dog plays with?") or were not labeled (e.g., "Can you show me what this one plays with?"). Children's inferences were significantly influenced by category membership as conveyed by the label. When no label was provided, children typically responded based on appearances (e.g., inferring that the misleading dog would play with a ball of yarn). However, with a label, children typically responded based on category membership (e.g., inferring that the mis-leading dog would play with a stick). In this study, the label did convey important, nonobvious information.

Welder and Graham (2001) have similar findings with toddlers sixteen to twenty-one months of age. In a series of three experiments, they presented their young participants with a generalized imitation task. On a given trial, a child first saw a novel object that was shown to have a novel property (e.g., a cloth-covered shape that squeaked when it was squeezed). The child then saw other objects varying in their similarity to the first (target) object: high similarity, medium similarity, or low similarity. Did the child attempt to squeak the other objects? If so, he or she would be credited with making an inductive inference from the target. The primary condition of interest was the surprised condition, in which the target object had the novel property, but the test objects were disabled so that they were unable to carry out the novel property. If children carry out the predicted action in this case (e.g., squeezing the toy), it can be assumed that they are doing so because they expect the toy to squeak—and not because the toy is actually squeaking (i.e., not because they enjoy producing the novel property). There were two other conditions as well which served as controls. In the interest-control condition, neither the target nor the test objects possessed the interesting property (e.g., neither squeaked). This condition served as a baseline to see how often children spontaneously engaged in the target activity (e.g., squeezing). In the predicted condition, both target and test objects possessed the interesting property. This condition served to keep children engaged in the task, as otherwise they might learn to expect that none of the test objects "worked."

Crucially for our purposes, each study included two between-subjects conditions: a no-label condition and a label condition. In the no-label condition, none of the items were labeled by the experimenter. This condition assessed the degree to which children extend novel properties on the basis of the perceived similarity between the test objects and the target objects. In the label condition, all the items in a set received the same label, either novel (e.g., "Look at this blint") or familiar (e.g., "Look at this ball"). (The novel objects were plausibly nameable by the familiar labels.) Of interest here was whether the label would encourage children to make more inferences. In other words, the contrast between the no-label and label conditions measures whether children treat words as indexing induction-rich categories.[2]

Welder and Graham (2001) found that, in the absence of labels, children generalized the novel, nonobvious property to others of like kind. Children assumed that two objects that were similar in shape also had the same nonobvious property. Most interesting for the current context, labeling the pictures had robust effects on children's inferences. Children performed more target actions on the test objects (e.g., squeezing) upon hearing a label than upon hearing no label. The condition difference held up for both novel labels (e.g., "blint") and familiar labels (e.g,. "ball"). Somewhat surprisingly, the effects of labeling were stronger with novel labels than with familiar labels—perhaps because the familiar labels were ones for which the novel properties typically do not occur (e.g., balls do not usually squeak; spoons do not usually rattle), and the corresponding typical functions (such as throwing for the "balls") were irrelevant.

In a further study, Graham, Kilbreath, and Welder (2001, 2002) obtained similar findings with children twelve to fourteen months of age. Children once again received a generalized imitation task with objects in a surprised condition (as well as the other two controls). Once again, hearing a novel label induced children to draw more inferences, as measured by their attempts to carry out the target actions that were demonstrated on the target objects (e.g., squeezing the ball-like object). This effect occurred only with test objects that were low in shape similarity to the target object. Test objects that were high in similarity to the target elicited a high degree of target actions whether or not the items were labeled; test objects that were wholly dissimilar to the target elicited very few target actions whether or not the items were labeled. As Graham, Kilbreath, and Welder note, it is especially compelling that children of this age demonstrated a sensitivity to language, given that they were only beginning to talk.

An anecdote about my youngest child, Benjamin, would seem to fit these results. One day when he was thirteen months of age (with only a few words in his productive vocabulary), we were sitting together on the couch when he started fingering a button on my shirt. I told him it was a "button," whereupon he started pushing down on it firmly with his index finger. It seemed as if he was treating it like other "buttons" (namely, those on the telephone, remote-control devices, and CD player)—as small protrusions that one pushes to make interesting things happen. And, crucially, it seemed that the word "button" conveyed that inference. Coincidence? Perhaps—but Graham, Kilbreath, and Welder's results would suggest it was not.

Control Studies

My collaborators and I have also conducted numerous control experiments to rule out the possibility of task demands and to determine the role of category membership (as opposed to superficial matching strategies) on children's performance. One primary concern with the initial studies was that children may have made use of the category information simply because they were attempting to please the experimenter. Upon hearing the experimenter provide identical labels for two of the pictures in a surprising way (with labels conflicting with appearances), the children may have reasoned that their own answers should "match" whatever the adult said. In other words, children may have used the words as cues to the experimenter's desired responses and attempted to match the experimenter's lead. This alternative account contrasts with the interpretation that we have made—that children used the words as cues to the category membership of the objects, and drew category-based inferences accordingly.

In order to tease apart these two accounts, we tested children on three sorts of scenarios: (a) the labels matched, but were uninformative with regard to category membership; (b) the labels matched, but the task did not require category-based induction; and (c) the labels mismatched, but children were able to determine category membership through other means. The "superficial matching strategy" model would predict label-based responding in (a) and (b) and either random or appearance-based responding in (c). In contrast, we predicted no label-based responding in (a) and (b) and consistent category-based responding in (c). See Table 2.3 for a brief sketch of the study designs.

In the control studies, children did not blindly follow the experimenter's labels. Children did not draw inferences when the property to be inferred was fortuitous (e.g., "fell on the floor this morning"; S. Gelman, 1988) or inconsequential (e.g., which color chip to place on a picture; S. Gelman and Markman, 1986). Children did not draw inferences when the animal was labeled with an adjective describing a transient state (e.g., labeling animals from contrasting categories as "sleepy" and "wide awake" instead of "bird" and "dinosaur"; S. Gelman and Coley, 1990), a description of a single property (e.g., "has andro in its blood" versus "has estro in its blood"), or a proper name (e.g., "Anna" versus "Beth"). Children did not draw inferences from nonsense words (e.g., "fep") when the categories to which they refer are perceptually heterogeneous (Davidson and Gelman, 1990).

Matching experimenter-provided labels were not even necessary for obtaining category-based inferences. Synonymous labels sufficed to induce category-based inferences (e.g., "bunny" and "rabbit"; S. Gelman and Markman, 1986). Even when

Table 2.3.   Control studies, category-based induction

(a) Design: Labels that do not reflect category membership

Label information	Example	Use of labels?
[1] temporary state labels	"sleepy"	no
[2] property descriptions	"has andro in its blood"	no
[3] proper names	"Sally"	no
[4] novel labels, no coherent category	"fep"	no
[5] preferences	"likes the color green"	no

(b) Design: Task that does not require category-based induction

Task	Example	Use of labels?
[6] noninference task	selecting plastic chips	no
[7] perceptual properties	"weighs ten pounds"	no
[8] accidental properties	"fell on the floor this morning"	no

(c) Design: Lack of identical labels for same-category instances

Label information	Example	Use of category?
[9] synonyms	"puppy" and "baby dog"	yes
[10] no labels, but subtle perceptual cues	leaf insect with head and legs	yes

Key: [1] S. Gelman and Coley (1990); [2] S. Gelman, Collman, and Maccoby (1986); [3] Heyman and Gelman (2000), study 3; [4] Davidson and Gelman (1990), study 1; [5] Heyman and Gelman (2000), study 3; [6], [9] S. Gelman and Markman (1986); [7] S. Gelman and Markman (1986); Heyman and Gelman (2000), study 2; [8] S. Gelman (1988), study 1; Heyman and Gelman (2000), study 2; [10] S. Gelman and Markman (1987)

labels were not provided, children drew category-based inferences when pictures included sufficient cues to detect category membership (e.g., they draw an inference from a beetle to a leaf insect, despite the leafy appearance of the latter, apparently because it has eyes and antennae; S. Gelman and Markman, 1987).

I describe three of the control findings in more detail, in order to illustrate the flexibility and sophistication of children's use of language on this task. One of these studies examined children's capacity to make category-based inferences in the absence of adult labels (S. Gelman and Markman, 1987), one examined the role of category coherence in children's inferences (Davidson and Gelman, 1990), and one examined the relative strength of category labels versus property predicates (S. Gelman, Collman, and Maccoby, 1986).

CATEGORY-BASED INFERENCES IN THE ABSENCE OF ADULT LABELS.   I argue that children's beliefs about category identity—not labels per se—crucially influence their inferences. Although adult-supplied labels are a particularly efficient and effective means of conveying category membership, they are not required. This point was particularly evident in an experiment that Ellen Markman and I conducted as a follow-up to our initial set of findings (S. Gelman and Markman, 1987). The study was designed to examine induction patterns in younger children (three-year-olds) and to assess more systematically the separate influences of labeling and object appearances.

In this study, three- and four-year-olds saw ten item sets. For each, a researcher taught children about a novel property of a single target picture (e.g., "See this cat? It can see in the dark") and then asked whether the property was true of each of four test pictures, in turn. There were four types of test pictures: (a) same category, similar appearance (e.g., a cat with markings similar to those of the target cat), (b) same category, dissimilar appearance (e.g., a cat with different markings, in a different position), (c) different category, similar apperance (e.g., a skunk with markings strikingly similar to those of the target cat), and (d) different category, dissimilar appearance (e.g., a dinosaur).

The experiment had three conditions designed to tease apart the effects of language and appearance. In the word-and-picture condition, all pictures were shown and named. In the word-only condition, all pictures were named but the target picture was not shown to the child. Instead, the experimenter simply said, for example, "I see a picture of a cat. This cat can see in the dark." In the picture-only condition, all the pictures were shown, but none were named. The word-and-picture condition and the word-only condition replicated the results described in the earlier study (S. Gelman and Markman, 1986), with children drawing more inductive inferences to items from the same category than to items from a different category, this time at both ages three and four.

For present purposes, though, my focus is on the third condition, the picture-only condition. We had designed the study with the expectation that children would simply rely on outward appearance and so show strikingly different results from those conditions in which the pictures were labeled. And indeed, results in the picture-only condition did differ significantly overall, with children tending to rely more on picture appearance than on category membership. The picture-only condition was the only condition of the three in which children tended to draw more inferences to the similar picture from a different category (e.g., the skunk) than the dissimilar picture from the same category (e.g., the different-looking cat).

However, there was another aspect of the data in the picture-only condition that was unexpected but highly revealing. There was a subset of items for which children correctly determined category membership on the basis of subtle perceptual clues (as confirmed by the names children provided for these items) and then proceeded to draw category-based inferences. In other words, on a subset of the items (three out of ten items at age three years; five out of ten items at age four years), children made nonobvious category-based inferences that did not require experimenter-provided labels. For example, the children appropriately drew inferences from a leaf insect to a black beetle, despite their dissimilar shape and color, because they were able to determine that both were "bugs" (see Figure 2.3). Conversely, children did not draw inferences from a leaf insect to a leaf, despite a striking similarity between the two, because they had attended to subtle featural differences (e.g., eyes and antennae on the leaf insect). When a separate group of children was later asked to name all the pictures used in the study, naming same-category instances with the same label (e.g., "bug" and "bug" for the leaf insect and beetle) correlated highly ($r = .77$) with the children's ability to draw category-based inferences. Those pictures that the children named in accordance with category membership were the ones for which the children also drew appropriate inferences.

Overall, this study illustrates that it is category membership, not label-matching

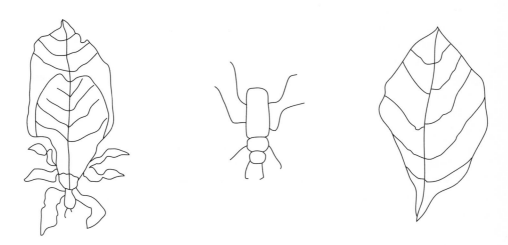

Figure 2.3.   Leaf insect, beetle, and leaf. *Source:* S. Gelman and Markman (1987).

per se, that determines the patterns of children's inductive inferences. Deák and Bauer (1996) have a similar finding: when four-year-olds were presented with unlabeled objects and an inductive inference task, they made taxonomic choices (of taxonomically related but dissimilar-looking objects) an average of 74% of trials, which was significantly above chance.

ROLE OF CATEGORY COHERENCE IN CHILDREN'S INFERENCES.   The results presented so far concern familiar categories (e.g., squirrel, cat) and therefore raise the question of whether children have a more general expectation that novel categories and labels likewise support the sorts of category-based inferences we have been studying. Natalie Davidson and I examined this question by studying children's inductive inferences within novel categories, such as gnulike animals with trunks (Davidson and Gelman, 1990).

In the first of a series of experiments, children were presented with stimulus sets that were comparable in design to those presented in S. Gelman and Markman (1987). Each item set included a target item (e.g., gnulike creature with a long trunk, called "a zav") and four test items (see Figure 2.4): (a) same label, similar appearance (e.g., another gnulike "zav"), (b) different label, similar appearance (e.g., a gnulike "traw"), (c) same label, dissimilar appearance (e.g., a long-necked "zav" with different fur, ears, and tail), and (d) different label, dissimilar appearance (e.g., a "pume" that looked like a cross between a moose and a giraffe). Naming and perceptual similarity were completely orthogonal to one another (e.g., the two "zavs" were as dissimilar from one another as they were from the "traw" and "pume"). Adult similarity ratings confirmed the design of the study. We can consider that "zav" is an incoherent category, in the sense that there is no internal coherence (correlated features) of the sort that Rosch et al. (1976) and Markman (1989) discuss.

The procedure was analogous to that of S. Gelman and Markman (1986). Children learned a new property (e.g., "This zav has four stomachs inside"), then were asked whether each of the test pictures had the property ("Does this traw have four stomachs inside, like this zav?"). In contrast to the earlier work with familiar categories, children based their inferences strictly on appearances and made no use whatsoever of the experimenter-provided labels.

There were two further experiments in which children did make use of label information. Both involved manipulations that affected the structure of the categories in question by strengthening their coherence. In one condition, we strengthened category coherence by relabeling the pictures with familiar labels. For example, "zavs" were now "cows," and the "traw" was now "a deer." (We also pretested the properties on a separate group of children, to make sure that children had no a priori assumptions regarding whether or not these familiar categories had the test properties—for instance, whether cows had four stomachs.) In this condition, when the pictures were given familiar category labels, children drew more inferences to pictures receiving the same label than to pictures with different labels. It

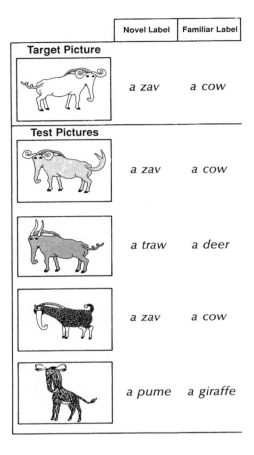

Figure 2.4. Sample item set. *Source*: Davidson and Gelman (1990). Reprinted with the permission of Elsevier Science.

seems that the items inherited coherence from the familiar labels. The category "cow" is already coherent, whereas the category "zav" is not. Accordingly, children were willing to use "cow" as the basis for novel inductions.

In a third experiment, we strengthened category coherence by dropping one of the two conflict items in each set (either [b] different label, similar appearance or [c] same label, dissimilar appearance). Although there was still an anomalous instance (e.g., a zav that was different in appearance from the other zavs), zavs overall were still more similar to one another than were zavs and the traw. In this case, too, within-category inferences increased significantly.

It was not the similarity of pictures taken individually that determined whether children used a word as the basis of induction, but rather the coherence of the set of pictures given the same name. Davidson and I concluded that conceptual grasp of the category being named, and not just the label itself, influenced children's expectations about a label.

CATEGORY LABELS VERSUS PROPERTIES.   Pamela Collman, Eleanor Maccoby, and I designed a study to examine the inductive potential of gender categories, although, as will become clear, the study also has implications for how category labels differ from properties (S. Gelman, Collman, and Maccoby, 1986). Preschool children learned new properties for specific boys and girls and were asked to say which property a new child would have, given a gender label that conflicted with the child's appearance. For example, on one item set, children saw a typical girl, a typical boy, and a boy with long hair (who resembled the girl) (see Figure 2.5; Table 2.4 presents the full set of items). They were told the gender category of each picture ("girl," "boy," "boy"), and then learned, of the typical girl and boy, that they had "estro" and "andro" in their blood, respectively. (The short names were used because pretesting indicated that the longer words estrogen and androgen were difficult for the children to remember.)

The key question was what the third child (the boy who resembled the girl) would have inside his blood. As with the studies of animal and substance categories that Markman and I conducted, children inferred many properties on the basis of category membership, ignoring conflicting perceptual information (e.g., in the example above, inferring that the boy with long hair would have andro in his blood). Specifically, 81% of children's inferences were based on gender category information, and only 19% of their inferences were based on perceptual similarity. Four-year-old children assumed that the gender categories "girl" and "boy" indicate nonobvious properties that extend beyond surface perceptual cues. (See also Berndt and Heller, 1986, and Martin, 1989, for evidence regarding the inductive potential of gender categories.)

One of the most interesting findings from this study involved the contrast between gender labels and gender-linked properties. In a second condition of the experiment, we reversed the labels and the properties. For example, rather than labeling the pictures as "boy," "girl," and "boy," the researcher instead said, "This one will grow up to be a daddy," "This one will grow up to be a mommy," and "This one will grow up to be a daddy." Then, children were taught the category labels for the first two items, and were asked to infer the category membership of the third picture ("Is this one a boy or a girl?"). In short, children learned properties and were asked to infer categories, rather than the reverse. Although these two modes of presentation were structurally equivalent, psychologically they were clearly distinct. Children more readily drew property inferences based on knowing the category label (81% of the time) than they inferred the category label based on knowing the properties (42% of the time).

Children's reliance on gender names as the basis for inductive inferences sug-

Figure 2.5. Sample item set. *Source*: S. Gelman, Collman, and Maccoby (1986). Reprinted with the permission of the Society for Research in Child Development.

Table 2.4. Full set of properties taught in S. Gelman, Collman, and Maccoby (1986)

Male	Female
has little seeds inside	has little eggs inside
has andro in his blood	has estro in her blood
has a little bag outside called a scrotum	has a little bag inside called a uterus
shoulders will get big and wide when he grows up	hips will get big and wide when she grows up
voice will get deep and low when he grows up	voice will stay the same when she grows up
will grow a beard when he gets older	will grow breasts when she gets older
goes pee standing up	goes pee sitting down
will grow up to be a daddy	will grow up to be a mommy
plays with trucks and does boy things	plays with dolls and does girl things

gests that children realized that gender is a category that captures clusters of enduring properties. Why did children fail to infer category membership from a nonperceptual property? Apparently children had little faith in the predictive power of a property. With rare exception, properties do not have the privileged status of category labels and so rarely overpower perceptual information. (The "rare exceptions" include those properties deemed to capture the category essence, such as chromosome information in the case of gender—at least for scientifically educated adults.) Given that attributes do not generally predict the category of an object, children may require specific knowledge that a property is relevant before they are willing to rely on it for classifying an object.

It is particularly interesting that children distinguished the properties from the category labels in this experiment, because several of the properties provided biological information that is (at least for adults) as informative as the labels. Growing up to be a mother is conclusive regarding the categorization of a person as female, as long as "mother" is interpreted in a biological sense. Despite the overwhelming extent to which these properties are closely tied to gender categories, they were considered less predictive than category labels.

Summary of the Basic Effect

The studies of category-based induction demonstrate two important points: children readily infer that members of a category share underlying, nonobvious properties, and language can be an important source of information identifying category membership (see also Markman, 1989). In other words, knowing the category label helps children draw important property inferences. Even when children do not initially realize that both a flamingo and a blackbird are birds, for example, language readily conveys this implication to children of preschool age. The category name is especially important for conveying category membership and inductive potential and for allowing children to learn and use categories that extend beyond perceptually salient features. It also appears that category labels have a privileged status relative to other sorts of information, such as nonlabel properties (see also chapter 8). Now that we have established the basic effect, I turn to questions regarding its scope and development.

LABELS VERSUS PROPERTIES, INDUCTION VERSUS CATEGORIZATION

One striking finding from the earlier results was that labels and properties appear to have a markedly different status for young children. Although in a logical analysis one could construe a label as simply one more property, even four-year-olds recognize a distinction, with implications for their reasoning. Recall that Pamela Collman, Eleanor Maccoby, and I found that children treat inferences from gender labels to properties differently from how they treat inferences from properties to gender labels (S. Gelman, Collman, and Maccoby, 1986). An important question concerns the generality of this effect. Is there a general principle that labels for kinds are a stronger inferential base than properties, or was this result specific to gender categories? After all, gender categories are highly familiar, even to young children, as were several of the properties used in the experiment. It is possible, then, that children have built up specific expectations about the relative strength of these particular categories and properties, rather than more-general expectations about the nature of categories versus properties (including those that are unfamiliar).

The possibility that there may be a more general distinction between labels and properties is an interesting one that would readily fit within an essentialist framework. A category label serves as a stand-in for the kind as a whole. In this respect, only essential properties (such as DNA in the case of animal kinds, or molecular weight in the case of chemical kinds) should be as powerful as the category label in guiding inductive inferences. However, given that essentialism tends to be a placeholder notion, with the child or adult not knowing exactly what the essence is, most of the time any given property will not be nearly as predictive as a label for the kind. Put somewhat differently: when given the category label, you can be certain that the instances have the category essence. When given a property, your certainty that the instances have the essence will depend on the extent to which you believe the properties are essential.

The distinction between the category label and a property can also be construed as a distinction between two sorts of tasks: induction (which entails inferences from a category or a category label to properties) and categorization (which entails inferences from properties to a category or a category label). In this section I present evidence that this distinction (construed either as a distinction between types of information, or as a distinction between types of tasks) is fundamental to young children.

Marianne Taylor and I found support for a distinction between category-based induction and other sorts of reasoning tasks (Taylor and Gelman, 1993). We contrasted category-based induction with similarity judgments and found that four-year-olds reliably made use of different sorts of information in the two tasks. Children saw triads of pictures of people varying in age and/or gender. Each triad included one target picture and two comparison pictures. For example, one triad depicted a baby girl (the target), a baby boy, and a woman. In the similarity condition, children were asked to point to the comparison picture that was "more like" the target. In the inductive-inference condition, children first learned a new property of the target (e.g., "This baby girl has nitons inside") and then were asked to point to the comparison picture that had the same property ("Which one also has nitons inside?"). Even though children in the two conditions saw identical sets of pictures, they responded with distinctly different patterns. The four-year-olds in the similarity condition used gender on 68% of the conflict trials, whereas those in the inductive-inference condition used gender on only 20% of the same trials. The comparison of conditions revealed that four-year-olds made a sharp distinction between what is salient (typically gender) and what supports an allowable inference (typically age).

Of course, gender is also a category with high inductive potential, as we have seen earlier (S. Gelman, Collman, and Maccoby, 1986). Gender categories do not reduce to superficial appearances. Given a contrast between gender and physical similarity (such as hair color and length), gender wins out. But age groupings have even higher inductive potential. Given a contrast between gender and age, age wins out. The distinction between a baby and a child, or between a child and an adult, is even more powerful than the distinction between male and female (keeping age constant). The main point to keep in mind, though, is the contrast between similarity and induction. Gender is perceived as more strongly marked and visible than its inductive potential would support. At least within this one domain, children honor a principled distinction between what something is like (similarity) and what properties it supports (induction).

More broad-based support for a distinction between category-based induction and categorization comes from Mitsumi Imai (1995). In a task modeled directly on S. Gelman, Collman, and Maccoby (1986), she presented Japanese preschool children with a series of thirteen triads that drew widely from a range of categories, including different types of animals, artifacts, and foods. For each triad, there was a target picture (e.g., blackbird), a taxonomic alternative (e.g., penguin), and a shape alternative (e.g., bat). Children were randomly assigned to one of two conditions.

In the property-inference condition, children learned novel words in "dinosaur language" for all three pictures (e.g., "fep" and "wap"), with the target and taxonomic alternative being given the same label. Then children learned a new property of each of the alternatives (e.g., that the penguin can see very far, and that the bat can hear from far away) and were asked which property was true of the target. This condition was equivalent to the category-to-property inference condition of S. Gelman, Collman, and Maccoby. In the word-learning condition, children learned a novel word for each of the two alternatives (e.g., "fep" and "wap"), and learned a new property about each of the three pictures (e.g., the penguin and blackbird were each said to see very far, whereas the bat was said to hear from far away). The property taught on the target matched the property taught on the taxonomic alternative. Then children were asked which label applied to the target. This condition was equivalent to the property-to-category-inference condition of S. Gelman, Collman, and Maccoby. Imai found that taxonomic inferences were higher in the property-inference condition than in the word-learning condition (73% versus 51%, respectively). Only the label-based property inferences were significantly above chance. Property inferences elicit different reasoning strategies than word learning.

In a thoughtful analysis, Deák and Bauer (1996) suggest that the relevant question in investigating children's categorization is not "Do children use perceptual or conceptual information?"—a question to which there is no simple answer—but rather "What are the contexts that lead children to make use of different sorts of information?" One of the factors they investigated is task type: whether the child is posed an inductive-inference question, of the sort detailed in this chapter, or a categorization question (e.g., "Which ones are the same kind of thing?," which they call a "taxonomic question"). Deák and Bauer conducted an intensive investigation, systematically varying labeling, item type (drawing versus object), and task type (inductive inference versus taxonomic question). Two findings are of particular interest here. First, as we have found (e.g., S. Gelman and Markman, 1986), labeling had a substantial effect on children's answers by increasing their rate of taxonomic responding, in some cases even doubling or tripling the rate of taxonomic choices (see Table 2.5). Second, preschoolers selected taxonomic choices more often when given an inductive-inference task than when given a categorization task. This task effect was limited to the condition in which children saw objects (not drawings) and no labels were provided.

Florian (1994) suggested that a full comparison of labels and properties requires a complete 2 x 2 design in which one examines inferences both from and to both labels and properties (see Table 2.6). Florian designed a series of experiments that included all four cells, focused on novel animal categories. For example, in the L → L cell, children would hear, "This animal is a trud [pointing to target animal], and this animal is a keech [pointing to probe animal]. This also is also a wug [pointing to target animal]. Do you think this keech is a wug, like this trud is a wug?" In contrast, S. Gelman, Collman, and Maccoby (1986; henceforth referred to as "GCM") examined only two of those cells, those involving mismatch between type of information and type of inference (cells L → P and P → L in Table 2.6, marked "GCM").

What are the predictions for the other two cells: when a label is supplied and a label is inferred (L → L), and when a property is supplied and a property is inferred (P → P)? Table 2.6 presents these predictions in rough form. First, consider property-to-property inferences. The essentialist account predicts that property-to-property inferences should be lower than label-to-property inferences, because only labels (not properties) directly reveal membership in a kind. Nonetheless, children should make at least some use of a novel property when making inferences about another property, because children also expect that properties form correlated clusters. To use Rosch et al.'s (1976) well-known example, knowing that an animal has claws rather than hooves greatly increases the probability that it has feathers rather than fur (see also Malt and Smith, 1984). Accordingly, I would predict some property-to-property inferences, but fewer compared to label-to-property inferences.

Now consider label-to-label inferences. Here the essentialist account makes no strong predictions. It does not predict higher L → L inferences than P → L inferences, because, as already discussed, labeling is governed by principles wholly distinct from those governing distribution of properties. Whereas properties tend to cluster, labels tend to contrast (see Clark, 1987). Once a person knows that two animals share a name, it may even be somewhat less likely that they will share

Table 2.5.   Mean percentage of taxonomic choices

	Drawing	Object
Categorization		
No labels	20	46
Labels	75	92
Inductive inference		
No labels	27	74
Labels	81	81

Source: Deák and Bauer (1996).

Table 2.6.   Predictions for conditions comparing labels and properties (where "low," "medium," and "high" refer to how much the information positively predicts the inference)

	Inferences are made about:	
	Label	Property
Information is supplied about:		
Label	L → L: low	L → P: high
Property	P → L: low	P → P: medium

a second name. At the very least, then, essentialism does not predict high L → L inferences.

Florian's studies were complex in design (four experiments, each with up to twenty-four different kinds of trials), and it is not my goal to present them fully. Instead, I will highlight a few main findings from the studies with children, describing aspects of the design as needed.[3] It is important to note that my interpretations of the results do not always conform to those of the studies' author.

Overall, matching verbal information (when target and test pictures matched in label or property) affected children's answers, whereas mismatching information did not. For example, if a child heard two different pieces of information (either labels or properties) for two similar animals, there was no significant effect on inferences, compared to a control condition in which no verbal information was provided. Because of this overall effect, the rest of what I report will focus exclusively on the trials in which children received matching information.

In two important respects, the data replicated the earlier work on category-based induction. First, as in GCM, label-to-property inferences (L → P) were higher than property-to-label inferences (P → L). Florian did not directly compare these two cells in her analyses, so it is not possible to determine whether these differences were statistically significant. However, the L → P advantage appears sizable. In experiment 2, where the precise numbers were presented, Florian found a mean of 62% for L → P inferences, compared to a mean of 34% for P → L inferences. The relative advantage of label-to-property inferences is predicted by essentialism.

The second respect in which the data replicated the earlier results is that shared labels boosted property inferences. Specifically, L → P inferences were significantly higher than a control condition in which no information was supplied (what I am calling the 0 → P condition). For example, in experiment 2, the percentage of inferences to the dissimilar picture doubled from the no-information control when a matching label was provided (31% in the no-information control; 62% in the matching label condition).

The one finding that did not conform to essentialist predictions was that property information boosted property inferences at least as powerfully as did label information. Specifically, although shared labels enhanced property inferences (L → P), shared property information enhanced them just as much if not more (P → P). However, it is important to keep in mind that the information-processing demands were highest in the property-to-property condition, where children had to keep track of three wholly novel properties (two properties for one picture and one property for a second picture), all while trying to decide on an answer regarding another property question. I suggest that the processing burden may have led some children to adopt a simple "matching" strategy in this condition (if the two pictures match on one set of properties, then the child guesses that they match on the second set of properties, too). Some support for this suggestion comes from the fact that this matching tendency was actually higher for children in experiment 2, who were on average six months younger than the children in Experiment 1 (3;10 versus 4;4). In any case, the comparison of L → P versus P → P inferences deserves further study.

The other notable finding from these experiments was that, as expected, inferences about labels were quite distinct from inferences about properties. Children's inferences regarding labels were uniformly low, whether the information supplied was a label (L → L) or a property (P → L). Neither of these conditions differed from the no-information control condition. Whereas properties were assumed to cohere in a correlated structure, labels were not.

SUMMARY.   We have evidence for a three-way distinction among similarity judgments, categorization judgments, and category-based induction (see also Rips, 1989, for a distinction between similarity and categorization). Category-based induction most reliably leads children toward taxonomic categories and away from conflicting appearances. Correspondingly, labels are treated as very different bases of information than properties. It is notable that these distinctions emerge so consistently by the time children are preschool age.

ESSENTIALIZED DOMAINS

My focus to this point has been primarily on animal categories, but new sets of issues arise when we consider other domains. I suggest that category-based reasoning appears broadly (not just for biological kinds, *contra* Atran, 1998) but not promiscuously for all categories (that is, it is reduced for artifacts, *contra* Carey, 1996). The data currently available on category-based induction outside the biological domain are slim but suggest that children construct domain-specific expectations about the structure of categories—expectations that tend to entail richer inferences for categories of natural kinds (including living things and natural substances).

First, consider artifacts. There is somewhat of a paradox in the discussion of artifact categories. Most essentialist accounts presume domain differences in essentializing, with living kinds and natural substances clearly construed in an essentialized manner and human artifacts less so (Markman, 1989; Keil, 1989; S. Gelman, 1988; see the bird-tchotchke example provided earlier).[4] An artifact category such as "cups" is unlikely to have a rich cluster of nonobvious properties that are intrinsic to the objects being classified. To the extent that cups have a causal essence, they are probably linked to the intentions of the humans who created them, rather than to properties inherent in the cups themselves (P. Bloom, 1996). Likewise, artifacts can participate in rich causal theories, including those in archaeology and cultural studies (Eakin, 2001), but such theories concern interactions between the object and the larger world, not properties intrinsic to the artifacts themselves (Keil and Richardson, 1999). Whatever commonalities are found within artifacts are ones that the human creators intended.

However, past studies arguing for the existence of correlated structure in categories have typically presented artifacts as the prime example. For example, Rosch et al.'s (1976) classic work on basic-level categories focused primarily on artifact domains (including furniture, toys, tools, and clothing). Rosch pointed out that categories within these domains, such as chairs, books, or screwdrivers, are notable for capturing clusters of correlated properties and high within-category similarity, including overall shape.

The resolution to this paradox, I suggest, is that Rosch focused on known properties, and induction by definition focuses on the unknown. I predict that despite the cluster of common properties richly described by Rosch for both animal and artifact categories, when it comes to further inferences, to inferences beyond what is already known, and to inferences about nonobvious or hidden properties, artifacts will separate from animal kinds, and differences will emerge. Artifacts will support some novel inferences, but they are quite limited compared to those of natural kind categories.

Surprisingly few studies have compared induction within animal and artifact categories directly. However, when natural kinds (including animals, plants, and—

in some studies—substances) are compared to artifact categories, children tend to draw more inferences within the former than within the latter (S. Gelman, 1988; S. Gelman and O'Reilly, 1988). This domain difference is found whether the properties concern internal parts, functions, or behaviors. However, the fact that there are quantitative differences between domains does not necessarily suggest a qualitative difference in children's reasoning about those domains. For example, children clearly draw at least some category-based inferences with artifacts. They draw more nonobvious inferences within an artifact category (e.g., from a straight-back chair to an armchair) than to unrelated items (e.g., from a straight-back chair to a fly).

Even for young children, the sort of labeling effects on induction discussed earlier can also be seen within artifact categories (see studies by Graham, Kilbreath, and Welder, discussed earlier). For example, when my son Adam was two years of age, I gave him a snack, a small tin that contained bite-sized chunks of fruit, along with a spoon. I told him that it was a "fruit cup." He then held the container up to his mouth and attempted to drink it. Ordinarily Adam would not have attempted to drink solid food; the word "cup" seemed to encourage a nonobvious inference.

A comparison that should be done (but has yet to be done in any systematic way) is to examine children's inferences about artifacts on a Gelman and Markman–style conflict task to determine whether artifacts, like natural kinds, permit inferences that override outward appearances. I am aware of only one study with this design (Davidson and Gelman, 1990), which found no difference between domains in children's category-based inferences. However, that study was unusual in focusing on novel categories and highly atypical instances. It will be important to reexamine this issue comparing living kinds, natural substances, and artifacts directly, with familiar categories.

One unexpected difference between natural-kind-based and artifact-based induction emerged in a study of superordinate level categories (e.g., animals versus toys; S. Gelman and O'Reilly, 1988). For animal and plant categories, inferences within the basic level were consistently stronger than inferences across basic-level categories (for example, children drew more inferences from one type of dog to another than from a dog to a rabbit). In contrast, for artifact categories, inferences across basic-level categories were often just as frequent as inferences within basic-level categories (e.g., children drew as many inferences from a train to blocks as from one train to another). This pattern held across both children (preschoolers and second-graders) and adults. At least on some items, participants apparently responded to the perceived substance out of which the artifacts were made. For example, one item set included trains and blocks, but the respondents construed them as questions about wood and metal, leading them to draw inferences from the wooden train to the blocks. When we examined how often participants showed this sort of pattern (making an inference to a superordinate match, but skipping either a basic-level match or a more typical superordinate match), they did so significantly more often for artifacts than for natural kinds (26% versus 14% in study

1; 38% versus 16% in study 2). This result suggests that artifact superordinates are less tightly structured than natural kind superordinates.

Gail Heyman and I also found a domain difference in children's inductive inferences about traits (Heyman and Gelman, 2000b). We found that three- and four-year-old children made more category-based inferences within the domain of people than within the domain of dolls. Specifically, three- and four-year-olds saw a series of triads that posed a conflict between outward appearances and novel trait adjectives. For example, children were shown pictures of two dissimilar girls, one described as "zav" and one described as "not zav." Then they saw a third girl who more closely resembled the "zav" girl but was described as "not zav." Children learned a novel feature of each of the first two girls (e.g., "wants to erkin [versus towket] when she is grown up"), and were asked to predict which property generalized to the third girl (e.g., "Does she want to erkin when she is grown up, like this girl who is zav, or does she want to towket when she is grown up, like this girl who is not zav?").

When asked to reason about people, children made adjective-based responses significantly above chance (5.31 out of 8 trials, or 66%). See Table 2.7 for the response patterns of individual children. Interestingly, however, the domain of people was treated as special. We found that children treated adjectives for people as more powerful than adjectives for nonpeople. We labeled the same drawings of human faces as either "people" (study 1) or "dolls" (study 2). For example, in study 1, one item would be introduced as "This girl is zav"; in study 2, the same item would be introduced as "This doll is zav." The properties for dolls were designed to be as similar as possible to the properties for people. However, some differences were introduced in order for the properties to apply sensibly to each domain. For example, when the triads were characterized as "girls" or "boys," one novel property pair was: "likes to play jimjam" versus "likes to play tibbits"; when the triads were characterized as "dolls," the corresponding novel property pair was: "is used to play jimjam" versus "is used to play tibbits." Whereas children drew adjective-based inferences an average of 66% of the time when the pictures were labeled as

Table 2.7.   Percentage of participants using a consistent adjective-based strategy, a consistent appearance-based strategy, or neither

	Strategy		
	Adjective-based	Appearance-based	Neither
Study 1 (person)	56	6	37
Study 2 (doll)	19	37	44
Study 3 (person condition)	58	0	42
Study 3 (doll condition)	26	11	63

Source: Heyman and Gelman (2000). Reprinted with the permission of Elsevier Science.

people, they drew adjective-based inferences only 41% of the time when the same pictures were labeled as dolls.

In a third study, the properties were identical across people and dolls (e.g., "always makes people laugh" versus "never makes people laugh" was used for one of the picture sets, both when it was described as portraying people and when it was described as portraying dolls; see Table 2.8 for the full set of properties). When the pictures were described as people, children used novel adjectives as the basis of inductive inferences 69% of the time (significantly above chance), but when the pictures were described as dolls, children did not show this pattern—they were at chance (mean of 58%). Everything in the two conditions was identical, except whether the pictures were referred to as "people" or "dolls." This result suggests that there is indeed something special about the domain of people in how children interpret novel labels.

It is striking that the materials presented to children were identical in the two cases—same pictures, same properties, same labels. The only distinction was a conceptual one: whether children construed the drawings as representing real humans, or instead construed the drawings as representing representations of humans. We hypothesize that the human-doll distinction does not indicate anything special about dolls, but rather reflects a more general domain difference between people and inanimate entities. Dolls are rather atypical artifacts, because they are sometimes treated as animate (during pretend play, for example), but it is thus all the more compelling that children differentiated between people and artifacts in this potentially confusing or borderline case.

Summary of Domain Issues

The data currently available comparing natural kinds (including animals, plants, and natural substances) and artifacts on an induction task suggest that natural kinds are construed as more "kindlike" than artifact categories, even by preschool children. Children tend to draw fewer inductive inferences within artifact categories than animal kinds. The results also reveal an important distinction between

Table 2.8. Properties used in study 3 (person-versus-doll study); Heyman and Gelman (2000)

Wears only old shoes / Wears only new shoes
Is found in the kitchen all the time / Is found in the TV room all the time
Always gets lost / Never gets lost
Is always staying clean / Is always getting dirty
Is always around books / Is always around music
Always falls down / Never falls down
Always helps people feel better when they are sad / Never helps people feel better when they are sad
Always makes people laugh / Never makes people laugh

---

people and dolls, in the expectations children hold. People are assumed to supply a richer basis than dolls for inductive inferences from adjectival descriptions.

What remains to be seen is where exactly the line is to be drawn. For example, is the category of people special, and distinct from all other categories (including animal kinds) in permitting adjectives as a basis for induction? Or are artifacts distinct from both people and animals in having less inductive potential? Which domain distinctions are found when reasoning about nouns, and which domain distinctions are found when reasoning about adjectives? When do these distinctions emerge, and how do they change developmentally? These are empirical questions that require further study.

PRIVILEGED LEVELS

Each object falls within multiple classifications. "Brown-backed gray squirrel," "gray squirrel," "squirrel," "mammal," "animal," "living thing," "physical object"— these are different ways of characterizing the same beast. Are all of these levels essentialized? Intuition suggests that the answer is no. It stretches the imagination to think that there is some hidden, nonobvious essence that characterizes "objects" as a class. At the other extreme, we are unlikely to posit a deep, enduring difference in kind between brown-backed gray squirrels and other types of gray squirrels. Differences exist, to be sure, but I suspect they are construed as rather superficial and not terribly predictive. Somewhere between those two extremes are the levels that are construed in an essentialist manner. Which levels are privileged for induction? The answer to this question has important implications for why categories promote induction.

Adult Studies of Category Levels

Coley, Medin, and Atran (1997) have made use of an ingenious method to study which levels are privileged for induction among adults. They taught people facts about an entire category at a given level (e.g., "All gray squirrels have enzyme X"), then tested the degree to which the fact generalized to the next higher level (e.g., "How likely is it that all squirrels have enzyme X?"). The goal is to look for the "elbow" in the inductive patterns—that is, the point at which inductive potential plateaus. In Coley et al.'s words, the privileged level is "the highest or most abstract level at which inductive confidence is strong" (Coley, Medin, Proffitt, Lynch, and Atran, 1999, p. 210). When this study is done both with U.S. college students at Northwestern University (NWU) and with Itzaj Mayan adults in the rainforests of Guatemala, there is clear agreement that a "middle" level of categorization—the "generic species" level—is privileged for both populations. These data are presented in Figure 2.6 (see Coley et al., 1997, for more extensive presentation).

So, for example, U.S. students readily generalize from brown-backed gray squirrels to gray squirrels (specific), and from gray squirrels to squirrels (generic), but

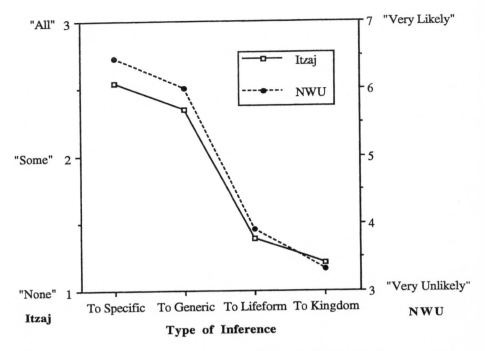

Figure 2.6   *Source:* Coley, Medin, Proffitt, et al. (1999). Reprinted with the permission of MIT Press.

not from squirrels to mammals (life form), or from mammals to animals (kingdom). Likewise, they generalize from northern rainbow trout to rainbow trout (specific), and from rainbow trout to trout (generic), but not from trout to fish (life form), or from fish to animals (kingdom). The Itzaj show the same patterns, though they were tested with categories indigenous to their environment (e.g., agouti, spider monkey).

Surprisingly, U.S. college students display a markedly different pattern on standard categorization measures. When U.S. undergraduates are asked to write down all the attributes they can think of for a given category, they treat the life-form level (e.g., bird, fish, tree, flower, or bush) as basic and privileged in the sense of capturing just as many features as lower-level categories. In contrast, the Itzaj treat the generic-species level as privileged. Put a slightly different way, the Itzaj are consistent across tasks (displaying greatest knowledge about the generic-species level and also treating this level as privileged with respect to induction), whereas the U.S. college students exhibit a surprising inconsistency.

Coley, Medin, et al. (1999) explain this discrepancy by appealing to a distinction between knowledge (as measured by Rosch's tasks, which required generating properties or identifying pictures) and expectation (as measured by tasks of inductive inference). They suggest that the college students expected properties to cluster at the generic-species level, even without a detailed knowledge base. Why? The key, Coley, Medin, et al. suggest, is the system of nomenclature: generic-species categories are named with a single label (e.g., squirrel, trout, oak, marigold, or sparrow). Levels below that are (in English and universally) typically marked as subtypes directly, by means of compound names (e.g,. "gray squirrel," "rainbow trout," "red oak"; see Berlin, Breedlove, and Raven, 1973). Adults—and young children (Gelman, Wilcox, and Clark, 1989)—recognize that compound nouns can indicate subordination in a hierarchy. The category level that is encoded in single lexemes receives privileged status:

> Labels may "stake out" a category, despite lack of specific knowledge about members of that category. . . . This may include the assumptions that the category will be coherent, category members will share many underlying properties beyond what meets the eye, and that in effect, there is "where the conceptual action is." In other words, *labels may signal categories that are believed to embody an essence.* (Coley, Medin, et al., 1999, p. 214; emphasis added)

To summarize: the Coley, Medin, et al. findings are extremely significant for three reasons: they reveal a level of categorization, the generic-species level, that is cross-culturally (perhaps universally) privileged with respect to induction; they demonstrate a gap between speakers' knowledge and their expectations, analogous to the argument I have been making with regard to children; and they implicate language as a potential influence on essentialist reasoning.

Child Studies of Category Levels

I will draw on Coley, Medin, and Atran's (1997) analysis to consider the issue with children. I predict that children, too, would rely heavily on linguistic cues to determine which level of abstraction is privileged. Specifically, they should draw most inferences from categories that are labeled with a single lexeme. This pattern may even be stronger in children than adults, as children have access to even less knowledge.

None of the developmental studies have made use of the methodology employed by Coley, Medin, and Atran, and so cannot be compared directly to the findings with adults. Instead, in the developmental studies, children learn a fact about an individual "target" object, then are given other objects, more or less related to the target, in order to track how far the fact has generalized (e.g., to others of the same subordinate-level category? to others of the same basic-level category? to others of the same superordinate-level category?).

By three or four years of age, children clearly honor the level of abstraction that is labeled monolexemically (corresponding to Rosch's basic level). Inferences to the basic level are more powerful than inferences to superordinate levels (S. Gelman and O'Reilly, 1988). And inferences to the basic level are not significantly less powerful than inferences to subordinate levels (Waxman, Lynch, et al., 1997), despite the greater similarity between the target object (i.e., the object on which the new fact was taught) and the subordinate-level match. For example, Waxman, Lynch, et al. (1997) find that children were as likely to generalize a new fact taught about a collie to a setter as they were to generalize it to another collie. The subordinate level could be highlighted only by providing additional manipulations (such as contrastive information to emphasize how subordinate-level categories are distinct from one another). Inductive inferences at both levels were clearly higher than inductive inferences to the superordinate level (e.g., from collie to caribou).[5]

With children younger than about two or three years of age, there is more controversy as to which level of abstraction children privilege. Mandler and Mc-Donough (1996) propose that below age two, children privilege a more abstract level for induction. The researchers use a generalized-imitation technique, in which a researcher models a particular action with a given object (e.g., giving a toy dog a drink from a cup), then gives the child an opportunity to model that action on either or both of a pair of additional objects (e.g., a different dog and a cat, or a bird and an airplane). In an important series of studies with fourteen-month-olds, Mandler and McDonough found that infants treated members of different basic-level categories as equivalent as long as they were within the same global category (either animals or vehicles). So, for example, fourteen-month-olds generalized drinking from a dog to a cat, a bird, and even an anteater (which was unfamiliar). They did not generalize across domains; for example, they did not generalize drinking from a dog to a vehicle, either familiar, such as a car, or unfamiliar, such as a forklift. McDonough and Mandler (1998) obtained similar results with nine- and eleven-month-olds. They concluded that fourteen-month-olds generally do not yet subdivide the domains of animals and vehicles into finer-grained categories (Mandler and McDonough, 1996, p. 331).

Mandler and McDonough also considered a potential counterargument: that the properties used (such as drinking or giving a ride) may have been more appropriate for global categories than for basic-level categories. After all, drinking is a property that applies generally to animals, not just to dogs; giving a ride is a property that applies generally to vehicles, not just to cars. From Mandler and McDonough's own work, we know that children can differentiate between different types of properties in their inductive potential (for example, restricting "drinking" to animates, but not restricting "washing" to animates). It is therefore important to examine the scope of children's inferences when they are provided with properties that properly apply only to a given basic-level kind. To address this issue, Mandler and McDonough ran a further study in which children saw basic-level properties modeled (e.g., chewing a bone was modeled on a dog and then tested on a goose; drinking was modeled on a cup and then tested on a frying pan). Fourteen-month-old children again failed to differentiate within the global categories. Only twenty-month-olds began to restrict their inductive generalizations to basic-level categories, and even then primarily within the domain of artifacts rather than animals or plants.

A plausible developmental story, and the one that Mandler and McDonough would tell, is that children initially form quite broad global categories, and do not treat basic-level categories as a basis of induction until about two years of age.[6] Mandler and McDonough acknowledge that infants can readily perceive differences between basic-level kinds (such as dog versus duck; see Eimas and Quinn, 1994) but argue that such differences are not treated as conceptually relevant. They theorize that development proceeds from general to specific, with children at first treating broad kinds as inductive bases and only gradually coming to treat basic-level kinds in this manner.

Mandler and McDonough's important results demonstrate several new things: that even infants are not limited to basic-level categories but instead have access to broader categories, that infants' inductive inferences need not conform to perceptual groupings, and that inductive inferences yield different results from other classification tasks.

Where I think the jury is still out, however, is whether global categories are somehow privileged for young children (those below twenty months, say), and conversely, whether basic-level categories are inaccessible to young children for induction. It is difficult to reconcile Mandler and McDonough's elegant experimental results with several observations:

1. By nine to twelve months of age, infants draw novel inferences from one object to another of the same kind, when the property is distinctive to that sort of thing (e.g., turning a special kind of can upside-down to make a funny sound) (Baldwin, Markman, and Melartin, 1993). Importantly, babies discriminate in their property inductions, rarely extending this expectation to toys of sharply different appearance.
2. Twelve-month-olds treat basic-level categories (e.g., cup, duck, car, bottle) as sortals, on a task that demands understanding these as different kinds of things (Xu and Carey, 1996).
3. Waxman and Markow (1995) found basic-level categorization in twelve-month-olds, using the same task Mandler and McDonough (1993) had used.
4. Children's first words appear by about thirteen months of age, and typically include names for basic-level categories (such as "dog," "cracker," or "ball"; Nelson, 1973). Also, children between thirteen and eighteen months are generally quite good at making at least one sort of category-based inference: reporting the distinctive sounds made by different animal kinds (e.g., a cow says "moo"; a dog says "woof-woof").

I illustrate the problem with an anecdote about my daughter, Stephanie, age sixteen months at the time. We were outside when Stephanie picked up a long, skinny pinecone. I named it for her: "That's a pinecone." She looked at me with a rather surprised look, and then raised the pinecone to her head and pulled it through her hair—combing (or should I say "coning"?) her hair with the cone/comb. It seemed that she heard "pinecone" as "pine-comb" and then inferred that it could be used in the same manner as other combs. If my interpretation is apt, then she mapped a category-specific function onto the basic-level kind "comb."

Based on these varied bits of evidence, I strongly suspect that children do have the capacity to treat basic-level categories as a basis of induction from their first uses of the corresponding words in language. What is still missing is an account of how such sensitivity can be reconciled with Mandler and McDonough's studies. Perhaps the right basic-level properties have not yet been studied in their tasks. It would be interesting, in this regard, to run the Mandler and McDonough studies again, supplying basic-level labels for the items as they are introduced. If my account is correct, then doing so should highlight the basic-level kinds, thereby inducing basic-level inductive inferences.

Conclusions

The induction task sheds new light on the question of privileged category levels. Both the adult data (e.g., Coley, Medin, et al., 1999) and the developmental data (e.g., Mandler and McDonough, 1998) find notable differences in performance and sensitivities when the task is an inductive inference task as compared to a test of category knowledge. As Coley, Medin, et al. point out, induction is a test of expectations, and expectations do not reduce to knowledge. For adults, the generic-species level (e.g., trout, maple, lark, deer) seems to be privileged for inductive inferences. The constancy of this finding across two very different populations that have different "basic" levels in a Roschian analysis is striking. This unexpected finding suggests the importance of language for guiding adults' inferences. The developmental question yields findings that are more debatable, especially for children younger than two years of age. Nonetheless, I have argued that there, too, the basic level is primary for induction.

SUMMARY

Induction is one of the most important functions of categories (E. Smith and Medin, 1981)—indeed it is arguably *the* most important function (J. Anderson, 1990). Categories serve not only to organize the knowledge we have already acquired, but also to guide our expectations and encourage inductive inferences about novel properties (Coley, Medin, et al., 1999).

Young children's category-based inferences are consistent with essentialism in two respects. First, the properties children infer from one category member to another concern internal features and nonvisible functions. Second, children draw inferences even when category membership competes with perceptual similarity. These findings demonstrate that category-based induction cannot be reduced to some general similarity metric (in contrast to Quine, 1977). This conclusion conflicts with standard accounts of children's categorization, which appeal to seismic shifts with age, from "perceptual" to "conceptual," from "concrete" to "abstract," or from "obvious" to "inferred." Even for young children, nonobvious properties are central to category-based inferences.

There is enormous subtlety and flexibility regarding when children do and do not make category-based inductive inferences. No simple rule can account for the patterns. Children are not using a simple matching strategy. They do not display a simple preference for either nouns or adjectives. The effect emerges not only with familiar labels, but with other labels, too; however, it does not emerge with all labels. The only explanation that satisfactorily accounts for the varied patterns of data is that children assess the extent to which entities are members of the same kind (often conveyed via a label or phrase, though not necessarily) and independently assess the extent to which the property in question is relatively enduring (rather than temporary or accidental). Category-based induction results only when the entities belong to a kind and the property is relatively enduring.

Most theoretical accounts of categories, though they do not specifically exclude the possibility of such inferences, do not provide a means of explaining them. For example, defining-features theories of categories assume that category-relevant features are finite and known; prototype theories assume that the relevant properties have been detected and observed (even when learning is automatic and nondeliberate). Inductive inferences, in contrast, concern what is not yet known.

We also have some clues as to why children succeed in category-based induction when in many respects they fail at constructing theory-based categories on their own. If we were to give these same children a set of stimuli, without language cues, and ask them to sort them using some kind of traditional measure (e.g., "put together the ones that go together"), we would expect them to perform poorly. Likewise, attention to subtle features would increase with age (see, e.g., Hatano and Inagaki, 1999). However, when they are given a categorization and asked to make inferences, even the youngest children we have tested have an expectation that items from the same category will share novel properties.

These data are consistent with an essentialist bias. However, by themselves the data in this chapter do not provide clear-cut evidence of essentialism. They could, for example, be accounted for in terms of a tendency to view categories as inhering in kinds, without children further assuming an underlying essential force (Strevens, 2000; see chapter 10 for arguments against this possibility). However, in conjunction with the studies reviewed in chapters 3 through 6, these data are, I argue, best accounted for in terms of an essentialist bias.

Chapter 3
Hidden, Nonobvious Properties

> Of course he's different. There are genes and energy in him from some-
> body else's body. Those things affect you.
>
> Wife of heart-transplant recipient, discussing changes her husband expe-
> rienced after receiving his new heart, in Claire Sylvia and William Novak,
> *A Change of Heart*

In this chapter I make the case that by four years of age children construct beliefs and assumptions about properties that are "internal, but . . . unknown" (to borrow from Locke) and that these beliefs have serious consequences for reasoning about what things are. This set of constructions contradicts standard views of children as focused on what is concrete, perceptual, and in the immediate context.

Explicit essentialist accounts given by adults characterize essences as invisible, distinct from outward appearances, and remarkably stable and resilient. I illustrate this point with the self-reported experiences of Claire Sylvia, who underwent a heart-lung transplant (Sylvia and Novak, 1997). Following the surgery, she described feeling changes in her behavior and emotions. For example, she began to crave beer and fried chicken—foods she had never liked before. She became more aggressive, independent, and confident, and for the first time walked with a swagger. Even her favorite colors changed, from pink and red to blue and green. Sylvia attributed these changes to characteristics of her donor, a young man named Tim. She said she felt "as if a second soul were sharing my body" (p. 107), and referred to "this new male energy" (p. 107). In speculating on what remained of the man who had donated his heart, she concluded, "Perhaps what still existed of Tim was his purer essence" (p. 169). Sylvia's therapist concurs: "'I am beginning to believe that some of Tim's essence has transmigrated to Claire. . . . If the transplant has somehow passed on elements of his temperament, personality, and identity, then psychological residues of the actual Tim L. (not just the image of 'Tim') may now inhabit Claire'" (p. 165). Others that Sylvia interviewed used very similar language: "I could feel his essence, his energy" (Harriet, wife of a heart donor, talking about meeting the recipient of her dead husband's heart; p. 218). "Anyone who receives a new heart is getting a big ball of subtle energy. Ancient cultures have known about subtle energy throughout history, and have viewed it as the vital force of all creation'" (Paul Pearsall, author; p. 225).[1]

What I find interesting about this account is not the question of whether or not it is true or even plausible, but rather how Sylvia (and others interviewed in the book) construe a personal essence: as nonvisible, internal, persisting through massive changes, and having the capacity to influence outward behaviors and preferences. It is both material (located in the heart, a flesh-and-blood bodily organ) and immaterial (an "energy" or "soul").

Children may or may not understand heart transplants in this manner, but by the time they have reached preschool age, children have a wealth of beliefs that closely approximate Sylvia's characterization of an essence. I will review three sorts of evidence: stability over transformations, boundary intensification, and nonobvious properties.

STABILITY OVER TRANSFORMATIONS

Although essentialism implies within-category similarities, somewhat paradoxically it is within-category differences that more strongly speak to essentialism: differences over time (from caterpillar to butterfly; from baby to adult human) and differences across instances (an ostrich and a hummingbird are both birds; a chihuahua and a Great Dane are both dogs). Maintaining category identity over striking observable changes constitutes evidence that the categorizer asserts some sort of underlying constancy. Essentialist reasoning is thus implicit in judgments that an animal's identity is retained over even dramatic transformations (Keil, 1989).

When do children appreciate the stability of identity over transformations? Once again, there is a "standard," traditional answer (that children do not grasp constancy until about second grade), and there are more sophisticated expectations that children reveal under more sensitive testing conditions (that children expect constancy by preschool age). I consider, in turn, studies of constancy, growth and metamorphosis, and origin of species.

Constancy Studies

Piaget demonstrated that preschoolers have considerable difficulty reasoning about transformations of physical quantities (e.g., volume, area, and length). These conservation tasks reveal a consistent error: preschool children tend to report that superficial changes alter the physical quantity. So, for example, mashing a ball of clay will cause it to weigh more, or pouring liquid into a tall, skinny container will cause there to be more to drink. When researchers first extended physical constancy tasks to matters of identity, children showed similar error patterns. For example, on gender constancy tasks, preschoolers reported that even superficial changes could modify gender identity. They said that boys can turn into girls, that girls can turn into boys, and that changes in hair style and clothing can affect gender (Emmerich, Goldman, and Kirsh, 1977; Kohlberg, 1966; Liben and Signorella,

1987). It is not until about second grade that children consistently pass either the Piagetian conservation tasks or the Kohlbergian gender constancy tasks.

To some extent these errors reflect task demands and infelicitous wording. For example, merely changing the order of item presentation leads to dramatic improvements in children's answers (Siegal and Robinson, 1987). On gender constancy tasks, the original order involved a repetitive series of questions, with the key gender constancy questions at the end. Siegal and Robinson reasoned that repeated questioning might lead children to infer that their initial answers were wrong, and so to change their answers by the end. For example, if they originally said (correctly) that a girl wearing a different outfit was still a girl, by the end of a series of questions about the same item, they might change their answer and say that the child was a boy. Presenting the key questions first should reduce this tendency to change answers. And that is just what the researchers found. Posing the gender-constancy questions first in the sequence led to much better performance in a sample of three- to four-year-olds (from 33% of the sample giving gender-constant responses on the task, in the original order, to 77% giving gender-constant responses on the task, in the reversed order). Others have also found gender constancy at earlier ages, using modified questioning techniques (e.g., A. Johnson and Ames, 1994).

However, modifying the instructions only goes so far. Even when the task is made very clear, there are cases when young children seem to find it plausible that a person can become a member of the opposite sex, that a cat can become a dog, and so forth. For example, deVries (1969) went so far as to present children with a live cat, whose face was then covered with a highly realistic dog or rabbit mask (either in view of the child or shielded from the child's view). DeVries not only asked children what the animal was, following the transformation, but also whether the animal could bark, whether it would like to play with a dog or a cat, what kind of food it could eat, and whether it had a dog's or a cat's insides. Children were also invited to pet the animal, in order to gauge how fearful they were of it. Three-year-olds seemed genuinely deceived by the masking procedure. Four-year-olds displayed at least some constancy after watching the researcher unmask and remask the cat, but were far from certain that the animal had not changed species. By five years of age, 75% of the children expressed "no more than momentary belief that the identity has changed" (p. 23).

Similar errors are reported by Keil (1989), who developed ingenious scenarios in which animals were described as being transformed by scientists to look and act just like some other species. Five-year-olds tended to say, for example, that a raccoon that was shaved, painted black and white, and implanted with an odor sac was now a skunk. Reliance on appearances decreased with age; children gave more essentialist answers as they grew older. By second grade, children preserved category membership on a majority of their judgments. Second-grade children also distinguished animals from artifacts, judging that for artifacts identity *is* skin deep, so that (for example) a coffeepot can be transformed into a bird feeder. (See also Rips, 1989, for similar findings with adults.)

Keil's data neatly demonstrate a powerful essentialism in children by second grade. But the findings with younger children are problematic. How can these findings be reconciled with an essentialist account of *early* cognition? I propose that children's difficulty reflects the placeholder nature of their essentialist understandings. They simply do not yet have the knowledge to figure out which sorts of transformations constitute kind-altering transformations and which do not. One of the things that need to happen for children to appreciate gender constancy fully is for them to have particular biological knowledge about sex (Bem, 1989). Likewise, one of the things children need in order to appreciate "species constancy" fully is to have particular biological knowledge about the implications and limits of the sorts of surgical operations that Keil's research assistants described. We adults realize that inserting a smelly sac into an animal will not disrupt its essence, but does a five-year-old? Apparently not. Perhaps it is not surprising that children have some doubts—after all, the scientist was doing invasive things to the innards of the animal. It is all the more impressive that second-graders discounted such actions. Yet until children have a more secure knowledge base, they can be mistaken about which properties are essential while still holding essentialist beliefs.

Even for adults, some transformations might plausibly lead to a change in kind. For example, if scientists were to alter the DNA sequence of a developing embryo, adults might agree that this change could result in a changed species. Certainly sex-change operations are construed by many to constitute essential changes (and to result in essential changes in behavior and personality; see D. McCloskey, 1999). With the unnatural and unfamiliar transformations described in some of these thought experiments, children are baffled as to which criteria to consider.

Another way of framing this point is that the transformation tasks require inferring categories from properties (e.g., "This animal has properties x, y, and z. Is it a skunk?"). As discussed in chapter 2, young children find this sort of inference task much more difficult than the converse task of inferring properties from categories (e.g., "This animal is a skunk. Does it have properties x, y, and z?"). The performance of the younger subjects on constancy tasks could reflect this difficulty rather than a lack of essentialism.

This analysis implies that children should perform better with familiar, highly practiced transformations (such as costumes) as opposed to unfamiliar transformations (such as appearance changes induced by injections). Children's greater knowledge about the consequences and reversibility of costumes should provide needed information when trying to gauge their effects on category identity. This is indeed what Keil (1989) found. When the transformation was one involving a costume change—even an extremely realistic costume change that wholly altered an animal's appearance—both kindergarteners and preschoolers consistently maintained that category identity was unchanged. A lion in a tiger costume is still a lion.

Children should also perform better when the property cues are so powerful as to provide unambiguous evidence regarding category membership. For example, if a child knows that an object is not alive, then no amount of salient perceptual cues should induce them to say that it is a real dog. This again is what Keil found when posing transformations that crossed ontological boundaries (e.g., a toy dog changed into what appeared to be a real dog). In each of three item sets, a transformation would have entailed crossing over the animate/inanimate divide. For example, when asked about a porcupine that became cactuslike in appearance (dyed yellowish green and injected with a substance that caused it to hibernate for years), five-year-olds answered that the animal in question was still a porcupine. These results argue against a developmental shift from perceptual to conceptual categories (Keil, 1989, p. 214).

Altogether, I interpret the results of constancy studies as showing that children as young as four years of age appreciate that the identity of animals and other natural kinds can persist in the face of massive transformations. What something is cannot be reduced to what something appears to be. Sameness of personal history over time trumps outward resulting appearances. Nonetheless, this appreciation can be disrupted by tasks that employ difficult and complex transformation processes.

Growth and Metamorphosis

Karl Rosengren, Chuck Kalish, Michael McCormick, and I examined children's understanding that identity is maintained over the natural biological transformation of growth (Rosengren et al., 1991). We reasoned that an important piece that may have been missing from prior research was consideration of the mechanism underlying transformations. In other words, children may be sensitive to whether the mechanism is a natural biological transformation or one that defies biological laws. Even though children report that some transformations lead to identity change, they may realize that natural transformations such as growth do not.

Rosengren et al. (1991) found that children as young as three years of age expected animals to undergo changes over time (via growth) without affecting identity, that children believed that such changes are strongly constrained (e.g., one can get bigger but not smaller over time), and that these changes are specific to the domain of living things. For example, three-year-olds, five-year-olds, and adults were shown a picture of an animal and were told, "Here is a picture of Sally when Sally was a baby. Now Sally is an adult." They were then shown two pictures, one identical to the original and one the same but larger, and were asked which was a picture of Sally "as an adult." (See Figure 3.1a.) In all age groups, the participants tended to choose the larger figure, showing that they expected the object to increase in size with growth.

By five years of age, children realized that animals can undergo metamorphosis without changing identity. In another experimental condition children saw a picture of a juvenile of a species that undergoes radical metamorphosis (such as a caterpillar). They then saw a picture of the same creature, only smaller (e.g., a smaller caterpillar), and a picture of a larger animal differing in shape (e.g., a

a.) Stimuli Set: Metamorphosis Bigger-Bigger

Baby

Adult

b.) Stimuli Set: Metamorphosis Bigger-Smaller

Baby

Adult

Figure 3.1(a) and **3.1(b).** Sample triads. *Source:* Rosengren et al. (1991). Reprinted with the permission of the Society for Research in Child Development.

moth). (See Figure 3.1b.) Again participants were asked to choose which picture represented the animal after it became an adult. Three-year-olds were at chance—itself a potentially intriguing finding, in that they did not simply prefer the similar-looking picture. By five years of age, children chose the metamorphosed animal significantly above chance levels, indicating a belief that an individual can naturally undergo even substantial shape changes over time yet retain its underlying identity. (See also Hickling and Gelman [1995] and Inagaki and Hatano [1996] for other work on growth concepts.)

Interestingly, when reasoning about race, too, children expect constancy over growth, despite a literature suggesting lack of race constancy. Hirschfeld (1996) notes that on standard constancy tasks, children treat race as inconstant and changeable (Aboud, 1988; Ramsey, 1987). Nonetheless, when children are asked about the natural processes of growth and inheritance, they expect race to stay constant. Hirschfeld posed conflicts between race and body build, between race and occupation, and between occupation and body build. For example, on one triad children viewed an adult black male dressed in a policeman's uniform (the target picture), as well as two comparison pictures: a white child in a policeman's uniform, and a black child dressed in a plain outfit (no uniform). Children were asked either a growth question (which of the two comparison pictures was the target as a child) or an inheritance question (which of the two comparison pictures was the target's child). In both the inheritance and the growth task, children three to seven years of age preferred race over body build (mean of 81% of trials) and preferred race over occupation (mean of 70% of trials), but showed no preference for occupation over body build (mean of 57% of trials). The selections did not reduce to overall similarity. A separate group of children who were given a similarity task (which of the comparison pictures looked most like the target) showed significantly different patterns of results. For example, they judged occupation as more perceptually salient than race, but race as more important for judgments of growth and inheritance.

Origin of Species

> You can't make a monkey out of me.
> You can't make a monkey out of me.
> I am human through and through
> All my aunts and uncles, too.
> And you can't make a monkey out of me. . . .
> But mankind is the same in all ages as today . . .
> No you can't make me out of a monkey.
> —Gentry Family, "You Can't Make a Monkey Out of Me"
> Victor Recording, 1926

Despite essentialist assumptions about category immutability, categories do in fact transform from one to another, most notably in evolution (Mayr, 1982, 1991). Yet children—and in some cases even adults—have trouble appreciating evolutionary accounts of species origins (see Evans, 2000, 2001, for review). How much children's difficulties lie with their resistance to viewing categories as changeable, or instead to other factors (e.g., complexity of the theory, lack of evidence, beliefs in creationism, difficulty understanding deep time) is unclear and deserves further study.

Samarapungavan and Wiers (1997) found that children avoid evolutionary accounts of species origins for quite some time even past the preschool period. In one detailed study of Dutch third- and fifth-graders (mean ages 9;4 and 12;3), researchers questioned children extensively about species origins and modifiability. Out of thirty-five children, seventeen were consistently essentialist in their answers across the experimental battery, and only three consistently provided accounts in which species could undergo change. Essentialist accounts led to answers such as the following. When asked, "How did peacocks get their long, colorful tails?" one child replied: "It just is that way. Peacocks always had long tails just like giraffes always had long necks." Likewise, when asked whether brown bears would develop white fur after living at the North Pole, another child answered, "No, brown bears will always be brown bears. They cannot become another bear."

Summary

Several studies with a variety of methods demonstrate that by four or five years of age, children treat a range of natural categories as resistant to transformation. These results would seem to contradict the classic claim that preoperational children (in Piaget's terms) fail to appreciate "constancy," and that identity remains constant over outward transformations. As in chapter 2, I invoke the distinction between knowledge and expectation (Coley, Medin, Proffitt, et al., 1999). The knowledge required to form an accurate classification is distinct from the rich expectations even preschool children hold about categories. These results need not imply a biological understanding of categories (see Solomon et al. [1996] for discussion), but they do suggest an essentialist one. By four years of age, children treat category membership as intrinsic and unalterable.

BOUNDARY INTENSIFICATION

We have just seen that even preschool children treat category boundaries as stable in the face of superficial transformations: classification of an item stands firm despite even radical outward changes. A second way that people may be biased toward treating category boundaries as stable is by treating instances as either in a category or outside a category, but not in between, and not to a partial degree. In Daniel Dennett's words, "Essences were definitive, and as such they were timeless, unchanging, and all-or-nothing. A thing couldn't be *rather* silver or *quasi*-gold or a *semi*-mammal" (1995, p. 36).

I should be clear about precisely what the prediction here is and is not. The claim is not that essentialism predicts absolute category boundaries 100% of the time, as some have suggested (e.g., Kalish, 1995). Why? Because, as people have come to accept, the world is an untidy place. Species can interbreed, substances have impurities, and biological processes can go awry. I could attribute essences to a category, with the concomitant belief that possession of the essence makes you 100% a member of the category, but also believe that essences can be combined or intermingled (consider mules—the offspring of horses and donkeys, and so neither 100% horse nor 100% donkey). Likewise, the world presents entities laced with "impurities" (consider polluted water—not 100% H_2O and so not 100% water). Biological processes can be disrupted at certain points during development; for instance, a child can be born neither wholly male nor wholly female. All of these cases are real-world examples of boundary-mixing. It is interesting in this regard that Kamp and Partee suggest that categories with absolutely sharp boundaries may be limited to abstract domains such as pure mathematics (1995, p. 172). It is presumably in abstract realms that the messiness of the real world does not interfere.

To repeat, the claim is not that an essentialist would turn a blind eye to such cases. Instead, I suggest two hypotheses: category membership should be distinct from typicality—that is, people should believe there is something above and beyond (or should I say "under and below"?) apparent features—and category boundaries should be treated as relatively more dichotomous (either/or, discrete, or nonfuzzy) than they truly are. Perhaps the best way to appreciate these predictions is to make an analogy to the categorical perception of speech sounds (Harnad, 1987; Wood, 1976). For humans (and a few nonhuman species as well), simple speech sounds such as "ba" and "pa" are perceived as discontinuously belonging to one or the other of a small number of categories, even though the physical information varies continuously. Sounds are not perceived as "kind of ba, kind of pa"—they are perceived as one or the other. However, even with categorical perception, it is not that people perceive no fuzzy boundary, but rather that people greatly reduce the fuzzy boundary compared to the variability in the physical stimulus (see Figure 3.2).

I am predicting what I call "boundary intensification" rather than "absolute category membership." If I am correct, then clearly essentialized categories (especially living kinds and categories of people) should be subject to boundary intensification in a way that other categories (such as human artifacts) are not.

When we look at real-world behavior, it appears to be strewn with examples of boundary intensification. The "one-drop" rule in racial classification is perhaps the most obvious example: someone who has one black grandparent and three white grandparents is considered black, not white; the converse is not the case (i.e., someone who has one white grandparent and three black grandparents is also considered black; Hirschfeld, 1996). A "fuzzy" situation in the world is decided in a nonfuzzy manner. Similarly, Jewish law indicates that the offspring of a Jewish mother and a non-Jewish father is a child who is 100% Jewish. Again, ambiguity in the world is resolved categorically. Gil-White (2001) discusses the example of the word *erliiz* in western Mongolia, which "connotes mixed ancestry but not mixed ethnicity . . . [suggesting] a reluctance to see the category boundary as a fuzzy one." (See also Nave, 2000, cited by Gil-White.) Treatment of intersexuals (those born with ambiguous genitalia) is typically rather extreme in the United States and can include surgery in infancy, with lifelong hormone replacement treatment

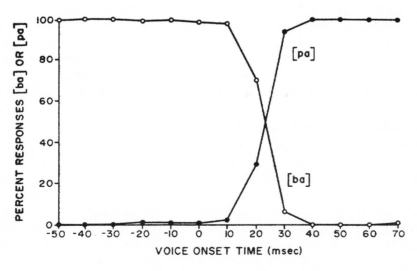

Figure 3.2. Categorical perception of "ba" and "pa" as plotted against the underlying physical continuum. *Source:* Wood (1976). Reprinted with the permission of the American Institute of Physics.

(Hird and Germon, 2001). This behavior can be considered a case of boundary in-tensification, an attempt to "fix" individuals at the border so that they fit more neatly into one gender category or another. More generally, membership in a vari-ety of social groups is accompanied by the addition of distinctive properties that serve to intensify category boundaries. So, females differ from males in so many conventionalized ways beyond biology: clothing, hairstyles, jewelry, makeup, even on which side of a shirt the buttons are attached.[2]

These examples seem implausible for artifacts. We in fact seem to relish and de-light in boundary-crossing with artifacts: creating telephones that look like Mickey Mouse, clocks that look like little birdhouses, belts that double as wallets, and a kitchen tool that both slices *and* dices. The fear or disgust that seems to accompany the "monster" hybrids in the animal domain (Douglas, 1966) is absent in the case of artifact hybrids. (I can think of only one exception: the hybrid toys created by the evil boy in the movie *Toy Story* were mightily creepy. The boy had recombined parts of his toys, for instance putting a doll head onto erector-set legs. However, these toys were all but animate: they experienced fear, followed directions, and moved autonomously. So the example seems more an illustration of animal hy-brids than of artifact hybrids.) Boundary intensification apparently does not re-flect a domain-general bias.

In this light it is important to consider the evidence of typicality judgments—that people reliably judge penguins to be atypical birds, for example. If typicality judgments faithfully reflect category membership, then several things follow: membership in a category is "graded" rather than binary, less than fully typical in-stances are only "sort of" members of a category, and the prediction of boundary intensification is falsified. However, it is now widely agreed that membership judg-ments need not reflect typicality. E. Smith and Osherson observe: "while most of us believe that penguins are atypical of birds, few of us doubt that they are in fact birds" (1988, p. 52; cited in Osherson and Smith, 1997). This point is discussed in numerous accounts (Armstrong, Gleitman, and Gleitman, 1983; Hampton, 1998; Kalish, 1995; Kamp and Partee, 1995; Lakoff, 1987; Malt, 1990; Murphy and Medin, 1985; Osherson and Smith, 1997; Rips, 1989; E. Smith and Medin, 1981; Williamson, 1994; Zadeh, 1982).

Assuming, then, that category membership need not reflect typicality, the main question of interest for this context is whether membership judgments are more closely linked to typicality for certain domains. Specifically, do essentialized cate-gories (such as natural kinds) show a sharper divide between typicality and mem-bership than less essentialized categories (such as artifacts)? In contrast to the pen-guin example, intuitively it does seem that some artifacts have less determinate category membership: the back seat of a car might be sort of furniture; an extra-large coffee mug without handles might be midway between a cup and a bowl (Labov, 1973).[3]

One way to test the prediction that category membership should be distinct from and more dichotomous than typicality is to gather both typicality ratings (e.g., "how good an example" of the category "birds" is a penguin?) and category membership ratings (e.g., "how clearly a member" of the category "birds" is a penguin?), and then to compare the two sorts of judgments. I would predict that, for natural kinds, category membership ratings would be more absolute than typicality ratings, whereas for artifacts there would be no difference between category membership ratings and typicality ratings. In other words, for natural kind categories, people should be more likely to give the endpoints of the scale when rating membership: a penguin is definitely a member of the bird category, even though it is not a very typical bird. For artifact categories, membership and typicality should be more closely coordinated.

Generally, researchers have found such an asymmetry between animals and artifacts (see Diesendruck and Gelman, 1999, for review). In one study, Gil Diesendruck and I asked a sample of forty-two undergraduates to provide either typicality ratings or category membership ratings for 293 different animals and artifacts. We found that membership ratings were consistently more extreme than typicality ratings, but only for animals. Take, for example, the category of mammals. College students judged 96% of the time that various examples were either definitely a member of the category "mammals" or definitely not a member of the category "mammals," including such atypical instances as mink, jaguar, bison, and skunk. Typicality ratings were much less polarized, with only 72% of judgments showing correspondingly extreme scores. Table 3.1 shows these data in more detail. The responses are broken down into six intervals, based on the mean typicality ratings provided. The purpose of doing so was to compare animals and artifacts when typicality was equivalent. Then, for each interval, we looked to see how often respondents rated an example as either definitely a member of the relevant category, or definitely not a member of that category. We can see that people consistently rated animals more definitely as belonging in or out of the corresponding category. For example, consider the interval between 6 and 7, in which items were judged as highly atypical (as might be, for example, "germ" in the category of insect, or "ashtray" in the category of furniture). Although these animal and artifact examples had equivalent typicality scores, people were much more certain about the category boundaries for the animal items than the artifact items. Whereas 87% of the time animals in this interval were rated as definitely either in or out of the category, only 56% of the time were artifacts in this interval rated as definitely either in or out of the category.

Kalish (1995) noted that adults do admit some flexibility in animal category boundaries; for example, they consider a mule neither "completely a horse" nor "not at all a horse," but rather a horse to some degree. Using this fact, he argued against an essentialist account of categories. However, as I argued earlier, essentialism is not incompatible with some fuzziness of boundaries. The example of "mule" is particularly telling, as mules are hybrids, biologically the offspring of two distinct animal kinds (horses and donkeys). And even in Kalish's own data, animals (not artifacts) typically displayed the predicted essentialist pattern: more extreme

Table 3.1.   Percentage of absolute membership ratings and mean typicality ratings by typicality intervals; Diesendruck and Gelman (1999)

Typicality Interval	Percentage of definitely a member		Percentage of definitely not a member		Mean typicality	
	Animals	Artifacts	Animals	Artifacts	Animals	Artifacts
1–1.9	92%	91%	1%	1%	1.5	1.6*
2–2.9	80	61*	4	5	2.3	2.5
3–3.9	55	38*	12	9	3.4	3.5
4–4.9	19	19	27	16*	4.3	4.3
5–5.9	9	6	53	35*	5.4	5.1
6–7	1	3	86	53*	6.5	6.3

* Asterisks indicate a significant difference between domains.

category membership judgments than typicality judgments. (See Hampton, 1998, for similar findings.)

Coley and Luhmann (2001) argue that judgments of category membership can also be contaminated by a rater's own lack of confidence in his or her own knowledge. For example, a rater might judge that an eel is not entirely a fish—not because they have a principled belief that category membership of fish is graded, but because they are expressing their own lack of certainty regarding what exactly an eel is. To get around this problem, Coley and Luhmann probed participants' judgments about whether an expert would be able to make an absolute judgment (e.g., "Would an expert be able to determine whether an eel is a fish?"). The items included 120 items drawn from four superordinate domains: living kinds, nonliving natural kinds, social kinds, and artifacts. The results replicated Diesendruck and Gelman's (1999) finding that category membership was rated as more absolute for living kinds and nonliving natural kinds than for artifacts. Moreover, they found that the relationship between typicality and expert judgments varied dramatically as a function of the superordinate domain. For social kinds and artifacts, typicality and expert judgments reliably correlated (R-squared of .83 and .64, respectively), indicating that even experts would be uncertain about the category membership of atypical items. In contrast, for living and nonliving natural kinds, there was no reliable correlation between typicality ratings and expert judgments (R-squared of .07 and .04, respectively), indicating that typicality does not reflect underlying category structure in these domains.

Further evidence for domain differences comes from the different kind of linguistic "hedges" for natural kinds (such as "planet") versus artifacts (such as "toy") (Malt, 1990). Undergraduates find it sensible for someone to say "According to experts, that's a planet" or "Loosely speaking, that's a toy," but odd for someone to say "According to experts, that's a toy" or "Loosely speaking, that's a planet." "According to experts" implies that some expert has a clear set of definitions to apply; "loosely speaking" implies that boundaries are permeable or flexible.

Malt (1990) also asked people directly whether category boundaries are a matter of degree or absolute. When she did so, once again natural kind boundaries were treated as absolute by most respondents whereas artifact categories were not. For example, if a hypothetical character came across something that seemed to be roughly halfway between a chicken and a turkey, people expected that it was probably one or the other (chicken *or* turkey), and that they would need to consult an expert to figure out which it was. Yet if a hypothetical character came across something that seemed to be roughly halfway between a chair and a stool, they expected that one could think of it as either one and could call it whatever one wants.

In a related set of experiments, Kalish (1998) found that preschool children tended to be realist about category boundaries, treating them as objective and not subject to disputes. For example, children judged that it is not acceptable for a puppet to classify a deer with a horse (versus another deer), or a hammer with a bat (versus another hammer). In other words, for basic-level animal and artifact categories, boundaries were viewed as objective and real.

Interestingly, a domain difference did emerge for superordinate-level categories, where children were decidedly more objective for animals than artifacts (Kalish, 1998). With animal superordinates, children were adamant that there is only one right way to classify a triad of pictures (e.g., a lion goes with a cat, not a dog). With artifact superordinates, children allowed that there was more than one right way to classify a triad of pictures (e.g., a bowl could go with either a pot or a barrel). As Kalish puts it, "children were inflexible in judging decisions about sorting animals. There was one right way to categorize an animal, just as there was one right answer to whether an act was morally acceptable or not." This inflexibility did not appear for artifact categories, which were treated as more arbitrary or a matter of convention. Similar patterns emerged in a replication study with adults: basic-level categories (both animals and artifacts) were seen as highly objective, and superordinate-level categories were seen as more objective for animals than for artifacts.

Another intriguing piece of evidence with children comes from a study by Keil (1989). The study was primarily designed to examine judgments on his transformation task (see earlier in this chapter), but also included a measure of whether ambiguous items (such as an animal with some tiger features and some lion features) would be seen as intermediate between two categories, or as strictly belonging to one category or the other. On each of five item sets, children from kindergarten, second grade, and fourth grade saw a series of drawings that varied gradually from at first resembling a typical instance of one category (e.g., tiger) to eventually resembling a typical instance of a contrasting category (e.g., lion). The intermediate stages looked truly intermediate, displaying features of each kind. The story that accompanied these gradual transformations described a series of external modifications (such as dyeing the animal's black stripes orange and using "hair tonic" to make hair grow around the animal's head) that were responsible for the appearance shifts. For each picture, the experimenter asked what the animals in the transitional stages were. Nearly all the children judged the intermediate animals as being either one kind or another, and rarely a mixture of both. Out of forty children, only five (mostly fourth-graders) suggested that the animals might be blends of two species. This tantalizing finding deserves more systematic follow-up. For example, did the experimenter explicitly raise the possibility of a mixture in the question posed to children, or was that possibility left for children to come up with on their own? Furthermore, it would be interesting to compare children's judgments of animals to their judgments in other domains, especially artifacts.

Summary

Studies with adults support the idea that adults treat animals and other natural kind categories as having relatively rigid boundaries, such that something is either in a category or outside a category, but not partly or sort of belonging in a category. I refer to this phenomenon as "boundary intensification." In contrast, classification of artifacts tends to follow typicality more faithfully. However, to my knowledge, this issue has not yet received direct study in children. We simply do not know whether children honor a distinction between typicality and category membership, as adults do. If my framework is correct, then children too should show this effect, treating membership in a category as more absolute and definitive than would be predicted by typicality ratings. Children may even be especially rigid about category boundaries.

A second type of boundary intensification has also been studied (and documented) in children. It involves rejecting category anomalies altogether. Rather than accepting category anomalies as full category members (thereby dissociating typicality from category membership), which was the version of boundary intensification studied in this section, one could pull the boundaries tighter so that only typical instances are included. An example of the first type would be deciding that a penguin is 100% bird; an example of the second type would be deciding that penguins are not birds whatsoever—that only robins, sparrows, eagles, and the like are birds.

Young children do seem to exclude atypical instances at a higher rate than do older children or adults (Nelson et al., 1978; Mervis and Pani, 1980), causing their categories to include a narrower range of instances. For example, four-year-olds will often say that a boy cannot wear a dress, whereas eight-year-olds acknowledge that a boy could wear a dress (though they do not like it) (Levy, Taylor, and Gelman, 1995). This phenomenon, though of interest in its own right, is separate from the issue of essentialism. Young children's preference for tight, tidy boundaries need not imply that boundaries are determined by something other than typicality or similarity. It is certainly possible to exclude atypical instances *and* to define categories in terms of superficial properties. For this reason, it will be important in the future to study boundary intensification in children by focusing the relationship between typicality and category membership.

Finally, there is support for a related phenomenon in both preschool children and adults: category boundaries are viewed as real and objective more for animals than artifacts (Kalish, 1998). Although this phenomenon is not strictly speaking a matter of boundary intensification, it does speak to the relative power and stability of category boundaries in the animal domain, both for adults and by preschool age.

NONOBVIOUS PROPERTIES

> All along people told me that I was going to have a boy. I even bought blue bedding for the nursery. Well, the baby came out, and the doctor cried, "It looks like a girl!" My first thought was: "Oh, my God! We have a boy that looks like a girl!"
>
> —Letter to *American Baby* magazine, May 2001

Appearances can be deceiving. This core belief is implicit in the behaviors of children and adults in the studies reviewed to this point. Despite older claims about the phenomenism of children (e.g., Piaget, discussed in Flavell, 1963), children do clearly grasp the appearance-reality distinction by four years of age. Flavell, Flavell, and Green (1983) posed appearance-reality conflicts to young children (for example, a fake rock made out of sponge—it *is* a sponge, but it *looks like* a rock), explained in clear and simple language just what the conflict was, and then asked children to report back both appearance and reality. Several findings are relevant to the present discussion:

- Although three-year-olds find this task rather difficult, by four years of age children do quite well. To reframe in the current context: not only can children learn categories that conflict with appearances, but they can reflect on this distinction (in a metacognitive way) and hold in mind simultaneously both aspects of the conflict (both appearance and reality).
- At no age, even three years, did children show a bias toward phenomenism (reporting just appearance, for both appearance and reality). In other words, children display no tendency to construe the world solely in terms of surface appearances. They were as likely to report that reality was apparent (e.g., that the sponge/rock looked like a sponge; intellectual realism error) as to report that appearances were real (e.g., that milk covered with a blue filter really was blue; phenomenism error).
- Children tended to rely consistently on reality when answering questions about object or event identity (such as the real or apparent identity of the sponge/rock), and to rely on appearances when answering questions about object or event properties (such as the real or apparent color of the

milk behind the filter) (Flavell, Flavell, and Green, 1983; Taylor and
Flavell, 1984). One way to describe this effect is to say that intellectual realism emerges more for category judgments than for property judgments.
Categories are seen as particularly stable and persistent in the face of conflicting perceptual information (akin to the distinction between categories and properties discussed in chapter 2).

Grasping the distinction between appearance and reality in a general sense does
not mean that one always recognizes false appearances, nor does it mean that one
has resolved the distinction correctly. I am reminded of Morison and Gardner's
(1978, p. 643) example of the child who said of the *Sesame Street* character Big
Bird, "I know that Big Bird isn't real. That's just a costume. There's just a plain bird
inside." Likewise, those who deny the moon landing have a firm grasp on the
appearance/reality distinction (for example, explaining that video footage of
the historic landing is an elaborate hoax perpetrated by the government), despite
having beliefs that most people today disagree with. The point, though, is that by
four years of age preschoolers appreciate that the appearance/reality conflict exists.
This basic appreciation has quite significant consequences for children's reasoning
about the nonobvious.

Preschool children also formulate the existence of invisible particles in their understanding of contamination and germs (Au, Sidle, and Rollins, 1993; Kalish,
1996; Rosen and Rozin, 1993; Siegal and Share, 1990), elements of reproduction
(Springer and Keil, 1991), or cooties (Hirschfeld, 2002). That children appear to
learn and accept such constructs readily is evidence against the notion that their
concepts depend on concrete, perceptually apparent properties.

Let me be clear: these constructs (germs, cooties, contaminants) are not
essences. They are not properties that characterize members of a given category.
(The one exception may be cooties, as they tend to be attributed to members of a
given sex—"girl cooties" or "boy cooties"—and so are category-linked.) Germs,
cooties, and contaminants are not responsible for kind-typical properties (e.g., a
dog's germs do not cause the dog to bark). However, that children appreciate such
entities argues that they have the capacity to formulate essences. It demonstrates an
attention to internal and nonobvious properties, and a willingness to accept constructs for which they have no direct or observable evidence.

From this general introduction, I turn now to studies examining specifically
children's understanding of internal parts and internal substance. Essences are
often portrayed as internal or compositional (e.g., the genetic code of an animal;
the chemical structure of an element). Even on a placeholder notion, I expect that
essences are assumed (by adults) to be relatively more internal than other properties. You may not know quite what it is that distinguishes one breed of dog from
another, but you presume it is hidden deep within the animals, not merely lying
atop their fur or skin. So it is important to discover how children think about the
insides of things, and whether they grant insides special status. At the same time, it

is important to keep in mind that insides are not equivalent to essences; essential similarities may also take the form of behaviors, functions, parentage, psychological makeup, or even intangible qualities such as a soul.

Internal Parts and Substance

The importance of insides can be seen among adults from a range of cultures. Consider, for example, that the dominant metaphor for kinship in the United States is blood ("blood is thicker than water"). In other words, a physically internal substance (blood) represents one's identity as a member of a biological family. When we talk about genes and DNA, we likewise represent them as internal. The United States is not the only culture for which internal substance stands for kinship. People of New Guinea also treat many substances (blood, semen, mother's milk, bone) as a metaphor of either kinship or shared gender attributes (Harriet Whitehead, personal communication; Whitehead, 1986).

Similarly, half a world away, the anthropologist Francisco Gil-White (2001) transcribed the following conversation with a group of Kazax men in Western Mongolia. In the midst of a conversation about nature-nurture conflicts, Gil-White asked the following: "If I stayed here, and learned Kazax, and Kazax customs, married a Kazax girl, and became a Muslim, would I still not be a Kazax?" Gil-White described the respondent's reply: "'Even if you do everything like a Kazax, and everybody says you are a Kazax, you still aren't a real Kazax because your parents are not Kazax. You are different inside.' And he pointed to his chest." The Kazax speaker seems to be asserting that "insides" are privileged over other properties: the innards of an person are identified with what is real, and what is common among members of a kind. Whether "inside" is meant literally or metaphorically is an issue I will examine in the studies that follow.

What about children? The very first child I tested on the category-based induction studies that Ellen Markman and I conducted was a delightful and articulate six-year-old named Amber. She was a bit too old to be included in the study proper, but I wanted to do a final run-through of the procedure before testing preschoolers. As we went through the twenty item sets, one by one, I observed with great interest that Amber consistently selected the category-based responses: the blackbird had the same property as the flamingo, not the bat; the tiny brown snake had the same property as the cobra, not the worm; and so on. At one point she stopped and explained: "All snakes are a little bit same and a little bit different. *Inside*, they're the same." As I scribbled down these words, I wondered whether they were the unusual insight of one particularly bright and inquisitive child, or whether just maybe they reflected a more general belief held in early childhood.

DISTINGUISHING INSIDES FROM OUTSIDES.   When we examine systematically the sorts of beliefs children hold about internal parts, we find that children clearly distinguish insides from outsides. Rochel Gelman (1987) asked preschool children what was on the inside and on the outside of various animate and inanimate objects, including humans, elephants, cats, dolls, and puppets. Children differentiated animals from inanimate objects on the basis of internal properties. They tended to say that animals had blood, bones, or other internal organs on the inside, whereas inanimate objects had material, mechanical devices, or nothing inside. Rochel Gelman proposed that children followed a "causal innards principle" for animals, such that the inside of an animal causes its self-generated movement (see chapter 5 for more discussion of this proposal). As indirect evidence for this principle, she found that children expected the insides of different animals to be very similar to one another and to differ from their outsides. In contrast, for inanimate objects children often reported that the insides were the same as the outsides (a "surface generalization rule"). For example, children might say that a doll has cloth on both the outside and the inside, whereas an elephant has skin outside and blood inside. Preschool children differentiate between animals and inanimate objects on the basis of nonobvious properties.

Children can also attend to internal composition when it conflicts with surface appearances. Henry Wellman and I (S. Gelman and Wellman, 1991) showed children triplets of items in which the target item and one test item looked alike but were from different categories (such as a pig and a piggy bank), and the target item and the other test item did not look alike but were from the same category (such as the pig and a cow). For each pair of test items, children were asked two questions (for example): "Which of these looks most like the pig?" and "Which of these has the same kinds of insides as the pig?" The first question required attention to surface similarity, the second to the less obvious property of internal constitution. Four-year-olds performed better than three-year-olds (78% versus 58% correct), but both performed better than chance—thereby accurately switching from surface similarity to internal constitution.

Wellman and I also conducted an analysis of error patterns that took into account how the children answered both questions for a given triplet (that is, both the "looks like" and "has insides" questions). Importantly, children were as likely to make realism errors (for instance, saying that the pig and the cow had the same insides *and* looked alike) as phenomenism errors (saying that the pig and the piggy bank looked alike *and* had the same insides). Similarity-based errors did not predominate. Children were able to consider both appearances and nonobvious properties in the same task, and not all errors were due to emphasizing outward similarity.

In describing the insides of a range of items, children tend to be roughly accurate, though incorrect in the details. Anne Watson O'Reilly and I (S. Gelman and O'Reilly, 1988) gathered descriptions of insides from preschool and second-grade children. See Table 3.2 for some examples. For living kinds (animals, plants, and other vegetation) children described living kind parts (liquids, organs, bones) 35% of the time, and artifact parts (stuffing, metal, fabric) only 1% of the time. This pattern was reversed for artifact items such as vehicles and clothing, where children mentioned artifact parts 59% of the time and living kind parts only 4% of the time.

Table 3.2.   A sample of children's descriptions of insides

Preschoolers (natural kinds)

   "Caterpillars have liquidy stuff inside."

   "A snake has . . . lots of teeny bones, right? so it can wiggle. 'Cause if it was one long bone, it would just have to slide."

   "They [carrots] have milk. Milk and wheat."

Second-graders (natural kinds)

   "Every dog has the same stuff, unless they're missing a tail or something. Just because [they] have different colors doesn't mean they have different stuff, because they're just growing dead cells of different colors."

   "Caterpillars have different kind of blood than spiders do."

   "Tomatoes have a lot of juice vitamins, and carrots have a lot of solid vitamins."

Preschoolers (artifacts)

   "Because blocks are wood—most blocks are wood. All blocks are wood."

   "They [dolls] all have cotton."

   "Teddy bears have feathers inside."

Second-graders (artifacts)

   "All chairs aren't the same. Some of 'em have metal, some of 'em have wood. Some of 'em have iron."

   "Robots have just like things that make 'em move their arms and their hands and walk."

   "Robots have lots of microchips."

Source: S. Gelman and O'Reilly (1988). Reprinted with the permission of the Society for Research in Child Development.

It is remarkable that children consistently distinguished the insides of living kinds from the insides of artifacts despite clearly lacking detailed knowledge (e.g., saying that carrots have milk and wheat inside, or that dolls all have cotton inside). This pattern suggests that children were constructing answers based on abstract expectations rather than repeating learned facts about specific entities.

Simons and Keil (1995) tested this possibility by asking three-, four-, and eight-year-old children to identify the insides of ten animals and ten machines, showing children visual representations (drawings, photographs, or jars of actual innards). The types of insides that were presented were of three sorts: animals, artifacts, and aggregate substances (e.g., a pile of rocks). Although children in all age groups, even three-year-olds, consistently answered differently for animals versus machines, they often were incorrect about precisely what these insides looked like. For example, a subset of the children at all three ages were unsure whether animals had animal insides or aggregate insides. Simons and Keil interpreted these data as showing that children have abstract expectations before concrete knowledge— what they term an "abstract-to-concrete shift."

In an unpublished study, Gail Gottfried and I found further support for Simons and Keil's interpretation by directly testing children's predictions about unfamiliar animals, plants, and machines. We reasoned that if children have abstract expectations that do not rely on concrete knowledge, then they should readily distinguish domains when presented with unfamiliar items, as long as they can identify the appropriate domain. In contrast, if children's grasp of insides rests on concrete knowledge, then they should perform poorly on unfamiliar items.

For this study, Gottfried and I selected a dozen items that had been pretested as recognizable by children as animals (e.g., a tapir), plants (e.g., a liverwort), or machines (e.g., an intercom), but incorrectly labeled at the basic level. Three- and five-year-olds were then asked to identify the insides of each item, selecting either from a set of three verbal choices (e.g., "bones, seeds, or wires") or from a set of three picture choices (e.g., bones, plant cells, or wires). Each set of choices included one animal-insides choice, one plant-insides choice, and one machine-insides choice. We found that four- and five-year-old children were consistently accurate at matching insides to domain. Three-year-olds had more difficulty, but even they were above chance on animals and machines. Preschoolers were able to infer the insides of a set of items they had never seen before, knowing simply that each was an animal, plant, or machine. It seems that the expectations children hold about internal parts and substance are abstractly tethered to the domain in question.

PRIVILEGED STATUS OF INSIDES.   The crucial question from an essentialist perspective is not just: do children understand that internal parts differ from external parts? but also, do children treat internal parts as somehow privileged? For example, when making inductive inferences or judgments about identity, are insides weighted more heavily than outsides? This task should be difficult for young children. We have already seen that children find it difficult to judge which of a set of properties is most relevant to forming a categorization (e.g., S. Gelman, Collman, and Maccoby, 1986). However, children may have a nascent understanding of the relative significance of internal properties if they are asked to consider the effects of their removal. Such a question causes children to focus not on the relative merits of a range of properties considered jointly, but rather on the question of whether "inner stuff" has important implications.

Henry Wellman and I investigated this question by asking children to consider a series of items that were transformed by having either their "insides" or their "outsides" removed (S. Gelman and Wellman, 1991). The test items were selected to be clear-cut examples (for adults) of objects for which insides, but not outsides, are essential, and included both animals and other sorts of entities including artifacts (see Table 3.3). For example, blood is more important than fur to a dog; the engine of a car is more important than the paint. As a control, we also selected a set of items for which the insides are not integral parts (containers, such as a jar or a refrigerator).

We asked four- and five-year-old children to consider three transformations: (a) removal of insides (e.g., "What if you take out the stuff inside of the dog, you know, the blood and bones and things like that, and got rid of it and all you have left are the outsides?"), (b) removal of outsides (e.g., "What if you take off the stuff outside of the dog, you know, the fur, and got rid of it and all you have left are the insides?"), and (c) movement (e.g., "What if the dog stands up?") as a control. For

Table 3.3.   Items used in S. Gelman and Wellman (1991)

Item	Insides removal	Outsides removal	Movement
Insides-relevant			
turtle	blood	shell	put in box
dog	blood and bones	fur	stands up
egg	runny stuff	eggshell	roll on table
banana	white part	peel	turn upside-down
car	motor	paint	turn around
book	pages	cover	turn over
pencil	black stuff (lead)	paint	drop on table
Containers			
jar	food	label	put in box
toy box	toys and games	paint	drag across room
refrigerator	food and shelves	paint	move to other side of kitchen

Source: S. Gelman and Wellman (1991). Reprinted with the permission of Elsevier Science.

each transformation, children were asked two questions: (a) identity ("Is it still a dog?") and (b) function ("Can it still bark and eat dog food?"). Results are shown in Table 3.4. Not surprisingly, children correctly reported that the identity of the containers (e.g., refrigerator) would not change if the insides were removed. The more interesting finding was with the other items: the children said that if the insides were removed, the identity and function of an object would change, but that if the outsides were removed, the identity and function would not change. Children judged insides to be more important, even when removing the outsides would sharply change the appearance of the object (for example, taking the shell off a turtle, or the fur off a dog).

Children understand that insides have a privileged status: their removal leads to loss of category identity and category-typical functioning. We cannot tell from these data whether insides are construed as kind-specific essences for children. For example, children may believe that the loss of blood, bones, and bodily organs will lead a dog to cease being alive, and by implication to be no longer a dog (and certainly no longer capable of barking or eating dog food). However, we cannot say one way or another, from these data, that whatever distinguishes a dog from a cat (say) is internal as well. Four-year-olds may still lack this understanding. In one study with twelve four-year-olds, children treated behaviors as more important than insides in determining the identity of an animal (Shipley, 2000, study 2). For example, an animal that was described as acting like a tiger (eats meat, roars, climbs trees) but possessing the insides of a camel (has the brain, lungs, and bones of a camel) was more typically judged to be a tiger than a camel. However, this result is inconclusive, since on an essentialist perspective the inner properties should

Table 3.4.   Results of S. Gelman and Wellman (1991) insides removal task: Mean percentage of responses affirming that identity or function changes

	Insides removal	Outsides removal	Movement
Identity questions			
Insides relevant	72	35	12
Containers	17	28	10
Function questions			
Insides relevant	92	29	15
Containers	20	23	7

Source: S. Gelman and Wellman (1991). Reprinted with the permission of Elsevier Science.

predict the outward behavior. Animals in which the inner properties fail to predict behavior are then anomalous, rendering any judgment in this case unclear.

Gil Diesendruck, Kim Lebowitz, and I have further found that preschool children can use internal properties as an index to naming (Diesendruck, Gelman, and Lebowitz, 1998). We conducted a series of studies that focused on a well-known word-learning error often referred to as the mutual exclusivity assumption (Markman, 1989; Merriman and Bowman, 1989), or the novel name/nameless category principle (Golinkoff, Mervis, and Hirsh-Pasek, 1994). Children have a powerful tendency to assume that words refer to nonoverlapping sets; more simply put, children tend to assume that each object has only one label. For example, children who know that a poodle is a "dog" will typically deny that it is a "poodle" or an "animal." We predicted that children would overcome this mutual exclusivity tendency if they learned that dogs and poodles, for example, share internal properties.

Three-, four-, and five-year-olds were taught new words for a series of animals or artifacts, then were tested on their interpretations of the new words. For example, children were shown two distinct kinds of squirrels (a typical squirrel and a flying squirrel) and were told: "This one [the flying squirrel] is a squirrel; it's a mef. This one [the typical squirrel] is a squirrel; it's not a mef." Before teaching the new word, the experimenter described how the two instances were alike. In the insides condition, the experimenter described internal properties (e.g., that the two squirrels had "the same stuff inside . . . the same kind of bones, blood, muscles, and brain"). In the control condition, the experimenter described superficial similarities (e.g., that the two squirrels were "the same size . . . [and live] in the same zoo in the same kind of cage"). The labeling phase alone provided all the information children needed to construct the hierarchy accurately. However, we knew from past work that children tend to collapse such a hierarchy into two mutually exclusive sets (e.g., S. Gelman, Wilcox, and Clark, 1989). The question, then, was whether the brief description of internal similarities would be sufficient to alter the children's patterns of word-learning.

The results demonstrated significant condition effects. In the control condition, with superficial similarities, the children typically treated the two labels (e.g., "squirrel" and "mef") as mutually exclusive ($M = 53\%$ of trials) and rarely gave the correct, subordinate interpretations ($M = 29\%$). In the insides condition, in which the items were described as sharing internal similarities, children overcame the error and gave fewer mutual exclusivity interpretations ($M = 36\%$) and more subordinate interpretations ($M = 38\%$). Children showed no condition effects when learning new labels for artifacts, whether the information concerned internal properties or common function. The use of internal information to constrain word learning was specific to animal kinds.

Diesendruck (2001) replicated this finding in Brazil with Portuguese-speaking children of widely varying sociocultural backgrounds: both middle-class four-year-olds, with background comparable to that of the U.S. four-year-olds, and children from *favelas* (impoverished neighborhoods surrounding the city). The results were in most respects very similar, with the same weakening of mutual exclusivity in the insides condition (see Table 3.5). This finding illustrates the generality of the effect across languages and across variations in sociocultural background.

GENES.   Although children in the studies reviewed above had received no formal instruction in biology and knew little about specific biological innards, they apparently were capable of learning about genes, in a rudimentary sense. In a study of five- and six-year-olds, Solomon and Johnson taught children that rabbits have bunnies (not dogs or cats or people) because "we all have tiny things called genes inside us that make us what we are . . . people have people genes and rabbits have rabbit genes" (2000, p. 88). In other words, children were explicitly taught a rudimentary, quasi-biological essentialist story of species differences.

Solomon and Johnson discovered that this brief lesson about genes influenced children's biological inferences in appropriate ways. For example, children in the instructional condition, compared to those in a control group who received no

Table 3.5.   Percentage of responses of each type by condition and group

	Correct (subord.)	Mutual exclusivity	Synonym	Other
U.S. middle class				
Internal	38%	36%	18%	8%
Superficial	29	53	10	8
Brazilian middle class				
Internal	56	26	13	4
Superficial	24	67	4	5
Brazilian *favela* residents				
Internal	27	19	38	15
Superficial	13	58	6	23

Source: Diesendruck, Gelman, and Lebowitz (1998) and Diesendruck (2001).

special instruction, more readily distinguished physical traits from beliefs, considering that the former but not the latter would be passed down from parent to child. It is remarkable that such young children, with so little in the way of a scientific foundation, were open to learning about the nonobvious construct of "genes."

Summary

In contrast to the usual picture of young children as focused on outward appearances, several researchers find that by three years of age, children distinguish insides from outsides, have correct general expectations about the contents of insides (i.e., how animals and artifacts differ in their insides), and treat insides as privileged with respect to identity, functioning, and word extension. This impressively rich body of expectations does not appear to be based on a concrete or detailed knowledge base. Instead, children seem to hold a framework assumption that the insides of living kinds are important.

Authentication

What kinds of evidence do children find relevant for authenticating an animal as a member of a given kind (e.g., a dog versus a wolf)? Does this evidence include nonobvious features? From a theoretical perspective, there is strong motivation for examining the kinds of authentication procedures children endorse, given my prediction that children should understand essences as an abstract placeholder notion before they have learned specific essential properties. As mentioned several times already, children's expectations can precede (and exceed) their knowledge (Coley, Medin, Proffitt, et al., 1999). I therefore predicted that children would have expectations concerning the way in which kinds differ before they have concrete knowledge of what properties specifically distinguish them. For example, children may expect that dogs and wolves differ in their internal parts before being able to state what those internal differences are.

To this point, studies examining links between insides and outsides have focused on ontological contrasts (e.g., animate versus inanimate) and leave open the question of whether children attribute kind-specific insides to different basic-level categories. For example, Simons and Keil (1995) as well as Gail Gottfried and I found that children posit different sorts of internal parts for animals versus artifacts, but this work does not address whether children believe that each basic-level animal kind (e.g., dogs versus cats) possesses its own unique internal structure. This issue is particularly important for the question of whether internal causal mechanisms are linked to specific kinds (generally assumed to be basic level). The literature contains contradictory hypotheses: Atran, Estin, et al. (1997) suggest that essences are at the level of genera-species (roughly, basic level) for adults. On the other hand, prior work suggests that the ontological-level contrast of living versus nonliving may be particularly crucial for distinguishing essences at the youngest ages (Keil, 1989). These opposing findings raise the possibility that there may be developmental change in which category level(s) are essentialized (from ontological to more specific levels).

The method of contrasting entities provides a potentially powerful tool for encouraging children to focus on different category levels. Preschool children are highly sensitive to the level of contrast between two objects (e.g., a Dalmatian is described differently, depending on whether it is contrasted with a bulldog ["Dalmatian"], a bird ["dog"], or a plant ["animal"]; Waxman and Hatch, 1992). We can therefore ask children to consider why an animal is classified as a dog versus a wolf, or why an object is classified as an animal versus a toy.

David Lizotte and I examined these issues in two studies with thirty-six five-year-olds and thirty-six college students (Lizotte and Gelman, 1999). For each trial, participants saw realistic color drawings of a pair of items (e.g., German shepherds) that looked nearly identical. They were told that the two items differed in some respect (e.g., one was an animal and one was a toy), and that their job was to figure out which item was which. Some of the contrasts were at the ontological level (one is an animal and the other is a toy). Some of the contrasts were at the basic level (e.g., one is a dog and the other is a wolf). And some of the contrasts were nominal (in name only) (e.g., one is Amanda and one is Melissa). The nominal contrast serves as a control, for which no information should be relevant.

The children were instructed that Charlie, the zookeeper, noticed that none of the cages in the zoo had name tags. He wanted to put the right name tags on each cage. But he discovered a problem: some of the things in the zoo looked "a lot alike," so he first had to figure out what they were. Children were then told that Charlie had some ideas about what to do in order to figure out what the various things were. The child's job was to say which of Charlie's ideas were good ones and which were silly. Children received six pairs of test items: two ontological, two basic level, and two nominal. For each pair, children were asked a series of four yes/no questions concerning various options (in random order):

- inspection of *insides* with X-rays and a microscope,
- knowledge of *origins* (for example, finding out who the parents of the animals were),
- observing *behaviors*, and
- knowledge of *age*.

These four identification procedures help tease apart different theoretical accounts of what participants are doing (see Table 3.6). One possibility is that children will think that items that look identical will in fact not be distinguishable based on any of these procedures. Although children certainly expect typical animals and toys to differ, and may expect typical instances of these basic-level kinds (such as dogs and wolves) to differ, these expectations could break down in the face of powerful perceptual information that breaches the boundary. This strong superficialist prediction would lead to a "no" bias (unfortunately, indistinguishable from

Table 3.6. Interpretable response patterns for Lizotte and Gelman study

Pattern	Behavior	Insides	Origins	Age
Superficialist	yes	no	no	no
Essentialist	yes	yes	yes	no
"Yes" response bias	yes	yes	yes	yes
"No" response bias	no	no	no	no

a response bias to say no to all questions). A weaker version of the superficialist prediction is that children will think that items will be detectable on the basis of outward behaviors, as these are immediately perceptible, but that none of the other means will be relevant. A third possibility, the essentialist prediction, is that children will think that the items will be detectable by a wide range of means—not just external behaviors, but also internal properties, behaviors, and origins. The inclusion of age questions helps to distinguish an essentialist prediction from an overall bias to say yes to all questions. That is, age is a control, since it is irrelevant to any of the contrasts we are examining.

To review: there were two sorts of controls built into the design: the age questions were included as a property that should not help authenticate the items at any level, and the nominal contrast was included as a contrast for which essentialist information should be irrelevant. For all other cells, a high response indicates appropriate use of an informational cue to distinguish kinds.

Figure 3.3 presents the data collapsed over the two versions of the experiment (which included slightly different versions of the questions). As predicted, adults endorsed behaviors, insides, and origins at a high rate at both the ontological and the basic levels. All these cells were significantly higher than the corresponding age questions, and all these cells were significantly higher than the corresponding questions regarding the nominal contrast. In other words, adults reported, for both ontological-level contrasts (is this an animal or a toy?) and basic-level contrasts (is this a dog or a wolf?), that information about outward behaviors, inner parts or substance, and parental origins were all highly relevant. This pattern fits the essentialist framework, in which kind differences should be detectable by a range of means, including nonobvious internal properties.

Data from children were similar though more variable. As with adults, children's responses varied by question for the ontological level and the basic level, but not for the nominal level. At both the ontological and basic levels, children tended to judge behaviors, insides, and origins as more important than age. Furthermore, for behavior, insides, and origins, children's responses were higher at the ontological and basic levels than at the nominal level. Putting all this information together, preschool children judged behaviors, insides, and origins as relevant sources of information to determining kind identity.

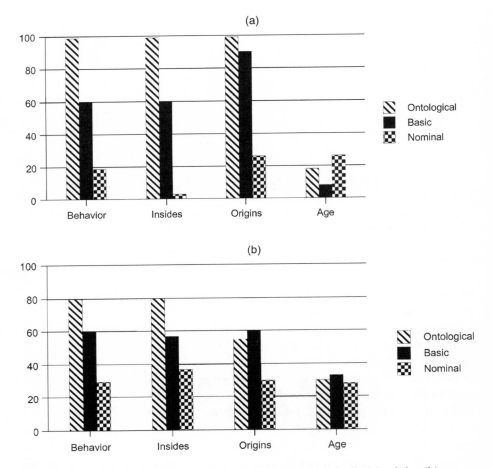

Figure 3.3. Results of Lizotte and Gelman (1999, unpublished): (a) Adults, (b) Children.

Overall, these data support the essentialist view for both ontological and basic levels, although more strongly for the ontological level than for the basic level. Both preschool children and adults considered internal parts relevant when seeking to determine the identity or authenticity of an item. Children were not simply endorsing insides due to a general bias that insides are somehow important. After all, age, too, is clearly an important dimension along which people and animals are sorted, but children typically thought it would be "silly" to consult the age of an item to figure out what it is. Furthermore, children were selective about which identities they thought were detectable by essentialist means: although ontological distinctions and basic-level distinctions can be decided on the basis of insides, the proper name that an animal receives cannot be decided on that basis. Children showed appropriate flexibility in their understanding of the value and limits of internal properties.

SUMMARY

In several ways, children privilege internal, nonobvious properties in their categories. I reviewed three sorts of evidence in this chapter. First, by four or five years of age, children often recognize that an animal cannot be transformed into another kind of thing (for example, a raccoon cannot become a skunk)—its category membership is stable over striking transformations. Second, preschoolers treat the boundaries of animal superordinates as more objective and real than the boundaries of artifact superordinates. And third, nonobvious properties, especially internal properties, are salient to young children and privileged in their determinations of what things are. The main message from this chapter is that children's categories cannot be reduced to salient perceptual cues, and that internal or nonobvious properties are significant in children's concepts.

These results are startling in view of traditional and recent claims about the nature of children's concepts. We learn in developmental psychology texts that children are tethered to the immediate concrete context, or in Flavell's words, "the widely held view that young children respond only to what is most striking and noticeable in their immediate perceptual field" (1977, pp. 79–80). Even when considering studies showing that young children can reason about nonobvious properties, students of cognitive development find it difficult to accept fully the implications of these results. Hampton (1998), for example, in reviewing findings "that children do not rely on purely *perceptual* similarity to define their concepts" (p. 141), including the work of Keil (1989), Carey (1985), and myself (S. Gelman, 1988), summarizes the data as such: "*The shift from perceptual to 'hidden' aspects of objects* is evidence of growing levels of knowledge on the part of the child, and an increase in the attention and importance accorded to deeper functional and relational kinds of attribute in concept representations" (p. 142; emphasis added). In other words, children's early sensitivity to "hidden" properties is seen as evidence of an earlier period of perceptually based categorization, despite unequivocal disavowals of this interpretation by those cited. For example, Keil (1989) explicitly rejects the notion that children are bound to an "animal sense of similarity" (Quine, 1977; Keil wittily dubs this "original sim"). The idea that children cannot look beyond surface appearances may be part of our entrenched and essentialized view of children (see also Siegler and Ellis, 1996, regarding scientists' essentializing of children). I have argued, in contrast, that this view of children is wrong. What we cannot say from these studies is what precedes children's understanding, below about three or four years of age. Perhaps Hampton is right, and children do initially rely on perceptual cues (though see Mandler, 1988, for a competing position). I take up this set of issues in more detail in chapter 9.

A caveat is in order, reflecting the imprecise relation between the tasks and methods reviewed in this chapter and the construct of essentialism. Each of the phenomena examined in this chapter is linked only indirectly to essentialism. For example, consider the issue of category boundaries. Although I am arguing for a relative heightening of boundaries in essentialized categories, Hirschfeld (1996) rightly comments that essentialism need not imply sharp boundaries: kinship is essentialized, but admits of degrees (for example, your second cousin is still essentially a family member, yet less centrally so than your sibling).

Likewise, although constancy over transformations does strongly imply an essentialist stance (showing that nonobvious properties are more central than superficial ones), constancy itself is not a necessary condition for essentialism. People can be essentialist even about categories they do not view as fixed over time. For instance, people appear to essentialize age groupings (babies, teenagers, old people), even though individuals move into and out of these groupings.

Finally, as already noted, essences do not reduce to insides. I have focused on material insides as relatively essential properties. However, at least for adults, essences need not be as tangibly perceptible as a heart or a brain. Anecdotal essentialist reports refer to immaterial essences as well, perhaps the most familiar for a Westerner being the soul. Recall the example of Claire Sylvia, at the beginning of the chapter. She (and others) made reference to an "energy," "essence," or "psychological residue" that persisted after the death of a heart donor. Are such conceptions available to children? In chapter 5, I return to the question of whether children might likewise appeal to a nonmaterial energy or force, by considering vitalism. Another way of gauging essentialism without direct appeal to insides is to examine children's conceptions of nature versus nurture. I turn to this issue next, in chapter 4.

Chapter 4

Children's Conceptions of Nature and Nurture

> When an American says that she is half Irish, one quarter Italian, and another quarter Mexican, she is not explaining the degrees to which she has mastered these different cultures, nor to which she chooses to participate or affiliate with them, but, rather, she is making a calculation based on the ethnicities of her grandparents.
>
> Francisco Gil-White, "Are Ethnic Groups Biological 'Species' to the Human Brain?"

Inheritance plays an important role in adults' everyday thoughts about social categories. When people think about identity, they often assume that properties are passed down from parent to child, independent of social or environmental influences. (One need not know anything about Mexican culture to consider oneself "one-quarter Mexican," in Gil-White's example.) In this sense we might say that social identity is construed as natural.

Natural categories exhibit properties determined by forces beyond human control. A cat cannot bark, sprout wings, or transform into an elephant, because category membership is determined and fixed by birth. Even if a cat wanted to bark, it could not do so—it is limited by its very nature. The stability of categories described in prior chapters may be due in part to beliefs about their natural basis.

For adults and some children, "natural" can be construed as "biological," and we can see this link informally in how people talk. Explicit construals of essentialism often recruit the language of biology: a ten-year-old girl in one of our studies explained that a boy will go fishing rather than put on makeup: "'Cause that's the boy instinct." A fifth-grader in another of our studies reported that a child born of not-too-smart parents but raised by smart parents would be not too smart, explaining, "It's in its genes." Another example was provided to me by a graduate student, Betsy A., whose father is Jewish and whose mother is not. She recounted with wry amusement that she was told by a potential beau, "I can't date anyone who's not a mitochondrial Jew." Nonetheless, "natural" does not necessarily mean "scientifically accurate." For example, I am aware of no fishing instinct located on the Y chromosome.

In this chapter I propose that children likewise view membership in certain categories as natural. I argue that young children appeal to inheritance and innate potential when they essentialize. They display rather elaborate beliefs that kinship overrides outward similarity, that inborn traits may be inherited, and that birth parents are more important than adoptive parents in determining how an animal or plant grows and develops. Whether and to what degree we wish to call these truly biological understandings is a controversial topic that I take up later, in chapter 6. The main point, in any case, is that children understand certain categories in terms of embodied, inherited, natural differences.

INHERITANCE

Kinship has a special status in young children's reasoning. Springer (1992) finds that children between four and eight years old appreciate that kinship is a special relation that allows projecting novel bodily or behavioral properties. He presented children with triads of animals in which kinship was pitted against perceptual similarity. For example, a target horse was shown with two smaller horses; one was highly similar but said to be not of the same family as the target, and the other was less similar but said to be the "baby" of the target. Children learned novel properties of the target (e.g., that a horse has hairy ears, or that a cow eats small weeds), and were asked in turn whether each of the other animals had the same property. Springer found that children projected the properties more often to the related-but-dissimilar animal than to the unrelated-but-similar animal. In a follow-up study, kinship was found to be more powerful than the purely social relationship of friendship. So, even when the unrelated animal was described as being the target's best friend, children granted kinship a privileged status, inferring more properties from parent to offspring than from one best friend to another. Springer also found that kinship-based inferences were specific to biological properties. For example, if children learned that the target horse got scratches on its legs while running through some bushes (a nonbiological property), they were no more likely to project this fact to its offspring than to its best friend. These findings demonstrate an awareness, quite early in childhood, that biological relationships have weightier implications than social relationships for a class of bodily processes. Although this understanding is still implicit (for example, children rarely supplied suitable explanations of their responses), it suggests the beginning of an understanding of biological kinship as a privileged relationship.

INNATE POTENTIAL

Inborn features also have a special status in children's concepts. Children treat inborn features as more likely than acquired features to be intrinsic to a species. Children predicted that unrelated members of an animal category would share abnormalities that were inborn, but not abnormalities that were acquired (Springer and Keil, 1989). For example, children reasoned that a bull was more likely to be born with a pink heart inside if other bulls that lived nearby had been born with pink hearts inside than if other bulls had a one-time accident that made their hearts pink.

Another way to gauge whether innate features are crucial to category membership is to ask whether changes in rearing conditions affect category identity or functioning. Researchers have studied these issues by using either an adoption task (e.g., S. Gelman and Wellman, 1991) or a switched-at-birth task (e.g., Hirschfeld, 1996). These tasks pose a nature/nurture conflict to children and ask them to choose which is more predictive. The basic idea is to describe an animal or child who at birth is either adopted by another family or is switched (accidentally) with another animal or child. The birth parents and the upbringing parents differ in some crucial dimension (e.g., race, species, personality trait). The question then is how the animal or child will turn out. If respondents predict that the animal or child will be like the birth parents, they are presumably using a nativist model. If instead they predict that the animal or child will be like the upbringing parents, they are presumably using an environmental model. (These sorts of thought experiments are not merely hypothetical to children. At least some children struggle with these issues spontaneously in trying to understand the world. For example, my son Adam, at age 7;4, asked me what would happen if Christian parents had a Jewish child: would the parents tell the child that Santa Claus is real?)

Henry Wellman and I found that nature wins out over nurture for four-year-olds' judgments about infant animals and plant seeds (S. Gelman and Wellman, 1991) (see Table 4.1). For example, respondents said that a baby kangaroo raised among goats will grow up to hop and have a pouch (see Figure 4.1). (All properties were pretested to make sure that children knew the answer when no conflict was presented—for example, they said that kangaroos are good at hopping and have a pouch and that goats are good at climbing and do not have a pouch. Furthermore, none of the questions could be answered by consulting the picture of the baby animal, which was depicted in such a way that the property in question was not visible.) Children very rarely appealed to the environment. We can think of this response as demonstrating robustness of the category despite external transformations.

One potential counterexplanation for these results is that children were simply reporting category associations: mooing and straight tails are associated with cows, and since the experimenter called the animal a "cow," it must moo and have a straight tail. However, this possibility seemed unlikely, because children consistently treated physical features as more malleable than behaviors. (This was a surprising result, as intuition suggests that adults would display the opposite pattern: greater malleability of behaviors than physical features.) For example, if a baby kangaroo was reared by goats, children were significantly more likely to predict that it would hop than that it would develop a pouch. This finding was not due to a difference in knowledge or associative strength. On a control task that presented no nature/nurture conflict, children were just as knowledgeable about physical properties as behaviors, and both types of features were equally associated with the

Table 4.1. Items used in S. Gelman and Wellman (1991) adoption studies

Item	Environment	Question
Animals		
rabbit	monkeys	long or short ears?
		rather have carrots or bananas?
tiger	horses	striped or plain fur?
		roar or neigh?
cow	pigs	straight or curly tail?
		say "moo" or say "oink"?
mouse	dogs	round or floppy ears?
		run away from or chase cats?
kangaroo	goats	have pouch or no pouch?
		good at hopping or climbing?
Plants		
seed from apple	flower pot	apple or flower?
seed from watermelon	cornfield	watermelon or corn?
seed from lemon	orange trees	lemon tree or orange tree?
seed from flower	strawberries	flower or strawberry?
seed from rose	dandelions	rose or dandelion?
seed from grape	coconut trees	grapes or coconut tree?
pit from peach	plum trees	peach tree or plum tree?

Source: S. Gelman and Wellman (1991). Reprinted with the permission of Elsevier Science.

categories in question. It seems that children's answers on the adoption task could not be reduced to category associations.

Nonetheless, we conducted a further control study to bolster our interpretation that responses were not due to category associations. In this control study, we asked children whether infant animals had each of the target properties when they were babies. We reasoned as follows: if children report that babies do not yet have their adult features, this finding would provide converging evidence that children are not just reporting category associations. It would also underscore that certain properties are viewed as not yet present in infancy yet inevitably developing even in the absence of environmental support.

A new group of four-year-olds was asked whether the infant versions of the animals had each of the test properties, with no environment specified (e.g., "Does this baby kangaroo have a pouch?"). The results clearly support an essentialist construal of our findings regarding physical properties. Four-year-olds attributed physical features to the infant animals only 40% of the time, which was significantly lower than the rate in the earlier study, in which four-year-olds attributed these same features to the same animal, *when it grew up*, 67% of the time (despite a contrasting environment). This result confirms that children's nativist responses in

Figure 4.1. Baby kangaroo and goats; S. Gelman and Wellman (1991). *Source:* Goats from Helweg (1978). Reprinted with the permission of Random House Children's Books, a division of Random House, Inc.

93

the earlier study could not be attributed to simple category associations. In contrast, children attributed the behavioral properties to the infant animals at a high rate, an average of 87% of the time. We cannot explain this difference between behaviors and physical features, but the impressive result with regard to physical features remains.

Carey and her collaborators (Carey, 1995; Carey and Spelke, 1994; Solomon et al., 1996) cautioned that a biological notion of innate potential is not required to account for these findings, and that at least some of the results might be attributed to children's expectations that identity is maintained over time. For example, because the animal was labeled as being a member of a particular species—such as a kangaroo—children may have simply assumed that it would continue to have kangaroo properties. This possibility does not undermine an essentialist argument, which indeed predicts that children will view properties as fixed despite environmental changes. However, for the question of whether or not children's understanding is biological, the critique is important.

Two further kinds of data undermine this critique. First, children report that seeds have innate potential, when the identity of the mature plant is neither present initially nor labeled by the experimenter (S. Gelman and Wellman, 1991). For example, by four and a half years of age, children reported that if a seed was taken out of an apple and planted in a flowerpot, an apple tree would pop out of the ground. Second, children have strong beliefs about the innate potential of people, even when they are not told the category identity of the adopted infant (Hirschfeld, 1995, 1996; Springer, 1995). In one series of studies, Hirschfeld (1995) showed preschoolers pictures of two families, one dark-skinned and the other light-skinned, whose newborns were inadvertently switched in the hospital. Each family took home and raised the other's infant. Children were then shown pictures of two school-aged children, one dark-skinned and the other light-skinned, and asked which was the child when he or she grew up and began school. Three-year-olds selected at chance, but four-year-olds relied overwhelmingly on a nativist reasoning strategy, choosing the child who matched the birth parents (not the adoptive parents) on skin color. Springer (1995) replicated this finding and extended it, demonstrating that five-year-olds believe that not only race but also a range of biological (though not psychological) properties are fixed at birth and immutable over the life span. Here again, the data support the essentialist interpretation. Children reasoned that category identity is determined at birth and impervious to environmental influences. In both sets of studies, an essentialist notion of innate potential governs children's expectations about racial identity.

Even when children fail to distinguish biological from nonbiological properties, they often display a "birth bias," reporting that offspring will resemble the birth parents despite immersion in the environment supplied by the upbringing parents. For example, S. Johnson and Solomon (1997) taught five- and six-year-olds about a horse raised by cows, and about a duck raised by chickens. They found that the modal response was a reliance on the birth parents. Out of sixty-four children, thirty-nine consistently showed a birth-parent bias (judging the offspring to re-semble the birth parent on at least ten out of twelve features), whereas only four consistently showed an adoptive parent bias (judging the offspring to resemble the adoptive parent on at least ten out of twelve features). The remaining children ei-ther showed an adultlike differentiation pattern (relying on the birth parent for physical properties and the adoptive parent for belief properties; $N = 4$) or showed a mixed pattern of responses ($N = 21$). The birth bias is inaccurate when applied to properties such as beliefs, yet it is consistent with an essentializing pattern.

Various researchers have extended this work to other kinds of properties that adults consider to be more environmentally determined, including language (e.g., English, Portuguese), gender-linked characteristics (e.g., wanting to play with dolls; see section titled "Gender" later in this chapter); and traits (e.g., shy, smart; see section titled "Psychological Traits" later in this chapter). Children's essentialist interpretations remain quite powerful even in domains where older children and adults have constructed more nuanced social-constructivist accounts. For exam-ple, Larry Hirschfeld and I conducted a switched-at-birth experiment using lan-guage as the contrast (Hirschfeld and Gelman, 1997). Preschoolers were told about two couples, one that spoke English and one that spoke Portuguese (with audio-taped speech samples provided to illustrate the contrast). As in Hirschfeld's and Springer's studies, the children were told that the newborn of each couple was switched with the infant of the other couple. Children then listened to two audio-taped speech samples, one in English and the other in Portuguese, and were asked to choose which language the switched-at-birth child spoke when he or she grew up. Although three-year-olds performed at chance, five-year-olds consistently se-lected the language of the birth parents.

GENDER

Young children are especially nativist about gender, compared to older children. Ullian (1976) interviewed six- to eighteen-year-olds about the causes of male/female differences and found that causal beliefs shifted with age from a biological orientation (focus on innate physical differences) to a socialization orientation (focus on social roles and obligations), and finally to a psychological orientation (focus on requirements of individual and interpersonal functioning). J. Smith and Russell (1984) reported a similar shift from a biological to a societal orientation in their interviews with seven- to fifteen-year-olds but found little evidence for a psy-chological orientation. For example, seven-year-olds most typically reported bio-logical or physical differences (e.g., "Boys have different things in their innards to girls") or normative differences (e.g., "Because God made them that way"). By the time a child reached age fifteen, socialization explanations were more common (e.g., "We do different things because it is the way we have been brought up"). Adult samples of parents (Antill, 1987) and college students (Martin and Parker, 1995) mentioned both biology and socialization in their explanations of gender differences. When asked which factor they saw as more important, both groups favored socialization (although a third of the parent sample viewed both as equally important). These developmental changes in explanations suggest that children especially view sex differences as fixed and inherent.

Taylor (1996) examined essentialist beliefs about gender in subjects ranging from preschool to college age. The task was again a nature/nurture task similar to those described above. Subjects were told about an infant boy who was raised from birth by his aunt on an island populated entirely by girls and women, or an infant girl who was raised from birth by her uncle on an island containing only boys and men. Participants were then asked to infer various sex-stereotyped properties of the boy or girl when he or she was ten years old (e.g., would he or she like to play with dolls? would he or she like to play football?).

The study yielded two notable findings. First, the youngest participants (four-year-olds) inferred that gender-linked properties were inherent in the child and not determined by the environment. For instance, they typically inferred that the boy raised with females would like to play football and would not like to play with dolls. Second, the youngest children provided the strongest evidence of essentializing, with socialization and interactionist explanations not emerging until about nine or ten years of age. Taylor (1993) found similar results in a second study that taught children unfamiliar gender-linked properties (for example, all the girls on one island like to play a game called fan-tan, and all the boys on the other island like to play a game called chuck-luck) and tested children's nature/nurture beliefs about the origins of these attributes (what does Chris [the child raised on the island with those of a different gender] like to play, fan-tan or chuck-luck?). In both studies, younger children professed stronger nativist beliefs about gender than did older children.

Marianne Taylor and I next examined children's causal explanations for their answer choices (Taylor, 1997; Taylor and Gelman, unpublished). Children were asked, with respect to a variety of biological and behavioral properties, not only whether nature or nurture would win out, but also why. Explanations are important because, as S. Johnson and Solomon (1997) point out, choices on a switched-at-birth task provide only indirect evidence regarding the reasoning process (see also Weissman and Kalish, 1999). Children could select a choice for reasons other than the contrast we had intended. For example, if those raising the child thought it was important to provide a gender-appropriate environment, they might treat the target child differently than the other children on the island (such as teaching the lone boy how to play football). In that case, seeming "nature" responses could actually reflect "nurture."

Accordingly, Taylor and I probed children's explanations. For example, children were asked why a girl raised with boys would have girl blood inside (versus boy blood inside; biological property), or why a girl raised with boys would prefer to play with a tea set (versus toy truck; behavioral property). In the first of two studies, five- and ten-year-old children were simply asked, in an open-ended way, to provide their own justifications. Table 4.2 lists a sample of the justifications chil-

Table 4.2.   Sample justifications

A girl raised with only boys and men

Wears a dress rather than a football shirt: "Because the boys have footballer clothes and the girls have those notchy things that go 'shake, shake' [pompons], and the girls have dresses—white dresses or pink." (Girl, age 5)

Grows up to be a nurse rather than a firefighter: "There's more of a chance she would want to be a nurse. Some females are firefighters, but whenever I watch *Rescue 911*, you see the males around there and the females for nurses." (Boy, age 10)

Likes to play with a tea set rather than a toy truck: "Because usually since she has a girl brain, she'd like to play with a tea set." (Boy, age 10)

Grows up to be a ballet dancer rather than a football player: "Because girls, a lot of girls, would more like to be a ballet dancer than a football player, and again it always depends on what she thinks." (Boy, age 10)

A boy raised with only girls and women

Plays with a truck rather than a tea set: "Because boys play with boy things and girls play with girl things." (Boy, age 5)

Wears army boots rather than hair ribbons: "Because he doesn't like them. Because he's a boy, and boys don't wear hair ribbons." (Boy, age 5)

Goes fishing rather than puts on makeup: "'Cause that's the boy instinct." (Girl, age 10)

Grows up to have a boy brain rather than a girl brain: "Because, you see, there's the difference in who gets boy brains and girl brains. Boy brains stay in the boy and girl brains stay in the girl." (Boy, age 5)

Source: S. Gelman and Taylor (2000). Reprinted with the permission of Routledge, Inc., part of the Taylor & Francis Group.

dren provided. As can be seen, children at both ages provided inherent and essentialist explanations for gender-stereotyped behavior, mentioning the brain, instinct, and desires to engage in sex-stereotypical behavior.

In a second study, 264 five-, seven-, and ten-year-old children ($Ns = 75, 89,$ and 100, respectively) received the nature/nurture scenarios described above and were asked for their explanations. However, this time we provided children with possible responses, which they were asked to endorse or reject one at a time. Possible responses included being born a certain way, being taught by others, learning, really wanting to, or others really wanting the child to. Here we report participants' justifications for their nature choices, that is, for those trials on which they said that a child would retain gender-characteristic properties. For biological properties, children nearly always (> 95% of the time) endorsed the mechanism of birth (being born a certain way), though the youngest children also sometimes endorsed wanting (51%) or learning (32%). This result validates our assumption that birth is interpreted as a biological mechanism. It also illustrates that even young children expect that different mechanisms can act in concert (e.g., innate tendencies and learning can work together; see also Marler, 1991).

We then turned to the behavioral properties (such as play preferences), which were our primary interest. When children gave category responses (in other words, reporting that a child raised with opposite-sex others would nonetheless show gender-stereotyped properties), they most often endorsed those mechanisms that involved the child himself or herself—really wanting to be a certain way (81%), learning to be a certain way (69%), or just being born a certain way (52%). Those that involved others (others teaching the child, or others really wanting the child to be a certain way) were deemed much less relevant (15% and 17%, respectively). These patterns were remarkably stable in children from five to ten years of age. Children endorsed both essentialist mechanisms (being born a certain way) and nonessentialist mechanisms (wanting, learning), but what the different mechanisms have in common is that they are self-guided and self-directed. Interestingly, children's endorsement of nonbiological mechanisms (such as learning and wanting) did not entail rejecting essentialist mechanisms. Children in all three age groups (five, seven, and ten) viewed both sorts of mechanisms as mutually operating. We conclude that when explaining the maintenance of gender-stereotyped properties, children consistently appeal to either inherent qualities in the person or outright essentialist accounts. This nativist bias is consistent with young children's powerful use of gender for making inductive inferences (S. Gelman, Collman, and Maccoby, 1986, discussed in chapter 2). With both nativist beliefs and inductive potential, children essentialize gender early on.

PSYCHOLOGICAL TRAITS

By late preschool, children reliably presume that innate propensities shape race, language, and gender, suggesting that children may hold nativist expectations about a broad range of phenomena. Psychological traits are also especially interesting to study (Heyman and Gelman, 2000). Because traits concern psychological rather than physical categories of people, they do not have the rich perceptual basis that one finds with basic-level animal kinds (e.g., "shy people" do not all look alike). Furthermore, the mental models adults use are intriguingly complex. Magazines for parents provide ample speculation about inborn personality characteristics in babies, yet at the same time provide advice on how to structure the environment so as to raise a calmer, more obedient, more intelligent child. Very little is known about how beliefs about trait origins develop in children. Until recently, the major focus has been on how stable or consistent children think traits are over time. Because children often seemed not even to acknowledge or appreciate the existence of traits, researchers saw no point in asking more broadly about trait theories. However, some findings suggest that children do possess early trait understandings (Eder, 1989; Heyman and Gelman, 1998). Given this research, the task of characterizing children's trait theories becomes timely.

Gail Heyman and I examined these issues using the switched-at-birth task. The literature does include a few studies that used the switched-at-birth task to study traits or other personal characteristics (Solomon et al., 1996; Springer, 1996). However, these studies are inconclusive about trait beliefs for two reasons. First, the kinds of personal characteristics differed from one another in how central they were to a person's identity (ranging from traits to preferences or beliefs), yet they were not analyzed separately. Second, the personal properties in these studies were presented alongside other kinds of properties. For example, the same child might have been asked to reason about traits, beliefs, and physical characteristics. The problem with this research design is that the context of the surrounding questions may have primed children to think about traits in one way versus another.

In contrast to past research, Heyman and I conducted studies that focused primarily on psychological traits. For example, in our studies we described nice people who pick up other people's trash, and mean people who throw rocks at dogs. A baby born to the nice people was raised by the mean people, and vice versa. The question was whether the baby would be nice, like the birth parents, or mean, like the upbringing parents. We conducted several studies with children as young as kindergarten age, up through fifth grade and adults. Trait properties included shy/outgoing, active/inactive, smart/not smart, and nice/mean. Physical characteristics served as a comparison, and included such things as ear shape and foot size. We systematically varied order: half the participants at each age got a physical characteristic as their first item, and half did not. One supplementary issue was whether thinking about physical characteristics first primes a more nativist way of reasoning.

Here I highlight three important findings. First, with age, psychological traits were increasingly differentiated from physical properties. Nonetheless, even kindergarteners distinguished the two kinds of characteristics. They consistently treated physical characteristics as innately determined, but their views of psychological traits were mixed. Second, the youngest children exhibited large order effects. Children who were asked about a physical characteristic first tended to judge properties as more biologically determined than children who were not asked about a physical characteristic first. In other words, if a child's first item was about hair texture, foot size, or ear shape, the child tended to focus on the birth parents for all the items. Yet if the first item was a psychological trait or belief, the child was much less likely to focus on the birth parents. This finding leads to an important methodological point. In some cells of the study design, children's responses did not differ from chance overall, but their performance varied substantially depending on how they were primed. This pattern of null performance overall but strong order effects might help explain why in past work some researchers found differences between biological and nonbiological properties and other researchers did not (Solomon et al., 1996; Springer, 1996). The order effect also suggests that young children's responses are malleable, and that children have access to (at least) two competing causal models.

A third and final point is that children had developed surprisingly rich conceptions of psychological traits in elementary school. We saw this development in their open-ended justifications, which we elicited and coded in one of the switched-at-birth studies. A certain portion of the time, when children did select the birth parents, they expressed rather powerful nativist theories, especially at nine to eleven years of age. Examples are the following explanations of why a child born to not-so-smart parents, but raised with smart parents, would be not-so-smart (with age group listed in parentheses):

(5–6 years old)	"He wasn't born to smart parents."
(6–8 years old)	"The family would try but the baby would always stay not very smart."
(9–11 years old)	"It will have trouble. It's in its genes."
(9–11 years old)	"You can change the way you act but you can't change the brain. If the baby was born to not-so-smart people, it couldn't learn things as well because it has a low I.Q."

Children's beliefs were sometimes more complicated than a simple yes or no. For example, one participant predicted that a child born to active parents but raised by inactive ones would turn out to be inactive, explaining: "The way they were raised. The child would want to be active but would be forced into not being more active and would get used to it." In other words, even when children chose the environment, they sometimes expressed that the environment was working against a natural tendency in another direction. Conversely, sometimes children talked about an innate potential that took environmental support to emerge, as in the following example from a participant speculating about a child who was born to smart parents but raised by not-so-smart parents: "The baby will not be smart at first, but in school it will get smart. The baby learns well because of the original parents. The new parents will be proud of the child for doing better than they expected." Especially given that adults appeal to a mixed model, the development of these theories in early childhood will be important to study in greater detail.

CROSS-CULTURAL EVIDENCE

Essencelike construals of kinds appear in a variety of cultures. For example, Errington (1989)

> describes how nobles in Luwu [of South Sulawesi] are so defined because of an invisible and inherited substance, "white blood." Since "white blood" is invisible, it can only be "read" through people's conduct (that is, elements such as the person's stance, demeanor, self-control, and entourage); it is one's conduct that demonstrates one's inner self. (Cited in Astuti, 1995, p. 470)

This example is interesting in its appeal to a nonvisible, causally efficacious, inherited inner quality.

Gil-White (2001) argues that essentialism can be found among the Torguud pastoralists of Western Mongolia. People predict that innate potential is more powerful than environmental influences and appear to link essences to something internal and hidden. On a switched-at-birth task, when asked to predict the ethnicity of a hypothetical child adopted by a different ethnic group, adults tended to report that identity is determined by descent rather than outward appearances. Gil-White also provides intriguing excerpts of conversations to support his claim of essentialist beliefs. For example, at one point he asked, "If an Uryanxai child was adopted by the Torguud, . . . would he be able to cast curses or not?" His informant replied, "That child doesn't know that his real parents are Uryanxai . . . so . . . he would be able to, but he wouldn't know it." That is a striking belief—that a person can have an inherited identity not known even to himself (much like J. K. Rowling's rendition of wizards, witches, and Muggles in the Harry Potter book series).

Atran, Medin, et al. (2001) used a version of the S. Gelman and Wellman (1991) inheritance task with Yukatek Maya-speaking children and adults in rural villages in south-central Quintana Roo, Mexico. Participants were given scenarios in which an animal (e.g., a cow) gave birth to a baby and died. Then the baby was taken to live with members of another species (e.g., pigs). Atran et al. improved the task in two major respects. First, the experimenter did not tell participants the species identity of the animal in question. For example, in one story participants heard, "One day a cow gave birth to a little baby." The offspring of the cow was never shown, and it was always referred to as "the baby" (never "the cow" or "the baby cow"). This wording gets around the problem mentioned earlier, that children might simply be reporting the maintenance of a (stated) identity over time. And second, the experimental questions probed novel as well as familiar properties, thereby allowing a test of whether children are using an inferential framework rather than reporting overlearned facts. For example, a familiar property of a turtle was "walks slowly"; a novel property of the turtle was "opens its eyes when afraid" (for half the participants) or "closes its eyes when afraid" (for the other half).

Results showed a strong and consistent tendency to attribute properties to the birth parents. For example, participants attributed known properties to the birth parent 71% of the time at age four to five years, 97% of the time at age six to seven years, and 98% of the time among adults. Similarly, participants attributed novel properties to the birth parent 69% of the time at four to five years, 83% at six to seven years, and 92% among adults. Such powerful adherence to innate potential is striking in a culture so different in many ways from the United States. Atran suggests nativist assumptions may be universal, albeit with local variations in content (Atran, Medin, et al., p. 35).

To be sure, essencelike construals vary in content across cultures. For example, the Tamil *kunam* are obtained from contact with the land rather than from inheritance (Daniel, 1984); the *bope* component, which Crocker (1979) describes for the Bororo, are generally found in all animals, rather than differing by species. Mahalingam (1998), investigating caste concepts in India, finds that individuals essentialize either more or less, depending on their location in the caste system. On a switched-at-birth task, high-caste (Brahmin) adults tend to infer that caste is fixed at birth, whereas adult members of the lowest caste (Harijan; so-called untouchables) tend to report that caste is determined by socialization. These sorts of variation nonetheless are consistent with the idea of essentialist beliefs across widely varying cultures and societies.

In contrast, Astuti (1995) describes what appears to be a nonessentialist belief system among the Vezo people of Madagascar. Their accounts of what it means to be a Vezo are based on a person's actions and where a person lives, rather than descent. "The term 'Vezo' does not indicate a trait of identity that is fixed and immutable, for people can move and thereby change their livelihood" (Astuti, 1995, p. 465). This belief system is expressed both in widespread talk and in performance on a switched-at-birth task (Astuti, 2000). Astuti summarizes this view as follows:

> I have described . . . the Vezo person as "transparent," for it is a person . . . with no intrinsic essence to it. Vezo-ness itself is not and does not become such a residue or essence since it is made anew and from scratch every day, through every act performed in the present. Vezo-ness is not inherent in the Vezo person; thus, if one were to search for Vezo identity "inside" the person, one would be unable to see it. To see what a Vezo person is one would have to look "outside it," at what the person does in the present—one would only be seeing a moment in an unceasing process of transformation. (1995, p. 477)

And yet even among the Vezo, essentialist construals seem to emerge:

- The Vezo have a word "kind" or "type" (*karaza*) that does appear to refer to essentialized natural kinds. In Astuti's words: "Membership of a karaza, whether of a class of objects, animals, or people, is based on intrinsic rather than acquired qualities; neither 'fishness' nor a specific kind of 'fishness' can be acquired, learned, or changed—a fish is born what it is. Similarly, a human being does not acquire or learn membership of a particular tomb or of the raza it contains but obtains it through descent" (1995, p. 467). In other words, although the Vezo do not consider themselves to constitute an essentialized kind, they construe other living things in this manner.
- When given a switched-at-birth task, in which a baby is described as being raised by adoptive parents, Vezo adults infer that physical properties (in contrast to beliefs) are fixed at birth and uninfluenced by the adoptive parents. For example, ear shape is that of the birth parents. So at least some qualities are construed as inherent and fixed at birth by adult Vezo.
- Most intriguingly from a developmental perspective, children six to thirteen years of age appear to be more nativist than adults. In a further experiment, children and adults again received a switched-at-birth task, but this time, instead of focusing on bodily or mental traits of individuals, the questions concerned traits associated with contrastive social groups,

such as occupation, religious beliefs, and (most important) social identity. For instance, the switched-at-birth task described a child of Vezo parents who was raised by Karany adoptive parents. The Vezo and the Karany are akin to "racial" groups in Western folk sociology. They differ in numerous respects, including religion, language, appearance, education, and occupation. When adults receive this task, 75% consistently attribute social identity, practices, and beliefs to the adoptive parents. Yet when children receive this task, 73% attribute these properties to the birth parents.

An additional contrast concerned that between the Vezo and the Masikoro. The Vezo typically fish, sail, and eat fish; the Masikoro, their immediate neighbors, typically cultivate, raise cattle, and eat grains. When contrasting the Vezo and the Masikoro, both children and adults considered nurture more powerful than nature. It is unclear why children treat the Vezo-Masikoro contrast as distinct from the Vezo-Karany contrast, though perhaps it should not be surprising. For U.S. children, too, not all social categories are essentialized. I would not expect the distinction between "farmers" and "fishermen" to be treated as inherited by young children in the United States, despite their essentializing of race and gender (see Hirschfeld's 1996 work contrasting race and occupation).

The point I wish to emphasize from the Vezo is that even in a culture that quite explicitly talks about social categories as created by actions and place, children essentialize at least some social groups.

A related study of nature/nurture beliefs focused on the Zafimaniry in a remote mountain village in eastern Madagascar (Bloch, Solomon, and Carey, 2001). As with the Vezo, adults in this culture report antiessentialist beliefs about human kinds. "Ethnographic work shows that the Zafimaniry believe that children come to resemble their parents, in great part, because of the house they grew up in, the environment in which they live, and the people with whom they have interacted (Bloch, 1993)." For example, Bloch reports that adults consider children to be "highly malleable to environmental influences . . . which will permanently affect the body and character of the child" (Bloch, 1993, p. 125). They construe children as only "potential persons," not yet fully formed (similar, perhaps, to how many in the West view a fetus).

Bloch, Solomon, and Carey (2001) provided thirty-two people (twenty-five children ages seven to fifteen, and seven adults) with a switched-at-birth task, modeled on Solomon et al. (1996). The results are interesting in several respects. First, despite the ethnographic descriptions, Zafimaniry adults' judgments on the switched-at-birth task are comparable to those of adults in the United States: they judge bodily traits as inherited and beliefs as environmentally given. This "differentiated" pattern is at odds with the suggestion (based on ethnographic description) that the Zafimaniry adults are extreme social constructivists. Instead, adult Zafimaniry have a notion of innate potential. Second, in contrast to the adults, children seven to fifteen years of age rarely showed such a differentiated pattern. Instead, they tended to have an adoptive-parent bias, reporting that a range of properties (including bodily traits, such as height) can be predicted by what the adoptive parent does or is like. The children's data do not fit the essentialist model.

Before we conclude that Zafimaniry children are nonessentialist, however, several considerations come into play. First, despite the forced-choice judgments of the children, their justifications suggest an awareness that bodily traits are not influenced by nurture. Justifications were coded as referring to any of several possible explanations, including birth origins (e.g,. "because he was born to the peasant") or nurture (e.g., "because he was taught"), among others. Most notably, participants (adults and children alike) never justified adoptive-parent choices of the bodily features in terms of nurture explanations. For example, they never explained that skin or blood color was imparted by teaching or upbringing. So there seems to be some differentiation of bodily versus mental traits, though it emerged more in justifications than in forced-choice responses. Second, the somewhat demanding version of the task could account for children's relatively poor performance. Springer (1996) and Hirschfeld (1996), focusing on middle-class children in the United States, have found that simpler tasks yield more essentialist construals at a young age.

Finally, children's responses may reflect confusion regarding who is of a different kind. That is, Zafimaniry children may essentialize certain categories (such as animal species or gender) but not others (such as ethnicity). If children lack sufficient knowledge of the city/village distinction employed in the switched-at-birth scenarios, they may consider both birth and adoptive parents to be members of the same kind, and so the variability may be understood as due to individual idiosyncrasies rather than to essentialized kinds (see also Weissman and Kalish, 1999, for the suggestion that "like produces like" might hold for properties diagnostic of a species, but not for properties that vary among individuals within a species). It would be interesting to rerun the experiment using category distinctions that are more clearly kind-based, such as gender or even animal species.

Conclusions from Cross-Cultural Research

On the one hand, essentialism is not just a Western invention. Widely varying cultures from different parts of the world seem to have come up with essencelike beliefs independently. On the other hand, cultures vary in (at least) how and for which categories essentialism is expressed. Differences emerge by at least six years of age (e.g., compare Solomon et al., 1996, with Bloch, Solomon, and Carey, 2001). More speculatively, there may even be cross-cultural variation in whether children essentialize at all. Though I have argued against this point, the data remain inconclusive. Taken as a whole, these findings support the argument that essentialism is an early cognitive bias that finds expression universally, but also point to the importance of factors outside children's predispositions that lead to variation in essencelike construals. I consider these environmental influences in chapters 7 and 8.

CONCLUSIONS

Children in these studies treat a range of categories—including animal species, gender, race, and at times psychological traits—as possessing inborn features, inherent in the animal or person, and passed down from parent to child. On this view, a kangaroo is born to hop. Even if it cannot hop at birth (because it is too small and weak), and even if it is raised by goats that cannot hop, and even if it never sees another kangaroo, hopping is inherent to kangaroos; this property will eventually be expressed. Likewise, a girl is born to play with dolls. Although there are some debates as to when precisely this understanding emerges, even on a conservative estimate it appears by about six years of age, and in some studies this understanding appears as early as age four. In this way, children "naturalize" certain categories, treating them as having a natural basis.

A naturalization model of category differences is not the only cognitive model one could possess. Recent cross-cultural work provides clear examples of alternative formulations. For example, one could view category identity as unformed at birth and malleable throughout the lifetime. However, even when such beliefs are explicitly articulated (e.g., in Madagascar), experimental investigations find essentializing of physical traits for certain categories. It seems that explicit ideology does not always match people's intuitive beliefs (see also Gil-White, 2001).

Many of the studies reviewed in this chapter are testing more than the idea that certain properties are inherent in an individual—they additionally test whether these properties are passed down from parent to child via inheritance. An inheritance model is not required of essentialism. One could be essentialist and believe that essences are transmitted by any one of a range of processes, including contact with land, or drinking breast milk, or eating special foods (processes that are invoked in some other cultures). I believe that these varying essentialist processes, though distinct from one another, all share three features: the essence is *transferable*, thereby accounting for how new members of a kind acquire their characteristics; transfer takes place *early in development*, so that the individual has the relevant properties in a formative period; and once the transfer has been accomplished, it is extremely *difficult to remove or change*.

Kinds versus Individuals; Types versus Tokens

Studies of innate potential have included two sorts of items: properties associated with a given category or kind, as with the examples above (e.g., is hopping an innate potential of kangaroos?) and properties associated with a given individual (e.g., is having brown eyes an innate potential of Ben?). We can think of the former as concerning types and the latter as concerning tokens (Jackendoff, 1983). These two kinds of items have generally been treated as equivalent, though they differ in ways that might have important psychological implications.

When we ask about the innate potential of an individual property, we focus on inheritance directly. We are asking, in effect, whether particular properties (such as eye color, height, and so forth) are inherited by the child from the parents. This question requires at minimum a grasp of inheritance. It also requires a theory of which sorts of properties are inheritable and which are not. For example, adults in the United States maintain that eye color is strongly inherited, whereas religious beliefs are not. However, there are also many properties for which we are uncertain, conflicted, or hold more complicated positions than simply attributing them wholly to either nature or nurture. For example, is a tendency toward obesity inherited? Probably it is to some degree, though there are competing theories out there. We also seem open to the possibility that properties once considered innately determined will in fact turn out to be more largely due to environmental factors, or vice versa. For example, work on temperament suggests a surprising degree to which innate potential plays a role in shyness. Some have even suggested that certain attitudes are innately determined (L. Ellis, 1998). Ellis argues that

> genetic factors incline many people to adopt sociopolitical attitudes that are associated with moral outrage when confronted with arguments that human beings inherently differ in their abilities to compete for social status. . . . People's attitudes . . . are influenced by genetics, and . . . one of the effects of these genes is to cause many of us to be highly resistant to any evidence supporting the hypothesis that genes have major influences on people's abilities to achieve high social status. (1998, p. 207)

(This article may or may not be a spoof—I'm not certain—but the very fact that it may be genuine illustrates my point that which properties are inherited is open for debate.)

Children could reject a nativist account because of their beliefs about the kind of property being considered, rather than due to a lack of nativist beliefs in general. Indeed, I suspect that children have trouble understanding that within-category variability is meaningful and required of any biological system. Therefore, children might view certain individually varying properties as accidental and unpredictable (much as adults might consider the property of having an odd or even number of freckles—as a bodily characteristic, but accidentally determined and not predicted by parental properties).

In contrast, when we ask about the innate potential of a category, we are asking how tight the link is between category membership and a given property. For example, what properties does a child have by virtue of being a girl? This question can (and at times will) be construed in terms of inheritance (e.g., a goat inherits goatlike properties from its parents), but in other contexts may not invoke inheritance at all. For some categories (such as gender), innate potential is not directly passed down by the parents (after all, a mother could give birth to either a son or a daughter) but rather is inherently fixed in the members of that category. In Taylor's (1996) work on the innate potential of gender-linked properties, no mention whatsoever is made of the birth parents. Instead, one could understand category-based innate potential by assuming that category-wide properties are fixed, immutable, and stable despite external factors.

It would be interesting to compare directly the innate potential of individual properties with the innate potential of category-based properties. For example, a given property such as neck length could be considered a marker of category membership (e.g., would a giraffe raised by pigs have a long neck?) or an individually varying property (e.g., would a human child born of long-necked parents but raised by short-necked parents have a long neck?). Similarly, skin color could be construed either categorically (as a marker of racial group membership) or individually (as individually varying skin tone within a racial group). One could present physically identical sets that are primed in either of the two ways, and ask children what property the offspring would have. I would predict greater use of innate potential for the category-based properties.

Chapter 5

Causal Explanations, Causal Determinism

> Human beings are theory builders; from the beginning we construct explanatory structures that help us find the deeper reality underlying surface chaos.
>
> Susan Carey, *Conceptual Development in Childhood*

> One of the things that theories do is to embody or provide causal linkages from deeper properties to more superficial or surface properties.
>
> Douglas Medin, "Concepts and Conceptual Structure"

We have seen in chapters 2 and 3 that people appeal to hidden, nonobvious features in constructing certain categories. But why should this be? Why are inner properties privileged? The essentialist proposal is that causes are more important than effects—and causes are more often internal, hidden, nonobvious than are effects (at least for natural kinds). People treat DNA as privileged, because they believe that it generates or constrains other, observable properties. The DNA of a fish causes it to have scales, gills, and a tail—not vice versa (the scales do not determine the DNA)—and so the hidden features are more central.

To give this point intuitive appeal, consider medical diagnosis. The physician does not seek to describe disease symptoms—which, after all, are just outward signs of some underlying disorder. Instead, the goal is to pinpoint the cause (and ultimately treatment) of the symptoms. Someone could hypothetically have measles without showing a rash, but one would not say that someone has measles if they have a rash caused by a different virus. Lugaresi, Gambetti, and Rossi (1966, p. 404; cited in Reznek, 1987, p. 32), when discussing a diagnostic puzzle regarding a neurological disorder, conclude: "It does not seem possible to answer this [taxonomic] question on the basis of clinical or even anatomical and clinical data, because, *a definitive classification is possible only when there is a knowledge of the intimate mechanism causing* the abiotrophic diseases in general" (emphasis added). (See also Thagard, 2000, for the importance of causes in people's explanations of diseases.)

Likewise, when we "diagnose" an animal as belonging to one species or another, we have the intuition that causes are central. Outward appearance is less telling than properties such as DNA or ancestry that cause such appearances. And for natural substances such as gold or water, chemical properties (such as H_2O) are definitive because they have causal powers.

My goal in this chapter is to argue for the centrality of causes in children's concepts. I do so in two different ways. First, I show that children's understanding of cause can determine which features are pivotal in the categories they form. Second, I show that children's explanations for category structure appeal to essences or essencelike constructs. I argue that the link between essences and categories follows from children's propensity to search for causes.

CAUSATION IN THE STRUCTURE OF CATEGORIES

I have suggested that causes are central to people's representation of categories. Yet two of the most prominent cognitive models of categories, the classical view and the prototype view, altogether ignore causal links among features. On the classical view, categories can be characterized by lists of necessary and sufficient defining features. On prototype views, categories are characterized by distance from a prototype. These two kinds of models differ from one another in important respects, but both can be considered similarity-based models, according to which category membership is determined by domain-general, acausal similarity (either similarity to a feature listing or similarity to a prototype; E. Smith and Medin, 1981).[1] Neither position considers causal links among features.

Similarity alone cannot explain why things belong to a given category. Murphy and Medin (1985) present two arguments for the inadequacy of similarity for categorization (see also Goodman, 1972). First, the similarity of any two objects depends on which properties of the objects are under consideration. Depending on what counts as a feature, any two objects could be as similar as any other two. A mouse and a lawnmower have indefinitely many features in common, because both weigh less than 500 pounds, are influenced by gravitational forces, can be found outdoors, are visible without magnification, and so on. Second, even if the set of possible attributes is somehow constrained, similarity judgments depend on the relative importance of those attributes. For example, both habitat and method of breathing may be important for classifying animals. If habitat is given more weight, whales might be classified with fish. But if breathing method is considered more important, whales would be considered mammals. Similarity alone is insufficient to hold categories together because it does not by itself provide adequate constraints on category membership. More is needed to constrain similarity, and to resolve questions such as what counts as a feature and which features are more central to a concept.

Theory-based approaches to categories are a response to these limitations. On a theory view, categorization often requires knowledge-rich, explanatory models. An intuitive example, supplied by Murphy and Medin (1985), concerns the hypothetical example of a man at a party who jumps into a swimming pool fully clothed. One might classify him as "drunk," not because of his physical resemblance to other intoxicated individuals, but rather because the categorization plausibly explains his behavior. The theory view does not replace prototype theory; instead, it argues for its insufficiency. That is, prototypes are accurate descriptions of the information people use to identify instances on many tasks. Importantly, however, the prototype is not the full story.

For adults, concepts are influenced by theoretical belief systems and cannot be characterized by statistical information alone (Heit and Rubinstein, 1994; C. Johnson and Keil, 2000; Keil, 1989; Murphy and Medin, 1985; Quine, 1977; Rips, 1989; Rips and Collins, 1993; see Murphy, 1993, 2002, for review). How subjects incorporate different features varies, depending on their theories about the domain (Wisniewski, 1995; Wisniewski and Medin, 1994). The probability of incorporating novel instances also depends on theoretical beliefs rather than statistical correlations (Medin and Shoben, 1988). In some cases a property equally true of two different concepts is more central to one than the other (e.g., "curved" is more central to boomerangs than to bananas, presumably because of its centrality to a theory of naive physics, even though in all our prior experience, "curved" is equally true of both concepts).

Implicit in this work is the idea that causes are central. Chuck Kalish and I argued that causal links determine which features are primary when a classification is constructed and extended (S. Gelman and Kalish, 1993). Specifically, we suggested that features that have causal implications will be weighted more heavily than features that do not. We also argued for asymmetry: causes are more central and defining than effects. Even given equal frequency, cause and effect features will be weighted differently. Although both cause and effect features participate in causal relations, causes should be viewed as more important. Ahn (1998) refers to this idea as the "causal status hypothesis."

Ahn and her colleagues have provided elegant evidence for the causal status hypothesis in adults by directly manipulating the causal status of features in artificial categories. The basic finding, over a series of studies, is that adults weigh the identical feature more heavily when it serves as a cause than when it serves as an effect (Ahn, 1998; Ahn, Kim, et al., 2000; Ahn and Lassaline, 1995). For example, in one item set, undergraduates learned of a novel category as follows: "Animals called 'roobans' tend to eat fruits, have sticky feet, and build nests on trees." Those in a causal background condition learned that the properties were causally linked: eating fruits tends to cause sticky feet because sugar in fruits is secreted through pores under the roobans' feet; having sticky feet tends to cause nest-building because roobans can climb trees more easily with sticky feet. Those in a control condition did not learn any causal links among the properties. Then participants rated a series of new instances. For example, they were told about an animal that likes to eat worms, has sticky feet, and builds nests on trees, and were asked how likely it was to be a rooban. Those in the causal background condition were least likely to consider an instance a rooban if it was missing the initial cause (in this example, eating fruit) and were most likely to consider an instance a rooban if it was missing the final effect (in this example, building nests on trees). Those in the control condition showed no differences among the test items.

In a second study, Ahn, Kim, et al. (2000) also found that the causal status of features influenced typicality ratings: items missing causal features were rated as less typical than items missing effect features. An intriguing aspect of this result was that it obtained even though the frequencies of the features were equated. A third study found that the causal status effect held up with a free-sorting task, in which instances were described but no categories were prespecified. Subjects viewed triads in which a target instance matched one option in a cause feature only, and matched another option in an effect feature only. For example, Samantha has low self-esteem (cause), which causes her to be depressed (effect); Marie has low self-esteem, which causes her to be defensive (matches Samantha in cause only); and June has been drinking, which causes her to be depressed (matches Samantha in effect only). When asked to categorize the items, college students relied on the matching-cause feature most often (Samantha and Marie were from the same category because both have low self-esteem). This effect disappeared in a control condition where people heard the same features but without any causal links (e.g., Samantha has low self-esteem and is depressed). The causal status effect also disappeared when the task involved rating similarity rather than categorization. Preference for causes did not reduce to an overall reckoning of similarity.

Summary

Statistical information is insufficient to account for the concepts of adults. A "theory" view of concepts argues instead that explanatory models and real-world knowledge play an important role. More precisely, causal features are weighted more heavily than other sorts of features in people's classification judgments. There is ample evidence for the causal status hypothesis in adults. I turn now to children.

CAUSATION IN CHILDREN'S CATEGORIES

Use of causal features could be the outcome of knowledge, experience, and cognitive maturity. If so, then we might expect a developmental shift in children's categories from similarity-based sorting early in childhood to more theory-based classifications as children gain expertise. This developmental progression is precisely what Quine (1977) proposed. However, I argue instead that causation is central to children's concepts from quite early on (see also Keil, 1989, 1994).

This position is plausible for several reasons. First, without theoretical commitments of some sort, it may be difficult for children to acquire concepts at all, let alone at the rapid clip that has been documented in studies of word-learning (Markman, 1989; Waxman, in press). Murphy (1993) suggests that theories help concept learners in three respects: theories help identify those features that are relevant to a concept, they constrain how (e.g., along which dimensions) similarity should be computed, and they can influence how concepts are stored in memory.

Concept acquisition may proceed more smoothly with the help of theories, even though the theories themselves are changing developmentally.

Second, recent work demonstrates that even infants are sensitive to causal relations when reasoning about events (see Schlottmann, 2001, for review). For example, children are aware of the causal implications of their own behaviors, preferring consequences that they control directly over those that are uncontrollable (see Parritz, Mangelsdorf, and Gunnar, 1992). A child interacting with a noisy mechanical monkey perceives it as mildly threatening when it moves unpredictably but enjoys it when she controls its movements herself (Gunnar-von Gnechten, 1978). Likewise, infants twelve and eighteen months old respond more positively to strangers who act in predictable ways that allow them more control than to strangers who are less predictable (Mangelsdorf, 1992). Findings such as these suggest that by a year of age, infants appreciate causal relations that involve their own agency.

Studies that specifically isolate cause also find sensitivity to causal relations in infancy. For example, Leslie and Keeble (1987) showed twenty-seven-week-old infants events that were either causal (one object colliding into another, causing it to move; also known as *direct launching*) or noncausal (an object changing color). After infants habituated to the display, they were shown the same event run backward. Leslie and Keeble found more recovery of attention to the backward causal sequences than to the backward noncausal sequences. In other words, infants viewed cause and effect as nonequivalent. The authors argued that this perception could not be due to spatiotemporal properties, but rather was specifically causal. In contrast, Oakes and Cohen (1990) failed to find an appreciation of causality in six-month-old infants. They did, however, find that ten-month-olds who habituated to a noncausal event (such as an object moving without being struck) showed more recovery of attention to a causal event (direct launching) than to another noncausal event (e.g., in which there was a time delay between when the object was struck and when it moved). In brief, appreciation of causality is in place by a year of age (see also P. White, 1995).

There is also growing evidence for the centrality of naive theories in children's classifications. Keil, Smith, et al. (1998) argue against the commonly held assumption that children's concepts are merely lists of features, and suggest instead that children attend to causal relations among features in constructing concepts. They asked five-, seven-, and nine-year-olds a set of counterfactual questions regarding novel animals and machines. After learning a series of facts about one exemplar (e.g., an animal called a "glick"), they were asked whether other instances could vary along each of a series of properties (including size, color, surface markings, and internal parts). Keil et al. found that even the youngest children weighted the properties differently, depending on whether the instances were animals or machines. For example, children assumed that members of an animal category would share the same color, number of internal parts, surface markings, and appearance of outside parts, but would vary in size and weight. Children showed the opposite pattern with members of a machine category. In short, children's judgments were not limited to tallying features in the exemplars.

Further indirect evidence comes from a set of studies that Chuck Kalish and I conducted some years ago (Kalish and Gelman, 1992). We found that three- to five-year-old children systematically predicted physical outcomes (such as how likely an object was to break) based on object substance (e.g., glass) rather than its object identity (e.g., frying pan). For instance, when asked whether a glass frying pan would or would not break when dropped, children reported that it would break. These same children consistently asserted that a frying pan (with substance unspecified) would not break when dropped. When the theoretical domain of interest involved physical principles such as breaking (which presumably enters into naive theories of matter; see C. Smith, Carey, and Wiser, 1985), children knew that material properties are more relevant than object type. To put it differently, children have learned the causal implications of material properties such as "made of glass" and use these implications as relevant.

In an additional study (Kalish and Gelman, 1992) we found that children could ignore material composition and make judgments based on object type when appropriate (e.g., deciding that a frying pan belongs in the kitchen because it is a frying pan). Children's theories seemed to determine which features were particularly important to a classification. To support this interpretation further, it would be important to obtain independent confirmation of the causal structure of the categories for children.

Barrett et al. (1993) demonstrated a more direct link between causality and categorization. They showed that children's intuitive theories help determine which properties and which feature correlations children attend to in their classifications. For example, in a task that required children to categorize novel birds into one of two novel categories, first- and fourth-grade children noticed the association between brain size and memory capacity and used that correlation to categorize new members. Specifically, exemplars that preserved the correlation were more often judged to be category members, and to be more typical of the category. The children did not make use of features that correlated equally well but were unsupported by a theory (e.g., the correlation between structure of heart and shape of beak). What was central to the feature weighting was the causal link between features, not frequency per se.

In a second experiment, Barrett et al. (1993) found that children treated the same set of features differently, depending on whether there was a theory-based link between pairs of the features. Again, "theory-based" correlation here apparently means "causally supported." Third-grade children were presented with stimuli that were described as either animals or tools, and then learned five properties about each category. When the category was described as an animal, children selectively focused on a subset of the properties that are relevant to animals: habitat (e.g., is found in the mountains) and physical adaptation (e.g., has thick wool).

When the category was described as a tool, children selectively focused on a different subset of properties that are relevant to artifacts, namely those involving function (e.g., can crush rocks; catches snakes).

Krascum and Andrews (1998) found that causal information had beneficial effects on even younger children's learning of novel animal categories. In their studies, four- and five-year-olds learned two animal categories ("wugs" and "gillies"), each possessing family resemblance structure. That is, members of each category shared a subset of features, all of which were visible and varying slightly from the category prototype. Each category could potentially be learned on the basis of perceptual similarity among category exemplars. In study 1, children were randomly assigned to one of two conditions. In one condition, children were taught a "theory" that provided an explanatory link among the features, for example, that gillies hide from predators, so that they have big ears to listen for predators, wings to fly up into a tree and hide, and a monkeylike tail to grip the tree trunk. In another condition, each feature was verbally highlighted, but no explanatory information was provided. In study 2, children were again randomly assigned to one of two conditions. One was again the "theory" condition of study 1; the other was a "features description condition" in which children were taught functions for each feature, but the functions did not cohere in a causal framework. For example, the gillies have big ears to listen to music, wings to fly up into a tree and sleep at night, and a monkeylike tail to pick up sticks. In both studies 1 and 2, the results were clear: children classified more accurately, both on immediate test and after a twenty-four-hour delay, when provided with the causal information, compared to either verbally highlighting without functional information (study 1) or verbally highlighting with functional information (study 2). The authors interpreted these results as supporting the idea that theories aid category-learning by enhancing children's learning of feature-category associations.

Gopnik and Sobel (2000) demonstrated that even two-year-old children attend to causal features. In their studies, two-, three-, and four-year-olds learned that a novel object with a novel name (e.g., "a blicket") had a certain causal power: placing the object on a machine would (apparently) cause the machine to light up and play music. The question of interest was how this information might affect categorization and induction for the children. In the categorization task, an initial object was labeled ("a blicket") and shown to activate the machine. Then the researcher demonstrated that various test objects also either had or did not have the causal property, and asked children which test objects were blickets. In the induction task, the researcher introduced children to the blicket and showed its causal influence on the machine, and then showed and labeled the test objects. In this condition, the key question was which test objects would activate the machine.

Even two-year-olds used causal information to guide both naming and induction. Importantly, they did so more than in a control condition, in which the blicket was associated with the machine's being set off but appeared not to cause it (i.e., in the control condition, the blicket did not touch the machine, and the researcher touched the top of the machine in a manner suggesting that he was activating it). In the strong case, when causal properties conflicted with appearance (e.g., an object identical in appearance to the blicket did not set it off, whereas one differing in shape and color did set it off), results were consistent with causal-based categorization, in three respects: at all ages children still used cause information more than in the control task; by three years of age, children used cause as much as perceptual information in the categorization condition; and by three years of age, cause won out over perceptual information, in an induction condition. The authors concluded that by two and a half years of age, children use causal information to guide categorization and naming. Some of the children even tried to peel back the outer covering of the blickets as if to figure out how they worked (appealing to internal parts) (Povinelli, 2000, p. 95, reporting personal communication with Gopnik).

It is interesting that children were not simply naming blickets on the basis of correlated properties they had encountered to this point. The researchers obtained differences between categorization and induction on their tasks that were consistent with the findings of S. Gelman, Collman, and Maccoby (1986), who found that category-based inferences about properties are more powerful than property-based inferences about categories (see chapter 2).

Not only are causal features more central than noncausal features, but also causal features are more central than effects (Ahn's "causal status hypothesis"). Ahn, Gelman, et al. (2000) taught seven- to nine-year-old children descriptions of novel animals, in which one feature caused two other features. Half of the participants learned three features of each animal (I will refer to them as X, Y, and Z) and the causal relations among them (the causal condition). The other half learned the same three features but no causal relations (the control condition). For example, one animal category was described as having blickem in its blood, small lungs, and purple skin. Children in the causal condition were told that one of the animal's features was a cause of the other two (e.g., "Blickem in their blood makes taliboos have small lungs and purple skin"). In order to ensure that children in each condition heard the stimulus words equally often, children in the control condition heard a repetition of the properties' names (e.g., "Did you understand? Taliboos have blickem in their blood, they have small lungs, and they have purple skin").

All participants were then presented with two options, one missing property X (i.e., the cause in the causal condition) and the other missing property Y (i.e., an effect in the causal condition), and chose which one was more likely to be a member of the target category. If children weight features based on their causal status, then children's preference for X should be greater in the causal condition (where it serves as a cause) than in the control condition (where it has no explicit causal role).

In the control condition, children did not show any preference for the missing-effect option (44%). However, in the causal condition, they favored the missing-effect option (74%) over the missing-cause option. Seven- to nine-year-olds, like adults, were more influenced by features that cause other features than features that are effects.

Summary

Causation is privileged in children's categorizations, in several respects. Properties that enter into causally meaningful links are better remembered and are treated as more central to the category than properties that are not causally meaningful. Even two-year-olds use causal features to categorize—on both naming and induction tasks—even when such features conflict with salient perceptual information. Finally, causes are treated as more diagnostic of category membership than effects (Ahn's "causal status hypothesis").

CAUSAL EXPLANATIONS

In this section I focus on causal explanations. If children are essentialists, they should search for underlying causes that result in observable features. They should assume there is some underlying nature that category members share and that causes them to be alike. For example, the essence of a tiger causes it to have stripes, large size, a capacity to roar, and the like. Children should invoke inherent, internal, or nonobvious properties especially for events and feature clusters that otherwise are in need of explanation. In other words, children should search for causes and impute essentialist causes to cover explanatory gaps (S. Gelman and Kalish, 1993). To argue for this position, I first review evidence that children search for underlying causes, then turn to children's explanations of natural kinds.

Causal Determinism

It is often argued that people search for causes and explanations. John Macnamara suggested that "the human mind is essentially an explanation seeker" (1986, p. 148). We are said to be causal determinists, seeking causes even for random occurrences. It is very tempting, in the face of one event following another, to assume that the two events are linked in a causal way. For example, one morning a few weeks ago while settling down to work, I pressed the power button on my computer, then a moment later heard a loud droning sound. I was certain that I had broken my computer, when it turned out that the sound came from a power saw that my neighbor was using outside. It was the timing of the two events (turning on the computer $\rightarrow$ droning noise) that gave rise to the illusion. This sort of impression is the basis of the sorts of superstitious rituals that ball-players engage in (such as wearing "lucky socks" before a big game). These cases are certainly guided and constrained by prior beliefs and expectations (for example, one is unlikely to assume that pressing the power button on one's computer is responsible for a neighbor's power saw turning on), but nonetheless reveal a hunger for finding and attributing causes.

There is indirect evidence that people search for causes (not just statistical regularities). When people are given the opportunity to seek information in order to explain an event, they ask for mechanism information (Ahn, Kalish, Medin, and Gelman, 1995). For example, suppose you were asked to find out why Dave would not eat rabbit meat on a particular (unspecified) occasion. If you were simply interested in determining the conditions in which an event occurs (the statistical regularities), then it would be sufficient to learn what events covary with the event in question. For example, you might ask "Does Dave usually eat rabbits?" or "Did other people eat rabbit meat on this occasion?" This is the classic theory proposed by Kelley (1967), sometimes referred to as the "ANOVA model," suggesting that people try to gain information about consensus, distinctiveness, and consistency in order to make attributions.

In contrast, if you were seeking the underlying causal mechanisms responsible for the event, you would generate plausible mechanistic accounts, which would lead to questions such as "Did Dave have a pet rabbit?" or "Did he have a toothache?" Ahn, Kalish, Medin, and Gelman (1995) found that these hypothesis-testing sorts of questions predominated in adults' responses. Even when we posed problems from wholly novel domains (by giving participants sentences containing phony words), still they tried to generate mechanistic hypotheses. For example, on reading "The fep mimbled the wug," a participant in the study might ask, "Is the fep mad at the wug?" making use of existing causal knowledge. They rarely resorted to asking covariation questions (e.g., "Did other things mimble the wug?" "Did the fep mimble other things?"). These results are also consistent with the finding that effects of covariation are greater when causal scenarios are more believable (Fugelsang and Thompson, 2000; Koslowski, 1996; P. White, 1989). What adults seem to be tracking is a mechanistic causal account, not feature correlations.

In contrast, it is interesting how little curiosity about causes is found in apes. Tomasello points out that chimpanzees require dozens of attempts before being able to use a tool correctly, when simply visually inspecting the tool would allow immediate success for someone who is thinking about causal mechanisms. For example, apes require much trial-and-error to figure out which of a set of sticks can be used to push food out of a clear tube. They do not immediately reject a stick that is too short, or a stick that is too wide. They can eventually, after much effort, learn which sticks lead to success, but they do not seem to consider the intervening causal links. (See also Povinelli, 2000.) Tomasello (1999) goes so far as to conclude, "nonhuman primates are themselves intentional and causal beings, *they just do not understand the world in intentional and causal terms*" (p. 19; emphasis added).

Children as young as two to three years of age perform much better on this sort of task (Tomasello, 1999; A. Brown and Kane, 1988; Bullock, R. Gelman, and Baillargeon, 1982). They make appropriate inferences about the intervening mechanisms that will or will not lead to certain outcomes (e.g., which type of stick will cause a series of dominos to topple). Even infants seem to *expect* causes: they gaze longer at events with no apparent cause, such as an object that moves on its own (Baillargeon, 1993). By preschool age, when children view an event that appears to violate known causal laws (e.g., a screen passing through a box), they attempt to dismantle the apparatus, apparently in search of a hidden causal mechanism (Chandler and Lalonde, 1994). They also endorse invisible causes. For example, upon viewing a radiometer (a device that spins when light is beamed on it), children as young as four years of age typically said yes when asked if there was "some invisible thing that goes from the light to the propeller" (Shultz, 1982).

Children also have surprising difficulty understanding random phenomena (as do adults; Langer, 1975; Rosenberg, 1997). Piaget and Inhelder (1975) showed children random devices such as spinners and found that the youngest children often insisted that they could predict where the pointer would fall. Metz (1998), in a study of kindergartners, third graders, and college students, found that randomness was difficult to grasp in all age groups. One of the difficulties was the tendency to impose an overly deterministic understanding of random events. For example, they report that it is possible to predict on what color segment a spinner will land, or which color marble will be selected next out of an urn. Metz suggests that children and adults alike may have a "deterministic epistemological set" (p. 344). See also Piaget (1930), Green (1978), and Kuzmak and R. Gelman (1986). The same kind of pattern is found when children are asked to explain adverse events, such as illness. Children tend to blame the illness on the victim, rather than consider that it happened randomly ("immanent justice"; Karniol, 1980; Kister and Patterson, 1980; Piaget, 1948; E. White, Elsom, and Prawat, 1978; Rosenberg, 1997).

Altogether, children act like causal determinists, actively expecting events to have causes (S. Gelman and Kalish, 1993). Young children seem to expect that the world is a predictable, orderly, knowable place.

CAUSAL DETERMINISM AND ESSENTIALISM.   I suggest that causal determinism in children contributes to essentialism. When children encounter events or features with no observable cause, children are inspired to search for inherent, nonobvious, or internal causes. These to-be-explained events might include, for example, the predictably constrained growth patterns of humans, other animals, or seeds; the lawful metamorphosis of caterpillars or tadpoles; the resemblance between parents and offspring; sexual dimorphism—the outward dissimilarity (but inner sameness) of males and females in certain species; or the feature correlations of living things, such that feathered creatures have wings, claws, and come from eggs, whereas furry creatures do not. When asking *why* birds hatch from eggs but kittens do not, or *why* babies grow into children not pigs (*contra* Lewis Carroll), or *why* children resemble their parents and not their best friends, whole classes of explanations fall short. These events cannot be satisfactorily explained by belief states or desires; they cannot be understood in terms of the principles of naive physics; they fall outside the realm of human actions or motivations altogether. Positing some sort of inherent, hidden cause would be a way of resolving the apparent contradiction between the lack of a visible cause and the need for all events to be caused. (See also Kornblith, 1993, p. 42, for elaboration of this argument.)

CHILDHOOD ARTIFICIALISM.   For the causal determinist account of essentialism to be plausible, children must recognize that certain classes of events are outside human control. Otherwise, children would have no impetus to search for inherent, unobservable explanations—they would have at their disposal a ready class of human intentional explanations. Yet this understanding is precisely what Piaget claimed children lack. On his account of "artificialism," children view humans as controlling all manner of events, including the construction of mountains, the clouds in the sky, and the existence of rivers and rocks.

Contrary to claims of childhood artificialism, Kathy Kremer and I found that children appropriately recognized that certain kinds of things are created by processes outside human control (S. Gelman, 1988; S. Gelman and Kremer, 1991). Humans were not viewed as all-powerful or the source of all worldly things. Children were highly accurate when directly asked, "Do you think people make X?" (where X was a remote natural kind, such as the moon or clouds; a familiar natural kind, such as a dog or salt; or a human artifact, such as a cup or car); see Table 5.1. Petrovich (1999) reported similar findings. Furthermore, preschool children also appreciated that living things are capable of healing by themselves, whereas artifacts require human intervention to be repaired (Backscheider, Shatz, and Gelman, 1993). These data argue against a stark form of childhood artificialism.[2]

Why then the contrast with Piaget's findings? Are the preschoolers of today simply more savvy than those of the 1920s, when Piaget conducted his research? Apparently not. It turns out that how the question is asked has a sizable effect on children's performance. Kremer and I included another task, in addition to the simple yes/no task reported above. This other task was modeled as closely as possible to Piaget's "clinical interview" method—a highly verbal, intensive questioning of children, asking them to explain in their own words where various entities came from. As with Piaget's interviews, at times the questions were misleading (for example, asking how something "is made," which could imply that there is "a

Table 5.1.   Mean percentage of correct responses to the yes/no question, as a function of age and item type

	Preschoolers	7 ½-year-olds	Adults
Familiar natural kinds	55%	79%**	93%**
Remote natural kinds	73*	92**	99**
Artifacts	95**	99**	100**

* Above chance by t-test, p < .05

** Above chance by t-test, p < .001

Source: S. Gelman and Kremer (1991).

maker"). This task yielded pages upon pages of conversation—but much of it made up by children on the spot. When asked to explain the origins of natural items, preschool children were as likely to propose some sort of human causation as a natural cause. It was not that the task led them to display no knowledge—even on this more taxing task, they clearly distinguished natural kinds from artifacts (preschoolers generated a human cause 80% of the time for artifacts, compared to about 20% of the time for natural kinds). Rather, children rarely were able to specify natural processes in response to the open-ended question. The following excerpt is from a child aged four years, four months, who in the process of groping for answers came up with increasingly artifactual possibilities:

Researcher: Where does the sun come from?
Child: God and Jesus.
Researcher: And how was it made?
Child: With fire.
Researcher: Where did they get the fire from?
Child: I don't kn—from a fire.
Researcher: From a fire? And how did it, what did they do to put the fire there?
Child: I don't—there was a fire in a house and then they came and got it, then put, made the sun.
Researcher: OK. Did they do that a long time ago?
Child: Yes.
Researcher: How long ago?
Child: Eighteen years.

Preschool children seem to know in a skeletal (to use R. Gelman's terminology), abstract (Simons and Keil, 1995), or framework way (Wellman and Gelman, 1988; Wellman, 1990) that natural kinds are not human-made, but they have not yet filled in the details of just how such sorts of items come into existence. When questioned intensively, they are prone to confabulation. On the rare occasions when children did come up with a natural explanation, it often was incorrect:

Researchers: Where do clouds come from?
Child: The sky.
Researcher: And how do they begin?
Child: Well, at night they go away and in the noontime, they are out. They come out again.
Researcher: OK. And how are they made?
Child: Um, out of rain and sun.
Researcher: And how does the rain make the clouds? The rain and sun?
Child: They mix up together.

Summary

Both children and adults tend to be causal determinists (assuming that events are caused), and even children recognize that natural entities are created outside the realm of human action or control. Putting these two pieces together, I propose that children "postulate unobservables" (in Kornblith's words) to account for why members of natural categories share similarities. This claim is a somewhat expanded version of Rochel Gelman's (1990) idea that children obey an "innards principle," an implicit understanding that animate entities have internal properties that enable them to move on their own. I turn now to studies examining these ideas.

Inherent and Internal Causes

What sort of unobservable cause might children impute to explain natural events or property clusters? If we were to ask college-educated adults in the Unites States, they might say that a tiger has stripes because of its DNA, or that an infant is male or female because of its chromosomes. Such explanations are both inherent (intrinsic to the tiger or infant itself) and internal (literally located inside the organism's body). Clearly young children do not have knowledge about DNA or chromosomes. However, they could appeal to inherent or internal causes in a nonscientific, nontechnical way.

Inherent causes entail the least theoretical commitment. They assume only that the cause is intrinsic to the organism or object itself—for example, a leaf changes color in the fall because "The leaf just makes itself change colors" or a rabbit hops because "Rabbits are made to hop" (S. Gelman and Kremer, 1991). One might argue that these are not really causes at all—certainly they are not mechanistic— yet they are noteworthy in locating the source of the property in the organism rather than in external forces. For example, "Rabbits are made to hop" implies that hopping is a property of rabbits, and not the outcome of the actions or wishes of people.

Living kinds have inherent properties in a second sense as well: they are the only sort of thing capable of goal-directed action (Opfer and Gelman, 2001; Opfer, 2000). Living things are capable of acting in ways that maintain their own integrity (e.g., plants can grow toward the sun; animals can pursue their own food), while nonliving things are not (e.g., a cup cannot roll to avoid being crushed). Living things have a capacity for directed action that does not require external forces. Even preschoolers appreciate a domain distinction in this teleological capacity, attributing goal-directed action more to animals than machines or simple artifacts (Opfer and Gelman, 2001).[3]

Internal causes go one step further in locating the cause specifically in some internal part or substance: batteries make a toy car move; muscles make a rabbit hop. Internal parts need not be essences; for example, neither batteries nor muscles are the essence of their respective category. However, such causes are interesting in implying that an internal, nonvisible feature is necessary for an outward set of properties. Internal properties are also often construed as more essential than outward properties (see chapter 3). So internal attributions can be viewed as a precursor to the sort of argument adults use when they attribute biological essences (e.g., "DNA causes a tiger to have stripes").

It is certainly not evident that young children would endorse inherent or internal explanations. Children may instead be biased to look for obvious visible causes, or they may overestimate the power of human action. There are documented examples of children attributing biological processes not to inherent properties but rather to external influences (e.g., eye color can be determined by a parent's wishes, Callanan and Oakes, 1992; see also Weissman and Kalish, 1999). Such reports tend to be anecdotal, however, so may not be representative. Furthermore, the characteristics investigated have been idiosyncratic, individually varying properties (e.g., eye color, shape of appendix) rather than species-typical properties (e.g., means of locomotion, body parts). Children may offer different sorts of explanatory accounts for individual- versus kind-relevant properties.

My collaborators and I have been examining these issues in a variety of studies that probe children's explanations of animal and artifact properties. The method is straightforward: the child is told or shown a particular property, then is asked to explain that property. We predicted that, for animals, children would attribute properties to the animal itself. Artifacts provide a comparison case where external causes are more appropriate.

Kathleen Kremer and I (S. Gelman and Kremer, 1991) asked children to explain species-typical properties and behaviors, such as, "Why do rabbits have long ears?" and "Why do birds fly?" We found that 72% of four-year-olds and 73% of first-graders spontaneously mentioned inborn dispositions, intrinsic nature, or growth at least once during the interview. For example, preschoolers said that a rabbit has long ears because "the egg made the [rabbit's] ears so that it had them when it hatched," or birds fly "because that's the way birds are made." Children mentioned these factors significantly more often when explaining properties of natural kinds (e.g., rabbits, flowers, or salt) than when explaining properties of human artifacts (e.g., cars, crayons, or phones).

Specific follow-up questions probed inherent cause (e.g., "Did a person make the long ears?" where the inherent response would be to say no) and internal cause (e.g., "Is there anything inside it that made the long ears?"). On this measure, children attributed inherent causes to natural kinds (not artifacts), but were at chance when answering questions about internal causes (see Table 5.2). Inherent causes seemed easier for children to grasp.

Gail Gottfried and I (S. Gelman and Gottfried, 1996) followed up on these findings by showing children events with or without a clear external cause (e.g., an item self-propelling across a table). If internal or inherent properties are the result of causal determinism, children should invoke them when an external cause is not available. We varied the presence of external cause in two ways: by varying (a) the

Table 5.2.   Percentage of trials on which participants attributed
properties to the targeted causes (human, internal)

	Person as cause		Inside as cause	
	Natural kinds	*Artifacts*	*Natural kinds*	*Artifacts*
Preschoolers	14%	68%	38%	40%
7-year-olds	20	78	50	62
Adults	5	96	71	26

Source: S. Gelman and Kremer (1991). Reprinted with the permission of the
Society for Research in Child Development.

structure of the event (half occurred by means of a visible human agent, half did
not) and (b) the ontological domain of the item undergoing movement (animal or
artifact). Artifacts are created and controlled by external agents, even when they
seem to be behaving on their own (e.g., the electric garage door is operated by a
remote-control device). In contrast, animals are self-sufficient and self-sustaining
(R. Gelman, Durgin, and Kaufman, 1995), even when their actions are under
someone else's control (e.g., digestion and respiration are largely beyond the control of others).

In this task, three- and four-year-old children saw videotapes of actual items either moving alone across a flat surface or being transported by a person and were
asked to explain how they moved. All items were unfamiliar to the children, so that
they could not simply rely on rote knowledge. We went to an exotic-pet shop and
videotaped, for example, a chinchilla hopping around its cage and a chameleon
walking on a rug. We bought unusual artifacts such as a wind-up toy sushi. For
those with wind-up mechanisms, we wound them up, let them go, and videotaped
their movements. For those without wind-up mechanisms, we attached a clear
plastic thread to each one and pulled on the thread; on the videotape, the object
was seen moving as if by magic.

By editing the videotapes, we made every item seem to start at a standstill, then
to move on its own. Children watched the videotapes and, after each one, were
asked how the item moved. Specifically, children received three causal questions
per item, tapping into two kinds of causes: internal cause ("Did something inside
this make it move?") and inherent cause ("Did this move by itself?" where the inherent response is "yes"; and "Did a person make this move?" where the inherent
response is "no").

The results are complicated, as seen in Table 5.3. For young children, both domain (animal versus artifact) and event structure (transported versus alone) mattered. First, we looked at the question about a person as cause. Children were
highly sensitive to the domain of the entity undergoing movement, even by age
three. They often reported that a person did not make the animals move, even
when the animals were visibly transported. In contrast, children often invoked a

Table 5.3.   Results from Gelman and Gottfried (1996)

	3-year-olds		4-year-olds		Adults	
	Alone	*Transported*	*Alone*	*Transported*	*Alone*	*Transported*
Person						
Animals	29	62	2	22	17	81
Wind-up toys	53	100	37	91	67	100
Transparent objects	33	96	26	96	72	100
Something inside						
Animals	42	56	44	57	69	83
Wind-up toys	51	44	62	42	86	0
Transparent objects	44	29	49	31	58	11
By itself						
Animals	98	73	96	91	92	83
Wind-up toys	82	42	71	13	47	0
Transparent objects	69	42	72	6	17	0

Source: S. Gelman and Gottfried (1996). Reprinted with the permission of the Society for Research in Child Development.

person as the agent of the artifacts' movement, even when the artifacts were moving alone. So even on the "person" questions, children were taking into account the causal implications of the domain. Children could have simply reported what was visible on the videotape (reporting that a person made the entity move, when a person was carrying it, and that a person did not make the entity move, when no person was visible), but they did not.

The questions about immanence ("Does it move by itself?") revealed that children were again responsive to both agency in the event and the implicit agency in the object. Children judged animate motion as self-caused, regardless of condition. Even when a person bodily carried the animal from one end of the screen to the other, three- and four-year-old children insisted that the animal itself was responsible. For the artifacts, what mattered was whether or not an external agent was shown. We consider the immanence responses to be genuine explanations and not simply redescriptions of the event, for two reasons: the domains differed significantly in how frequently immanence was invoked, and some children spontaneously referred to the self as the causal agent (e.g., "Itself made it move").

The next question is how children construed this inherent causal force, and specifically whether children thought of it as a physical, internal part. As shown in Table 5.3, children's responses to the insides question were much less clear than their responses to the other two questions. Children did not appear to localize the cause in any concrete internal part, nor did they show significant domain differences. In contrast, adults said "something inside" caused animal movement, whether or not the animal was moving by itself or being transported by a person. They also attributed "something inside" to artifact movement—but only when the objects were moving alone.

However, two small pieces of evidence suggest that children may link internal cause to external movement for artifacts. Both pieces of evidence came from children's open-ended comments. First, when children saw the artifacts moving, they sometimes talked about internal parts as potential causal mechanisms: "Hey, look! This is funny. It's moving by itself. Something's in it." "How does it move by itself? Some kind of electric?" The other piece of evidence has to do with how children described the insides of the artifacts. After children viewed each event and answered the yes/no questions, they were asked to describe the insides of each item. For animals, the insides were described in the same way regardless of condition: muscles, bones, blood, brains, and so forth. For artifacts, though, children gave different kinds of descriptions in the two conditions. When people transported the artifacts, children often described the objects as being empty inside or as having nonfunctional parts, like wood. But when the artifacts moved on their own, children were significantly more likely to describe mechanical or electrical internal causes (e.g., gears, batteries, or electricity).

Would we then want to say that children are essentialist about artifacts? After all, batteries are hidden, internal mechanisms that give rise to surface behaviors. I would say no, for two reasons. First, batteries, though internal, are not inherent. The artifact is not behaving by itself. Second, artifact innards may (proximally) cause movement, but they are not responsible for other outer properties—in contrast to animals, where the innards cause not just movement but also the morphology, preferences, behaviors, and ultimately the very being of the thing.

INTERNAL CAUSE VERSUS INTERNAL PREREQUISITE.   To this point, one puzzle is that children failed to attribute internal causes to animals. Children may be reluctant to attribute internal causes to animals if doing so implies that the internal parts have their own agency. Saying that internal parts "make" an animal move might be giving more agency to the parts than to the animal itself. Accordingly, Melanie Nyhof and I proposed that perhaps children would view internal parts as necessary for self-directed movement, even if they are unwilling to state that such parts "make" an item move.

To test this proposal, we provided children with a series of twelve unfamiliar entities (four simple artifacts, four complex artifacts, and four animals), each of which was assumed not to move on its own. It was crucial to the design of the study that the children expected the items not to move. We wished to manipulate children's assumptions regarding whether or not each item could undergo movement, then measure whether their attributions of insides changed accordingly. We were testing, in effect, whether children would impute certain kinds of insides only when the entity was seen to be capable of self-generated motion.

We preselected items on the basis of four-year-olds' responses to a task devised by Massey and R. Gelman (1988), asking them to report whether each of a series of pictured objects could move up a hill by itself. Only those items that children consistently reported could *not* move up a hill by themselves were included. The simple artifacts were familiar items such as a ball; the complex artifacts were all representations of animals (with faces and other animate features); the animals were all without discernible faces or other animate features (see Table 5.4 for complete list of items). By including items for which animacy and featural information conflicted (the complex artifacts), we provided a strong test of children's sensitivity to animacy independent of apparent surface cues.

We tested 38 four-year-olds and 35 adults. At each age, participants were randomly assigned to one of two conditions: a moving condition in which each test item moved on its own, or a still condition in which each test item did not move. Children first received an easy warm-up task to ensure that they understood the meaning of "inside" and "outside." For example, they were shown a cup with a penny inside of it and a block next to it, and were asked, "What is inside the cup?" All children performed extremely well on the pretest.

In the main task, participants were presented with each of the twelve test items individually, as well as three familiar baseline items (a person, a computer, and a rock). For each test item, participants viewed a brief video clip of the item either moving (moving condition) or not moving (still condition), followed by a series of questions. (The baseline items were presented without video clips, as we assumed that children would already possess strong beliefs concerning the capabilities of each.) For each item, the first question was always an open-ended question concerning what the item had inside, then the remaining six questions concerned whether the item had each of the following: blood, muscles, batteries, wires, energy, and power. All of these questions were of the form: "Does it have X inside of it?" where X was the relevant internal part (e.g., blood, wires, or energy). We predicted that children in the still condition would assume that the items had none of these properties. Of interest was what children in the moving condition would do. Would they now infer that these items do have either animate (blood and muscles) or inanimate (batteries and wires) innards? If so, we would infer that such internal parts have causal force for children.

The questions concerning energy and power were exploratory, to see if children would appeal to these more abstract, placeholder notions. Because the data from energy and power are unrelated to the issue at hand concerning concrete internal parts, I will defer discussion of these results for a later section, titled "Vital Force ("Energy") as a Causal Placeholder."

Table 5.4. Items used in S. Gelman and Nyhof study

Simple artifacts	Complex artifacts	Animals
Ball	Furby	Jellyfish
Block	Mr. Potato-Head	Lettuce slug
Beanbag	Teddy bear	Stick insect
Book	Fly	"Blob"

Before turning to the results of the test items, I first present the baseline data, to ensure that the properties we had intended to be domain-specific were indeed attributed to the predicted domains (blood and muscles for animals; batteries and wires for artifacts). As shown in Table 5.5, the four-year-olds showed sharp domain distinctions, with blood and muscles attributed to the person almost exclusively, and batteries and wires attributed to the computer almost exclusively.

I now turn to the data from the test items (see Table 5.6). Four-year-olds expected significantly more internal parts for moving than nonmoving items (see Table 5.5). Moreover, their expectations were distinctly domain-specific: biological parts (blood and muscles) for animals, mechanical parts (batteries and wires) for complex artifacts. The results are especially striking given that the complex artifacts had faces whereas the animals did not. Children had to make use of other perceptual cues to decide on which internal parts went with which items, presumably

Table 5.5. Baseline items, four-year-olds' and adults' mean percentage endorsement for each property set, as a function of domain and condition; S. Gelman and Nyhof

	Person	Computer	Rock
4-year-olds			
Blood/muscles	97%	1%	1%
Batteries/wires	3	89	1
Adults			
Blood/muscles	100%	0%	0%
Batteries/wires	7	77	0

Table 5.6. Four-year-olds' and adults' mean percentage endorsement for each property set, as a function of domain and condition; S. Gelman and Nyhof

	Animals		Complex artifacts		Simple artifacts	
	Still	Moving	Still	Moving	Still	Moving
4-year-olds						
Blood/muscles	17%*	34%*	10%	9%	2%	3%
Batteries/wires	1	3	17*	40*	3	8
Adults						
Blood/muscles	42*	70*	3	3	1	3
Batteries/wires	1	0	23*	96*	0*	15*

*Asterisks indicate a significant condition effect (still versus moving).

a combination of movement quality and static perceptual details, such as substance type. Adults showed similar patterns of results, though with more clear-cut condition differences.

We argue that children viewed the internal parts as causing autonomous movement. This interpretation is consistent with the fact that children attributed the queried parts to these items only after viewing them move autonomously. Alternatively, autonomous movement may have enabled children to classify the items more accurately (as animate or machine, depending on the item), and it was that classification that underpinned children's attributions of internal parts. Yet such an interpretation begs the question of why children would assume that certain inside parts "go with" being a machine or being an animal, even when the usual cluster of perceptual cues (e.g., presence of a face) were not provided. If children used autonomous movement to classify the items, then they must have recognized that being an animal does not necessarily entail having a face, but does entail having certain internal parts. On either interpretation, children viewed the internal parts as important.

SUMMARY.   Rochel Gelman has hypothesized that children maintain an "innards principle," according to which animals move on the basis of their own inner power (R. Gelman, 1990; R. Gelman et al., 1995). Data from preschool children support this notion in two respects: first, children endorse a notion of inherent cause—a cause whose source is the object itself—that applies to animal kinds. In other words, children assume that animal properties are somehow due to the animal itself. Second, children attribute domain-specific internal parts to self-moving items, for both animals and complex machines (though not for simple artifacts). It is unclear whether these internal parts are specifically viewed as causing autonomous movement, or are more generally viewed as linked to animals (in the case of blood and muscles) or complex artifacts (in the case of batteries and wires).

The weaker evidence for attribution of internal causes suggests that children may possess a skeletal sense of self-generated cause before they have learned about specific internal causal mechanisms. For children the causal essence may not reside in any particular internal part. Children may have an abstract or framework understanding before a specific one (R. Gelman, 1990; Simons and Keil, 1995; Wellman and Gelman, 1988).

Vital Force ("Energy") as a Causal Placeholder

Children seem to think that members of an animal category share something inherent, but they do not always know quite what. Here I examine specifically the possibility that children view "energy" as a causal placeholder in their emerging essentialism (but see Inagaki and Hatano, 2002, pp.121–122, for a different position regarding the relation between essentialism and vitalism).

Inagaki and Hatano (1993) have suggested that young children are initially "vitalist" in their reasoning about biological processes. They describe vitalism as involving two components: the transmission or exchange of a vital force (sometimes translated as "energy") in living things, and the personification of bodily organs. In a series of innovative studies, Inagaki and Hatano found evidence for vitalism in young Japanese children. Children were asked to select the best explanation for a series of biological phenomena (such as breathing). For each phenomenon, the researchers supplied three possible explanations: intentional, vitalistic, and mechanical. For example, one question was: "Why do we take in air?" The choices were (1) "Because we want to feel good" (intentional); (2) "Because the lungs take in oxygen and change it into useless carbon dioxide" (mechanical); and (3) "Because our chest takes in vital power from the air" (vitalistic). Six-year-olds, eight-year-olds, and adults were tested. Six-year-olds preferred vitalistic explanations (54% of the time). The older children and adults preferred mechanistic explanations, but still appealed to vitalism (though more at age eight than among adults). A small number of children even supplied vitalistic explanations spontaneously, for example: "If blood does not come to the hands, they will die, because the blood does not carry energies to them"; "We wouldn't be able to move our hands, because energies fade away if blood does not come there" (Hatano and Inagaki, 1999, p. 341).

Sue Morris, John Taplin, and I pointed out that vitalism appears in Western thought as well as Japanese philosophical tradition (S. Morris, Taplin, and Gelman, 2000). Vitalism was used until recently to account for the distinction between living and nonliving things. Vitalists argued that living organisms possess a rather mysterious force or fluid that exists throughout the body and operates according to laws that are independent of physics or chemistry (Mayr, 1988, pp. 12–13). However, the construct of vital force remained unspecified, and was rightly criticized as masquerading as an explanatory concept while failing to provide a genuine causal mechanism for biological events. Vitalist accounts faltered in Western biological thought by the 1920s and 1930s as increasingly detailed mechanistic biological explanations became available. From a scientific perspective at least, vitalism became discredited.

There are some intriguing similarities between the notion of vital force in traditional Western thinking about biology and that in Japanese philosophy. However, the similarity appears primarily with respect to the first of the two components mentioned earlier: ascribing a vital force to living things. The two traditions differ regarding organ agency (e.g., a heart pumps blood in an intentional way), a belief found in Japanese philosophy but not in Western vitalistic thought.

Morris, Taplin, and I designed a series of studies to investigate whether English-speaking children and adults in a Western society would also appeal to vitalist accounts, and what role each of the two components (vital energy versus organ agency) would play in these explanations. We replicated Inagaki and Hatano's findings with English-speaking children ages five and ten years (see also J. Miller and Bartsch, 1997): vitalist explanations predominated at age five years and remained highly endorsed at age ten. Even adults judged vitalist responses as plausible on some items.

In a follow-up study, we examined which component of vitalism was more important: the transfer of energy, or the psychological agency of a body part. For example, a participant might hear: "When we have a cut finger, what makes it get better?" or "When we have a cut finger, what happens when it gets better?" The energy response choice was, "Our cut finger uses energy to get better," whereas the organ-intentionality response choice was, "Our cut finger wants to get better." When the two possibilities were pitted against one another, transfer of energy prevailed. At each age (five, ten, and adult), participants preferred the energy response over the organ-intentionality response.

In a third study, participants could endorse or reject each of three vitalist sorts of explanations: energy-based, organ-want, and organ-think. For example, the question "What happens when we move?" was followed by three separate questions, in counterbalanced order: "Do our muscles use energy to move?" (energy-based), "Do our muscles want to move?" (organ-want), and "Do our muscles think about moving?" (organ-think). Once again, children strongly endorsed energy-based explanations at each age, although they also endorsed organ-desire explanations (see Table 5.7).

Children might have endorsed "energy" simply because it is a quasi-familiar term that sounds scientific. However, we argued against this idea by conducting a small follow-up study in which we asked children the same questions, but substituting "electricity" for "energy." Fifteen kindergartners (mean age 5;6) participated in this control study. For example, the question regarding a cut finger was, "Does our cut finger use electricity to get better?" We reasoned that "electricity," like "energy," is a scientific-sounding word that would be somewhat but not wholly familiar. If children preferred the energy explanation simply because the word sounds sophisticated and scientific yet at the same time familiar, then children should endorse electricity explanations as well. However, if children reject electricity explanations, we can more confidently conclude that children in the earlier studies endorsed a vitalistic concept. In fact, children overwhelmingly rejected the "electricity" explanations (mean level of endorsement was 17%, below chance by t-test, $p < .001$). It is unlikely, then, that children preferred the "energy" response choice for tangential reasons.

Table 5.7.   Percentage of trials supporting energy, organ-want, and organ-think explanations as a function of age; S. Morris, Taplin, and Gelman (2000)

	5 years	10 years	Adults
Energy	91%	86%	83%
Organ-want	86	80	53
Organ-think	34	27	2

Morris, Taplin, and I suggest that children and adults appeal to vital energy as a causal placeholder within a naive theory of biology, until they learn more scientifically accurate mechanisms (if they are ever acquired; Au and Romo, 1999). Energy transmission satisfies their belief that biological effects are caused and may also motivate the search for a more detailed biological explanation. However, children do not necessarily understand energy in the same way as do adults. It is also not clear from these results whether children construe energy as specifically biological. They may conceive of energy as a general causal force that is invoked to explain, for example, why one ball moves after being hit by a second ball, as well as biological events. They may even consider intentionality as a type of psychological energy, which has an effect on person activity that is comparable to the effect that biological energy has on biological activity.

To explore children's understanding of vital causes, Melanie Nyhof and I included two questions in our study of causal prerequisites (reported in the earlier section titled "Internal Cause versus Internal Prerequisite"). As a reminder: in this study children and adults saw a set of twelve test items (animals, complex artifacts that resembled animals, and simple artifacts) in one of two conditions, either moving or still. After viewing a videotape in which the item either did or did not move (depending on its condition), participants were asked a series of questions regarding the insides of the items. Of particular interest here, we included two questions intended to tap children's understanding of vitalism: "Does it have energy inside of it?" and "Does it have power inside of it?" (in counterbalanced order). We had originally intended these two questions to be equivalent means of tapping into a single vitalist construct, but they showed quite distinct profiles.

The distinction between the two questions is especially apparent in responses to the familiar baseline items: a person, a computer, and a rock (see Table 5.8). As can be seen, participants strongly endorsed *energy* for the person item, and *power* for the computer item. This finding is itself interesting and worthy of replication with a larger sample of familiar items. Given the clear differences between energy and power on the baseline items, I present the data from the test items broken down separately by question (see Table 5.9). Power and energy show divergent patterns here as well. Most clearly, power is linked to autonomously moving complex artifacts, for both children and adults. Although these results must be viewed as preliminary, given the relatively weak statistical power they provide, they suggest overall that children and adults link energy to familiar animals and link power to both familiar and unfamiliar (but autonomously moving) complex artifacts.

Gail Gottfried and I conducted a study to examine more closely how energy compares to a more specific "insides" causal account, and whether energy can be construed as domain-specific (as hinted in S. Gelman and Nyhof). There were three major differences between this study and the previous work that Nyhof and I had conducted: we rephrased the question so that it provided a more direct test of whether energy was construed as a cause (as opposed to merely linked with a category); we rephrased the question so that it did not presuppose that energy is inter-

Table 5.8. Baseline items, four-year-olds' and adults' mean percentage endorsement for each property set, as a function of domain and condition; S. Gelman and Nyhof

	Person	Computer	Rock
4-year-olds			
Energy	89%	38%	12%
Power	38	64	12
Adults			
Energy	100%	77%	37%
Power	77	94	26

Table 5.9. Four-year-olds' and adults' mean percentage endorsement for each property set, as a function of domain and condition; S. Gelman and Nyhof

	Animals		Complex artifacts		Simple artifacts	
	Still	Moving	Still	Moving	Still	Moving
4-year-olds						
Energy	34%	55%	34%	54%	8%	10%
Power	10	37	21*	71*	8	8
Adults						
Energy	87	90	87	53	26†	54†
Power	58	47	26*	84*	19	19

*Significant condition difference (still versus moving), $p < .02$

†Significant condition difference (still versus moving), $p < .05$, one-tailed

nal; and we included a broader range of properties, not just movement. One of the properties included was "sitting still," which is particularly interesting when comparing domains, in that animals continually require energy even to sit still, whereas artifacts typically require energy only when behaving in some way.

Participants were preschoolers, second-graders, and college students. Children saw a set of color photographs, one each of three unfamiliar animals (e.g., a cavy) and three unfamiliar machines (e.g., an electric razor).[4] These photos were selected on the basis of pilot testing, in which children in a separate group were able to identify the ontological kind of each picture (as animal, plant, or machine), but unable to identify its specific, basic-level name. It was important that children be able to identify the ontological kind, so that we could test whether children's vitalist accounts were domain-specific. However, we did not want children simply to report what they knew about particular kinds—hence the unfamiliar basic-level categories.

For each picture, participants first learned two properties. The animal properties were "move," "sit still," and "grow" (with each property attributed to two of the animals). The machine properties were "move," "sit still," and "make beads" (with each property attributed to two of the machines). Following presentation of each property, subjects were asked a question about the cause of the characteristic described. In the insides condition, the question was, "Does it use its own insides to X [e.g., move]?" In the energy condition, the question was, "Does it use its own energy to X [e.g., move]?" So, for example, on one trial participants would see a picture of a cavy and hear, "This animal can move. Does it use its own insides to move?"

The results confirmed the predictions: participants in all three age groups accepted that there was some sort of "energy" that caused important animal properties, at above-chance levels (see Figure 5.1). Furthermore, energy was construed as domain-specific at all three ages: it was endorsed more for animals than machines. It was not until age eight that children additionally endorsed concrete "insides" as causally responsible. These data confirm R. Gelman's and Simons and Keil's expectations that children construct an abstract framework understanding before filling in the details with concrete knowledge.

SUMMARY.   By preschool age, children have constructed a domain-specific explanation for the source of biological properties. There is little consistent evidence that preschoolers, unlike eight-year-olds and adults, have isolated particular internal parts as causally relevant. However, like these older age groups, they seem to view domain-specific internal parts as prerequisite to autonomously moving animals and complex artifacts. They also appear to have a causal framework in which "energy" plays a causal role. Children appeal to energy as a source of important animal properties, including movement, growth, and even simply sitting still.

One caveat is in order. There appears to be a mismatch between the mechanisms that children endorse on this sort of task (when the experimenter provides possible explanation choices) and the mechanisms that they spontaneously produce. For example, although children in the present set of studies tended to endorse vitalistic explanations for biological processes, children do not spontaneously offer vitalistic explanations (Inagaki and Hatano, 1993; J. Miller and Bartsch, 1997). Au and Romo (1999) interviewed over 300 children ranging in age from five to fifteen, asking them to explain in their own words several biological phenomena: the clinical course of a cold, inheritance, food spoilage, and HIV/AIDS transmission. Children talked about mechanical causality most of the time but almost never offered vitalistic explanations. Vitalism seems to provide an

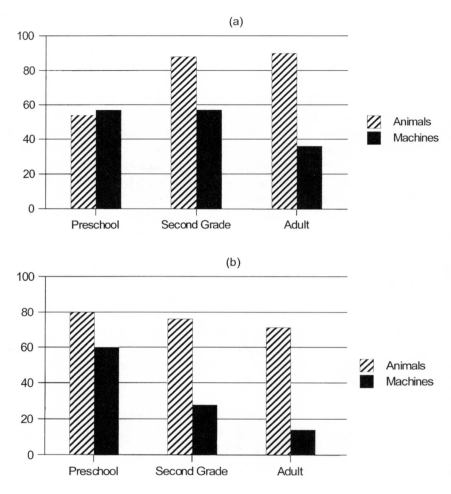

Figure 5.1. Mean percentage of "yes" responses; Gottfried and Gelman (unpublished); **(a)** Results from the "insides" questions; **(b)** Results from the "energy" questions.

explanatory framework that children find plausible and that they are willing to accept and endorse—yet not one that they spontaneously construct themselves. They can recognize an appealing explanation when they hear it, but they cannot yet generate a coherent explanation expressed in these terms.

What sort of entity do children construe "energy" to be? It is presumably invisible (corresponding to no particular bodily part or substance) and inherent (as children endorsed the idea that an animal uses "its *own* energy" to move, grow, or sit). Energy also appears to be domain-specific, as both children and adults appealed to energy more for animals than for machines. These properties suggest intriguing parallels to vitalist accounts found in different cultures. However, these initial findings raise many additional questions: do children construe energy as biological, psychological, or neither? How many different kinds of energies are thought to exist, and at what taxonomic level? For example, do children think that each species has its own unique kind of energy (one for horses, a different one for cows, and so on), or is there is single "animal" energy that spans all animal kinds? And what ontological kind does energy belong to: is it a substance, power, or information? Carey suggests that in Japanese philosophy, vital force is undifferentiated among these three ontological kinds (1996, p. 201). Is this also true of young children's beliefs?

The finding that "energy" (in all its vagueness) is endorsed before specific insides argues against the idea that children are constructing an understanding based on particular pieces of concrete knowledge (either observed or imparted by others). Instead, children have the outlines of the sort of explanation that is plausible—a framework or placeholder notion that guides their expectations.

Conclusions

Causality is central to children's categories in two distinct ways. First, by two years of age children view causes as vital to what something is. Features that are causes are more core than other sorts of features. Causes are more important than mere associations; causes are also more important than effects. Furthermore, features that are causally coherent (meaning that they fit together in an explanatory framework) are weighted more heavily than features that are equally available but not participating in a network of causal explanations. This first point can be restated as follows: concept learning cannot be characterized in terms of theory-neutral feature tabulations. Frequency alone cannot determine any of these results.

Second, causality is central to children's categories in that children provide consistent, domain-specific causal explanations for the properties that members of a category share. Even three-year-olds attribute animal actions to the animal itself, rather than to an external force (inherent cause). By four years of age, children appeal to "energy." By middle childhood, children appeal to "insides." These findings have important theoretical implications. Fodor has argued that the evidence for childhood essentialism could instead be taken simply to show that "young children are deeply into appearance/reality distinctions." Both Keil's transformation studies and Carey's (and my own) data that insides are more important to a thing's identity, could be accounted for in such terms. Fodor goes on to suggest: "What's further required, at a minimum, is the idea that what's 'inside' (or otherwise hidden) somehow is causally responsible for how things that belong to the kind appear; for their 'superficial signs'" (1998, pp. 154–155; emphasis added). The studies reviewed here provide initial evidence that preschool children indeed meet this requirement.

Psychological essentialism does not imply full-fledged explanatory theories, but rather theoretical commitments in the sense of adherence to nonobvious entities that cause observable structure. In the case of animal kinds, children appeal to inherent and vitalist causes. An important change from preschool to middle childhood is in the change from a placeholder understanding (an animal causes its own movement, due to some sort of energy) to a more precise understanding of internal cause.

Chapter 6

Conclusions to Part I

Chapters 2 through 5 offer powerful converging evidence for childhood essentialism. By the end of the preschool years, children assume that a variety of categories

- have rich inductive potential,
- are stable over outward transformations,
- include crucial nonobvious properties,
- have innate potential,
- privilege causal features,
- can be explained in terms of inherent and internal causes, and
- are real.

Collectively, these strands make a compelling case for essentializing by preschoolers. Children display evidence for both elements of essentialism presented in chapter 1: treating certain categories as richly structured kinds, and assuming that some as-yet-undefined causal placeholder is responsible for the structure of such categories.

In this chapter I consider four central issues that span the various phenomena detailed in the previous chapters: (a) which domains are essentialized? (b) is essentializing of living kinds biological, on either a naive-biological or correct-biological construal? (c) what is the role of statistical information in essentialist reasoning? and (d) what is individual essentialism and how does it compare to kind essentialism?

WHICH DOMAINS ARE ESSENTIALIZED?

Which categories are essentialized and, by implication, which domains? This question is closely tied to the matter of where essentialism comes from. For example, if essentialism is tightly constrained to all and only living kinds, then we might posit it as a component of a folk biological module. In contrast, if essentialism is broadly found within all domains, then we might suggest that it is a consequence of some very general cognitive processes. The question also has implications for theories of concepts: Can we posit one overarching theory for all concepts, or do we need to honor important distinctions?

Looking across chapters 2 through 5, the answer at first appears to differ depending on the phenomenon under consideration (see Table 6.1). For example, only living things exhibit innate potential, whereas categories in a broad range of domains have inductive potential. Causal features are central for both living kinds (see, for example, Ahn [1998, 1999]) and at least some artifacts (Gopnik and Sobel [2000] blicket-detector experiments), though in domain-specific ways. For living kinds the causal features are intrinsic to the object (e.g., tiger DNA causes tigers to have stripes), whereas for artifacts the causal features are extrinsic (e.g., the causal features of a blicket detector involve an interaction between the blicket and the machine). Essential nonobvious properties might at first appear to be special to natural kinds (functional parts for living kinds; microscopic structure for both living kinds and natural substances). Yet not only do complex machines seem to contradict this notion (e.g., computers arguably have essential internal processing chips), but also simple artifacts, in that the creator's intentions appear to determine artifact naming (P. Bloom, 2000; see more in chapters 9 and 10).

Despite such complexity, the patterns can be summarized by noting that the evidence for essentialism is (a) unambiguous for natural kinds and many social kinds, and (b) decidedly more mixed for artifacts. For example, although all categories have at least some inductive potential, the depth and range of that inductive potential seems qualitatively greater for, say, hyenas than greeting cards. If essen-

Table 6.1.   Evidence for essentialism across different types of concepts

	Inductive potential	Stability	Nonobvious properties	Cause	Boundary intensif.	Innate potential
Living kinds (ex.: cats)	high	high	high	high	high	high
Nonliving natural kinds (ex.: gold)	high	high	high	high	??	n/a
Ethnicities (ex.: Jews)	high	high	high	high	high	high
Social kinds (ex.: doctors)	high	medium	high	high	??	low
Simple artifacts (ex.: pencils)	medium	low	noninherent	noninherent	low	n/a
Machines (ex.: computers)	high	??	high	??	low	n/a
Noncoherent .(ex.: tchotchkes)	low	low	low	low	low	n/a

tialism entails the privileging of nonobvious properties, we see essentialism across domains. Tigers, gold, and pencils all are understood in terms of an underlying reality that does not reduce to outward appearance (internal composition, in the case of tigers and gold; creator's intent, in the case of pencils). But if essentialism additionally entails the assumption that these nonobvious properties are inherent in the item itself and revealing about richly structured categories, we see essentialism specifically within the domain of natural kinds.

To see why essentialism is domain-specific, consider pencils. Causal history tells us that something is a pencil—but this causal history is quite shallow in what it implies about commonalities *among* pencils. Something is a pencil because it was created with the intent of being a pencil—a nonobvious and underlying property, yes. But this property is not very useful with respect to making inferences about others of the same kind, nor does it lead to some of the other essentialist consequences (boundary intensification, stability over transformations, or categorical realism). In the case of artifacts, we seem to have a causally potent historical path but little else in the way of an essence or notion of kind. Whereas causal, nonobvious features are construed as inherent for natural kinds (the tiger's DNA, the chemical structure of gold), they are external or relational for artifacts (the intentions of the person who created the pencil—perhaps reflected in some quality of the object itself, but not literally in or of the pencil).

Still, it is deeply telling that essentializing-like processes are found across domains. Such processes argue for the centrality of nonobvious properties and appearance/reality distinctions in children's concepts. Essentializing is domain-specific in application, yet rooted in domain-general cognitive tendencies. We essentialize not because we have special processes dedicated to processing the biological domain. Rather, there are general mechanisms that can be applied broadly—for example, when tracing historical paths. I develop this argument in greater detail in chapter 11.

IS ESSENTIALISM A BIOLOGICAL CONCEPT?

I have already reviewed the arguments for why essentialism is not wholly biological, as essentialism extends to the nonbiological domain, including natural substances such as water or gold. But what about essentializing of the living world? Does this constitute biological reasoning?

Children expect categories to reflect natural processes by about four years of age, which certainly precedes their knowledge of detailed biological mechanisms, DNA, genes, and the like. It seems then that naturalizing of categories does not require or build on scientific biological knowledge. Can we therefore assume that essentializing of living kinds is not biological? The answer to this question depends in part on what one means by "biological." If "biological" means that one understands the correct mechanisms underlying biological processes such as growth, illness, or contagion, then preschool children fall far short (Au and Romo, 1999;

Carey, 1985; Solomon et al., 1996). On this criterion, even older children and adults may fall short (Au and Romo, 1999). However, if an initial biological theory is construed to mean one in which there is a realm that is distinct from human activities or mental states and that is specific to living things, then the data do largely support this understanding.

Let me elaborate. Children seem to struggle with just how nature fits in with other modes of theorizing (such as religion and science). Consider a friend of my son Adam, who repeatedly insisted that Mother Nature is God's sister. Given the debates that followed between the two first-graders, it seems very unlikely that this statement was intended as a metaphor. Instead, I think my son's friend meant literally that Mother Nature and God are siblings, and that nature is the same sort of thing as God (a supernatural being). And even though Adam vociferously disagreed, he also distinguished nature from a scientific realm:

Adam (age seven):   Chipmunks can go wherever they want in nature.
Adam's dad: How about the moon?
Adam: That's not nature, it's science.

On the other hand, children recognize that living things have natural origins (e.g., a dog is not made by a person; S. Gelman and Kremer, 1991), that biological processes are independent of human intentions (e.g., a child cannot stop growing just by wanting to; Inagaki and Hatano, 1993), and that biological entities can heal themselves (Backscheider, Shatz, and Gelman, 1993). In all of these respects, certain entities—ones that adults recognize as biological—engage in processes that are independent of human actions or desires.

I still need to explain why esssentialist talk recruits the language of biology. As seen in chapter 4, for example, adults and even grade-school children refer to "instinct," "genes," and other biological constructs when essentializing both biological and social categories. Yet even here, we need not assume that essentialism recruits scientific biology. When people appeal to biology, they often do so in ways that reveal fundamental misunderstandings. Consider, for example, a story reported in the *Ann Arbor News* on March 21, 2001. A middle-aged man who had been adopted at birth discovered that his biological parents had met as patients in a psychiatric hospital in Ypsilanti. His mother had suffered brain damage from childhood encephalitis; his father had suffered from a head injury resulting from a car accident, also in childhood. The reporter continues, in a somewhat bemused fashion: "Despite the fact that McClain's biological parents' mental problems stemmed from incidents in their lives—sickness and an accident—McClain believes he may have inherited a tendency to depression from at least his mother. 'I think it answers (questions) about some problems I've had in my life,' he said." This example suggests that an essentialist line of reasoning (mental problems from the biological parents were passed down to the child) is disguised as biology. See also E. Anderson and Jayaratne (1998) for examples of deeply misguided biologizing of social categories.

Why does essentialism of living kinds draw on the language of biology when it is not based in scientific biology? Biology appeals to people because it includes at least three crucial essentialist elements: (a) biological processes are *natural* (outside the realm of human control); (b) biological properties are *inherent* (inborn, and located within the individual); and (c) pursuit of biology entails a *search for unobservables*, including causally powerful unobservables. In all three of these respects, there is a dovetailing of naive folk-essentialist beliefs and biology as a science.

Where a true biological account of species differs from an essentialist account of species is in at least the following:

1. Biological species are defined by criteria that are *population-based* (not individual-based). For example, species differences are determined by interbreeding populations, not by inherent properties of individual members of the species (Sober, 1994).
2. Biological categories reflect *promiscuous realism* (Dupré, 1993) rather than a single identity for each. Each organism falls into multiple classification schemes, each of which has a valid basis in reality. There is no single organization scheme that applies to all biological categories.
3. Biological categories *evolve and change over time*, in contrast to the essentialist assumption that categories are fixed and unchanging (Mayr, 1991). (See chapter 11 for more discussion.)

To repeat, my argument is not that essentialism derives from scientific biological knowledge. Instead, folk biology is a framework that captures several essentialist assumptions: that certain properties are inherent in an individual, present from birth, and resistant to modification from outside forces. Essentialism of living kinds entails the belief that nature contributes more than nurture to the development of an organism. Children use the language of biology not because they are drawing from their biological knowledge to construct essentialist theories, but rather because they are modifying and assimilating biology to fit essentialism. The result is a folk biology that is strongly essentialist.

This analysis has implications for the ongoing debate regarding whether children undergo theory enrichment or theory change in the domain of biology (e.g., Carey, 1995; Hatano and Inagaki, 1999; Inagaki and Hatano, 2002; Keil, 1994; Wellman and Gelman, 1998). Several core tenets of a folk-biological theory seem firmly in place by the preschool years, as mentioned earlier: that living kinds entail processes that are natural and features that are inherent and nonobvious. In this sense, folk biology appears to be a domain distinct from both folk psychology and folk physics, by an early age. Over developmental time, folk biology undergoes enrichment in the fleshing out of this framework theory, but the fundamental structure does not change in childhood. Where we sometimes see genuine theory change is in the adoption of Darwinian evolutionary theory, though even here many adults may never fully drop their essentialist assumptions that contradict evolution.

The distinction between folk biological theory and scientific biological theory also helps demystify the following paradox: If people seek causes, explanations, and nonobvious properties, then why is adults' knowledge in many domains so shallow, incomplete, and wrong? If there is any doubt as to the truth of this last part of the paradox, we need look no further than the fundamental attribution error (Nisbett and Ross, 1980), error-laden reasoning heuristics (Kahneman, Slovic, and Tversky, 1982), and gaps and flaws in logical analyses (Johnson-Laird and Byrne, 1991). One resolution to this paradox, I think, is that people crave causal stories but generally are not very good at gathering and evaluating evidence (Kuhn, 1989). The scientific impulse is powerful even in childhood, the scientific method eludes many of us. Another reason is that people tend to be satisfied with rather shallow explanations (Keil, 1998). I might wish to know why an acquaintance is avoiding me at a party. Is he angry with me? Nearsighted? Shy? Once I make an attribution (let us suppose I decide that he is shy), I will often be satisfied with that. I do not then seek, in an infinite regress, the cause of his shyness, down to the intricacies of the biochemical predispositions and familial contexts that led to this state. Similarly, when reasoning about biological species (as well as social kinds), children appeal to underlying essentialist causes without constructing highly accurate biological models.

THE ROLE OF STATISTICAL INFORMATION

Young children and even infants are remarkably capable of using statistical regularities in the environment to organize and make sense of the world. For example, eight-month-old infants attend to transitional probabilities between pairwise syllables in an unbroken speech stream to detect wordlike units (Saffran, Aslin, and Newport, 1996; see also Christiansen, Allen, and Seidenberg, 1998; Gomez and Gerken, 1999; Kirkham, Slemmer, and Johnson, 2002; Maratsos and Chalkley, 1980; Marcus, 2000; and Shi, Werker, and Morgan, 1999, for other examples of early statistical learning). A question then arises: could children's essentialist responses be the result of statistical tallying of cues?

The question has not yet been studied directly. It would be interesting, for example, for someone to attempt to model the various phenomena reviewed above using statistical information alone. However, I suggest that a statistical tallying process will be of limited use in explaining the sorts of data reviewed in the prior chapters. An informal example with crows and computer printer cartridges begins to illustrate the problem. As far as I know, crows and the outer case of printer cartridges are always black. If statistical information were the source of essentialist presumptions, then color should be essential to both crows and printer cartridges. Yet color is essential to neither, because it is a consequence of other, more fundamental properties (genetic material of crows, human design for printer cartridges). Moreover, the color of crows is the consequence of something more essential than is the color of printer cartridges, as evidenced by intuitions about their stability (crows will continue to be black, whereas printer cartridges may be purple or yellow or polka-dotted in the future). The moral is that centrality of a feature cannot be deduced from its frequency—a point nicely demonstrated with adults by Medin and Shoben (1988).

Similar arguments can be made about determination of cause (see the examples and discussion in chapter 5), boundary intensification (which misrepresents statistical cues by, for example, minimizing within-category variability and exaggerating between-category differences), and attributing features to nature versus nurture (since the overwhelming amount of evidence available to people confounds nature and nurture).

It also seems that when statistical information comes into conflict with more categorical representations, the latter often wins out. I provide an extended illustration by considering category-based induction (as discussed in chapter 2), which for adults is modified by information regarding the variability of the evidence supplied. To give two notable examples: a small sample is (normatively) a less powerful basis of induction than a large sample, and a homogeneous sample is (normatively) a less powerful basis of induction than a heterogeneous sample (but see Lo et al., 2002, for a dissenting view). Furthermore, preexisting beliefs about the diversity of a property with respect to a category also influence inductive patterns. For example, we can confidently determine the chemical composition of gold from just a single sample, but we cannot determine the height of trees from just a single tree. We may think of this sort of information, involving sample size and diversity, as statistical information.

Although most people have numerous biases and deficiencies when reasoning about statistical evidence (e.g., Kahneman, Slovic, and Tversky, 1982), college-educated adults are sensitive to statistical information such as sample size and diversity when forming category-based inferences. Take an example from Nisbett, Krantz, et al. (1983). The researchers told adult subjects to imagine that they were on an unexplored island, that they saw a sample of one, three, or twenty islanders called the Barratos, and that the islander(s) in the sample had brown skin. In another example participants were again given a sample of one, three, or twenty Barratos, but in this case participants learned that the islander(s) in the sample was (were) obese. The participants were then asked to estimate what percentage of all Barratos on the island were either brown-skinned or obese. When judging obesity, the size of the sample mattered: participants were more willing to generalize obesity from three exemplars than from one, and from twenty exemplars than from three. They required a greater amount of evidence (namely, more obese islanders) in order to generalize that property. Yet when judging skin color, sample size had little effect on the degree to which adults generalized the property. A sample of one brown-skinned Barratos was enough for most adults to infer that all the Barratos on the island were brown-skinned. It would appear that adults had preexisting beliefs concerning the variability of skin color versus body type in a group of people.

There are two competing hypotheses regarding how children might perform on such tasks. On one view, children will be particularly sensitive to statistical variability in the input. As mentioned earlier, even infants are remarkably sensitive to statistical patterns in input language (Aslin, Saffran, and Newport, 1998; Marcus, 2000; Saffran, Aslin, and Newport, 1996; Shi, Werker, and Morgan, 1999) and in category construction (Younger, 1990). Similarly, certain theories of word acquisition presuppose that children track statistical regularities between features of the input language and real-world features (e.g., L. Smith, Jones, and Landau, 1996). Statistical information is available even in the absence of a large knowledge base, and so might be ideally suited for use by children, who have relatively impoverished knowledge compared to adults.

A competing account states that when the task entails induction from a sample, and that sample can be construed as representing a kind category, children will tend to ignore statistical variability, instead focusing on category membership.[1] On this second model, children will readily generalize from a single instance, even though such information is a relatively weak inductive basis. In effect, children will tend to treat category-based inferences on the model of adults with the brown-skinned Baratos: as a tightly bound, homogeneous grouping.

Carey (1985) found that six-year-old children tended not to use diversity when reasoning about biological properties. For example, when taught that both dogs and bees have a spleen, their inferences to other animals were no higher than when taught that only dogs have a spleen. Carey suggests that children relied on similarity to one or the other animal (p. 161). In a follow-up study, six-year-olds and adults were taught that both dogs and flowers have golgi. Here, some children appeared to attempt to discover the general category that encompassed both dogs and flowers, but such attempts were inconsistent.

I have further investigated these issues in collaboration with Alejandro López, Grant Gutheil, and Ed Smith. We gave children simple induction tasks in which the samples presented to children varied in their statistical power. Before presenting the design of these studies, I first need to explain briefly the theoretical model and evidence that formed the foundation for this work, the similarity-coverage model proposed by Osherson et al. (1990).

Osherson et al. amply demonstrated that adults (undergraduates in the United States) prefer certain sorts of inductive judgments over others. Adults received inductive "arguments"—premises and conclusions in written form—and were asked to judge which of a pair of arguments was stronger. For example, when presented with two samples of mammals (e.g., "cats and buffaloes have nesium inside" versus "cows and buffaloes have omentum inside"), adults were more likely to respond that a kangaroo possessed the property of the more diverse sample (cats and buffaloes) than of the more homogeneous sample (cows and buffaloes). This effect is known as the diversity phenomenon. Likewise, given a larger sample (e.g., "pigs, wolves, and foxes have ulnar arteries inside") versus a smaller sample (e.g., "pigs and wolves have cesium inside"), adults were more likely to say that a gorilla had the property of the larger sample. This effect is known as the monotonicity phenomenon. Altogether, adults consistently demonstrated thirteen reasoning phenomena.

These phenomena are all explained under an umbrella model, the similarity-coverage model (SCM). Osherson et al. argue that adults' use of sample size and diversity is based on their understanding that the larger and/or more diverse samples "cover" the category in question more effectively than those that are smaller and/or more homogeneous. Coverage can be roughly defined as the degree to which the members of a category sample are similar to all the members of the category in question. In the examples earlier, cats and buffaloes together are similar to a wider variety and greater number of mammals than are cows and buffaloes. In the same manner, the larger sample of pigs, wolves, and foxes is similar to a wider variety and greater number of mammals than the smaller sample restricted to pigs and wolves. Osherson et al. argue that when adults are presented with inductive tasks of this type, they first determine the most specific category that includes all the exemplars in question (the "inclusive category"; mammals in these examples), and then determine the degree to which each sample covers that inclusive category. Use of monotonicity and diversity information therefore requires that one have available the relevant inclusive category, and that one can calculate coverage based on that inclusive category. (See Sloman, 1993, for an alternative model.)

The model, in its emphasis on similarity, might at first appear to conflict with my findings with Ellen Markman described in chapter 2. In fact, however, the SCM accounts for such results by positing that children make use of assumptions along the lines of, "If two animals are both members of the same natural category, they probably feed their young the same thing" (E. Smith, 1989), thereby invoking category membership as a basis of the inference.

Alejandro López, Grant Gutheil, Ed Smith, and I were interested in discovering whether this model is developmentally basic (i.e., found even in young children), or whether these principles emerge gradually over development. We investigated several inductive reasoning phenomena in kindergarten and second-grade children (López et al., 1992). The arguments were stated aloud, with corresponding line drawings to help children remember the information and focus on the task. For example, in one diversity item, children saw pictures of a cat and a buffalo, and learned that cats and buffaloes have nesium inside. They also saw pictures of a cow and a buffalo, and learned that cows and buffaloes have omentum inside. They were then shown a picture of a kangaroo and were asked what kangaroos have inside, nesium or omentum. In another version of the task, the premises were the same, but this time children were asked what "all animals" have inside, nesium or omentum.

Kindergartners' inductive judgments were unaffected by either sample size or diversity, for either specific (kangaroos) or general (all animals) conclusion arguments.[2] In contrast, second-graders made use of both sample size and diversity information, but only for general conclusion arguments. López et al. (1992) suggested that children's difficulty computing coverage could reflect that the study focused on the superordinate-level category "animal." Young children have notorious difficulty reasoning about superordinate categories on many tasks (see Inhelder and Piaget, 1964; Markman and Callanan, 1983; Rosch et al., 1976; and Waxman, 1991, for children's difficulty with superordinate-level categories). Even the older children may have found it difficult to generate the superordinate category given a set of diverse exemplars (e.g., cats, buffaloes, and kangaroos). Support for this latter interpretation includes the fact that the older children did make use of sample size and diversity when the superordinate category was supplied by the experimenter (i.e., the specific conclusion arguments), and so the children did not have to generate that category themselves.

Grant Gutheil and I set out to test this possibility more directly, by examining children's use of monotonicity and diversity in basic-level categories (e.g., "frogs" instead of "animals"). Participants were second- and third-grade children and adults. Each participant saw a series of item sets in which two samples of animals were contrasted with one another. There were three distinct types of item sets:

- single versus homogeneous (e.g., one box turtle versus five box turtles);
- homogeneous versus diverse (e.g., five box turtles versus five dissimilar turtles: box turtle, sea turtle, snapping turtle, etc.); and
- single versus diverse (e.g., one box turtle versus five dissimilar turtles).

These three types of items enabled us to test children's sensitivity to monotonicity and diversity, both singly and combined. For each item, children viewed a pair of samples and learned a new fact about each one (e.g., "This turtle has small speckles on its stomach"; "These five turtles have no speckles on their stomachs"). Children then saw another member of the same basic-level category that was dissimilar from all the samples (e.g., a perceptually dissimilar turtle) and were asked which property it would have (e.g., "Here's another turtle. Do you think this turtle has small speckles on its stomach like this [single exemplar] turtle, or no speckles on its stomach, like these [five exemplar] turtles?").

Unlike adults, children failed to modulate their inferences in response to information concerning the number or heterogeneity of training exemplars (see Table 6.2). We reasoned that children may have attempted to use the similarity between premise and conclusion to draw these inferences, and so we conducted a follow-up study in which the conclusion picture was held up facing the experimenter and never shown to the child (e.g., "I'm looking at another turtle. Do you think this turtle has small speckles on its stomach like this turtle, or no speckles on its stomach, like these turtles?"). In this condition, children still made no use of sample size or diversity when they were presented separately. It was only when sample size and diversity were combined that children made use of such information. Children's persistent difficulties support the proposal that children up through nine years of age have difficulty recognizing the importance of sample size and diversity information when making inductive inferences about category members. It is only

Table 6.2. Mean percentage of responses in which participants employed monotonicity or diversity

	Children Study 1	Children Study 2	Adults
Single versus homogeneous	47%	47%	63% †
Homogeneous versus diverse	60	57	77**
Single versus diverse	60	70*	93**

† Greater than chance, $p < .05$, one-tailed

* Greater than chance, $p < .05$

** Greater than chance, $p < .01$, two-tailed

Source: Gutheil and Gelman (1997).

when both size and diversity information are combined and other strategies
are unavailable that eight- to nine-year-old children take this information into
account.

On these tasks, children have persistent difficulty using sample size and diversity information. What is the source of their difficulty? The problem is not necessarily an inability to appreciate diversity. Rather, Gutheil and I suggest that children
overestimate the power of a single example to guide induction. In past work it had
been found that for a range of properties, a single exemplar is often sufficient to
generalize the property to other category members (S. Gelman and O'Reilly, 1988;
Macario, Shipley, and Billman, 1990). The salience of category membership may
have overwhelmed any information concerning the size or diversity of the samples
provided—despite the perceived variability of these properties for adults in these
studies. In other words, children may have assumed that a property true of one
animal is true of other animals in the same basic level category. We speculate that
young children's focus on the category as determining the scope of induction may
lead them to ignore other relevant information, such as sample size and sample
diversity.

Do children wholly lack a diversity heuristic, or instead do they have access to
diversity-based reasoning in other contexts? It is interesting in this regard to consider the findings of Coley, Medin, et al. with Itzaj Mayan adults in Guatemala. The
failure of Itzaj adults to use diversity *as intended by the experimenter* (i.e., based on
similarity) could be traced to their use of ecological considerations instead, including specific ecological knowledge such as range and habitat. At times they did use
diversity, but it was based on ecology rather than similarity. The Itzaj adults also
successfully used diversity in a real-world (noncategorical) reasoning task:

"Imagine you want to buy several bags of corn from a given person. Before buying
them, this person will show you only two cobs of corn to check whether all the corn is
good. Do you prefer him to show you two cobs from one and the same bag, or do you

prefer him to show you one cob from one bag and another cob from another bag?"
(Coley, Medin, et al., 1999, p. 220)

On this task, the Itzaj did prefer the more diverse sampling strategy (one cob from each of two bags). However, Coley, Medin, et al. did not test children on this task. If children also use diversity when reasoning about sampling diseased corn from two bags, but fail to do so when reasoning about animal kinds, then their beliefs about the inductive potential of categories may be hampering their use of statistical information.

If the comparison to the Mayan adults is apt, then children may not be incapable of using diversity; rather, other strategies may get in the way. Indeed, two recent sets of experiments (Heit and Hahn, 2001; Lo et al., 2002) show that under certain circumstances, children do use diversity at a surprisingly young age. Heit and Hahn (2001) gave children problems such as the following:

- [picture of a girl playing with three Barbie dolls]: These dolls all belong to Danielle.
- [picture of a girl playing with a china doll, a stuffed doll, and a Cabbage Patch doll]: These dolls all belong to Jane.
- [picture of a baby doll]: Who does this doll belong to, Danielle or Jane?

All of the items involved children possessing or interacting with objects. The researchers found that children preferred the diverse sample (for example, judging that the baby doll belonged to Jane). Even five-year-olds could detect evidential diversity and use it to make novel inferences. This result is important and unexpected.

There are many differences between this task and those used in prior studies (e.g., domain of the categories, content of the properties, number of pictures, and absence of overlap between diverse and nondiverse training sets). Heit and Hahn did not attempt to isolate which factors were responsible for the change in performance. However, children may have been helped by construing the study as a thematic-matching task rather than a property-induction task. Because all the properties concerned a person owning or interacting with the target objects, children may have converted the task to one in which they were attempting to determine which group the target object should belong to, rather than which property a target object possessed. In other words, the task encouraged thematic links (among the objects in a set; for example, that the different dolls were used together in a single context—being played with by a single child) rather than property inferences (e.g., which property each doll individually possessed, independent of thematic context).

Treating the task as a thematic link entails detecting the diversity or homogeneity of items among a set and determining whether a novel item "goes with" a homogeneous versus a diverse set. What the task does *not* require, and wherein I would argue children's difficulty lies, is determining how to extend properties attributed to one set of individuals versus another. On this speculative analysis, Heit and Hahn's experiments tapped into the first set of skills (calculating diversity versus nondiversity and matching a picture thematically to one versus the other set) but not the second (inferring a novel property). There is some support for this distinction in that children do perform quite differently on tasks entailing inductive inferences versus categorization, as seen in chapter 2 (the section titled "Category Labels versus Properties" and the section, presented later, titled "Labels versus Properties, Induction versus Categorization").[3]

Lo et al. (2002) present data that further complicate this discussion. In experiment 1 of their paper, the authors found that preschool children failed to use diversity at above-chance levels—a finding consistent with López et al. (1992) and with G. Gutheil and Gelman (1997). However, in three other studies (experiments 2 through 4), with preschool children from the United States and Taiwanese preschoolers and third- through fifth-graders, children preferred diverse premises far above chance. In some of the experiments, children were presented with a "detective" task, in which fictional children evaluated the strength of different clues. For example:

> "Detectives Max and Morgan wanted to know if all animals have thick blood. Both of them found some clues. Max found that lions and tigers have thick blood. Morgan found that lions and rhinos have thick blood. If they wanted to know whether *all animals* have thick blood, which one is the better clue? Is this the better clue, that lions and tigers have thick blood? Or is this the better clue, that lions and rhinos have thick blood?"

Another version of the task, used in experiment 4, presented simplified wording:

> "Suppose you are curious about animals, so you decide to study them. If you want to know whether all animals have thick blood, which would be the better clue, that lions and tigers have thick blood, or that lions and rhinos have thick blood?"

With either kind of wording, children with a mean age of four to five years of age made use of diversity consistently.

Why the striking contrast with earlier work? I hypothesize that the answer again lies in the task. Lopez et al. and G. Gutheil and Gelman presented children with competing properties, either of which could have generalized to the conclusion category. In such a case, children would have to go through three steps to reason based on diversity: (a) generate category-based inferences from sample 1, (b) generate category-based inferences from sample 2, and (c) compare the strength of (a) and (b) to determine which sample provides a stronger inductive base.

In contrast, Lo et al. presented only one property and employed a task that explicitly encouraged cue evaluation. This ingenious method thereby focused children directly on evaluating which of two samples was a better basis of induction. By focusing them on cue evaluation rather than property inference per se, the task may have freed children to evaluate the strength of the competing samples. It will be interesting to compare directly the two sorts of tasks to determine whether this methodological difference was responsible for the variation in performance.[4]

SUMMARY.   I suggest that children's frequent failure to use diversity information may reflect their tendency to focus on categorical information to the exclusion of other sorts of information (including statistical). In this sense, children's sensitivity to categories as the basis of induction is a reasoning bias that, though useful much of the time, results in systematic errors. I have argued that the two sets of studies in which young children can use diversity are notable for focusing children away from category-based induction: in one case (Heit and Hahn, 2001) the task is converted to one which children can solve by forming thematic groupings, and in another case (Lo et al., 2002) children are explicitly asked to evaluate sources of evidence directly, thus bypassing the need for them to first form inductions from the category. These interpretations remain speculative, as more evidence is needed directly comparing the different methods to disentangle when children do and do not use diversity in their inductive reasoning.

At the same time, it is not inconsistent to be an essentialist about categories (expecting nonobvious properties to cohere, and to be explained in terms of a hidden causal force or entity) and yet to use statistical information to guide reasoning. Certainly an essentialist does not expect members of a category to be identical with respect to all properties. Even properties that are tightly linked to a kind (e.g., flying, for birds) can be construed as typically linked to an animal's essence without being exceptionless (Prasada, 2000). Representing such variability with any accuracy will require attention to frequencies, feature correlations, and other statistical information. Even for young children, statistical regularities may provide a rich database for developing categories (Younger, 1990). I would suspect that statistical information is particularly valuable in the task of identifying members of a category (see, e.g., Mervis and Rosch, 1981). By late elementary school age, children clearly make use of statistical information to guide their category-based inferences—and there is no evidence that children stop being essentialist at this age. My point here is that children's concepts do not reduce to a representation of the statistical patterns that are present in the environment. The essentialist representations they construct are more than the sum of such computations.

ESSENTIALISM OF KINDS VERSUS ESSENTIALISM OF INDIVIDUALS

To this point I have discussed essentialism as an assumption about kinds: that the world has natural discontinuities that are richly informative about nonobvious properties, and that these nonobvious properties give rise to outward similarities. These assumptions apply especially to categories of natural kinds, including plants, animals, and natural substances.

A similar set of assumptions seems to extend to how people reason about individuals. Specifically, with individuals, too, people attribute hidden, nonobvious causal properties that impart identity. A particularly clear example is Claire Sylvia's discussion of heart-lung transplants. Recall from chapter 3 that people undergoing such transplants often talk about some invisible "essence" or "energy" from the donor that persists through massive transformations (including the donor's death). There are also scattered accounts of an individual "essence" in contexts as diverse as psychotherapy, eulogies, naming, and religion. To sample from these, I typed the words "individual" and "essence" into an online computer search, which generated approximately 822,000 entries. For example, in one Web site (www.emerging-essence.com), a practitioner promises a commitment to "journeying to the core of your very being." Another Web site suggests that eulogies can capture "the essence of the individual." Yet another discusses "the divine essence in your name," noting that such essence is both physical and spiritual. At this point we know too little about the details of such beliefs, how coherent they are, how much they commit to a causal ontology, how widespread such beliefs are in the adult population, and how and when they emerge in development.

There is a related sense in which a notion of "individual essentialism" applies quite broadly, not only to construals of people but also to concepts of artifacts, natural kinds, famous works of art, and even everyday objects. In all these cases, people favor historical paths over outward properties when determining what something is. This tendency can be considered a version of essentialism: historical paths are nonobvious properties that take precedence over outward features, and historical paths have causal implications (e.g., the origins of an individual person implicate his or her biology; the origins of a work of art have ramifications for its outward features). By privileging historical paths, people say in effect that an underlying, hidden reality determines identity.

There are several pieces of evidence confirming that people do reason in this way. First, patterns of naming generally reflect the importance of historical continuity. As Kripke observed, we typically continue to give the same name to someone as she grows (with the remarkable changes from infancy to old age) or undergoes other outwardly massive transformations (e.g., due to pregnancy, bodybuilding, illness, head-to-toe tattooing, or fashion "makeovers").[5] Second, when undergraduates are given thought experiments in which they consider items with anomalous historical paths (for instance, a man who looks and acts like John F. Kennedy but served as prime minister of Britain; or a statue that looks just like Auguste Rodin's *The Thinker* but was formed inadvertently by the accidental spilling of some molten metal), they determine identity to large degree on the basis of the historical path information (Sternberg, Chawarski, and Allbritton, 1998). For example, they almost never judge that the JFK look-alike could be JFK. Third, when preschool children are asked to reason about works of art (P. Bloom and Markson, 1998; S. Gelman and Ebeling, 1998) or everyday artifacts (S. Gelman and Bloom, 2000), they likewise grant special significance to historical paths. For example, an object that looks very much like a knife is much less likely to be called "a knife" if it was described as having been created by accident than if it was described as having been created intentionally. Apparently, historical path (creation with the intent of becoming a knife) is critical for determining what something is, even for preschoolers. (See chapter 9 for a more extensive discussion of these studies.)

Does individual essentialism constitute merely a minor wrinkle on kind essentialism—the same phenomenon though varying in scope—or instead is it a substantively different sort of thing? I suspect that essentializing of individual people recruits much the same cognitive mechanisms as essentializing of natural kinds. The attribution of an immutable hidden energy or invisible force is remarkably similar across these examples. However, kind essentialism takes one crucial step beyond individual essentialism. With kind essentialism the person assumes that the world is carved up into preexisting natural categories. Individual essentialism seems not to require any such commitment to kind realism. The naive realism of essentialism would be lost if we were to lump together individual and kind essentialism. Likewise, the domain-specificity of essentialism would be lost were we to consider just those commonalities shared by individual and kind essentialism.

Nonetheless, it is a notable fact that attention to underlying nonobvious historical paths is found across ontological types—individuals *and* kinds—in people's reasoning about everything from pencils to Elvis Presley; from the Empire State Building to pigs; from diamonds to the Mona Lisa. This broadly general attention to underlying properties once again suggests that essentialism may arise from domain-general cognitive tendencies (see chapter 11).

CONCLUSIONS

In this chapter I have summarized the multifaceted evidence for essentialism in young children, noting that the patterns across a wealth of studies converge to present a picture of children as treating natural kinds (and many social kinds) as richly structured with nonobvious causal features. Although essencelike construals can be found broadly across domains, they are markedly more consistent and compelling for categories of natural entities. I have argued that essentialist construals cannot grow out of a simple tallying of features and are unlikely to reflect even more sophisticated statistically based reasoning. This conclusion implies that essentialism is the result of certain reasoning biases, an "essentializing mind," as it were. In part II I look more directly at the mechanisms that do—and do not—contribute to essentialism.

PART II

MECHANISMS OF ACQUISITION

Chapter 7

What Parents Say—and Do Not Say—about Essences

Voici mon secret. Il est très simple: on ne voit bien qu'avec le coeur. L'essentiel est invisible pour les yeux. [Here is my secret. It is very simple: It is only with the heart that one can see rightly; what is essential is invisible to the eye.]

Antoine de Saint-Exupéry, *Le Petit Prince*

Whenever I present my research on childhood essentialism at conferences or colloquia, people want to know *why* children essentialize, and more specifically, what parents are doing to put such ideas into their children's heads. I invariably hear questions along the lines of the following: "Children must be getting this from what their parents say, right?" "They learn about essentialism from books and TV, don't they?" Though not explicitly stated this way, the assumption seems to be that children would not come up with these ideas on their own. As Carey put it: "It is natural to propose that humans learn about the world by observing it: we learn that bodies fall by watching them fall; we learn that insults make people angry by watching people react to insults; we learn that 2 + 2 = 4 by observing two sets of two things combine into one set of four things" (1996, pp. 202–203). On this empiricist view, children learn about essences by observation, either direct or indirect—including the stories told by their parents. This view is appealing in many respects (though Carey goes on to reject this "natural" position). After all, children believe many other sorts of surprising things (the existence of Santa Claus and the Tooth Fairy, for instance) because they are told to, and they are trusting. Also, if parents transmit these beliefs to children directly, then we do not have to grapple with the disquieting implications of the possibility that children are somehow biased to construct stereotypes.

It is true that explicit essentialist accounts abound in classic and popular stories for children. The quote from *The Little Prince* at the beginning of this chapter is one of the most obvious examples. But there are many others, not quite so obvious yet still heavily essentialist. One of my favorite essentialist stories as a child concerned a king who posed a contest to his daughter's suitor. The suitor was shown two bouquets of flowers, identical in appearance. However, as the king informed the suitor, only one of the bouquets contained real flowers. The other contained exquisite, human-made fakes. The task of the suitor was to select the real flowers. If he did so, then the princess and the kingdom would be his. If he did not, then he would be banished or killed (I no longer remember which). The suitor examined the bouquets over and over with increasing dismay as the minutes ticked by; he simply could not tell which of the two was real. But then he saw that a small bee had entered the room unnoticed through an open window. As the suitor held his breath and watched, the bee silently landed on one of the bouquets. The suitor, trusting the instincts of the bee, selected that bouquet—and won the contest.

The story of the king and the flowers is clearly an essentialist tale. The implicit premises include: origins are central to identity; how something is classified cannot always be determined by outward appearances; and nonetheless, despite the fallibility of outward appearances, a nonobvious difference between categories remains and can be detected, even if detecting the difference is beyond the capacity of an ordinary person. And there are other essentialist tales. "The Ugly Duckling" is oft told and neatly essentialist: appearances are deceiving, and innate potential overrides a contrasting upbringing. Likewise, *Stellaluna* (Cannon, 1993) concludes that a bat is truly a bat, no matter how hard it may try to be a bird, even if it is raised by birds and believes itself to be a bird. Disney's *Lambert the Sheepish Lion* (Disney, 1977) is a similar tale about a lion cub raised with sheep, who believes himself to be meek and mild until a wolf threatens the flock—and Lambert's fierce nature comes through to save the day.

I cannot resist describing one more essentialist story: *The Sneetches* (Seuss, 1961). I quote below from a description given by Paul Bloom (personal communication). In this story,

> there are two types of Sneetches—those with stars, and those without—and the ones with stars are snooty and superior, and the ones without are miserable and depressed. Then a character arrives on the scene (Sylvester McMonkey McBean) with a machine that can add stars to the bellies of those that don't have any, and so the Sneetches without stars pay money for this. Now everyone has stars! The interesting thing is that, despite their perceptual identity, the groups clearly remain. The ones who originally had stars are enraged that they are now identical to those who had stars added, and they pay dearly to have their stars removed, so they will look different again. And so on. [A frenzied cycle of adding and removing stars continues until everyone is so confused that they no longer know who is who, the presence or absence of stars becomes meaningless, and all Sneetches live together in harmony.] But to follow the story, you need the Kripkean intuition that just because the groups are *defined* as "those with stars" and "those without," someone can remain a member of these groups regardless of whether or not they have stars.

But not all stories told to children are essentialist. The input that children hear is more complicated, and the acquisitional account is correspondingly more interesting. At the same time that children hear about the Little Prince, the Ugly Duckling, Stellaluna, and the Sneetches, they also hear stories such as *Horton Hatches the Egg* (Seuss, 1940). In this classic Dr. Seuss tale, a conscientious elephant named

Horton sits on an egg for days and weeks while its mother flies about the world on her own business. When the egg finally hatches, Horton is rewarded for his efforts: the creature that emerges is part bird, part elephant. *Babe, the Gallant Pig* (King-Smith, 1983) is another popular antiessentialist account: a brave little pig raised by herding dogs becomes the best sheepdog of them all. *Stuart Little* (E. B. White, 1945) is a somewhat mixed tale from an essentialist's perspective, but suggests that humans can give birth to mice (or to children who look awfully much like mice).

The problem with anecdotes is that they do not provide a representative look at what children are exposed to. It is also a problem that all these anecdotes concern fictional stories, because we know very little about how or whether children incorporate fictional worlds into their beliefs about the nonfictional world. Maybe children treat none of these stories as relevant to their reasoning about real life. The present chapter details a systematic investigation. We find some surprising results in terms of what parents do say about essences—and what they do not say. But I do not wish to get too far ahead of myself. First I need to lay some groundwork.

CONCEPTUALIZING THE QUESTION OF ORIGINS

The simple empiricist view alluded to at the beginning of the chapter might be rephrased as something like the following: children learn whatever they are told (or observe). Yet surely this account cannot be the full story. For one thing, it begs the question of why adults would be telling children an essentialist story to begin with. But equally problematic is the fact that children can be remarkably resistant to counterevidence. (To be sure, they are also susceptible to misleading suggestions or questions.) A classic example of this resistance includes the Piagetian training studies that demonstrated repeatedly that children cannot learn fundamental concepts (such as conservation of weight) simply by being told the correct answer. The stereotyping literature is also replete with examples of children and adults twisting their recall of events to fit prior biases (Liben and Signorella, 1987). Studies of folk theories likewise demonstrate powerful reasoning biases that contradict even direct instructions (Kaiser, McCloskey, and Proffitt, 1986). It is clear, then, that even young children can be active processors of information, and not merely passive recipients.

I illustrate this resistance to counterevidence with a bit of essentialist reasoning from my daughter, Stephanie, when she was about three and a half years old. She had been playing with a set of blocks that included a stylized dog and cat. Their faces were nearly identical, though only the cat had eyelashes. Later that day, Stephanie announced that "hes" don't have eyelashes; only "shes" have eyelashes. I then asked my husband to come into the room and take off his glasses. "Look at Daddy," I said. "Does he have eyelashes?" Stephanie looked right into his eyes and said, "No. Daddy's a 'he,' and 'hes' don't have eyelashes." Rather than change the theory to fit the evidence, my daughter ignored the evidence that disconfirmed the theory.

The problem of developmental origins is considerably complex, but as a starting point I assume that essentialism most likely requires both biases in the child and cues in the environment. The rough argument for biases in the child is that children and adults from widely varying environments essentialize. As we have seen in some of the previous chapters, children in impoverished neighborhoods in Brazil (Diesendruck, 2001), Torguud adults in Western Mongolia (Gil-White, 2001), and Vezo children in Madagascar (Astuti, Solomon, and Carey, cited in Astuti, 2000) show remarkable commonalities with middle-class children and adults in the United States, in their assumptions about living kind categories. Without some predisposition toward essentializing, it is difficult to see why children would converge on common beliefs in such radically varying environmental conditions (including ones in which explicit antiessentialist accounts are provided by the adults; Astuti, 2000).

However, cues in the environment are undoubtedly critical. There is cross-cultural variation in the degree of essentializing, how it is expressed, and for which categories. Bloch, Solomon, and Carey (2001) found that the Zafimaniry in Madagascar showed little essentializing of people (though notably they did essentialize nonhuman animal kinds). They reported, for example, that a person of one group (which we might gloss as a racial group) adopted by members of another group would take on the identity of the adoptive parents. Even within a culture, the degree of essentializing is not constant. As we have already seen, within the Indian caste system, mode of reasoning depends on one's own position in the hierarchy (Mahalingam, 1998). Even on the most nativist accounts, environmental input must play some role, because at the very least we have to learn which categories to essentialize, given that people in different cultures have different sorts of beliefs about categories such as caste or occupation.

These complex findings tell us that both child biases and environmental input must be having some sort of effect. It is important to avoid dichotomizing explanations of category acquisition and development into "learned versus innate." Explanations do not lie along a unidimensional continuum (Marler, 1991). Parental input and child biases may work together toward a common goal (Markman, 1992), with children's interpretive biases and parents' structuring of the input acting in consistent and mutually reinforcing ways. The real question is: how much of an effect does input have, and by what means?

There are at least three possible sorts of environmental cues that children could (in principle) use: perceptual information, explicit talk, and implicit cues from language. I say "in principle," because I am not assuming that such cues necessarily exist, nor that children are necessarily capable of noting and making use of such information even if it does exist. Rather, in this section I consider these as potential sources of information only.

Perceptual Information

Perceptual information includes observable property clusters, in the Roschian sense. For example, upon noting that cats share a variety of observable features (shape, body parts, fur, type of movement, and a tendency to sleep on laps), a child might be inclined to treat cats as a natural kind about which further inferences can be made. A category such as "furniture" would have much less coherence and would not so easily elicit a kind construal. Although perceptual information would presumably be relatively unvarying across cultures, there is cultural variability in the sorts of perceptual discriminations available concerning certain human kinds (depending on how heavily emphasized and embellished they are, both visually and behaviorally). A blatant example of cultural embellishment is with gender categories, where male/female differences are exaggerated by means of clothing, haircuts, jewelry, make-up, speech patterns, and gait. In some societies, differences in social groups are marked by permanently altering the growth patterns of a developing child, as with cranial deformations (to exaggerate ethnic differences) or foot binding (to exaggerate gender and class differences). At times a society perceptually marks social categories by imposing an identifying symbol on members of a minority group. For example, the Nazis forced German Jews to wear a yellow Star of David, and the Taliban rulers ordered Hindus in Afghanistan to wear an identity label and dress in yellow clothes.

Explicit Talk

Explicit talk includes not only the sorts of folk tales and movies already mentioned at the start of this chapter (such as "The Ugly Duckling"), but also conversations about the real world. Parental explanations of appearance/reality distinctions or category anomalies could potentially appeal to essentialism: "Birds and bats look the same on the outside, but inside they're different in ways you can't see." To examine the role of explicit talk, we would first need detailed information about the sorts of explicit essentialist statements that parents actually provide when talking with their young children.

Implicit Cues from Language

Naming ("This is a bird") seems to "invite" children to form categories (Waxman and Markow, 1995). Parental naming patterns influence categorical structure by demarcating category boundaries. Naming as it interacts with perceptual information could also be informative. For example, if a child hears the same name applied to varied things ("birds" for hummingbirds, eagles, ostriches, and penguins), she might infer that these widely disparate animals have some nonobvious properties in common. Callanan (1990) proposed that parental descriptions may help children learn not just which features or kinds of features to associate with a particular category, but also which categories are coherent and can be expected to share many features. For example, when a parent describes vehicles as "things that move," the child may learn not only that movement is typical of vehicles, but also that vehicles as a class have common properties (even when the information is misleading, as in the example above). In other words, parental descriptions convey information both by their content (i.e., which features correspond to which categories) and by their form (i.e., making statements about the category as a whole versus specific category members, thereby focusing on category coherence).

Parental naming strategies could provide indirect cues as to which names are essentialized. For example, the way superordinates are introduced suggests that they are less central to the identity of an object than are basic-level terms. In particular, parents "anchor" superordinates at the basic level (e.g., when teaching "animal," parents are more apt to say, "This is a cat; it is an animal" than simply "This is an animal") and generally fail to use superordinates to name just a single object (Blewitt, 1983; Callanan, 1989). In this way, different ways of speaking to children may do more than teach new vocabulary; they may be a means of marking which words map onto essentialized kinds.

The next step is to determine the availability of such evidence. My focus here is on the information from social cues: explicit and implicit talk. Is essentialism transmitted to children directly, or do children have beliefs that are not found in the input?

PARENTAL PICTURE-BOOK READING

This chapter reports the data from a project I conducted with John Coley, Karl Rosengren, Erin Hartman, and Athina Pappas: an intensive analysis of conversations between mothers and children as they looked through picture books (S. Gelman, Coley, Rosengren, et al., 1998). In this study, we invited a series of forty-six mother-child dyads to our on-campus laboratory, escorted them to a homey, comfortable room (complete with colorful wall decorations and a cozy couch), provided them with simple picture books to look at and discuss, and otherwise left them to their own devices. (See Table 7.1 for an overview of the study design.) We selected a book-reading task because book reading is a common activity in this culture and provides a context in which information about categories is most likely to be imparted (Lucariello and Nelson, 1986). We videotaped the conversations through a one-way mirror, made careful transcriptions of the conversations that took place, and exten-

Table 7.1. Overview of study's design

	Study 1	Study 2	Study 3
Participants	16 mother-child dyads	14 mother-child dyads	16 mother-child dyads
Child age range	32–38 months	32–40 months	18–23 months
Child mean age	35 months	35 months	20 months
Books	Custom-designed	Commercial	Custom-designed
Domain of books	Animals, artifacts	Farm animals, trucks	Animals, artifacts
N books per dyad	2	2	1

Source: S. Gelman, Coley, et al. (1998). Reprinted with the permission of the Society for Research in Child Development.

sively coded the videotapes and transcripts. These are the humblest of data, gleaned by listening in on the conversations between preschoolers and their parents.

We were interested in two questions. First, do mothers directly teach children the content of essentialist beliefs? Do they teach them, for example, that insides are more important than outsides; that characteristics can be inherited and inherent; or that for some categories, all instances are alike? Second, do mothers convey that certain categories are inference-promoting kinds? Do they focus on objects not as individuals but as members of a category?

In studies 1 and 3, we set up a context that should be most conducive to talk about essences. Each page in the picture books had appearance/reality contrasts: two bats and a bird; two horses and a zebra; two eels and a snake; and so forth. (All pictures were labeled [e.g., with "eel" lettered beneath each eel] so that parents would know the identity of each item.) One picture book focused on animals; the other focused on artifacts. The books were created to control for familiarity, within- and between-category similarity, and likelihood of discussing various kinds of links among items. So, each page included four target items: two instances of the same category (e.g., two horses), one instance of a contrasting category (e.g., zebra), and one item thematically linked to at least one of the two same-category instances (e.g., barn). The books used in studies 1 and 3 are described in Table 7.2. Study 2, in contrast, used commercially available picture books (Helweg, 1978; Mc-Naught, 1978). We included these in order to get converging evidence from books that are more ordinarily encountered in typical mother-child conversations. The mothers were simply told to look through the books with their children as they ordinarily would. They were unaware that we were especially interested in talk about categories or category essences.

A few words about the participants: this was a highly educated sample. All of the mothers had at least some college education, and 78% had at least an undergraduate degree. This was also a highly literate group. On average, parents reported reading to their child about one or two times per day and to have over sixty-five books for that child in the home. The children visited the library over once a month, on average. The mothers read on average over an hour per day, and each of the families subscribed to over six newspapers and/or magazines, on average. In this respect, the sample probably provides a high estimate of the nature and extent of parental essentialist input.

We coded over 3,000 on-task utterances from the mothers (roughly ten utterances per mother per page). There was a great deal of information in the tapes: nearly 40% of these utterances included information that went beyond labeling. As we had hoped, children made abundant naming errors, and consequently mothers had ample and explicit opportunities to explain to children why their classifications were in error. Thus, the data represent not only how mothers talk about categories, but also how they justify categorizations that are in dispute. We scrutinized the videotapes for possible clues in the input language and gestures.

Rather than spin out the tale of our results like a mystery story, with the denoue-

Table 7.2.   Content of books used in studies 1 and 3, by page

Target #1	Target #2	Contrast	Thematic
Animals			
horse	horse	zebra	barn
squirrel	squirrel	chipmunk	acorns
cat	cat	raccoon	ball of yarn
seal	seal	walrus	ball
bat	bat	bird	cave
crab	crab	lobster	pail
dolphin	dolphin	shark	hoop
eel	eel	snake	seaweed
anteater	anteater	aardvark	anthill
Artifacts			
desk	desk	table	chair
book	book	magazine	bookcase
car-clock	clock	toy car	batteries
boot-car	car	boot	traffic light
sneaker	sneaker	thongs	socks
Snoopy phone	telephone	Snoopy doll	notepad
wok	wok	pot	vegetables
safe	safe	refrigerator	money
tongs	tongs	compass	ice

Note: Each row represents a particular page (e.g., horse, horse, zebra, and barn were all on a single page).

Source: S. Gelman, Coley, et al. (1998). Reprinted with the permission of the Society for Research in Child Development.

ment carefully hidden till the end, I will give away the results up front: we found that the mothers did not provide explicit talk about essences. For example, they spent little attention on nonobvious, internal parts, or explicitly detailing the scope of novel properties. However, they did provide much implicit talk about kinds.

EXPLICIT ESSENTIALIST STATEMENTS

The first question was whether mothers provided explicit information that could directly teach children about essences. To review: four-year-olds assume that disparate members of an animal category are alike in nonobvious ways. They also have strong expectations about insides, kinship, origins, teleology, and the appearance/reality distinction (see chapters 2 through 6). So if children are essentialists because their parents train them to be, we would expect to hear mothers say things like the following hypothetical examples:

"All":   "Did you know that all bats give milk to their babies?"

Insides: "This dog has blood and bones inside. He needs them if he wants to stay strong and healthy."

Kinship: "The kitty has stripes because her mommy and daddy have stripes."

Origins: "That bird came from an egg that grew inside her mama."

Teleology: "Polar bears are white because that helps them hide in the snow."

Appearance/reality: "Birds and bats look the same on the outside, but inside they're different in ways you can't see."

We coded the data on the basis of these a priori hypotheses. Here is a sampling of what the mothers actually said, for each of these coding categories. These are typical actual examples:

"All":   "I think . . . roosters all have that thing."

Insides: "Batteries go in the car and the other car and the clock."

Kinship: "There's the mother cat and there's the aby."

Origins: "That's where we get our milk. The cows give us all the milk that we drink."

Teleology: "Look at his nose. That's for eating ants."

Appearance/reality: "These look like snakes, but they're called eels."

The actual examples mothers provided are substantially sketchier than the hypothetical examples. Equally important, these kinds of statements were extremely rare (see Table 7.3).

Table 7.3. Mean percentage of utterances containing explicit essentialist properties, for mothers (for all three studies), as a function of domain; S. Gelman, Coley, Rosengren, et al. (1998)

	Study 1		Study 2		Study 3	
	Animals	Artifacts	Animals	Trucks	Animals	Artifacts
Animal properties						
"All" for whole category	0	0%	0.18	0	0	0
Insides	0	0.58	0	0.63	0	0.19
Kinship	0.07	0	5.90*	0*	0	0
Origins	0.07	0.06	1.33*	0.24*	0	0
Teleology: self	0.15	0	0.13	0.24	0.21	0.18
Appearance reality	1.36*	0.65*	0.24	0.19	1.14	0.18

Note: Asterisks indicate a significant domain difference within a study.

Consider insides, a topic of immense importance in children's judgments of identity, word learning, and causal inferences (see chapters 3 and 5). Parents rarely talked about insides, and when they did, it was exclusively for artifacts (typically batteries). For example:

Mother: And the batteries make the clock go, right?
Child: Yeah.
Mother: And the batteries go inside a toy car too and make it go, right? And this, look at this one. This is a car-clock. So this is a combination of the clock and the toy car. And the batteries all go in this one to make it work. Pretty neat, huh?

Likewise, even though children draw a rich set of inferences based on category membership—for example, inferring that a blackbird feeds its young the same diet as a flamingo, because both are birds—parents almost never expressed the scope of a property in explicit categorical terms (using the word "all" to refer to the whole category, such as "all birds"). They used the word "all," but almost exclusively in ways that did not involve reference to an entire category. Some of these uses were context-bound, referring to all instances on the page (e.g., "All those words begin with A, don't they?" referring to "aardvark," "ant," and "anthill"); other uses were nonquantification (e.g., "You eat them all up"). Across the three studies, out of 120 maternal uses of the word "all," only 2 referred to an entire category. Of the 118 other uses, 27 referred to some specific context of instances, and 91 referred to nonquantificational uses.

Children also have a rich set of beliefs about kinship, origins, teleology, and appearance/reality conflicts. On some of these topics, mothers provided reasonably substantial amounts of input, particularly for appearance/reality conflicts, origins, and kinship. Also, mothers discussed these topics significantly more often for animals than artifacts. Even here, however, the language children heard was sketchy, incomplete, and (we argue) incapable of teaching children essentialism. For example, consider appearance/reality conflicts. Mothers never resolved appearance/reality contrasts in terms of internal parts, inheritance, or the like. Rather, they tended to note the conflict, then go on to the next topic.

Child: That's kangaroo [pointing to aardvark].
Mother   Well, that looks like a kangaroo but it's called an aardvark.
Child: Aardvark.
Mother: There's a white horsie and a brown horsie.
Child: And a zebra.
Mother: Right, a zebra. Looks like a horsie, doesn't it, with stripes.

Mother: Do you know what that one is?
Child: Ummm.

Mother: I don't know if you know what that one is.
Child: That's a snake.
Mother: It looks like a snake, doesn't it? It's called an eel. It's like a snake, only it lives in the water. And there's another one.

Despite the sparseness of these statements, they may be informative. For example, appearance/reality contrasts could imply that there is some (unspecified) quality or qualities that differentiate snakes from eels. The point here, though, is that this potentially informative input is implicit, not explicit. It would then still be up to the child to figure out what form those qualities might take.

What about origins? In study 2, origins were the most frequent of the "essential" properties we coded. However, it turns out that nearly all the references to origins concerned a single fact: where milk comes from. The following is a typical example:

Mother: Do you know where the milk comes from?
Child: The cows.

When it comes to essentialist implications of animal origins (e.g., that identity is given at birth, that parenthood trumps environment, or that animals are not made by humans and therefore have property clusters that must be explained in terms of inherent causes), children seem to be left to their own devices.

Kinship was also one of the most frequent essentialist topics of study 2 and so deserves special mention. That kinship references occurred almost exclusively in study 2 is not surprising, as it was only in study 2 that the books depicted clear family groupings (e.g., a mother cat with a litter of kittens). Both mothers and children were eager to identify which animals on a page were the babies, the mommy, or the daddy. Children even made guesses about kinship relations in the absence of much knowledge, as the example below illustrates:

Mother: A turkey, these are all turkeys.
Child: This must be a baby one.
Mother: Think that's a baby turkey?
Child: And this one too probably is.
Mother: They're pretty big for being babies, aren't they?
Child: Mmmhmm. These are mommies. This is a daddy-mommy.
Mother: OK, it can only be one. A daddy or a mommy. It can't be both.

The vast majority of the kinship talk was limited to a few topics: establishing which picture was which (where is the mommy? the baby?), naming the subkinds (e.g., male goats are called "billy goats"), and analogizing to human roles. Here is a fairly typical example of identification and naming subkinds:

Mother: Do you know what baby goats are called?
Child: Um, what?
Mother: Baby goats are called kids.
Child: Look, he's daddy.
Mother: Yeah, that's a daddy.
Child: That's a mom.
Mother: Yeah, I think you're right.

Both mothers and children at times analogized from animal kinship relations to humans:

Mother: So that's why they don't have any horns, because they're not grown up yet.
Child: Why? But this one is grown up [child is pointing to adult sheep with no horns].
Mother: You know what? I'll bet you that's a mom.
Child: I bet you, too.
Mother: Because they don't say that moms have horns, just the dads.
Child: Daddy does—my daddy doesn't.
Mother: No, I don't think he does. Do you know why?
Child: No.
Mother: Because he's not a sheep.
Child: Uh-uh. You don't because aren't sheep.

Mother: [Pig page] Look at this. I think this one's the daddy. "Hi, guys, I'm goin' off to work now. Anybody want to shake hands?" The mom stays home and take care of the babies, make sure everybody get their breakfast.

These sorts of examples suggest a tendency to talk about kinship as a social/emotional relationship—albeit with physical correlates (e.g., the presence or absence of horns or udders and the size of the babies relative to the mother). Occasionally kinship utterances included mention of biological properties (e.g., baby cows drink their mother's milk; baby ducks come from eggs), yet these were stated as isolated facts, and none were directly essentialist.

Summary

Mothers in our middle-class sample did little, if anything, to teach their children explicitly about essentialism. They simply did not go about teaching their preschool children directly about essential properties. They did not say things like "All birds have bird essences" or "Eels aren't snakes because all eels have certain kinds of parts inside that snakes don't have." It's not really surprising that mothers never mentioned DNA, chromosomes, or internal bone structure, given the age of these children. But it is perhaps more surprising to discover that mention of insides at all was rare, and focused on artifacts more than animals (e.g., batteries). Mothers in our studies did not use "all" as a universal quantifier, even though the word was plentiful in their speech. To the extent that mothers' input in our laboratory reflects their behavior with books at home, it seems implausible that children learn essentialism from this kind of direct statement.

Although one might argue that it would be difficult for parents to talk about such properties (either due to an insufficient knowledge base for these categories, or because the vocabulary for talking about them would be too advanced for a young child), we would suggest that such statements need not be arcane or highfalutin. Some of the justifications obtained *from children* in previous research provide a model for the kind of input that would be simple yet informative (S. Gelman and Markman, 1986, 1987; S. Gelman and O'Reilly, 1988). To quote from some four- to seven-year-olds: "Snakes are a little bit the same and a little bit different. *Inside* they're the same." "That's the way rabbits are, because that's how they are when they're born." "All flowers have nectar in 'em." "A snake has . . . lots of teeny bones, right? So it can wiggle. 'Cause if it was one long bone, it would just have to slide." "Every dog has the same stuff [inside]. . . . Just because [they] have different colors doesn't mean they have different stuff." Input of this sort was exceedingly rare.

Still, the implicit work may be important. For example, mothers' talk about kinship suggests that family relations are not purely social, but are also linked to physical properties such as horns or size. Linking kinship to physical properties is potentially important, because it tells the child (implicitly) that kinship is different from wholly social relationships such as friendship. Kinship talk also indicates that animals that are outwardly very similar can nonetheless be importantly different (e.g., male versus female), and that animals that are outwardly very dissimilar can nonetheless be importantly the same (e.g., parent and offspring). They convey— implicitly—conflicts between appearance and reality. We turn next to consider systematic ways in which mothers seem to provide implicit essentialist information.

IMPLICIT EMPHASIS ON CATEGORIES

Although explicit reference to essences was rare, mothers often stressed the importance of categories using more subtle devices. These were not essentialist statements per se; they did not convey that a nonobvious quality or substance was causally responsible for outward appearances. However, they did reveal a focus on taxonomic kinds. In particular, mothers frequently did two sorts of things that placed implicit emphasis on categories: they linked together two or more individuals of the same kind, in talk or gestures; and they talked about generic categories.

Linking Together Two or More Individuals

Pictures on a page can be considered individually ("Oh, there's a baby cow"). They can also be linked together ("These are special snakes that swim in underwater" [pointing to two snakes]). Mothers often talked about or gestured toward groups of two or more individual objects, linking them together as the same kind of thing.

Mother: What's that?
Child: Cow?
Mother: Well, it looks like—it's kind of big, isn't it? But it's really, these are both the same thing. What's that thing?
Child: Hmmm, a horse.
Mother: And how many horses are there?
Child: Two.
Mother: Right.

Mother: Boy, these are—you do not know these animals. This is an anteater. An aardvark. Can you say that?
Child: Aardvark.
Mother: Yeah, and this is an anteater, too. See, there are two anteaters.

There were several systematic patterns in how these relational statements and linking gestures were used. They disproportionately focused on taxonomically related individuals (e.g., two horses) rather than individuals that were related thematically (e.g., horse and barn) or contrastively (e.g., horse and zebra). Recall that the design of Studies 1 and 3 was such that we could chart the probability of producing each of these sorts of linkages by chance alone. Same-category links, both verbal and gestural, were far more frequent than any other kinds of links.

The patterns found with relational statements and linking gestures were qualitatively distinct from the patterns found with statements about and pointing gestures toward individual objects. For example, relational statements that drew together two pictures on the page were by far most common for the two same-category instances (e.g., the two horses) rather than for any other combination of two pictures. In contrast, statements about items taken individually tended to be higher for either the contrasting-category member (e.g., zebra) or the thematic associate (e.g., barn) than for either of the same-category instances. Much the same finding appears with gestures. Whereas gestures linking pictures were by far most common for the two instances of the same kind (e.g., gestures linking horse$_1$ and horse$_2$ were much more common than gestures linking any other two pictures), points to single objects were equally frequent for each of the four pictures on a page (e.g., horse$_1$, horse$_2$, zebra, and barn). By focusing on an item as one of a group, mothers may subtly convey taxonomic information.

DOMAIN DIFFERENCES IN LINKING OF MULTIPLE INDIVIDUALS.   Given that natural kind categories are, on the whole, more richly structured than artifact categories (S. Gelman, 1988; Keil, 1989), we hypothesized that mothers would talk differently about animals versus artifacts. In fact we found pervasive domain differences in all three of the studies. Mothers provided more relational statements for animals than for artifacts, and related both members of the target category (e.g., both horses) more often for animals than for artifacts. This difference occurred not only in maternal speech but also in gestures: mothers linked together same-category instances in their gestures more frequently for animals than for artifacts. An important control for these domain differences arose in maternal talk and gestures about individual items: when mothers talked about or pointed to pictures considered singly, no consistent domain differences emerged. In other words, the domain differences involved category structure, not just information about individuals. Altogether, then, maternal input makes available a wealth of information about the importance of taxonomic categories and also differentially emphasizes the importance of categories for animals versus artifacts.

To return to the issue with which I began this section, we can conclude that maternal input does provide children with a rich albeit subtle database regarding category structure. The statements and gestures that link together two or more instances of a category are interesting in several ways: taxonomically related instances are drawn together more than any other kind of instance, attention to same-category membership is stronger for animals than for artifacts, and the distribution of talk about groups (of two or more) differs from the distribution of talk about individuals. This sort of information could encourage essentialism; children may notice that two animals that look very different get the same name, and that two animals that look very similar get different names. However, two caveats are important to keep in mind. First, the input here is very implicit. The child would need to bring much to the table in order to extract essentialism out of these fragmentary cues. Second, we do not know whether children pick up on this information.

Generic Noun Phrases

The most dramatic sort of reference to more than one individual was the generic construction, in which the speaker talked about the category as a whole—*chipmunks* as a general kind, not any individual chipmunk or individual set of chipmunks. Generic noun phrases in English are expressed with bare plurals (e.g., "*Bears* hibernate in winter"), definite singulars (e.g., "*The elephant* is found in Africa and Asia"), or indefinite articles (e.g., "*A male goose* is called a gander"), and are accompanied by verbs that are typically nonpast and nonprogressive. Because there is no one-to-one relation between form and generic function, meaning and context are required in order to reach a generic interpretation (e.g., "the elephant" may refer to a particular elephant or to the kind). Generics are distinctive in referring to a category as an abstract whole, rather than referring to an individual or group of individuals (Carlson and Pelletier, 1995; Lawler, 1973).

SEMANTICS OF GENERICS.   Lyons suggests that generics can often be translated roughly as "generally," "typically," "characteristically," or "normally" (though not as "necessarily"). Unlike statements using "some," generics invoke the entire category. Yet unlike statements using universal quantifiers such as "all," "every," or "each," generic statements often allow for exceptions (Lawler, 1973, p. 329; McCawley, 1981). The statement "Birds fly," for example, is considered true, even though penguins, emus, and ostriches cannot fly. In contrast, "*All* birds fly" is false. As a consequence, generic statements are perhaps more powerful than utterances with universal quantifers. Whereas even a single counterexample would negate the generalization "All boys play with trucks," the generic statement "Boys play with trucks" can persist in the face of numerous counterexamples. In the extreme case, generic statements may be false of most or all previously encountered instances (e.g., racial or ethnic stereotypes). Therefore, generics are potentially more robust as input than statements explicitly generalizing to the entire category.

The degree to which generics allow for exceptions varies considerably, such that generics cannot be equated with any particular quantifier, such as "most." For example, the statement "Birds lay eggs" is true, even though less than half the bird population does so (excluding male birds and chicks). The generic "The trout reaches a length of 30 cm." is also true, even though less than 5% of all trouts reach this length (thanks to Herey, 1985, for this example).

Generic statements refer to kinds (Carlson, 1977), or to individuals as representatives of kinds (Herey, 1985). The generic statement "Birds lay eggs" can be paraphrased as "Birds are a *kind of* animal such that the mature female lays eggs" (Shipley, 1993). Shipley (1993, p. 278) proposes that a generic statement such as this, "which presupposes the conceptualization of the class of birds as a single entity, should enhance the psychological coherence of the class of birds for that reason." Mayr (1991, p. 42) likewise suggests: "He who speaks of 'the Prussian,' 'the Jew,' 'the intellectual' reveals essentialistic thinking. Such language ignores the fact that every human is unique; no other individual is identical to him." Generics may be a subtle but effective device used by parents to convey that members of a taxonomic category share properties.

Generics express qualities that are relatively essential, enduring, and timeless (Carlson and Pelletier, 1995). Properties stated generically are not essential in the sense of being true of all instances of the kind, yet they are relatively more essential than nongenericized properties. For instance, although it is not essential that seals bounce balls (neither all seals nor only seals bounce balls), it is a distinctive, nonaccidental property of seals. In contrast, nongenerics ("*These bats* live in a cave," "*My cat* caught two mice," "There are *some dinosaurs* in the museum") refer to accidental, transient, or contextually bound properties. Properties that by definition refer to the category as a whole, such as "extinct" (also known as "kind-level-predicates"; Herey, 1985) can be predicated only of generic noun phrases—again illustrating the link between generics and nonaccidental properties. Accordingly, we can say that dinosaurs are extinct, but we cannot say that a particular dinosaur or set of dinosaurs is extinct.

Generics also express properties that are normally true of instances of a given kind. "Normally true" implies "naturally, inherently true," at least in the case of natural kinds (Prasada, 2000). For example, consider the generic sentence, "Dogs have four legs." In Prasada's terms, four-leggedness is "part of the 'blueprint' that the process of growth or creation is trying to implement, and thus in normal circumstances caused by it" (p. 129).

GENERICS IN THE MATERNAL DATABASE.   Table 7.4 contains examples of generic noun phrases drawn from our database. Generic noun phrases refer to a category (e.g., bats) as an abstract whole. They do not just refer to pictures on the page; they refer to the larger category of which the instances on the page are just examples. Generics refer to kinds (see also Shipley, 1993; Wierzbicka, 1994, on kinds).

In our sample, most of the mothers produced at least one generic statement (90% of the mothers of thirty-five-month-olds; 69% of the mothers of twenty-month-olds), and many produced several. Mothers averaged about 3.27 generics per 100 utterances (see Table 7.5). Although this percentage may seem low, I argue that it represents a substantial and potentially salient amount of input to children. Nouns can function in many different ways, including generic reference, singular definite reference, general definite reference, nonreferring definite reference, distributive general reference, collective general reference, specific indefinite reference, and nonspecific indefinite reference (Lyons, 1977, pp. 177–197). Given this variety of functions, any given noun phrase type will constitute only a small fraction of speech. Accordingly, even the most salient of noun phrase types will occur in less than the majority of utterances. (Analogously, although food is a highly salient and important concept for young children, mention of food appears in much less than half of their utterances, because there are many competing topics of conversation.)

Table 7.4.   Sample generics produced by mothers; S. Gelman, Coley, Rosengren, et al. (1998)

"Bats are one of those animals that is awake all night."
"That's not the ocean, but they do live at—seals live in the ocean really."
"Roosters are man chickens, male chickens."
"A wok is how people in China cook. Well, actually, a wok is how people in America cook like Chinese people."

Table 7.5.   Frequency of maternal generics (as mean percentage of on-task utterances); S. Gelman, Coley, Rosengren, et al. (1998)

	Animals	Artifacts
Study 1	5.15	1.44
Study 2	5.30	0.82
Study 3	6.05	0.85

In order to determine the relative salience of generics, it is therefore misleading to consider the proportion of speech containing generics, and more meaningful to consider the absolute frequency of such speech. As mentioned earlier, 83% of the mothers produced at least one generic in the brief session, which typically lasted no more than about fifteen minutes. (In contrast, only 56% of the mothers talked about numbers, and only 37% of the mothers referred to object shape.) During this session, each mother produced on average approximately 189 utterances, 3% to 4% of which were generics (i.e., 7.25). By extrapolation, this suggests that children would typically hear over 30 generics per hour, if placed in a comparable context. Indeed, the rate at which generics are produced in maternal speech is comparable to the rate at which mothers produce causal language (Hickling and Wellman, 2001) and exceeds the rate at which children produce genuine psychological references to thoughts and beliefs at six years of age (Bartsch and Wellman, 1995). In our own sample, the rate of generic usage was greater than the rate at which mothers talked about object size (3.09% of utterances), color (1.96% of utterances), number (0.77% of utterances), shape (0.35% of utterances), or texture (0.22% of utterances). By contrast, truly rare linguistic forms, such as the dative passive, would be found much less frequently.

Mothers talked about the category as a whole even when all they could see on the page was a single instance ("That's a chipmunk. And *they* eat the acorns"; "And this is *a seal*. And *they* clap their hands together like this" [emphases added]). Mothers (and at times children) moved seamlessly from considering a single instance to generalizing about the broader kind (see examples below). It is as if the speaker were saying (implicitly): there is an entire class of things just like this one.

Mother: And here's an aardvark.
Child: Oh.
Mother: Mmm.
Child: What's he eat?
Mother: I don't know what they eat. Maybe they eat ants, too, or bugs.
Child: Oh.
Mother: I think they have long tongues.
Child: Oh.
[In this example, the child makes a specific reference; the mother responds with a series of generics.]

Mother: Well, there's this, this animal that I've never met before.
Child: What is it?
Mother: He's called an aardvark.
Child: What do they do?
Mother: You know, that's a good question. I'm not that familiar with aardvarks. We're going to have to look it up and see if we can find out more about aardvarks. Or maybe we can ask somebody.

[In this example, the mother is specific; the child responds with a generic, which the mother then picks up on.]

DOMAIN DIFFERENCES IN GENERICS. Mothers' generics were strikingly domain-specific, appearing significantly more frequently for animals than artifacts (M percentage of coded utterances containing a generic was 5.50% for animals and 1.04% for artifacts). The domain differences in generic usage cannot be attributed to frequency of talk about animals and artifacts overall, since we controlled for that by calculating percentages of coded utterances. They also cannot be attributed to familiarity with the category, similarity among category members, thematic relatedness among category members, or amount of maternal talk. We controlled for similarity and thematic relatedness by selecting the stimulus materials from a larger set of items that were pretested on adults, and we controlled for familiarity and amount of talk by conducting analyses that took into consideration the amount of talk and maternal ratings of child familiarity. The domain differences are also unlikely to be attributable to lack of sufficient knowledge about the artifacts. Mothers certainly knew several category-general properties true of each artifact depicted (including its parts, function, thematic associates, and appearance), and mentioned many of these properties in reference to particular objects and contexts. Importantly, though, mothers typically failed to mention these properties in generic form.

Why, then, did animals elicit so many more generics than artifacts? We interpret this result as reflecting conceptual differences between animal and artifact categories. Animal categories are more "kindlike" than categories of artifacts (see Keil, 1989; S. Gelman, 1988). Where direct comparisons of animals and human-made artifacts have been conducted, clear domain differences appear as early as age three or four years. These comparisons include studies of internal parts (R. Gelman, 1990; Simons and Keil, 1995), object identity (Keil, 1989), inheritance (Hirschfeld, 1995; Springer, 1992), origins (S. Gelman and Kremer, 1991; Keil, 1989), self-generated movement (R. Gelman et al., 1995; Massey and Gelman, 1988), and spontaneous growth and healing (Backscheider et al., 1993; Rosengren et al., 1991).

The beliefs children express include the following: Animals have richly structured internal parts that differ from their exteriors and cause self-generated movement; simple artifacts have the same parts inside as outside, and their inner parts are unrelated to movement. For animals, transformations cannot influence the item's identity; for artifacts, changes can alter identity. Animal properties such as skin color and build are inherited from biological parents; for artifacts, no such inheritance process is possible. Animals originate by means of a natural, self-generated, inherent process; artifacts originate by means of a human or humanlike "other" who creates the item (P. Bloom, 1996). In animals, growth and healing are highly patterned, predictable processes stemming from the animal itself; in artifacts, size changes and mending are less predictable and require external agents of change.

On the assumption that mothers construe animal kinds as more richly structured than artifact kinds (deeper similarities, greater coherence, and all the rest), they should more easily conceptualize animal categories as abstract wholes, and hence use generics. Consistent with this interpretation, maternal generics were much more domain-specific than generics found in the written texts of the books used in study 2. Recall that study 2 used two commercially available picture books: one about farm animals and the other about trucks. Coding of the texts of these books revealed many generics in both the farm animal and truck domains (Ms = 67 versus 50 generics per 100 coded utterances, respectively), with no significant domain differences in generics found in the texts. The domain difference in maternal speech was tilted much more heavily toward animals, suggesting the importance of maternal conceptual biases. Maternal biases may in turn inform children's acquisition of the very same animal/artifact distinction.[1]

POSSIBLE FUNCTIONS OF GENERICS.   There are at least three potential functions that generics may serve for young children. (See chapter 8 for more evidence and discussion.) First and most obviously, generics may teach children particular category-wide generalizations. From maternal generics, children can learn particular facts concerning animal vocalizations, habitat, diet, behaviors, and so forth. Because these properties are predicated of the kind as a whole, they may become more central to children's conceptual representations than they would be if they had been stated nongenerically. Furthermore, because these facts are stated generically (rather than as universal quantifiers), they may be particularly robust against counterevidence (e.g., "birds lay eggs" allows for male birds, whereas "all birds lay eggs" does not; Krifka et al., 1995; Lyons, 1977). Even erroneous properties stated generically, such as stereotypes concerning gender or race, may be more difficult to counter and erase than erroneous properties stated absolutely.

A second potential function of generics may be to imply that members of a category are alike in important ways, even beyond the particular properties mentioned in the generic statements. In other words, hearing generic statements about a category may lead children to treat this category as one about which indefinitely many category-wide generalizations could be made. Generics may serve this function even when the information is relatively superficial (e.g., "Little rabbits are called kits"), or when little or no new information is provided (as with questions, for example, "How do they [bats] sleep?"), because the generic form itself implies that category members are importantly alike. If so, then there should be measurable effects of introducing novel categories with generics as opposed to nongenerics. This suggestion fits with recent experimental evidence that when teachers emphasize category membership in the classroom—even in seemingly superficial ways—children hold more stereotyped social beliefs (Bigler et al., 2001).

Shipley likewise proposed that a grouping becomes a "kind" (i.e., richly structured, inference-promoting) when a person "projects a property onto individual members of a class" (1993, p. 270). In other words, when a person learns a new property of a category as a whole, that category is hypothesized to cohere in novel ways. Shipley suggests that a generic statement such as "Birds lay eggs," "which pre-supposes the conceptualization of the class of birds as a single entity, should en-hance the psychological coherence of the class of birds for that reason" (p. 278). For example, the child may then hypothesize that she can make numerous other novel inferences about the class of birds.

A third possibility is that overall amount of generic talk may foster or inhibit es-sentialist reasoning. That is, variation in frequency of generic expression (whether it be individual variation, or variation that correlates with some other factor such as language or culture) could conceivably influence essentializing more broadly. Consider a child who hears plenty of kind terms, but exclusively in reference to in-dividuals ("Here's a soft kitty," "Baby Ben can't use that cup yet," "Those flowers could use some water"). Now consider a child who hears plenty of kind terms, but with generics mixed liberally in ("Kitties are so soft," "Baby Ben can't use cups yet," "Flowers need water"). It seems at least possible that extravagant use of generics might encourage a focus on individuals as representing kinds.

CONCLUSIONS

Despite a wealth of studies detailing children's category knowledge, very little is known about *why* children have an essentialist bias. A critical piece of the puzzle would seem to be the nature of the information children encounter. Do parents teach essentialism to their young children—either directly or indirectly? The work described in this chapter characterizes maternal talk in a middle-class U.S. sample, both to provide a descriptive database and to make inferences about the role of children's contributions.

We found a mismatch between maternal speech documented in this project and children's knowledge as revealed in prior experimental tasks. Although children have a rich set of beliefs about insides, teleology, and animal origins (see chapters 3, 4, and 5), mothers provided almost no corresponding input about these topics. We found no evidence that mothers teach essentialism to their children. This finding is particularly striking, given that studies 1 and 3 used books that were specifically designed to focus mothers on category boundaries and deceptive appearances. From other evidence (mothers' appearance/reality statements and children's frequent naming errors), we know that the specially prepared picture books succeeded in providing appearance/reality conflicts; nonetheless, these books did not foster much discussion of nonobvious properties. It seems that children may be largely constructing essentialist beliefs themselves based on indirect evidence.

Essentialist talk in the input was implicit rather than explicit. Mothers implied, with their gestures and relational statements, that certain objects go together; and with their generics, they implied that certain categories promote inferences. They did not explicitly state that categories are richly structured, or that category mem-bers share nonobvious essences; nor did they talk about properties shared by all category members. These findings suggest that if maternal input exerts an influence, it is of two sorts: mothers teach children about kinds, not about essences, and mothers help children identify which categories are richly structured. I briefly expand these points below.

Kinds versus Essences

The present data do not support a developmental story that says children build up beliefs about category structure from particular facts about internal, nonobvious similarities shared by particular instances of particular categories. Rather, children seem to have a general understanding that categories are important, inference-promoting, richly structured entities. This "framework," "skeletal," or "placeholder" understanding gets filled in with specifics only later (R. Gelman, 1990; Medin, 1989; Wellman, 1990). Recall the distinction from chapter 1, between kinds and essences. Kind information conveys that different instances cohere into a richly inference-promoting category (Gopnik and Meltzoff, 1997; Schwartz, 1977, 1979), without explaining the basis of the category, or what nonobvious substance or property holds the category together. In contrast, essentialist information conveys the underlying causal force that holds the category together, be it material substance such as DNA or something else (soul, vital force).

The input characterized in these studies is of the first sort: it conveys that animals are sorted into kinds, but does not describe or explain the basis of kind membership. The findings are therefore consistent with Simons and Keil's (1995) proposal that children proceed from abstract to concrete rather than the reverse. Maternal input provides an abstract framework in which taxonomic categories (particularly taxonomic animal categories) are important, but little specific information regarding precisely how or why.

Keil (1998) suggests that children may play an important role in the parental strategy of relying on sketchy input and avoiding detailed didactic explanations: children are easily "satiated" (as are we all) by explanatory regress (Harre and Madden, 1975). "Rather than try to load the child down with what would ultimately be an impossible burden of detail, the parent is instead showing the child how to approach various domains and allowing the child to proceed to discover the details at her own pace" (Keil, 1998, p. 152).

Keil provided an amusing example of what happens in the rare instance when a parent does attempt a more explicitly didactic strategy. In trying to explain to their two-year-old why grasshoppers hop, one child's parents discussed contracting leg muscles at great length, with an earnestly detailed exposition. Keil concluded:

> The child looked ever more like a captive, eyes darting about for any alternative venue, and finally got up and ran over to a stream. The parents, noticeably exhausted from their intense efforts at explicit instruction, looked at each other in frustration, the father finally suggesting that perhaps their son was not really interested in biology and that they should try something else, like chemistry. They went over to the stream and started explaining the molecular nature of water. (Keil 1998, pp. 149–150)

The point here is clear: detailed, explicit teaching is unlikely to find a receptive audience in a toddler or young preschooler.

Identifying Richly Structured Categories

Maternal input is potentially most useful in helping children figure out *which* categories are richly structured. The input from mothers in the present studies is redundantly informative about distinctions between animals and artifacts. The suggestion that subtle features of maternal input exert an influence could help explain how children in different cultures distinguish among categories of different types. Children must learn the classifications of their culture—for example, that certain racial or ethnic distinctions are perceived as "deep" in their society, but that other social contrasts are not.

At this point it is important to clarify two things about these suggestions. First, positing that maternal input influences concept acquisition does not mean that children are passive recipients or blank slates. I am suggesting quite the opposite. Biases in maternal input can converge with children's conceptual biases (Markman, 1992). The implicit nature of the input suggests that maternal and child biases probably do converge: if children are making use of the input, they must have sufficient orienting biases to allow them to pick up on subtle cues.

Second, although parents of these young children provide little explicit essentialist talk, I suspect that eventually parents do talk with their children about domain-specific properties that inform naive theories (for example, that members of an animal kind tend to be alike with respect to bone structure, inheritance of eye color, innate potential for height, and so forth). As children get older, particularly as they encounter biological information in schools, parents are likely to provide much information to help children elaborate their biological theories. These facts may be details that get filled in, after children have initially established that certain categories are richly structured.

Generalizability Issues

The present study of mother-child conversations is just a first step, and raises questions concerning the generalizability of these results. One question is whether the input provided in these book-reading contexts reflects the input children receive in other contexts. It is possible, even probable, that specifically focused contexts would elicit from mothers more talk about biological processes, internal parts, or nonobvious similarities. For example, a book about the internal workings of the human body would undoubtedly yield talk about internal biological parts, and a book about adoption would probably foster discussion of origins, innate potential, and kinship relations. It is also quite possible that children's spontaneous questions provoke relevant explanations and information (Callanan and Oakes, 1992). For example, discussion of family resemblance could imply essentialism ("You have your Grandpa's nose"; "Blood is thicker than water"). Yet even here, unless the information gets considerably more explicit, more is left unsaid than said. For example, saying "You have your Grandpa's nose" could still leave open the possibility that the resemblance was passed down by nonessentialist means, such as intentions or shared activities.

A second issue regarding the generalizability of these results concerns how parents from other cultural backgrounds talk about essentialism. Parents from different cultures show substantial variability in how they talk to their young children (Heath, 1983; Lieven, 1994; Schieffelin and Ochs, 1986). It is striking that our highly educated sample did not provide more explicit input. After all, we might expect such a sample to provide talk that is especially didactic and precise. I suspect, therefore, that explicit essentialist talk to children is rare throughout the world. What is less clear is whether the implicit devices detailed here are found broadly across cultures (though see chapter 8 for cross-cultural evidence of generics in child-directed speech).

Summary

In speech and gestures to young children (twenty and thirty-five months of age), mothers provide much information beyond simple labeling. This information is subtle yet potentially highly informative: mothers link together different category instances (in relational statements, generics, and/or gestural links) without being explicit about how these instances are alike in important and nonobvious ways. Mothers do not seem to teach children directly that categories have essences. However, maternal input does suggest that certain categories have inductive potential, by focusing on certain objects not just as individuals but as members of a larger category. These data suggest possible mechanisms by which a notion of "kind" is conveyed in the absence of detailed information about category essences.

The mothers we studied emphasized category relations, but they did not explicitly illuminate or elaborate on them. On the one hand, it is interesting that a variety of subtle devices were frequent even in input to the younger children (twenty-month-olds). On the other hand, it is interesting that the input was not very explicit, given that our participant sample was highly educated and placed great value on books and literacy. One might expect a sample such as ours (primarily middle class, college educated, and sufficiently motivated to participate in research without compensation) to engage in relatively sophisticated talk, with relatively high levels of discussion and explanation. Instead, our results suggest that the input functions in a specific way: it implies that certain categories are important, without explaining their underlying or biological basis.

To be clear, however, that such input is available does not necessarily mean that it is used by children. I follow up on some of these findings in chapter 8, where I examine how children respond to the language devices parents use most frequently.

Chapter 8

Essentialism in Language

> If Adam had called a camel a camel, then this particular combination of
> sounds expressed and contained the camelness of camel, the essence of
> camel.
>
> Robert South, seventeenth-century Anglican preacher, paraphrased in
> Hans Aarsleff, "Language and Victorian Ideology"

In this chapter I make the case that language exerts important influences on essentialist reasoning. This argument is potentially precarious. Some very persuasive arguments have been mustered to suggest that language should have no substantive role in the formation or structure of essentialized categories (e.g., Pinker, 1994). Arguments *against* linguistic effects on concepts include the following important observations. Language does not appear to be necessary for forming categories, since prelinguistic infants acquire many categories (Balaban and Waxman, 1997; Mehler and Fox, 1985), and even use categories to form inferences about unknown properties (Baldwin, Markman, and Melartin, 1993; Hayne, Rovee-Collier, and Perris, 1987). Young children treat categories in essentialized ways, long before the introduction of formal schooling or scientific principles (S. Gelman and Coley, 1990). Also, as we saw in chapter 7, parents provide little or no direct instruction about essences in their ordinary conversations with children (S. Gelman, Coley, Rosengren, et al., 1998). To some extent, then, children construct essentialist beliefs spontaneously. Finally, there are striking cross-cultural similarities in conceptual organization in speakers of widely varying cultural backgrounds (Atran, 1990; Berlin, 1992). These similarities appear to include an appeal to category essences. The picture that emerges—of essentialist beliefs early in childhood, universally attained in the absence of instruction—suggests a robust capacity that spontaneously develops rather than an acquired set of beliefs that are susceptible to varying linguistic input.

Why then would I wish to argue for the importance of language? Because two additional points lead to the conclusion that essentialism is not *wholly* a wired-in capacity, and that language can bolster essentialist tendencies. First, as discussed in chapter 7, there is cross-cultural variation regarding which categories support rich inferences and essentialist accounts (e.g., Bloch, Solomon, and Carey, 2001). A striking example is caste in India, which is essentialized more among upper-caste

than lower-caste individuals (Mahalingam, 1998). A person's occupation is likewise treated differently in different historical periods: essentialized in nineteenth-
century Britain (Thompson, 1963), but treated as relatively superficial by preschool
and elementary school children in the United States today (Hirschfeld, 1996). Similarly, class can be viewed either as fluid and circumstantial or as deeply rooted and
essential. Consider the following discussion, which contrasts class distinctions made
in the current-day United States with those made in early-twentieth-century Peru
(e.g., *gente decente* [respectable people] versus *gente de pueblo* [common people]):

> [Peruvian class terms] referred to sorts of people rather than to locations in a fluid
> social structure. Unlike such terms as upper, middle, and lower class, which might de-
> note momentary economic status, *gente decente* and *gente de pueblo* were *moral* cate-
> gories, signifying intrinsic qualities, not transitory circumstances. By using these
> terms, Latin Americans constructed a vision of society in which status was clearly as-
> cribed: either one was born *decente* or one was not. Respectability was a matter of
> blood and character, innate and unchanging. As a result, the distinction between
> *gente decente* and *gente de pueblo* tended to be seen in rigidly dualistic terms, follow-
> ing an "us and them" logic that left scant middle ground. . . . [Members of the soci-
> ety] shared the same linguistically constructed assumption that decency reflected
> some inner essence. (Parker, 1998, pp. 24–25)

Obviously, cultural variation in essentialism cannot be innately determined. We
must therefore look toward other means of expressing and conveying cultural differences in belief systems. Language is one potential means of conveying cultural
beliefs.

In addition, language has at least two expressive functions that are directly relevant to the inductive potential of categories: conveying membership in a kind (e.g.,
by labeling an entity with a common noun, or by referring to kind membership
with the word "kind"), and expressing scope of a proposition (e.g., with logical
quantifiers, such as "all," "some," or "most," or with generic noun phrases, such as
"*Bears* hibernate in winter"). I propose that these two functions of language cannot be expressed nonlinguistically. There is simply no unambiguous way to carry
out either function without words for things. For example, it is difficult to imagine
how a nonlinguistic species could convey that a legless lizard *really is* a lizard, even
though it looks outwardly just like a snake. With language, however, such a concept
is elegantly expressed (e.g., "This is a lizard"). Likewise, no process of enumerating
and displaying examples can convey unambiguously that all birds have hollow
bones, whereas this is an uncomplicated linguistic effort. Given the relevance of
these functions for induction and category-based reasoning, the relative ease of
conveying these functions via language, and the difficulty of expressing them by
nonlinguistic means, there is reason to suspect that language plays a role in the
structure of people's categories.

My goals in this chapter are to lay out the claims and linguistic devices (as there
are different, competing theoretical arguments in the literature for how language

leads to essentialism), as well as the developmental evidence. I discuss two primary ways that language seems to affect the construction of essentialized kinds. One is by conveying membership in a richly structured category (naming), the other is by expressing the scope of a proposition (generic noun phrases). I then contrast these with two forms that, although potentially relevant to essentializing, are not used to essentialize (the word "kind" and universal quantifiers). I end by cautioning that, despite the importance of language, there is no compelling evidence as yet that language creates an essentialist stance, or that essentialism requires language.

NAMING

One recurring idea is that essentialism is somehow linked to names for things (see also the discussion in chapter 2). Here I need to be clear that by "naming" I mean labels for kinds (words such as "dinosaur," "tiger," or "New Yorker"), and not labels for individuals (such as "Emily" or "Bertrand") or nonlabeling words (such as "bereft" or "crunchy"). Historically, names were thought to reflect essences in a true and fundamental way, as in the quote from Aarsleff that began this chapter. More recently, this view has been modified as a psychological claim to argue that names are erroneously assumed to reflect essences. As Haslam puts it: "One commonly voiced account of essentialist thinking is that it reflects the mistaking of verbal sameness for underlying nonverbal sameness, the idea that what is denoted by a single label must itself be a single kind of thing" (1998, p. 305). Likewise, Mayr suggests:

> Essentialism's influence [on pre-Darwinian philosophers] was great in part because its principle is anchored in our language, in our use of a single noun in the singular to designate highly variable phenomena of our environment, such as mountain, home, water, horse, or honesty. Even though there is great variety in kinds of mountain and kinds of home, and even though the kinds do not stand in direct relation to one another (as do the members of a species), the simple noun defines the class of objects. (1991, p. 41)

Similarly, Piaget proposes that "in learning the names of things the child at this stage believes it is doing much more. It thinks it is reaching to the essence of the thing and discovering a real explanation" (1929, pp. 61–62). These views suggest that there is a bias or error in the power that people assign to words.

Sperber also argues that essentialism is triggered by cultural input in the form of labels. He suggests that merely hearing a noun label for a living thing is sufficient to provoke an essentialist construal of that species (1996, p. 144). Carey further suggests that category labels do not merely reflect essentialism, but in fact are the root of essentializing:

> Essentialism, like taxonomic structure, derives from the logical work done by nouns. The child has a default assumption that count nouns are substance sortals, i.e. nam-

ing concepts that provide conditions of identity during the maximal lifetime of an entity . . . the application of every count noun carries with it the idea that the identity of the entity picked out by the noun is unchanged in the face of surface changes. I submit that biological essentialism is the theoretical elaboration of the logical-linguistic concept, substance sortal. (1995, p. 277)

Although Carey is not specific about the process by which essentialism appears, this quote seems to suggest something like the following: a fundamentally accurate understanding of how words work (that they typically pick out context-independent kinds, such as "person," rather than context-specific concepts, such as "ticket holder") is extended and somehow taken too far, so that children assume that nouns refer to kinds that are fixed, unchanging, and determined by underlying features. One point that is not clear in Carey's account is whether the original impetus to look for kinds depends on language, or whether it is a prelinguistic capacity that gets strengthened by means of language. For example, would people who are not exposed to conventional systems of naming (such as deaf individuals not exposed to sign language; see Goldin-Meadow and Mylander, 1990) also exhibit essentialism?

Similarly, Waxman (1999; Waxman and Markow, 1995) argues that words serve as "invitations to form categories." As Waxman suggests:

Words focus infants' attention on commonalities among objects, highlighting these especially in cases where the perceptual or conceptual similarities may not be as apparent as at the basic, or folk-generic, level. . . . This can have dramatic consequences, inviting the child to notice deeper and more subtle commonalities than those that served as the initial basis of the grouping. In this way, naming may itself help to advance the child beyond perceptible commonalities among objects, pointing them toward a richer appreciation of the deeper, nonperceptible commonalities that characterize human concepts. (1999, p. 269)

In this section I want to consider just what is meant by saying that essentialism is linked to naming. I will argue that names are important for conveying to children membership in a kind, and so indirectly tell children when and what to essentialize, but that there is no evidence yet that names also encourage children to essentialize (as argued by Carey and Mayr). Although children treat certain names as reflecting essentialism (see below), I suspect that essentialism does not require naming in a fundamental way. Essentialism as a cognitive principle probably does not derive from naming. Instead, naming plays a secondary—though important—role.

Names Tell Children Which Individuals Belong to the Same Kind

Labeling is a pervasive and powerful way of conveying category membership to young children. As we saw in chapter 2, children can make use of words to redraw category boundaries (S. Gelman and Markman, 1986). To the extent that a category is essentialized, then, labeling tells children which entities share an essence. For example, naming a pterodactyl "a dinosaur" (despite its birdlike appearance) changes the type of inductive inferences young children make about the animal (S. Gelman and Coley, 1990). The naming effect is particularly relevant in border-line or atypical cases, in which a nonlinguistic analysis might diverge from label-ing. Children show these effects as early as twelve months of age—the very initial stages of word learning (Graham, Kilbreath, and Welder, 2001, 2002).

Examples of this effect can be found in natural interactions outside the labora-tory as well. For example, Shatz describes a time when her grandson Ricky, age twenty-one to twenty-two months, saw a panther at the zoo. As she tells it, Ricky's initial reaction was to say, "Meow, meow." His mother explained, "That's a panther. It's more like a tiger than a cat." Ricky responded, "Grrrrr." Shatz concluded:

> Thus, Ricky was able to make use of Alice's [mother's] words to infer that, even though an animal may look like one thing, if it *is like* another thing, it will behave like the other thing. . . . Ricky's example suggests that, although appearance is an im-portant clue about how to categorize the world, even before age two, children dis-cover more subtle organizations than those based on appearance alone. Names for things are important clues to categorization. (1994, p. 71)

I would add that Alice's use of a new name for the animal ("That's a panther") may have been crucial in convincing Ricky that the animal was "more like a tiger than a cat." The label told Ricky that not only was the animal *like* another thing, it *was in fact* another thing.

In these examples, labeling works by invoking a known category (such as "dino-saur"), and conveying that item X belongs to that category. Words like "dinosaur" are entrenched kinds for children. It is unknown how the category initially came to be treated as richly structured, but language has the nontrivial role of expressing what belongs in that kind. In these examples, category labels are communicating kinds, not constructing them. Words for nonkinds (words such as "sleepy" or "Sally" or "likes the color green") do not have this power.[1]

Children treat category labels as real, not as arbitrary conventions (Piaget called this "nominal realism"; Piaget, 1929; Markman, 1976). One seven-year-old child worried aloud that since nobody lived at the time of the dinosaurs, it would be im-possible to know if the names we use for them are the right ones; for example, maybe the brontosaur should actually be called the triceratops (Gail Heyman, personal communication). (When I mentioned this anecdote to a nine-year-old I know, her response was, "I don't think they have the wrong names, because they found the fos-sils and stuff"—once again revealing the nominal realist assumption that there is a right or wrong name.) It is this assumption that labels reveal the true identity of a thing that leads to rich category-based inferences in such young children.

Names Tell Children Which Categories Are Kinds

An immediate question that arises is whether the power of names is restricted to familiar, entrenched labels that have already proven themselves to have inductive potential (labels such as "tiger" or "dinosaur"), or whether even wholly novel labels can serve this function (labels such as "tapir" or "kinkajou"). Both Davidson and Gelman (1990) and Graham, Kilbreath, and Welder (2001) found that novel labels can be interpreted as inference-rich. But what is the nature of the generalization children have formed? Clearly not all words map onto essentialized kinds—a point I argued in chapter 2 when I reviewed the numerous control studies in which certain types of words failed to promote inductive inferences.

Some of the descriptors or phrases that do not seem to indicate essentialism to children include: temporary states (e.g., "sleepy"), preferences ("likes the color green"), proper names (e.g., "Sally"), and property descriptions (e.g., "has andro in its blood"). This collection suggests perhaps a general distinction between common nouns and other parts of speech (adjectives, proper names, verbal phrases). In other words, children may have a general assumption that common nouns refer to essentialized kinds (as implied by both Carey and Mayr).

There are two wrinkles in this formulation. First, the generalization runs into an immediate snag with count nouns that are poor candidates for essentializing: count nouns that refer to superordinate-level categories (such as "a pet"), count nouns that refer to contextually limited groupings (such as "a passenger" or "a ticket holder"), count nouns that refer to shape (such as "a square"), and (perhaps) count nouns that refer to human artifacts (such as "a cup"). I will set aside the issue of artifacts for now, as they raise a complicated set of side issues (including the possibility that artifacts may indeed be essentialized, just differently from natural kinds; see chapters 6 and 11). But what about "pet," "occupant," and the like? Words such as these demonstrate that there is not a foolproof, airtight link between formal cues—such as those marking nouns—and essentialism.

However, the problem shrinks to manageable proportions when we note that by at least three years of age children expect that the first count noun they learn for an object will be its basic-level kind name (Hall, 1993; Hall and Waxman, 1993; Markman, 1989). Parental input supports this assumption, by which I mean that parents typically teach the basic-level count noun for an object before introducing superordinate level names or situated-restricted words (Callanan, 1985; Hall, 1994). Furthermore, when a count noun refers to a group of objects with no perceptual coherence (those with as much between-category similarity as within-category similarity), children treat the label differently, and do not expect it to have inductive potential (Davidson and Gelman, 1990).

I suggest the following modified proposal: children may provisionally assume that the first count noun they learn for an object is its basic-level kind-referring name (e.g., "dog"—not "pet," "Fido," "passenger," "friend," "oblong," or "plaything"). For relevant domains (such as animal and plant species, natural substances, and human kinds), it is this privileged class of names that receives essentialized status. This provisional assumption is "soft," in the sense that it will be dropped in the face of strong contradictory evidence (for instance, if the initial set of exemplars lack perceptual coherence). It is not a hard-and-fast constraint.

Even so, such an assumption would place a great deal of power into the hands of language.

The second wrinkle, namely, a need for empirical data, is a bigger one. There are two sorts of data we would need to see: that speakers have an assumption that extends beyond familiar, entrenched labels, and that speakers have an assumption that is limited in scope and excludes non-count-noun form classes. Below I review the available evidence from adults and children.

PRIVILEGED STATUS OF COUNT NOUNS FOR ADULTS.   There is now growing evidence that nouns may carry implications beyond other linguistic expressions (see Gentner, 1982). Markman (1989) hypothesizes that referring to a category with a noun conveys that a category (1) supports more inferences, (2) provides more essential information, (3) is central to the identity of an object, (4) is relatively enduring and permanent, (5) is organized into taxonomies, and (6) is unique and nonoverlapping with other categories. In a nutshell, category labels (e.g., "tattletale," "nerd") seem intuitively to tell us what an entity is, not just what an entity is like (Markman, 1989). Many properties that could be construed as temporary states ("Sally didn't clean up her room today") may seem more enduring and fundamental when expressed in the form of a category label ("Sally is a slob"). In contrast, referring to a category with an adjective implies that it supports fewer inferences, provides less essential information, is less central to an object's identity, and so forth.

Some indirect evidence for this semantic contrast between nouns and other expressions comes from a study of compound nouns in English (Clark, Gelman, and Lane, 1985). Using an elicitation task, Eve Clark, Nancy Lane, and I found that preschool children express enduring links between two objects with compound nouns, whereas they express temporary links between two objects with other descriptive phrases. For example, a tree with branches ending in pencils might be called a "pencil-tree" (noun), whereas a chair with a toy duck sitting on it might be called a "chair with a duck on it" (descriptive phrase). Only the stable, intrinsic property is captured in a noun; the momentary juxtaposition is expressed by other means.

Ellen Markman and Ed Smith (cited in Markman, 1989) tested these ideas directly in a series of studies with adults. On one task, participants were asked to list properties of a series of categories. Depending on the condition, categories were either nouns (e.g., "an intellectual") or adjectives (e.g., "intellectual"), matched for semantic content. Subjects listed more properties of the nouns than of the content-matched adjectives (Ms per item of 4.0 versus 3.1, respectively). On another task, subjects were given a direct contrast between nouns and adjectives and asked which was more important and why. These adults judged nouns as conveying more powerful information than adjectives, and often explained their choices by suggesting that the noun was more enduring and central to category identity.

In an honors thesis conducted at the University of Michigan, Cristine Cunningham Reynaert conducted a follow-up to Markman's study, focusing on language for mental and physical illnesses (Cunningham, 1999). Reynaert compared three kinds of wording: nouns (e.g., "He is a schizophrenic"), adjectives (e.g., "He is schizophrenic"), and possessive phrases (e.g., "He has schizophrenia"). She hypothesized that nouns would be most powerful, as in Markman and Smith's work, and that adjectives would be more powerful than possessive phrases. Saying that someone "is" something seems to imply permanence; saying that someone "has" something seems to imply that it could be temporary. (These intuitions already guide informal practices. For example, one colleague was asked by an editor to substitute the phrase "children with autism" for "autistic children." He was told that "autistic children" implies that autism defines the identities of the children in question, whereas "children with autism" implies that autism is one of many possible facets of the children.)

On one task, ninety-six University of Michigan undergraduates were given triads of descriptors, describing the same illness in one of three forms: count noun (e.g., "She is a diabetic"), adjective (e.g., "She is diabetic"), or possessive phrase (e.g., "She has diabetes"). Twelve triads were supplied, listing twelve different illnesses, half mental and half physical (see Table 8.1). For each triad, participants asked to rank-order the strength of the three statements, as "strongest," "middle," and "weakest."

For mental illnesses, there were powerful wording effects. As predicted, nouns ("is a") were rated most strongly ($M = 1.68$ on a scale of 1 to 3, with 1 being strongest), adjectives were intermediate ($M = 2.03$), and possessive phrases were weakest ($M = 2.29$). All three wording types were significantly different from one another. Participants gave justifications that supported their judgments, for example, "A *neurotic* labels him and defines him, just *neurotic* tells us something about him but doesn't define him. *Has neurosis* makes it sound like a cold—not the kind of person he is." "Being an asthmatic is saying you definitely have asthma and it is a part of you." "Both [is and is a] sound like it's her identity. The weakest [has] sounds like more of a diagnosis, rather than a statement claiming who she is."

Surprisingly, there were no significant wording effects for physical illnesses. However, this null result may be due to the nouns being unfamiliar in several cases

Table 8.1.   Items used in Reynaert and Gelman study

Mental disorders	Physical disorders
Alcoholism	Arthritis
Anorexia	Asthma
Manic-depression	Diabetes
Neurosis	Epilepsy
Psychosis	Hemophilia
Schizophrenia	Paralysis

(e.g., "a paralytic," "a hemophiliac," and "an epileptic" are all unusual). For example, one participant wrote, "I think people know 'paralyzed' better than 'paralytic' and think of it [paralyzed] more strongly." Overall, the results suggest a subtle variation in strength implied by the form in which an illness is expressed, with nouns most powerful, adjectives intermediate in power, and possessive phrases weakest.

PRIVILEGED STATUS OF COUNT NOUNS FOR CHILDREN.   Novel category labels are important sources of information for children, compared to conditions in which they hear no labels at all (Balaban and Waxman, 1997; Markman and Hutchinson, 1984; Waxman and Hall, 1993; Waxman and Markow, 1995). Children are also sensitive to linguistic form-class (e.g., nouns versus adjectives) in some cases as early as two years of age (R. Brown, 1957; S. Gelman and Taylor, 1984; Hall, 1994; Hall, Waxman, and Hurwitz, 1993; Katz, Baker, and Macnamara, 1974). For example, children appropriately assume that a novel noun refers to a class of like objects, whereas a novel adjective refers to a single property.

However, I know of only a few studies that directly contrast nouns with other parts of speech, in terms of essentialist sorts of inferences. Hall and Moore (1997) directly contrasted adjectives and nouns, and found that preschool children and adults distinguished adjectives and nouns on the basis of form class alone. In their studies, children heard familiar color terms in either adjective or noun form, applied to a set of novel creatures. For example, in one experiment, the distinction between nouns and adjectives was supplied morphosyntactically: e.g., "This is a blue one" (adjective) versus "This is a blue" (noun). In further experiments the distinction was supplied phonologically: e.g., "This is a blue bírd" (adjective) versus "This is a blúebird" (noun). Children were then asked to judge which of two pictures was also "a blue one" / "a blue bird" (adjective condition) or "a blue" / "a bluebird" (noun condition). Participants chose between pictures depicting either an object-kind match (the same creature or bird but now covered with a red substance) or a property match (a different creature or bird that was blue in color). Both four-year-olds and adults used lexical category (noun or adjective) as the basis of their judgments. On hearing an adjective, participants typically selected the property match, whereas upon hearing a noun, participants typically selected the object kind match. One way of interpreting these results is to say that nouns led to judgments of greater stability—that is, object identity was preserved with nouns but not adjectives.

Gail Heyman and I designed a study to test whether lexicalization per se—that is, characterizing a person or object with a classificatory label—carries implications beyond the literal information conveyed. In a sense this study is a follow-up to the Markman and Smith work with adults, only we focused on children. Specifically, we compared labels with roughly equivalent verbal descriptions. Labeling may imply that the information provided is particularly stable and immutable. Giving a label may reify a category in a way that other ways of referring to the same information does not. We find intuitive support for this hypothesis in noting that labels can be separated from the behaviors they describe (e.g., "I believe in equal rights for women, but I'm not a feminist").

A classic example comes from the case of John Rocker, a baseball player for the Atlanta Braves who was roundly criticized for making a racist comment in an interview. When he later tried (unsuccessfully) to explain himself, an ABC News reporter asked him directly, "Are you a racist?" Rocker replied: "Absolutely not. . . . You hit one home run in the big leagues, it doesn't make you a home run hitter. . . . To make one [racist] comment like this doesn't make you a racist." In these cases, a label conveys that someone is a member of a category (with implied stability and centrality to identity), whereas the behavioral description conveys that someone has a particular attribute (with implied temporary status and distance from central identity). (Rocker's line of reasoning concerning the relevance of a single action, however, seems disingenuous. On analogy, would someone who kills just one person not be a murderer?)

Interestingly, Gail Heyman's daughter Alison spontaneously invoked a similar distinction at four years of age, when she was recounting a problem she was having with a boy named Gabriel. She told her mother, "Gabriel didn't just hurt me! He hurt other kids, too! He is *a hurter*! Right, mom? He is *a hurter*." Alison implied that "a hurter" is someone who habitually hurts people, perhaps even (if I might be permitted some interpretive leeway here) someone for whom hurting is an intrinsic aspect of their nature.

To date, nearly all studies of lexicalization effects have focused on familiar labels. With known words, it is difficult to tease apart effects of the information conveyed in the label from effects of the label form itself. Distinguishing between these factors is crucial for understanding why lexicalization and essentializing are linked. It could be that concepts so important as to be essentialized are prime candidates for lexicalization because of their salience, frequency, and stability. If that were the case, then lexicalization might have no cognitive effects. Gail Heyman and I (S. Gelman and Heyman, 1999) examined whether the linguistic form itself is sufficiently powerful to produce inferences of stability. We tested this possibility by using novel nominalized phrases, to prevent listeners from simply retrieving previously learned meanings. During the experimental sessions, four child characters were described. Each was described as having an idiosyncratic characteristic (e.g., loves to eat carrots). Then, each was described with either a novel noun (e.g., "She is a carrot-eater"; label condition) or a descriptive phrase (e.g., "She eats carrots whenever she can"; verbal predicate condition). Each characteristic was chosen as one that could be construed as either temporary or stable. We hypothesized that labels would imply greater stability of the characteristics. Children were then asked a series of questions designed to assess their judgments of the stability of the characteristic, over time and across contexts.

Participants were five- and seven-year-old children, randomly assigned to either a label condition or a verbal predicate condition. Each participant received four item sets. For each item set, participants heard a three-sentence description, followed by a set of four test questions. The three-sentence description included the character's name and age, a distinctive behavior that the character characteristically engages in, and either a noun label (label condition) or a description in the form of a verbal predicate (verbal predicate condition). For example, for one story, the description was as follows: "Rose is eight years old. Rose eats a lot of carrots. (She is a carrot eater [label condition].) (She eats carrots whenever she can [verbal predicate condition].)" The verbal predicates were designed to restate the information in the previous statement in a slightly different form. The labels were designed to refer to the same information, using a single compound noun phrase.

Aside from the carrot-eaters item, the other items concerned a boy who thinks creatures live on other planets (a creature believer), a boy who wakes up early (an early waker), and a girl who really loves guinea pigs (a guinea-pig lover). (By the way, although these labels may seem a bit whimsical, real-world counterparts really do exist. I recently read an article in the *Ann Arbor News* about members of the Flat-Earth Society, which referred to "Flat-Earthers" and "globalists.")

The four test questions for each item set concerned the stability of the key property (e.g., eating carrots). They concerned past behavior ("Did Rose eat a lot of carrots when she was four years old?"), future behavior ("Will Rose eat a lot of carrots when she is grown up?"), behavior with no family support ("Would Rose eat a lot of carrots if she grew up in a family where no one liked carrots?"), and behavior with family opposition ("Would Rose stop eating a lot of carrots if her family tried to stop her from eating carrots?").

Responses were scored as 1 for each stable response ("yes" to the questions regarding prior behavior, future behavior, and no family support; "no" to the question regarding family opposition), 0 for each nonstable response ("no" to the questions regarding prior behavior, future behavior, and no family support; "yes" to the question regarding family opposition), and 0.5 for each "don't know" response. As predicted, children expected significantly greater stability in the label condition than in the verbal predicate condition (see Table 8.2). To examine whether these effects hold for each of the four item sets, we examined responses for each item set separately. In every case, the label condition was significantly higher than the verbal predicate condition.

To summarize the results of this study: by five years of age, children judged personal characteristics as more stable when they were referred to by a noun ("She is a carrot eater") than by a verbal predicate ("She eats carrots whenever she can"). Children in the label condition predicted that characteristics were more stable over time and adverse environmental conditions. This finding is consistent with a range of other findings showing that people possess strong stereotypes of social categories encoded in labels (Darley and Fazio, 1980), and that nouns are particularly important for implying that a category is richly structured (Hall and Moore, 1997; Markman, 1989). These findings also extend beyond previous work in showing that labels differ from verbal phrases that convey the same information. The present findings are also noteworthy in that all the characteristics were relatively novel

Table 8.2.   Mean percentage of predictions that the characteristic would be stable, as a function of age, condition, and
property type; S. Gelman and Heyman (1999)

	Condition	
Property type	Label	Verbal predicate
5-year-olds		
Past	70%**	62%
Future	82***	63
No family support	69**	54
Family opposition	79***	71**
7-year-olds		
Past	73**	71**
Future	77***	65**
No family support	66*	48
Family opposition	76***	66*

Notes: Each mean was submitted to a t-test to determine whether it
deviated from chance performance (50%).

   * $p < .05$

   ** $p < .01$

   *** $p < .001$

(e.g., carrot eater, creature believer). Children were not retrieving rote meanings,
but rather were making use of a general rule that they applied to these novel noun
phrases. Heyman and I concluded that lexicalization (in the form of a noun) provides important information to children regarding property stability.

Conclusions

Labeling is an important mechanism for expressing kind membership (and indirectly essentialism) to young children. This effect is quite general, revealed both in
children's reasoning about familiar category labels (such as "a bird" or "a dinosaur") and in children's reasoning about novel category labels (such as "a fep" or
"a blicket"). Children's use of familiar category labels suggests an implicit, powerful realism concerning well-known kind terms. Their use of novel category labels
suggests a ready sensitivity to formal linguistic cues, from a remarkably young age.
Both cases demonstrate that labeling has special implications.

However, the formal cues are not sufficient to explain the data. There is not a
simple, perfect link between nouns and essentialized kinds. Labeling cannot wholly
solve the problem of how children decide which categories to essentialize, as some

common nouns do not map onto natural kinds (e.g., "passenger," "pet"). Nouns are also not the only means of conveying kind membership, as adjectives such as "shy" and "smart" serve the same function (Heyman and Gelman, 2000b). Children make use of a theory-based understanding: they attempt to calculate which words map onto kinds by using whatever information is at hand, including (but not limited to) formal morphosyntactic cues. I will have more to say about this issue in chapter 9. (See also P. Bloom, 2000.)

Some readers may wonder how I can argue that count nouns promote essentialist thought, at the same time that I insist that essentialism is domain-specific in its application (see chapter 6). After all, count nouns are used for all domains, including such obviously nonessentialized artifacts as containers and wickets. Why then do we not essentialize containers and wickets? Because naming links to essentialism only indirectly. Names per se do not imply essentialism. Rather, a name is one clue that the entities being named have shared category membership and form a kind. Children's domain-specific assumptions about the nature of kinds combines with their assumptions about naming, to yield essentialist effects. To return to the carrot-eaters study: the label "carrot eater" implies a coherence and stability to the category of people who eat carrots whenever they can. However, this implication in part follows from our assumptions about kinds of people. I suspect that if we were to conduct a parallel study with artifacts (e.g., regarding tools that are "carrot dicers" rather than people that are "carrot eaters"), no labeling effects would emerge.

There are still many questions remaining, all concerning in one sense or another the scope of children's reasoning. We still do not know, for example, what sorts of essentialism are linked to naming, beyond the documented effects. Specifically, supplying a name encourages children to form inductive generalizations and treat a category as stable over time. Do names also encourage children to assume—at least in certain domains—that a category has a biological basis, that it is innately determined, passed along from parent to child, and localized in the brain?

We also know little about the differences between different linguistic forms, in the richness of concepts they imply. Perhaps there is a hierarchy, with common nouns most reliably anchored to essentialized kinds, followed by adjectives, followed by verbal phrases. Or it may be that the clues offered by linguistic form class become less reliable and more contextually variable once one moves away from common nouns.

Another unresolved issue is whether different domains make use of different sorts of linguistic cues for their expression. Adjectives, for example, may be much more potent when referring to human traits than when referring to nonhuman characteristics (a possibility suggested by the data Gail Heyman and I gathered, comparing construals of people versus dolls; Heyman and Gelman, 2000a). I also suspect that effects of linguistic form will be more effective for domains in which outward perceptual cues are more ambiguous. For example, social categories seem less clear-cut and more open to alternative construals than do animal species. Consequently, social categories may be more susceptible to language effects on children's conceptualizations. (See Diesendruck, in press, for more extensive arguments for interactive effects of domain and language.)

Finally, and most important: does naming play a role in constructing an essentialist stance to begin with? The data reported to this point concern the conditions under which children of a given age either do or do not draw essentialist sorts of implications from labels. They have not stepped back to ask the more challenging question of why lexicalization and essentialism are linked to begin with.

I will return to this question in the conclusions to the present chapter and in chapter 11. But my brief response to the question, for now, is skeptical regarding the role of language in constructing an essentialist stance. To see why, let me first suggest what the naming-as-driving-essentialism position might look like. If naming were to play a critical role in the initial formation of essentialism, it would presumably be along the lines sketched out by Mayr and others, and summarized by Haslam: names draw together, and imply sameness among, unlike things (penguins and robins are "birds"; Great Danes and chihuahuas are "dogs"). Children may confuse verbal sameness with nonverbal sameness (in Haslam's phrase). They may come to assume that entities with no outwardly observable commonalities must share something in common—something that is hidden and unobservable, yet important enough to warrant a label.

The problem I have with this sort of account is the following: why should children accept these labels as kind-referring to begin with? Why, for example, should children treat the robin-referring "bird" as the same kind of thing as the ostrich-referring "bird"? They could treat them as they do proper names or homonyms—as words that are coincidentally extended to unlike things, with no further implications. Children do not draw name-based inferences from one child to another just because both are called "Lily," they do not draw name-based inferences from a flower to a child just because both are called "Lily," and they do not draw name-based inferences (as far as I know) from baseball equipment to a flying mammal just because both are called "bats" (see P. Bloom, 2000, for more extended discussion). My daughter, Stephanie, at preschool age gave a clear example of assuming that two ontologically distinct things do not form a coherent kind, despite sharing a name. One night at dinner she observed, "Isn't it funny: 'chicken' sounds just like 'chicken'!" At first I didn't understand and asked her to repeat herself. After she did, I asked whether she meant that the chicken that we eat sounds like the chicken that says "buk-buk." She said that yes, that was what she meant. I then made the mistake of explaining that this is because the chicken we eat *is* the chicken that says "buk-buk," at which point she threw the piece of chicken she was eating across the table and became an avowed vegetarian for the next couple of weeks.

My point is that children would (hypothetically) have the option of ignoring same-namedness, if they did not *already* have the insight that unlike things can belong to the same natural kind. In order to benefit from naming, children need first to have some fairly deep insights into how naming works. (See also Wittgenstein, 1953: "One forgets that a great deal of stagesetting in the language is presupposed if the mere act of naming is to make sense.") Labeling is an important *cue* for children's essentializing, but it is unlikely to be its *cause*. I suggest that there are several more likely sources of initial essentialism, including infants' rich inferential capacities, even before the emergence of language (see more discussion in chapter 11). On this view, essentialism is initially a nonlinguistic assumption that is intensified by language and that over time comes to be cued by words.

GENERIC NOUN PHRASES

The second linguistic expression I consider is the generic noun phrase (e.g., "*Dogs* bark," "*A giraffe* is an animal," or "*The hippo* is a four-legged beast"). Initial discussion of generics appeared in chapter 7. Generics are potentially important for conveying generalizations about shared properties of category members (Carlson and Pelletier, 1995). They can do so in at least two ways. First, they involve properties that are definitional, recurrent, or lawlike (Dahl, 1975), and generally true of the prototype. Thus, they are useful for making predictions and may be particularly important for conveying that categories have rich structure. Second, they make reference to objects as a category, rather than objects as individuals (see Lyons, 1977). For example, "Dogs are friendly beasts" refers to the category of dogs, rather than any particular dog or group of dogs. Indeed, some properties are true *only* of the category, and not of any individual, such as, "Dinosaurs are extinct" (no particular dinosaur or dinosaurs can be extinct—only the species).

Children and adults use knowledge about kinds to form overarching hypotheses ("over-hypotheses") that apply generatively to novel categories, for example, "each kind of animal has its own characteristic sound" (Shipley, 1989, 1993). Children appear to generate such over-hypotheses on the basis of experience with a limited set of familiar kinds, which then allows them to generate novel inferences about unfamiliar kinds (e.g., that armadillos have a characteristic sound), even in the absence of any further information about that kind (e.g., without knowing anything about armadillos other than that they are a kind of animal).

There are at least three conditions that must be met for generics to play a role in early essentialism: they must be available in the input to young children, they must be used in ways that map onto relevant conceptual distinctions (distinguishing kinds from other categories), and they must be understood by young children. In the remainder of this section, I argue that all these criteria are met in early childhood. These results are surprising in light of two traditional assumptions about children's language: that parent-child conversations focus on the here and now, and that children's concepts focus on the immediate, concrete present. Both of these conclusions must be revised in light of the findings I report below.

Frequency of Generics in Child-Directed Speech

Until recently there was little direct psychological study of generics, nor any reports of their distribution in adult or child speech. Yet in categorization research, generics frequently appear in experimental materials, perhaps with an implicit recognition of their significance (e.g., Abelson and Kanouse, 1966; Kanouse, 1987; Kanouse and Abelson, 1967; Rips, 1975; Waxman, Shipley, and Shepperson, 1991; Waxman, Lynch, et al., 1997).

There are also anecdotal reports of generic usage (though not typically characterized as such) in studies of children's and/or parents' spontaneous comments. For instance, in her examples of how parents introduced novel categories to their preschool children, Callanan (1990) included generic statements such as, "They [hummingbirds] sort of make a humming sound" or "A mixer is what we use to mix things up in the kitchen." Similarly, Shipley (1989) mentioned that, in her studies, preschool children (some as young as three years of age) referred to animal kinds with generic statements including: "Dogs go ruff-ruff and them have long tails" or "Animals can't talk." Likewise, Adams and Bullock (1986) found that parents of three-year-olds provide generic statements such as, "They [penguins] live at the South Pole and they swim and they catch fish."[2]

These informal reports suggest that generics are used in ordinary speech. Likewise, one primary finding from chapter 7 was that generics were ubiquitous in child-directed speech during picture-book reading. Nearly all of the mothers in our study made at least one statement including a generic noun phrase during the brief session. Mothers used generics for both relatively familiar categories (e.g., "*Kitty cats* love to unravel yarn") and relatively unfamiliar categories (e.g., "*A wok* is how people in China cook. Well, actually, *a wok* is how people in America cook like Chinese people"). They talked about the category as a whole even when all they could see on the page was a single instance ("That's a chipmunk. And *they* eat the acorns").

Table 8.3 shows the frequency of generics in maternal input, from several independent studies, and confirms that generics are common in the speech that young

Table 8.3.   Maternal input regarding generics

Study	N	% Ss producing Generics	Language	Activity	Domain	Mean % generics
[1]	46	83%	English	book	animals	5.50%
			English	book	artifacts	1.04
[2]	26	92%	English	book	animals	11.00
[3]	24	100%	English	book	mixed	3.28
			English	toy play	mixed	0.65
	24	88%	Mandarin	book	mixed	1.64
			Mandarin	toy play	mixed	0.18

Key: [1] S. Gelman, Coley, Rosengren, et al. (1998), 20 and 35 months; [2] Pappas and Gelman (1998), 30 and 45 months; [3] S. Gelman and Tardif (1998), study 2, 20 months. (Study 1 included contexts that varied by language; study 2 controlled for contexts across languages and so is reported here.)

children hear. Mothers consistently produced more generics regarding animals than artifacts, controlling for the amount of speech in each domain. This distributional difference suggests that mothers favor generics especially for richly structured kinds (see chapter 7 for more discussion of this point).

Distribution of Generics versus Nongenerics with Respect to Number

I suggested earlier that, if children are to make use of generics in implying essentialized kinds, then generics must differ systematically in meaning from nongenerics. One subtle piece of evidence that generics are conceptually distinct from nongenerics comes from how number (singular versus plural) matches or mismatches nonlinguistic context. In the picture-book-reading task described in chapter 7, mothers showed an occasional mismatch between the number of available category instances and the plurality of the noun phrase used (S. Gelman, Coley, Rosengren, et al., 1998). Specifically, mothers at times used plural generics even when only a single instance was visible in the picture (e.g., "That's a chipmunk. And *they* eat the acorns"). Similarly, sometimes mothers shifted between singular and plural forms (e.g., "Did you know when *a pig* gets to be big, *they're* called hogs?"). This pattern is striking, because on the surface it would appear to be a blatant error: reference to a single individual with a plural noun. However, I suggest that the "error" is in fact not an error at all, but rather reflects the semantics of generic nouns. Specifically, both singular and plural forms refer to the generic category. For example, "they" in the chipmunk utterance refers not to the chipmunk identified in the previous sentence, but rather to chipmunks as an abstract kind. If my interpretation is correct, then these mismatches suggest that generics are not tied to a particular set of instances present in the immediate context but rather refer to the category as a larger whole.

In order to argue that generics refer to categories as distinct from individuals in the immediate context, two alternative explanations need to be ruled out. First, the use of plural noun phrases in the context of a single instance could simply be an error. Parents may occasionally use the wrong form, due to forgetfulness or slips of the tongue. For example, a mother may have intended to say "*it eats* the acorns," but said "*they eat* the acorns" instead. Second, the number mismatch may reflect use of "they" as a gender-neutral pronoun. Because it was not possible to detect whether the animals in the picture book were male or female, perhaps participants, uncertain of whether to say "he" or "she," opted for "they." If either alternative account is apt (errors or gender-neutral pronouns), then we should find the same mismatch between plural noun phrases and single-exemplar contexts with nongeneric utterances as with generics. For example, if the gender interpretation is correct, then parents should just as often say things like, "See this bat? *They* came from the cave over there" (i.e., using "they" in a nongeneric sentence) as "See this bat? *They* live in caves" (i.e., using "they" in a generic sentence). In contrast, if the number mismatch pattern is distinctive to generics, it would provide indirect evidence for a conceptual distinction between generic and nongeneric constructions.

To summarize, if generics and nongenerics are semantically and conceptually equivalent, then they should not differ from one another in the distribution of linguistic form (singular versus plural) across depicted contexts (individual instance versus multiple instances depicted on a page). However, if generics and nongenerics are semantically and conceptually distinct, then their distributions should differ, with generics eliciting more plural forms in single-instance contexts.

Athina Pappas and I designed a study to address this issue (Pappas and Gelman, 1998). Pappas conducted this study as an undergraduate honors thesis under my supervision. She asked mother-child pairs to look through picture books about animals. She had specially created the books so that each page included either a single instance of a category (e.g., one crab) or many instances of a category (e.g., many crabs), in this way manipulating contexts by varying the number of items on a page. There were sixteen pages per book: eight pages depicted a single animal on each; eight pages depicted many (twelve to fifteen) animals of a given category on each. The number of instances were counterbalanced across books (e.g., book A included one crab and many rabbits; book B included many crabs and one rabbit).

Twenty-six mother-child pairs participated, with children ranging in age from twenty-three to fifty-seven months (mean age thirty-eight months). Participants were seated in chairs at a table and told that they would be given a picture book for them to look through and talk about as they typically would at home. Pappas videotaped the sessions; a set of assistants later transcribed the videotapes. A coder then identified all noun phrases (proper nouns, common nouns, pronouns, and adjectival noun phrases) referring to the target items—for example, on the rabbit page, all noun phrases referring to rabbits, whether depicted on the page or not. Utterances containing the target noun phrases were then coded for number (singular versus plural) and generic status (generic versus nongeneric). The data are presented in Table 8.4.

Both mothers and children produced generics in different contexts than nongenerics. Whereas the linguistic form of nongenerics closely matched the number of pictures in the context (with singular noun phrases typically used for single-instance pages and plural noun phrases typically used for multiple-instance pages), such was not the case for generics. Page type had no effect on the form of generic utterances. Generic plurals were used just as often in the context of single-exemplar pages as in the context of multiple-exemplar pages, at times resulting in the sort of "mismatches" described earlier. For example, in one transcript, the mother referred to an individual ostrich as "ostrich," and the child replied, "They stink," using a plural pronoun following reference to an individual.

Although we had predicted that generics would be relatively more independent of context than nongenerics, the size of the effect was rather surprising: for generics, linguistic form was wholly independent of context, as measured by number of

Table 8.4. Mean percentage of coded utterances containing generic and nongeneric noun phrases (NP) as a function of speaker, age, page type, and linguistic form; Pappas and Gelman (1998)

	Generics		Nongenerics	
	One instance	Multiple instances	One instance	Multiple instances
Mothers				
Singular NP	1.42	1.08	38.00	21.2
Plural NP	5.42	3.38	2.08	26.8
Children				
Singular NP	0.04	0.08	19.69	9.8
Plural NP	1.04	0.58	0.58	12.61

items on the page. In other words, mothers and children were no more likely to access the larger category when presented with many instances than when presented with just one. The fact that even a single instance of the category could trigger a generic utterance suggests that children and parents were thinking about individual animals in two ways, both as individuals and as instantiations of a kind. In summary, generic noun phrases differ in their semantics and conceptual organization from nongeneric noun phrases, both in the input to young children and in children's own speech.

Generics in Mandarin Child-Directed Speech

Formal analyses suggest that generics are not peculiar to English but are expressed in a variety of languages (Carlson and Pelletier, 1995). In this section I discuss generic usage in Mandarin.[3] Mandarin poses a particularly interesting contrast to English, given claims in the literature that it is especially unsuited to generic expression. It therefore provides an especially strong test of the generality of generics in input speech.

Mandarin lacks three of the grammatical distinctions used to identify generics in English: articles, plurality, and tense. A fourth grammatical distinction (aspect) does not always appear in Mandarin, and is even ungrammatical with some verb types (Li and Bowerman, 1998). As a consequence, there are sentences in Mandarin that could be translated as either generic or nongeneric in English (Krifka, 1995). For example, the following sentence:

xiao3	ya1zi	yao2yao2bai3bai3	de	zou3	lu4
little	duck	waddlingly	DE	walk	road

could be translated in any of three different ways:

- The duck is waddling,
- The ducks are waddling, or
- Ducks waddle. / A duck waddles.

Only the third is generic. We cannot conclude, however, that Mandarin fails to express generics. There are subtle semantic and pragmatic cues that may help clarify the status of an utterance (Krifka, 1995). The absence of specific number, time, or place markers can imply a generic interpretation—in Mandarin as well as English. Nonetheless, because Mandarin lacks articles, plurality, tense markings, and (sometimes) aspect, the expression of generics is less overt in Mandarin than English. Thus, the difference between English and Mandarin in generic expression is a matter of degree rather than a qualitative difference.

There is in fact a long-standing but previously untested claim that these linguistic differences lead to corresponding conceptual differences in how speakers of Mandarin versus speakers of English think about generic kinds (A. Bloom, 1981; Moser, 1996). A. Bloom (1981) states the linguistic relativity hypothesis most starkly. He asserts that Chinese has no mechanism for signaling generic concepts (p. 38) and suggests:

> Perhaps the fact that English has a distinct way of marking the generic concept plays an important role in leading English speakers, by contrast to their Chinese counterparts, to develop schemas specifically designed for creating extracted theoretical entities, such as the theoretical buffalo, and hence for coming to view and use such entities as supplementary elements of their cognitive worlds. (p. 36)

Bloom's suggestion has two parts: (1) a claim that generics have no means of expression in Chinese, and (2) a claim that this linguistic difference leads to corresponding conceptual differences. Yet, on his own admission, Bloom had insufficient evidence for this position (p. 36). Specifically, to provide preliminary support, he presented a single sentence to 110 Taiwanese subjects: "Dai4shu3 shi4 chi1 luo2bo de dong4wu4"[4] [(The) kangaroo(s) is/are (a) turnip-eating animal(s)]. Subjects were asked whether the sentence, "in addition to referring to an actual kangaroo, to some actual kangaroos or even to all actual kangaroos, might have an additional interpretation, for example, as a conceptual kangaroo" [guan1nian4 shang4 de dai4shu3]. A positive response to this question was deemed evidence of a generic interpretation. Thirty-seven percent of the subjects said yes, which Bloom interpreted as a low number, and most of the "yes" responders already knew English, suggesting that their interpretation could have been influenced by their knowledge of English, rather than a functional knowledge of generics in Mandarin. Bloom inferred from these results that Chinese speakers have difficulty grasping generic concepts, though he cautioned that further research is needed.

This initial study, though intriguing, raises a variety of questions (see also Lucy, 1992, for a related critique). First, it requires a difficult metalinguistic judgment. The question itself is ambiguous (what is meant by a "conceptual kangaroo"?) and likely to lead to confusion. Second, the experiment included only Mandarin speakers tested in Mandarin. Because there was no comparison group of English speakers, it is difficult to know whether 37% agreement is relatively high or low, and impossible to draw cross-linguistic conclusions. We cannot assume that English speakers would perform any differently.

Another limitation is that, in his analysis of English, Bloom focused on the definite singular form of the generic ("the X"), and did not discuss either the indefinite singular form ("an X") or the bare plural construction ("Xs"). One can form generics in English using any of these three forms (e.g., "the kangaroo is a turnip-eating animal"; "kangaroos are turnip-eating animals"; "a kangaroo is a turnip-eating animal"). I suggest that the notion of "a conceptual kangaroo" is sensible only when one focuses on the definite singular form of the generic (which, incidentally, is the least commonly found form in ordinary speech; Pappas and Gelman, 1998). When considering plural generics (e.g., "Kangaroos are turnip-eating animals"), it no longer seems apt to regard the generic noun phrase as referring to a conceptual individual. Plural generics call to mind the category as a whole (e.g., the category that includes most or all kangaroos), rather than a single abstract entity (e.g., a conceptual kangaroo).

Finally, in an anecdotal example provided by Bloom to illustrate lack of generic understanding, one speaker provided evidence that I interpret as potential sensitivity to generic concepts. The example concerns an adult speaker with "a very modest command of English" who claimed not to understand the question about a conceptual kangaroo. However, Bloom went on: "From the generality of the content of the statement and the lack of any kangaroos in the vicinity or previous mention of any, she inferred that the sentence must be referring to plural kangaroos; in fact, to all kangaroos [suo3you3 de dai4shu3]." I suggest that this capacity to differentiate between particular kangaroos in specific contexts and the set of all kangaroos nicely captures the distinction between nongeneric and generic interpretations. Unfortunately, it is not clear how frequently people reached this interpretation, as Bloom did not report (and appears not to have asked) how many of the 110 speakers interpreted the sentence as referring to the set of all or most kangaroos. In sum, Bloom argues that generic concepts are less available to speakers of Mandarin because they cannot be expressed in Mandarin. However, support for this hypothesis was weak and unconvincing.

Moser (1996) put forth a different set of claims, focusing on both ancient and modern Chinese. He suggested that generics *can* be produced in Mandarin, but that generic concepts are less accessible to metacognitive awareness because they are less overtly marked. This aspect of Moser's argument, though intriguing, was untested. Moser did present some preliminary evidence that speakers of Mandarin were not random in their interpretation of unmarked nouns. When Mandarin speakers were asked to substitute either singular or plural third-person pronouns for nouns that English speakers would consider generic, they were often consistent across speakers for a given sentence (though variable across sentences). For example, for the word "kangaroo" in the sentence "Kangaroo is/are turnip-eating animal," participants selected the third-person singular pronoun (ta1) 66% of the time, whereas for the word "panda" in the sentence "Panda is/are on the verge of extinction" they selected the third-person plural pronoun (ta1-men) 63% of the time. However, these data are difficult to interpret, without either baseline comparisons of some sort (e.g., from speakers of a language that marks generics overtly), or predictions regarding which interpretations will be reached under various conditions. Most problematic for our purposes, either singular or plural pronouns could be consistent with a generic reading, and either could be consistent with a nongeneric reading.

We are left with some powerful claims in the literature regarding the semantic and/or conceptual implications of how generic expression varies cross-linguistically—but little in the way of compelling or relevant data. To address this lack of evidence, Twila Tardif and I conducted a cross-linguistic study of generic noun phrases, comparing speakers of English and of Mandarin (S. Gelman and Tardif, 1998). We had two primary questions: whether generics could be identified in Mandarin, despite the cross-linguistic differences in how transparently they are expressed, and if so, how frequently they appear relative to English.

We examined generics in two data sets. The first included at-home interactions between parents and their children that were captured on audiotape. The English-language data were kindly supplied to us by Erika Hoff; the Mandarin-language data were gathered by Tardif. The Mandarin-speaking participants were ten children and their families, all residing in Beijing. Children averaged 21.7 months of age with a mean sentence length in morphemes (MLU) of 1.82. Of the ten children, five had parents who had professional or semiprofessional occupations; five had parents who were manual or semiskilled laborers with no more than a high-school education. Audiotaping contexts included both indoor and outdoor toy play, mealtimes, dressing, social interchanges, and occasional book-reading episodes. The English-speaking participants were twenty mother-child pairs from Wisconsin. One group ($N = 10$) was matched to the Chinese sample in age ($M = 21.7$ months); the other group ($N = 10$) was matched to the Chinese sample in MLU ($M = 1.63$). Within each group, five of the children had parents who were characterized as "upper middle class" and five had parents who were characterized as "working class."

The second dataset was gathered with the purpose of equating contexts across languages. We gathered child-directed speech from twenty-four English-speaking parents in Ann Arbor, Michigan, and twenty-four Mandarin-speaking parents in Beijing, China, interacting with their twenty-month-old children. Each parent-child pair was videotaped for thirty minutes. Mothers and children spent ten minutes looking through a picture book, ten minutes playing with ordinary toys (e.g., blocks, stuffed animals), and ten minutes playing with mechanical toys, with the three activities presented in counterbalanced order. The physical contexts (including play materials) were identical across languages.

In both data sets, each videotape was transcribed and coded by native speakers in the relevant language, with a bilingual coder for reliability. We did not code pronouns, given that Mandarin is a pro-drop language (that is, subject nouns are not mandatory, so that where in English we might say "It runs," in Mandarin the utterance might be simply "Runs"). All other noun phrases were coded in two ways: as generic or nongeneric, and for domain.[5] Sample generics included: "*Baby birds* eat *worms*" (English) and "*da4 lao3shu3* yao3 bu4 yao3 *ren2*?" (Do *big rats* bite *people* or not?) (Mandarin). We found that generic noun phrases could be reliably identified in both English and Mandarin (with agreement between coders of well over 90% in each language).

We validated our coding by giving a subset of the English utterances (appropriately translated as needed) to both English- and Mandarin-speaking adults. The utterances were selected so that generic and nongeneric noun phrases were equated in animacy (half of each were animate, half inanimate), subjecthood (half were sentence subjects, half were not), and number in English (half were singular, half plural); these three factors were fully crossed. The task was to read each sentence and indicate whether the target noun phrase was true of "one" member of the category, "a few" members of the category, or "most/any" members of the category. Overall, speakers in both languages strongly agreed with our coding, typically interpreting nongeneric sentences as referring to "one" or "a few" instances, and typically interpreting generic sentences as referring to "most or any" instances. English speakers showed more interindividual consistency than Mandarin speakers, however, suggesting that formal cues do provide important disambiguating information.[6]

The primary results appear in Table 8.5. Despite very different formal devices for expressing generics, patterns were remarkably similar across languages. Generics were frequent in Mandarin as well as English (for example, in study 2, 83% of the Mandarin-speaking mothers and 100% of the English-speaking mothers produced at least one generic during thirty minutes of play with their twenty-month-olds). In both languages, generics were more frequently expressed for animals than for other domains. These cross-linguistic similarities argue that generic concepts are robustly expressed in the speech to small children. Interestingly, however, generics were significantly more common in English than Mandarin, suggesting that language-specific differences in how transparently generics are marked may affect frequency of use.

The frequency with which mothers produced generics was highly sensitive to interactional context. Mothers consistently produced more generics during the book-reading activity ($M = 2.46\%$ of utterances) than during free play with toys ($M = 0.41\%$). There are many possible explanations for this difference, but one that I find most provocative is the idea that book reading encourages mothers to focus on objects as kinds rather than individuals. Pictures are more easily construed as representations than are real objects (even toys; DeLoache, 1991), and so may encourage more talk about the kinds that they represent. In contrast, toys are

Table 8.5.   Mean percentage of maternal utterances including a generic noun phrase, by data set, language group, and domain; S. Gelman and Tardif (1998)

Data set 1

	Mandarin	English-MLU match	English-age match
Animals	0.09	0.25	0.26
Artifacts	0.05	0.06	0.18
Other	0.03	0.15	0.35

Data set 2

	Mandarin	English
Animals	0.37	0.88
Artifacts	0.22	0.46
Other	0.07	0.18

more easily construed as objects in their own right (even though in fact they are also representations), and so may encourage more talk about the ongoing activity. Interestingly, the book-reading context also elicits proportionally more nouns and fewer verbs, relative to the toy play contexts (S. Choi, 2000; Tardif, Gelman, and Xu, 1999). Contexts that encouraged nouns also seemed to encourage generics, whereas contexts that encouraged verbs did not. The important point here is that factors that sway the interpretation of an entity (as representing a kind versus as an individual object) are associated with more versus fewer generics.

As can be seen in Table 8.6, the distribution of generic noun phrases differed markedly from that of nongeneric noun phrases in both languages. Whereas generics appeared significantly more often for animals than for artifacts, nongenerics appeared significantly more often for artifacts than animals. This result tells us that the domain differences in generic use cannot be due to differences in

Table 8.6.   Mean percentage of maternal utterances including a nongeneric noun phrase by data set, language group, and domain; S. Gelman and Tardif (1998)

	Mandarin	English
Study 2		
Animals	12.30%	11.68%
Artifacts	16.73	19.34
Other	5.01	5.66

the salience of each domain. It is also interesting that there were no language differences in the frequency of nongenerics.

The results suggest an interaction between cognitive universals and language-specific effects. Most important, we argue for cross-cultural (probably universal) properties of generic concepts that are expressed with linguistically different constructions. However, we also found that generics were expressed more frequently in English than Mandarin. It will be interesting in future work to see whether children learning Mandarin acquire generics differently or later, given the lower frequency of generics in the input and their relatively greater ambiguity of expression.

SUMMARY OF GENERICS IN CHILD-DIRECTED SPEECH.   Generics refer to kinds and as such are of special interest in considering the sorts of implicit input children receive about essentialism. Generics are highly frequent in ordinary child-directed speech. In each study we have done, nearly all the mothers produced at least one generic, most produced several, and some produced dozens. Generics appear in speech to the youngest children we have studied (twenty-month-olds). They are found in two languages that express generics quite differently (English and Mandarin). The ubiquity of generics in child-directed speech raises the question of whether generics might even be more commonly used when speaking to children than when speaking to other adults. Generics also appropriately signal which kinds are more (versus less) richly structured, as indicated by the context sensitivity of their use: used more for animals than artifacts, and more in book-reading contexts than in toy-play contexts. But are they used by children? This question of course cannot be answered with an exclusive focus on adults. We turn now to the data from children.

Generic Production in Children's Speech

In this section I describe the evidence to date for children's production of generic noun phrases in spontaneous speech. I make two major points with the production data: generics are produced as early as two years of age, though the frequency increases markedly between two and three years; and generics are distributed differently from nongenerics by their earliest use, suggesting appropriate semantic interpretation by two years of age.

Jonathan Flukes and I analyzed transcripts from the longitudinal CHILDES database organized by Brian MacWhinney and Catherine Snow (1985, 1990).[7] Subjects were eight children (ages two to four years) followed longitudinally. The researchers who contributed the data were Lois Bloom (1970), Roger Brown (1973), Stan Kuczaj (1976), Brian MacWhinney (1991), Jacqueline Sachs (1983), and Catherine Snow. Table 8.7 summarizes the data set.

We included only those files in which child MLUs were at least 2.5 for three taping sessions in a row, in order to ensure that children had command of the appropriate syntactic devices, such as plurality and determiners. We first conducted a computerized search for all utterances containing plural nouns, mass nouns, or

Table 8.7.   Data set used in CHILDES study of children's generics

Child	Researcher	2 years	3 years	4 years
Abe	Kuczaj (1976)	X	X	X
Adam	R. Brown (1973)	X	X	X
Naomi	Sachs (1983)	X	X	X
Ross	MacWhinney (1991)	X	X	X
Nathaniel	Snow	X	X	
Peter	L. Bloom (1970)	X	X	
Mark	MacWhinney (1991)		X	X
Sarah	R. Brown (1973)		X	X

nouns preceded by the article "a" or "an," as these are possible generic constructions.[8] Altogether we identified nearly 45,000 relevant noun phrases. Then we
coded each noun phrase as generic or nongeneric, and for domain. For domain, we
made a three-way distinction between animals or animal parts (e.g., butterflies,
people, firemen, elephants, ghosts, bones, and feet), artifacts (e.g., shoes, money,
toys, cars, houses, and pirate hats), and all other domains (e.g., yogurt, rainbows,
flowers, jokes, and parties). Intercoder agreement on identification of generics was
97%; coding of domain was over 90%.

We coded for generics using a combination of morphological, semantic, and
pragmatic cues. In order for a noun phrase to be coded as generic, it had to meet all
of the following criteria: appropriate form of the noun (bare plurals, plural pronouns, or singular noun phrases preceded by an indefinite article), appropriate
form of the verb (present nonprogressive tense), and absence of individuating information (for example: number ["three dogs"], reference to a specific time point
["yesterday," "tomorrow"], possessives ["my rice"], deictics ["these cars"]). Any
one of these cues taken individually would be insufficient to result in a generic
coding. For example, "Those birds like to fly" uses present nonprogressive tense,
but would not be coded as generic because the noun phrase has the wrong form.

For comparisons across ages, we analyzed data from only the four children for
whom we had data at all age levels. For analyses within an age group, we examined
all children with data at that age. See Table 8.8 for examples from the youngest age
group (with generic noun phrases in italics). Further examples included the following (with generic noun phrases in italics): "That shirt's not for *girls*" (Ross, 2;7);
"*Animals* eat *berries* and *they* eat *mushrooms*" (Abe, 2;9); "*Indians* live in Africa"
(Adam, 3;3); "*Bad guys* have some guns" (Mark, 3;7); "Don't play with *guns*"
(Sarah, 4;10). Many of these sentences are deceptively simple and ordinary. What
makes them distinctive is not their content (after all, they rarely mention hidden
essences or invisible core properties), but their scope. These generic utterances
refer to kinds, not individuals (either singly or collectively). If we can assume that
generic constructions mean the same thing to children as to adults (see studies
below for evidence to back this position), then even a sentence as simple as "I don't

Table 8.8. Sample generics, age two

Child	Age (yrs.; mos.)	Generic topic	Utterance
Abe	2;11	animals, pomegranates	Do animals like pomegranates?
Adam	2;8	penguins	Oh no, they do fly?
Naomi	2;11	doggies	Doggies do poop.
Nathaniel	2;6	mushrooms	Eat them.
Peter	2;9	milk, a cow	Milk comes from a cow.
Ross	2;10	shampoo	He don't like shampoo.

like brown rice" (Abe, 2;6) refers to the generic kind of "brown rice," predicating a relatively enduring psychological attitude toward the category as a whole.

The children readily talked about categories as kinds using generic noun phrases (see Table 8.9). The eight children we studied produced over 3,000 generic noun phrases during the sessions recorded between ages two and four years, with higher rates of generics over time. All six of the two-year-olds we studied produced generics. By age four years, generics constituted nearly 4% of children's total utterances (including both searched and unsearched utterances). We do not yet know why the developmental increase occurred. It may reflect a conceptual change in the early preschool years. Specifically, a developmental increase may occur in how readily children think about categories abstracted from context. Alternatively, the change might reflect increasing syntactic skills during this age range. Four-year-

Table 8.9. Relative frequency of generic noun phrases in the naturally occurring speech of children in the CHILDES data base, as mean percentage of total utterances and as mean percentage of searched utterances (mass nouns, plural nouns, and indefinite singular nouns only) within each domain

	Age 2 (N = 6)	Age 3 (N = 8)	Age 4 (N = 6)
Generics as mean percentage of total utterances			
Animates	0.33%	1.24%	1.82%
Artifacts	0.12	0.37	0.59
Other	0.39	0.57	0.77
TOTAL	0.83	2.17	3.18
Generics as mean percentage of searched utterances within each domain			
Animates	4.52%	9.69%	13.05%
Artifacts	1.64	3.91	7.83
Other	3.20	4.56	5.01
Total number of generics	361	1,563	1,172

olds have better control over the syntactic devices needed to create generics, such as articles, plurality, and tense (R. Brown, 1973).

Children's generics were domain-specific. At each age, children produced significantly more generics for animals and animal parts than for artifacts or other domains. This pattern was consistent across children: when controlling for the number of searched utterances in each domain, six of the eight children provided more generic nouns for animates than artifacts at every age, one of the children showed the pattern in two of the three age periods, and the eighth child showed this pattern at one of the two ages for which we had data. To put this another way, out of twenty comparisons (four children with data at all three age periods, and four children with data at two age periods), eighteen showed a higher proportion of animate generics than of artifact generics. These results are consistent with the interpretation that children view animal categories as more richly structured than categories of artifacts.

Before concluding that children have an animacy bias, it is important to conduct an analysis of children's baseline speech. We wished to make sure that children's animacy bias in generics was not simply due to an abundance of animate noun phrases overall. To address this question, we computed a proportion score for each domain that was the number of generic noun phrases in that domain divided by the number of total coded noun phrases *in that domain*. In this way, each child's data serve as his or her own control. As shown in Table 8.8, even controlling for baseline frequencies of speech in each domain, children strongly preferred to use generics for animals and animal parts. This difference was significant even at age two.

Although animals and people are biological entities, categories of animals and people are not necessarily biological. A sizable subset of children's generics referred to nonbiological social kinds (including teachers, poor people, cowboys, "Italy people," strangers, good little girls, Naomis, bad people, carpenters). The data therefore suggest that children produced more generics for the animate domain, rather than that children produce more generics for the biological domain.

SUMMARY.   By two and a half to three years of age, children readily produce generics, with distributional patterns that distinguish them from nongenerics. Whereas children tend to produce more generics for animals than inanimate objects, there is no such preference for nongenerics. Whereas nongenerics tend to match the nonlinguistic context in terms of number (singulars used in the context of a single picture, plurals used in the context of multiple instances), generics are typically independent of the nonlinguistic context (e.g., plurals used in the context of single instances as well as multiple instances) (Pappas and Gelman, 1998). These patterns are what we would predict from a semantic analysis. Generics refer to categories with relatively more richly correlated structure (such as animals), and their meaning is not tied to any depictable or present nonlinguistic context.

Children Assign Appropriate Semantic Interpretation to Generics

I turn now to more direct evidence concerning young children's semantic interpretation of generic noun phrases. Inhelder and Piaget suggested, rather pessimistically, that early in development children "cannot choose between the individual (the same substance displaced) and the generic (the same category of phenomena)" (1964, p. 4). Although others have convincingly dispelled the more extreme version of this claim (that children cannot distinguish repeated instances of an individual from multiple instances of a kind; Karmiloff-Smith, 1977; Maratsos, 1974), there remains the question of when children grasp the subtle conceptual implications of generic knowledge (see also Prasada, 2000).

Generics have two important semantic features. First, they are generally true, and so are distinguished from indefinites (e.g., "*Bears* live in caves" is generic; "I saw some *bears* in the cave" is indefinite). The distinction between a generic reading and an indefinite reading is particularly critical because the same form of the noun phrase can be used for both (e.g., "bears" in both examples above). Second, generics need not be true of all members, and so are distinguished from universal quantifiers (e.g., "all," "every," "each"). In two studies described below, Michelle Hollander, Jon Star, and I examined whether children appreciate these features.

GENERIC SCOPE: YES/NO TASK.   Hollander, Star, and I conducted a study that focused directly on what generics mean to young children, by examining their scope of application (Hollander, Gelman, and Star, in press). Recall that, for adults, generics are distinctive in implying broad category scope (e.g., "Birds fly" is generally true of birds) yet allowing for exceptions (e.g., penguins). Thus, generics are distinct from both "all" (e.g., "All birds fly") and "some" (e.g., "Some birds fly"). Our study was modeled after an experiment conducted by C. Smith (1980), which had focused on children's interpretation of "all" and "some." In Smith's study, children four to seven years of age received a series of questions regarding properties of familiar categories. One-third of the properties were true of all members of the category in question (what we will call "wide-scope properties"); one-third were true of some members of the category ("narrow-scope properties"); and one-third were true of no members of the category ("irrelevant properties"). Children were asked about each category-property pairing with either the word "all" or the word "some" (e.g., "Do all girls have curly hair?" versus "Do some girls have curly hair?"), and their yes/no responses were recorded. Smith found that by age four, children appropriately distinguished "all" and "some" at least some of the time.

We predicted that, if given the same task with questions presented in generic form, children would treat generics as partly like "all" and partly like "some." In particular, we predicted that children would accept both "all" properties and (to a lesser extent) "some" properties as true in generic form.

Three-year-olds, four-year-olds, and adults each received three blocks of questions (generic, "all," and "some"), in counterbalanced order. Each block consisted of twelve questions: four concerning wide-scope properties (e.g., "Are fires hot?"), four concerning narrow-scope properties (e.g., "Do girls have curly hair?"), and four concerning irrelevant properties (e.g., "Do fish have branches?"). Each property was rotated through each of the three wording conditions, so that the specific content was not confounded with a particular condition (e.g., across children, a given question would be "Are fires hot?," "Are all fires hot?," or "Are some fires hot?").

The three-year-olds showed no sensitivity to wording condition, so here I report just the data from four-year-olds and adults. These results can be seen in Table 8.10. There was a significant interaction between question and property type. With the wide-scope properties, children were more likely to answer "yes" in response to "all" and generic questions, than in response to "some" questions. There was no significant difference between "all" and generic on these items. In contrast, with narrow-scope properties, children were more likely to answer "yes" in response to "some" and generic questions, than in response to "all" questions. There was no significant difference between "some" and generic on these items. Finally, for both generic and "all" questions considered separately, children were more likely to affirm wide-scope properties than narrow-scope properties. There was no significant difference between wide-scope and narrow-scope properties for "some" questions.

To conclude, children interpret generics as being reducible to neither "all" nor "some." Like "all," generics are appropriate for category-wide generalizations (e.g., "[All] fires are hot"). Yet like "some," generics are appropriate for properties true of a subset (e.g., "[Some] girls have curly hair"). Although generics can be said to be midway between "all" and "some," they are also more "all"-like, in that children endorse generics more often for wide-scope properties than for narrow-scope properties (like "all," but unlike "some").

These results with four-year-old children are consistent with a semantic analysis in which generics imply broad generalizations but also allow for exceptions. I want to take a moment to point out the ways in which these distinctions (between

Table 8.10. Mean percentage of "yes" responses; Hollander, Gelman, and Star (in press)

	"All"	"Some"	Generic
Four-year-olds ($N = 18$)			
Wide-scope properties	92	78	92
Narrow-scope properties	23	77	64
Irrelevant properties	6	7	6
Adults ($N = 38$)			
Wide-scope properties	84	91	94
Narrow-scope properties	3	100	61
Irrelevant properties	1	3	0

generic and "all," and between generic and "some") are subtle and so provide a powerful test of children's grasp of generic implications. The distinction between "all" and generics is subtle in that both noun phrase types imply the category as a whole, differing only in their commitment to every instance. At times generics are indistinguishable from "all," being used to convey properties true of every category member (e.g., "Dogs are mammals"). Nonetheless, generics allow for the possibility of counterexamples in a way that "all" does not. The distinction between generics and "some" is subtle in that the bare plural form has dual functions, at times referring to generics (e.g., "*Bears* like to eat ants") and at times referring to an indefinite plural (e.g., "I saw *bears* in the park yesterday"). Unlike generics, the indefinite plural is comparable to a noun phrase with "some" (i.e., "I saw bears in the park yesterday" is comparable in meaning to "I saw some bears in the park yesterday"). Given these potential confusions—on the one hand between generics and "all," and on the other hand between generics and "some"—it is all the more impressive that four-year-olds distinguish among the three forms.

GENERIC SCOPE: ELICITED PRODUCTION TASK. Star, Hollander, and I conducted a study similar in logic but differing in design (Hollander, Gelman, and Star, in press). Here, children (mean age 4;10) were asked to produce their own utterances, under the guise of giving information to Zorg, an alien puppet from outer space. The prompts children heard employed one of three kinds of cues: generic (e.g., "What can you tell Zorg about dogs?"), "all" (e.g., "What can you tell Zorg about all dogs?"), or "some" (e.g., "What can you tell Zorg about some dogs?"). To keep children's attention and interest, we showed them a line drawing of each entity after they gave their verbal descriptions. An analogous paper-and-pencil version of the task was developed for adults.

Elicited production is a more demanding task than the yes/no task described above. Instead of simply assessing the truth value of a series of utterances, children were required to generate properties on the basis of linguistic cues alone. Good performance on this task requires that children have sufficient access to generic knowledge to produce it on demand. It also requires that they demonstrate sensitivity to the linguistic prompts, and resist any tendency they may have to describe kinds in terms of prototypes on the one hand, or salient exemplars on the other.

Transcripts of the elicitation sessions were prepared, and coding proceeded in a series of steps. First, each utterance was broken down into propositions (e.g., "They play with string and chase a mouse" was considered two separate propositions: play with string, chase a mouse). Next, each proposition was coded for consistency between the linguistic form of the experimenter's prompts and the linguistic form of the child's response. For example, if a participant received a generic prompt but gave a property that was prefaced with "Some . . . ," the proposition would be considered inconsistent with the prompt. On this measure, 80% of the propositions were consistent with the experimenter-provided prompts. Focusing just on those utterances that were consistent, we had an independent group of adults rate the frequency with which each property was true of the category in question. Adult raters were blind to the purpose of the ratings, to the linguistic prompts that were provided by the experimenter, and to the linguistic format in which the property was expressed. (So, for example, "some dogs are furry," "all dogs are furry," and "dogs are furry" would all be rendered as "are furry" for the adult raters.) We then averaged the adult ratings for each property, and determined for each child subject the mean rating assigned to the properties they generated, for each of twelve categories.

Both children and adults were sensitive to the linguistic prompts provided by the experimenter, although in slightly different ways (see Table 8.11). Whereas adults distinguished all three forms from one another ("all" > generic > "some"), children distinguished "some" from the other two forms only ("all" = generic > "some").

It is somewhat surprising that on the semantic interpretation (yes/no) task, children treated generics as intermediate between "all" and "some," but on the elicited production task, children treated generics as equivalent to "all." However, we suspect that this result may largely reflect the difficulty of producing properties that are true of all members of a category (e.g., Mervis and Rosch, 1981). One would be hard pressed to list features that are true of all shirts, other than that they are worn (which is typically listed in the generic condition as well). In addition, at times children provided properties that, taken collectively, described all category members, but taken individually did not (e.g., one child said that fish are "kind of sparkly and kind of just grayish, and brown and blackish, and purple, silver, gold, pink"). The important similarity across the studies is that generics were clearly distinguished from an indefinite "some" interpretation—despite the fact that both bare plurals and mass nouns are used for both generic and indefinite utterances.

Generics Constrain Children's Inductive Inferences

Generics serve not only to express information that is already known, but also to convey important expectations to others. I hypothesized that generic language would convey to children the potential scope of inductive inferences.[9] Jon Star,

Table 8.11. Mean scope ratings, production task; Hollander, Gelman, and Star (in press)

	"All"	Generic	"Some"
Children			
People	73%	78%	71%
Animals	65	69	50
Artifacts	61	66	47
Adults			
People	80%	74%	64%
Animals	91	87	75
Artifacts	91	85	70

Jonathan Flukes, and I conducted a study to examine whether and how children make use of information in generics as compared to other linguistic expressions to direct their inductions (S. Gelman, Star, and Flukes, 2002). We focused specifically on the three types of noun phrases investigated in the studies described above: generics (e.g., "*Dogs* have four legs"), universal quantifiers (e.g., "*All bears* have claws"), and indefinite plurals (e.g., "*Some turtles* have spotted shells").

Thirty-seven children (M = 4;7) and thirty-six adults participated in the study. We presented a series of animal categories, one at a time. For each page there was a target question (e.g., for the category "bears," the question page said, "Which ones like to eat ants?"). There were six category exemplars to choose from. All were either highly or moderately typical of the category. (Atypical instances were not included, as we were concerned that the children might not accept them as category members.) Children learned what the pictures were (e.g., "Here is a page of bears") and received a clue to help them answer the question. The clues varied in linguistic form, for example: "All bears like to eat ants," "Some bears like to eat ants," or "Bears like to eat ants" (generic). Across items, the wording was varied within subjects.

The induction rates for the "all," generic, and "some" conditions were all significantly different from one another (see Table 8.12). However, these differences interacted with age. Both children and adults were sensitive to the wording in the inferences that they drew. For adults, generics were treated as equivalent to "all," whereas for children, generics were treated as less powerful than "all" but more powerful than "some." These developmental differences suggest two conclusions: that preschool children were sensitive to generic noun phrases as fostering inductive inferences broadly within a category, but that they favored a more conservative interpretation of generic noun phrases than did adults. Specifically, four-year-olds were less willing to generalize from a generic statement to the category as a whole.

In order to determine whether adults made *any* distinction between "all" and generics, we conducted a follow-up study with adults only, in which participants were asked to judge, on a scale of 0–100%, what proportion of the category had the novel property in question, in each of the three wording conditions. This task has the advantage of allowing adults to consider the full range of exemplars—not just moderately to highly typical instances, but atypical instances as well. Another advantage is the more finely grained rating scale. With this task, adults did recognize a semantic distinction between "all" (100%) and generics (84%)—a modest, though reliable difference.

Table 8.12.   Mean percentage of pictures selected on induction task; S. Gelman, Star, and Flukes (2002)

	"All"	Generic	"Some"
Children	92%	75%	62%
Adults	95	94	64

We do not yet know at what age interpretation of generics changes from the more conservative reading favored by four-year-olds to the more generous reading favored by adults. However, we speculate that the caution displayed by the children may be adaptive, given the frequency with which generics appear in parental speech. Children's awareness that generics admit exceptions could help prevent overly broad generalizations.

Summary of Generics

The findings reviewed above argue for an early-emerging capacity to produce and interpret generics, and by extension, to readily consider and converse about abstract kinds. The data can be summarized as follows:

- Generics are a frequent topic of conversation, both in speech addressed to young children (as young as twenty months of age) and in children's own speech (by two years of age). By age four, children also readily produce generics on command, with an elicited production task.
- Generics map onto conceptual structure in interesting ways, for both adults and children. Generics are expressed more frequently for animals (including people) than for artifacts. Also, the syntactic number with which generics are expressed is independent of real-world context (e.g., plurals in the context of a single instance); in contrast, for nongenerics, syntactic number closely matches the real-world context (e.g., plurals in the context of multiple instances).
- The patterns obtained in English (frequency in parental input, domain specificity, and differences between generics and nongenerics) replicate even in a language with very different formal means of expressing generics, namely, Mandarin Chinese.
- Children sensibly interpret the semantics of generics, treating them as broader in scope than "some," but allowing for exceptions (unlike "all"). Children do not confuse generics with indefinites, despite the fact that a single form of the noun phrase (bare plurals; mass nouns) can be used for either meaning.
- In their inductive inferences, too, children treat generics as broader in scope than "some" but narrower in scope than "all."

Altogether, these findings argue for an early-emerging capacity to produce and interpret generics as kind-referring expressions.

HOW DO CHILDREN LEARN GENERICS?

Here I lay out rather explicitly the nature of the acquisitional challenge posed by generics, focusing first on the problem of generic knowledge (which information to generalize, and to which kinds), and then on the problem of generic language (which utterances are kind-referring). This extensive preamble is important in order to highlight the depth of the puzzle that generics pose for a theory of acquisition. Then I consider the nature of the learning mechanism required for children to display the proficiency detailed above. I consider seriously the possibility that lower-level mechanisms could account for generic acquisition, and reject that possibility in favor of a "theory theory" account.

Induction Problems Posed by Generics

Generics pose two sorts of induction problems for learners. Both are subsets of the more general problem of induction discussed by Plato and Hume, among others.

1. When encountering any phenomenon (e.g., a child sees a picture in a book of two horses eating hay), how can the child know if this observation generalizes to others of the same kind? For example, do horses in general eat hay, or just the horses in this book? Relatedly, the child must determine which broader kind to consider. For example, is it more appropriate to infer that horses eat hay, that farm animals eat hay, or that animals eat hay? I refer to this set of issues as *the problem of generic knowledge* (see Prasada, 2000).

2. A second, related inductive problem concerns language interpretation. When hearing an utterance, how can children determine whether the speaker has a generic interpretation in mind or something else? For example, a caregiver may say to a child either "The horses are eating hay" or "Horses eat hay." How is the child to figure out which utterance is kind-referring? I refer to this as *the problem of generic language*. Children must solve both induction problems if they are to have a full understanding of generics.

Problem of Generic Knowledge

Prasada concisely states the problem of generic knowledge: "how do we acquire knowledge about kinds of things if we have experience with only a limited number of examples of the kinds in question?" (2000, p. 66). For example, how is it that we possess such rich and varied beliefs (horses eat hay; lima beans are detestable; Midwesterners are friendly; birds lay eggs; cars are expensive)?

The knowledge or beliefs expressed in generics concern *kinds* and cannot be reduced to knowledge of statistical regularities (Prasada, 2000). Generics can be paraphrased in ways that statistical statements cannot (Prasada, 2000). For example, Shipley (1993) gives the example that "Birds lay eggs" roughly means "Birds are a *kind* of animal such that the mature female lays eggs" (discussed in chapter 7). In contrast, "45% of birds lay eggs" does not mean "Birds are a kind of animal such that the mature female lays eggs." Generic propositions express potentialities of the kind, which will be true of varying amounts of a category depending on the predicate. For example, "Dogs are mammals" is true of 100% of dogs, "Birds lay eggs" is true of less than half of all birds, and "Cats live to be twenty years old" is true of probably less than 10% of all cats. Yet all are sensible generic utterances. Relatedly, there is no single statistical statement that corresponds to generics. "All" does not work, because generics admit of exceptions. "Most" and "usually" do not work, because generics can be true of less than half the category. And "some" does not work, because generics can be true of all members of a category.

We also do not systematically sample the evidence before making a generic statement. Generic propositions can be constructed on the basis of objectively insufficient evidence, even a single example (Macario, Shipley, and Billman, 1990). I could conclude that "lima beans are detestable" after sampling lima beans just once. Yet it would be anomalous to conclude that "90% of lima beans are detestable" on the basis of a single tasting. What allows us to go from a sample of ten, or even one, and to generalize to the kind as a whole (representing an untold multitude of instances)?

Even frequent experience cannot provide unambiguous evidence for a generic belief.[10] The induction problem would persist even if we had extensive experience with members of a kind, because no amount of personal experience or direct contact can give us access to the kind in its entirety. Even in the case of, say, an endangered species with only four living exemplars on earth, experience with each and every existing instance would not give us access to the kind as a whole, because the kind includes past, future, and potential instances. The problem of generic knowledge is all the more difficult in that counterexamples do not invalidate generic beliefs (see also McCawley, 1981; Prasada, 2000). If I assert that Midwesterners are friendly, and you argue that they are not, I am not going to back down if confronted with the existence of an unfriendly Midwesterner. Certainly stereotypes (which typically entail generic beliefs about human kinds) persist despite little or no direct supporting evidence.

Indeed, I would claim that generics can never be displayed, except symbolically. Jackendoff (1983) points out that conceptualizing an object as a category member (what he calls a concept of "type") is an abstraction: unlike a concept of an individual (i.e., a concept of "token"), it cannot be represented in a concrete image or fully embodied in any set of real-world individuals.

Although one can talk about the distinction between a kind and members of a kind, one cannot directly demonstrate or illustrate the distinction. For example, one can show a child one (specific) dog, but one cannot show a child the generic class of dogs. Likewise, one can never demonstrate, with actual exemplars, photos, or drawings, the distinction between a generic kind (rabbits) and a plurality of instances (some rabbits). As Waxman notes: "it would be logically impossible for caretakers to assemble together all members of an object category to model explicitly the extension of the category name" (1999, p. 243). Thus, generic noun phrases exemplify in especially sharp relief the well-known induction problem discussed by Quine (1960) when considering naming.

The problem of generalizing from a particular example to a kind is compounded by ambiguity regarding which kind to consider. Each object is at once a member of a varied set of categories (the same entity is at once Marie, a cat, a pet, a mammal, a vertebrate, and a physical object), thus raising the question of how one selects the level of abstraction to which a property applies (e.g., the body temperature of your pet cat). The human capacity to generalize brings with it the question of how this capacity is constrained (Goodman, 1973). In sum, although generic knowledge is a ubiquitous feature of human thought, it requires inferential leaps that extend beyond what we can know directly from our senses.

Problem of Generic Language

In addition to the conceptual issues raised above, the question of how children identify an utterance as generic is exacerbated by the complexity of mapping between formal and semantic cues. Simply put, in the case of English generics there is no one-to-one mapping between form and meaning. Command of the generic/nongeneric distinction in English requires, at the very least, morphosyntactic cues, contextual cues, and world knowledge. All of these factors are important to expressing and interpreting generics; none is individually sufficient.

MORPHOSYNTACTIC CUES.   In English, generics can be expressed with the definite singular, bare plural, indefinite singular, or definite article plus adjective (Lyons, 1977):

a. *The bird* is a warm-blooded animal.
b. *A cat* has 9 lives.
c. *Dinosaurs* are extinct.
d. *The elderly* need better health care.

They can be contrasted with nongeneric expressions such as the following:

e. *The bird* is flying.
f. *A cat* caught 2 mice.
g. There are *dinosaurs* in that museum.
h. *The elderly man* crossed the street.
i. *The bears* are huge.

There is overlap in the formal properties of the noun phrases in the generic and nongeneric examples, with (a), (b), and (c) matching (e), (f), and (g). Thus, generics in English are not uniquely identified with a particular form of the noun phrase, but instead are cued by a variety of additional means. At least four morphosyntactic cues help a speaker identify an utterance as generic or nongeneric: determiners, number (i.e., singular versus plural), tense, and aspect.

Determiners and number jointly operate to indicate genericity. In English, a plural noun phrase preceded by the definite determiner ("the") cannot be generic. For example, "Bears are huge" readily admits of a generic reading, but "The bears are huge" does not. Neither determiners nor number alone indicates whether or not a noun phrase is generic. However, it is the interaction of the two (i.e., definiteness plus plurality) that provides information regarding genericity. Aside from this restriction, generics can use definite or indefinite articles, can be singular or plural, and can include both naming expressions ("The elephant likes peanuts") and describing expressions ("A cat that has stomach trouble eats grass") (examples from Bhat, 1979, p. 139).

Tense is also an indication of genericity. With the exception of the historic past (e.g., "*Woolly mammoths* roamed the earth many years ago"), past-tense utterances are not generic. For example, we distinguish between "A cow says 'moo'" (generic) and "A cow said 'moo'" (nongeneric). Likewise, "The lion is ferocious" can have either a generic or a nongeneric reading, whereas "The lion was ferocious" has only a nongeneric reading.

Finally, *aspect* is an important cue in English for distinguishing generic from nongeneric interpretations. For example, a statement in the simple present, such as "Cats meow," is generic, whereas a statement in present progressive, such as "Cats are meowing," is nongeneric.

To summarize so far: in English, some of the formal cues relevant to whether a noun phrase is generic include articles, plurality, tense, and aspect. The cues can compete (e.g., "A cat caught two mice" has a potentially generic noun phrase but a decidedly nongeneric verb), in this example with the nongeneric verb winning out in the semantic interpretation. A striking example of how the cues interact can be seen with the following set of sentences:

- Do you like the mango? (specific)
- Do you like mango? (generic)
- Would you like mango? (indefinite ["some"])

Whether or not the noun phrase includes the determiner is not decisive, nor is the verb decisive. It is the combination of the determiner and the verb that is important. However, even here the formal cues are not entirely decisive, as can be seen when we consider "Would you like mango, if you were a monkey?" (which could have a generic reading, even though the first portion is identical to the nongeneric indefinite sentence). Even when we consider all formal cues simultaneously, they are often insufficient to determine with any certainty whether a noun phrase is generic or not. This issue is elaborated below.

CONTEXTUAL CUES.   Contextual cues are also central to the identification of generics. The structure of the sentence is important, as well as extrasentential information that surrounds the utterance in discourse. Compare the two examples that follow:

- Dingoes live in Australia.
- There are dingoes in Australia.

The first implies a generic reading: dingoes (as a kind) live in Australia. The second implies a nongeneric reading: some dingoes live in Australia, while others may live elsewhere. The relevant distinction here is neither the form of the noun phrase nor the tense or aspect of the verb, but rather the sentence construction.

A second sort of contextual cue involves the resolution of anaphoric references involving "they."

- "This is a tapir. They like to eat leaves."
- "These are my tapirs. They like to eat leaves."

The first "they" implies a generic reading (the class of tapirs), because there is no specific plural entity in the linguistic context. By contrast, the second "they" implies a particular reading (my tapirs). In both cases, "they" refers to a plurality, but in the first example the plurality is one that is alluded to and inferred, rather than present in the immediate context. This rather subtle implication is one that children will need to master.

A further influence concerns the semantic context, as established by prior speech and knowledge. For example, consider the two rather fanciful scenarios below:

Person 1:   What color fur do blickets have?
Person 2:   A blicket has purple spots.

Person 1:   Something in this room has purple spots. What is it?
Person 2:   A blicket has purple spots.

Intuition suggests that a generic reading is more likely in the first case than in the second (which more powerfully supports an indefinite interpretation than a generic interpretation). (Prosody is also likely to vary in these cases. In the first case, heavier prosodic emphasis would probably be placed on "purple spots," whereas in the second case, greater emphasis would probably be placed on "blicket.")

WORLD-KNOWLEDGE CUES.   World knowledge influences generic interpretation, even when formal cues are kept constant, because we know a great deal about which properties, events, and states concern individuals, and which properties, events, and states concern kinds. For example, ownership ("having") is a state that implies that something *in particular* is owned. One typically cannot have or own an entire kind. Yet enjoyment ("liking") is a state that can take as its object either an individual or a kind. With this distinction in mind, compare:

- I have rice.
- I like rice.

"I have rice" refers to an indefinite sample of the kind (equivalent to "some rice"). "I like rice" implies a generic kind.

Likewise, the predicate can influence interpretation of the noun. Some predicates (e.g., "are extinct") require a generic reading. But the importance of semantic information is more widespread. Compare the following two sentences:

- A horse is vegetarian.
- A horse is sick.

Both examples have a noun phrase "a horse" that is indefinite singular; both have a predicate that is present nonprogressive. However, whereas the first example could readily be interpreted as kind-referring (meaning that horses usually or ordinarily are vegetarian), the latter is unlikely to receive a generic reading. Being sick is (typically) predicated of individuals rather than of kinds.

Yet this analysis is complicated even more by content knowledge. "A pot is dirty" is unlikely to be interpreted as generic, yet "A pig is dirty" could very well be generic. Pigs as a class, but not pots as a class, are reputed to be dirty by their nature. I am not suggesting that morphosyntactic cues are irrelevant here. For example, "Horses are sick" sounds odd, as the form pulls strongly for a generic reading whereas the content pulls strongly for a nongeneric reading, leaving it difficult to interpret. Tense, too, though a fairly reliable marker of whether an utterance is intended to be generic, is fallible. The historic past provides an exception to the generalization that generics are present tense. For example, "Saber-toothed tigers roamed the earth many years ago" is stated in the past because the species is extinct, but the utterance is still generic. We reach a generic interpretation by means of world knowledge.

Precisely which properties are interpreted as more or less generic is itself a nontrivial cognitive question which is beyond the scope of this discussion. The relevant point, and one to which I return later in the chapter, is that children use naive theories to make this determination.

SUMMARY.   A wealth of factors—including a cluster of morphosyntactic cues (regarding determiners, plurality, tense, and aspect), discourse context, world knowledge, and perhaps prosody—appear to determine whether an utterance receives a generic or nongeneric reading by adults. Later I return to the question of *why* generics receive such varied expression. For now, this discussion highlights the daunting inductive task that children face in acquiring the means for producing and interpreting generics in English.

One question raised by this analysis is how it relates to the claim that generics motivate essentialist thought. If children need conceptual information about the world in order to interpret a noun phrase as generic or not, then wouldn't this point undermine the argument that children use generics to figure out what is and is not an essential kind? My answer is no: real-world knowledge and contextual information are useful for identifying generics, but identifying generics does not require a priori knowledge of the kinds themselves. To illustrate, consider the following sentences (with apologies to Lewis Carroll):

a. I like toves.
b. Toves are extinct.
c. I have toves.
d. The toves gyred and gimbled.

"Toves" is a nonsense word with no semantic content, so I have no knowledge about what they are. Despite lacking any knowledge of toves, I am able to determine which of the above sentences are generic and which are nongeneric. In part I do so on the basis of morphosyntactic information (in (d), the nongeneric status of the utterance is signaled by the form of the noun phrase ["the" + plural noun] as well as the tense of the verbs), and in part I do so on the basis of knowledge of the verbs ("like" and "extinct" in (a) and (b) signal that they are generic; "have" in (c) signals that it is nongeneric). The amount of information is very rich indeed, even with a wholly novel noun phrase. If children likewise can make use of such information, then they can use generics to figure out when categories are referred to as kinds.

How Do Children Solve the Inductive Puzzle of Generic Language?

The expression of generic kinds in language must be learned in childhood. It is not innate (as seen by cross-linguistic variation), yet it is available within the first few years of life. What is the acquisitional process? I have already argued rather extensively that adults use multiple sorts of information to identify an utterance as generic or not. Below I report evidence on some of these cues that children make use of. Specifically, I focus on children's sensitivity to formal cues, including noun morphology (e.g., to distinguish "What color are birds?" [generic] from "What color are the birds?" [nongeneric]), and their sensitivity to contextual cues (e.g., to distinguish "Here's a bird; what color are they?" [generic] from "Here are two birds; what color are they?" [nongeneric]).

FORMAL CUES.   Among the multiple formal cues that are relevant to the generic/nongeneric distinction, the use of determiners is one of the most direct, as they are part of the noun phrase itself. Recall that bare plural nouns may be generic (e.g., "What color are *birds*?"), whereas plural nouns with a determiner generally cannot (e.g., "What color are *the birds*?"). Maratsos (1974, 1976) found that even three-year-olds are sensitive to some of the semantic distinctions between "the" and "a" (definite versus indefinite), though he did not study how these forms map onto generic versus nongeneric interpretations.

Lakshmi Raman and I studied whether children display sensitivity to this formal distinction (S. Gelman and Raman, in press). Our task was very simple. For each of a series of items, we showed participants a realistic drawing of two entities, for example, a picture of two penguins. The entities were chosen to be atypical or unusual in at least one salient respect. For example, penguins are unlike typical birds in that they cannot fly. Then we posed a simple question about the atypical dimension (e.g., flying, in the case of the penguins item). Crucially, the question was presented in either generic form ("Do *birds* fly?") or nongeneric form ("Do *the birds* fly?"). We predicted that if the presence or absence of the determiner signals whether the noun phrase is generic or not, then participants will answer with reference to the broader category in the bare-plural case, and with reference to the pictured exemplars in the determiner + noun case. In other words, children should answer "yes" to the bare-plural question about birds and "no" to the determiner + noun question about birds.

Sample exemplars and questions are listed in Table 8.13. We tested four-year-olds and adults on twenty items, and two- and three-year-olds on twelve of the twenty items. In each age group, half the items were presented in generic form and half in nongeneric form, with items intermixed throughout the testing session. We counterbalanced which items were generic and which were nongeneric, across participants within an age group.

Children in all three age groups passed this task with flying colors (see Table 8.14). When they heard, "Do the birds fly?" they typically said "No," sometimes adding that they are penguins. But when they heard, "Do birds fly?" they said "yes" or "usually." Despite the fact that the context strongly pulled for a nongeneric reading, they used the formal cues to differentiate generic from nongeneric interpretations. The adults also did extremely well. Nearly all of them answered quite differently, depending on whether or not a determiner was in the noun phrase. An interesting point, however, was that the two adults who did *not* show the distinction were both bilingual, with a language other than English as their first language. So, the cues to generics are available early in development, but they are subtle enough that a nonnative speaker sometimes has trouble picking up on them.

CONTEXTUAL CUES.   As discussed earlier, although formal cues are important to identifying an utterance as generic or not, they are insufficient. In the next study, Lakshmi Raman and I sought to establish when in development children make use

Table 8.13.   Sample items; Gelman and Raman (in press)

Picture	Question
2 red birds	What color are (the) birds?
2 three-wheeled cars	How many wheels do (the) cars have?
2 penguins	Do (the) birds fly?
2 star-shaped cookies	What shape are (the) cookies?
2 tiny elephants	Are (the) elephants big or small?
2 loafer shoes	Do (the) shoes have laces?

Table 8.14. Mean percentage of responses; Gelman and
Raman (in press)

	Category-wide	Specific	Other
2-year-olds (N = 17)			
Generic	49%	27%	23%
Nongeneric	7	77	17
	*	*	
3-year-olds (N = 16)			
Generic	64	16	20
Nongeneric	5	83	11
	*	*	
4-year-olds (N = 16)			
Generic	59	21	20
Nongeneric	9	82	9
	*	*	*
Adults (N = 25)			
Generic	76	11	13
Nongeneric	2	96	2
	*	*	*

* $p < .01$

of contextual cues. We exploited the fact that mothers often make generic state-ments in the context of a single instance (e.g., pointing to a single squirrel and say-ing, "They like to eat acorns"; S. Gelman, Coley, Rosengren, et al., 1998; Pappas and Gelman, 1998). We hypothesized that this combination of a single referent with a plural noun phrase indirectly suggests a generic interpretation, whereas either a single referent with a singular noun phrase or a plural referent with a plural noun phrase would not. In other words, the mismatch situation (one referent, plural noun phrase) should yield a generic interpretation, whereas the match situations (either both singular, or both plural) should yield nongeneric interpretations. Table 8.15 displays the predictions more explicitly. Neither the picture cue by itself nor the linguistic cue by itself signals whether the interpretation is generic or not. It is only by using a combination of contextual and linguistic cues that generics can be differentiated from nongenerics.

To test our predictions, we first conducted a study with adults, comparing all three types of situations to one another. Each adult received three kinds of items: mismatch (one referent, plural noun phrase), singular match (one referent, singu-lar noun phrase), and plural match (two referents, plural noun phrase). Each item depicted one or two atypical entities (such as a tiny elephant), and each question concerned the dimension along which the item was atypical (such as the elephant's size).

The logic of this study required that the atypical dimension be one that was idiosyncratically true of the particular instance(s), and not generally true of an en-

222 Mechanisms of Acquisition

Table 8.15. Study design; Gelman and Raman (in press)

No. of referents	Noun phrase	Predicted interpretation
1	"they"	generic
1	"it"	nongeneric
2	"they"	nongeneric

tire subtype of the category. Otherwise, the question would be ambiguous. For example, a generic interpretation of "Do they fly?" in the context of a penguin could refer either to birds in general (in which case the answer would be "yes"), or to penguins (in which case the answer would be "no"). By including only idiosyncratically atypical items (such as a three-legged dog), there is no known subtype or natural kind of which the atypical dimension would be generically true. Such items enable a cleaner contrast between generic and nongeneric interpretations.

A sample set of items is shown in Table 8.16. On each item, the experimenter first showed the picture, saying, "Here is an X" or "Here are two Xs" (depending on how many items were present; X was the category label, e.g., "elephant"). Then the key question was presented in both written form and read aloud by the experimenter. For each question, adults wrote down a response; the responses were later coded independently by two researchers, with well over 90% agreement. Each response was coded as either "category-wide" (for example, "big" for the elephant question), "specific" (matching the picture; for example, "small" for the elephant question), or "other" (e.g., "big and small"). We predicted that the mismatch items would lead to category-wide responses, whereas the singular and plural match items would lead to specific responses.

The results bore out the predictions (see Table 8.17). The mismatch trials, with a plural pronoun in the context of a single exemplar, led to more generic interpretations than match trials. This result was upheld for adults as well as three- and four-year-olds. The results from two-year-olds were more mixed. These data establish that children make use of both formal and contextual cues to determine genericity. The cues to generics do not reduce to a particular set of linguistic forms. In

Table 8.16. Sample items; Gelman and Raman (in press). All are presented here in mismatch form.

Picture	Question
Short-necked giraffe	Do they have long necks or short necks?
White apple	What color are they?
Square balloon	What shape are they?
Tiny elephant	Are they big or small?

Table 8.17.   Mean percentage of responses; Gelman and Raman (in press)

	Category-wide	Specific	Other
2-year-olds			
Mismatch	45%	33%	21%
Singular match	25	48	27
Plural match	33	52	15
3-year-olds			
Mismatch	74	17	8
Singular match	15	73	12
Plural match	15	63	22
4-year-olds			
Mismatch	82	11	7
Singular match	17	73	10
Plural match	45	50	5
Adults			
Mismatch	48	48	4
Singular match	4	92	4
Plural match	6	92	2

the next section I consider what theoretical account could explain this developmental capacity.

How Do Children Learn Generics?

I suggest that the acquisition of generics cannot be explained in terms of simple associationist theories, but instead requires that young children make use of naïve theories.

PROBLEMS WITH STATISTICAL ASSOCIATIONIST MODELS.   If children use a low-level learning mechanism to acquire generics, then they would presumably keep a statistical tally of formal linguistic cues as they match to real-world features. Children then would come to expect certain properties to co-occur with specific linguistic frames. Such an automatic, associative mechanism would operate independently of reflective thought. Or, to rephrase in colloquial English, the child over time "soaks in" the statistical regularities present in the input. L. Smith, Jones, and Landau stress the importance of concrete properties in the process of word use and interpretation. To quote: "Young children's naming of objects is principally a matter of mapping words to selected perceptual properties" (L. Smith, Jones, and Landau, 1996, p. 144; see also chapter 9 for more discussion).

There are two major problems with proposing that children are detecting correlations between linguistic cues and concrete perceptual properties in order to learn generics. First and most obviously, there are no concrete perceptual properties associated with an utterance being generic. Even if there were concrete properties that correspond to the base word (e.g., perhaps "apple" is associated with a round shape; but see Chapter 9 for counterarguments), no such concrete perceptual properties signal whether the conceptual representation is generic or nongeneric. To illustrate, consider the mother who solicitously asks her two-year-old, "Do you like the mango?" as the child is tasting mango for the first time. Now consider a second mother who solicitously asks her two-year-old, "Do you like mango?" as the child is tasting mango for the first time. The nonlinguistic contexts are identical; the conceptual implications are quite different.

The second problem with a statistical learning model for learning generics is that there is no 1:1 mapping between linguistic form and meaning—even for young children. There is nothing even approaching a 1:1 mapping. Two-year-olds in our analyses of the CHILDES data used multiple forms for generics (singular noun with determiner "a," mass noun, bare-plural noun, pronoun), and each of these forms was used for both generic and nongeneric utterances (e.g., sometimes bare plurals were generic, sometimes bare plurals were indefinite; the same was true of "a" plus singular nouns).

A proponent of the statistical learning view might propose that children are instead attending to a multiplicity of cues "out there" in the input language and situation—not 1:1 cues, but perhaps a grid of cues that, taken together, signal genericity to the child. For example, perhaps determiners, number, tense, aspect, and prosody together form the relevant linguistic cues. The problem here is twofold. First, it is not clear that there is any sort of finite set of cues that determine genericity; rather, there seems to be an open-ended variety of ways in which world knowledge and context can combine in novel ways to imply a generic or non-generic interpretation. This situation contrasts with, say, the distinction between count nouns and mass nouns in English, which are rather reliably cued by a small set of formal features. Second, we would still be left trying to come up with a possible set of nonlinguistic contexts that would be "associated" with these cues. In the absence of a specific proposal of how learning generics would work (along the lines of the proposed count noun/mass noun distinction supplied in L. Smith, Jones, and Landau, 1996), it is difficult to accept—or even evaluate—such a possibility.

At the very least, the analysis of generics provided in this chapter greatly complicates the question of how one would implement an acquisitional process that depends entirely on lower-level learning mechanisms. I am skeptical that such an analysis is possible.

AN ALTERNATIVE PROPOSAL: MULTIPLE CUES AND NAIVE THEORIES.   Before sketching out my proposal, I first take a brief detour to ask *why* generics are marked in such a complex and subtle manner. If generics are so important, why do they not receive a single, unambiguous marker in English (or other languages)? The reason, I propose, is that generics are marked more by their absence than by their presence. Generic interpretations result when utterances are neither particular nor indefinite. In other words, generic interpretations are the default, at least by three years of age. There are many devices in language for indicating that something is particular, and it would be extraordinarily difficult (perhaps impossible) to enumerate them all. These include form of the determiner, precise number, deictics (including pointing), tense, and so on. All these devices serve to locate an utterance within an identifiable context (*this* place, *that* time, *those* entities). Generics contrast with specific utterances in that they cannot be pinned down to a context—they hold generally over time and situations. Thus, there is not a limited set of features or contexts that corresponds to the set of generic utterances. Rather, language users assume that an utterance is generic unless that interpretation is blocked—and there are many ways to block it. In fact, the more cues a speaker has at her command, the better. Multiple sources of information—including naive theories—are required, given how generics work.

This view is admittedly speculative and runs counter to the more usual model positing that children's early language is focused on the "here and now." Nonetheless, it could also help explain how generics are learned in languages that do not make use of determiners, tense, and other morphosyntactic markers used in English. Speakers in languages such as Mandarin still map a generic/nongeneric distinction onto utterances, but they are using nonmorphological cues to identify specificity and resolve ambiguity. In that sense, English and Mandarin are not so different from one another. It would be interesting to know how generally this analysis applies across languages.

What are the implications of this view for acquisition? In learning generics (at least in English), the child's task is not to acquire a particular form, nor to map one formal set of cues onto a set of properties in the world. Rather, the child's task is to filter out the specific. Children can do so most successfully by considering multiple cues, given the breadth and variety of means of indicating specificity. Such cues would at the least include morphosyntactic information and theory-based inferences. Presumably they would also include prosodic information (e.g., stress) and conventions of discourse (e.g., governing anaphora). Given how readily children grasp generics early in life, and the ease with which children produce generics in multiple syntactic forms, it would appear that even young children are likewise forming a mental model of the utterance as an integrated whole to determine whether there is any indication of specificity. Any indication of specificity could be enough to block a generic interpretation.

Another prediction is that as soon as a child learns that a particular cue marks an utterance as specific, she will readily recruit that information to mark an utterance as nongeneric. For example, the determiner "the" powerfully guides adult speakers toward nongeneric interpretations (though there are exceptions, such as "The early bird catches the worm"). Recall that 91% of English speakers interpreted "*The* tractor doesn't have a nose" (emphasis added) as nongeneric, whereas only 22% of Mandarin speakers did so when the sentence was translated into Mandarin (with no determiner; analogous to "Tractor not have nose"). Interestingly, children distinguish definite from indefinite (using "the" versus "a") by three years of age (Maratsos, 1974). I predict that children can likewise recruit this distinction for differentiating generic from nongeneric utterances. Specifically, if one were to conduct a microgenetic study (Karmiloff-Smith, 1992; Kuhn, 1995; Siegler and Crowley, 1991) examining the use of determiners to mark definiteness and genericity, one should find that children immediately extend the distinction to generics as soon as the definite/indefinite distinction is mastered. Their knowledge that the determiner "the" is specific should lead children to assume that definite noun phrases cannot be generic. Consistent with this prediction, children do not at first use definite singulars ("The early bird catches the worm") as generic.

In brief, I propose that acquisition of the generic system in any language requires a theory-driven assessment of which utterances pick out specific referents and which do not. All sources of information (formal, semantic, pragmatic, and world knowledge) relevant to marking specificity will be important. In future work it will be of interest to explore how different sources of knowledge interact. However, the suggestion that children use multiple cues does not imply that children use all the information adults do. Presumably adults have access to a richer set of linguistic and pragmatic skills to mark an utterance as generic or nongeneric, and I suspect that developing this full set of skills will be a time-intensive and gradual process.

Which Is Primary: Generic Concepts or Generic Language?

What sort of cognitive and/or linguistic capabilities could support children's sustained interest in and ease with generics? Relatedly, which comes first: generic concepts or generic language? On the "concept-first" view, the conceptual notion of kind arises nonlinguistically, with generic noun phrases merely reflecting this conceptual structure. This view maintains that children possess an innate or early-emerging notion of kind (e.g., Gopnik and Meltzoff, 1997; Macnamara, 1986) as well as a rich reserve of nonlinguistic generic knowledge, and generic language merely reflects and expresses this conceptual knowledge. Alternatively, the "language-first" view proposes that generic language plays a role in the formation of kind concepts. In its strongest version, generic knowledge would not exist without language. A. Bloom's (1981) analysis of generics in Mandarin versus English would fall within this position. Carey and Xu's (1999; Xu, in press) work on kind concepts, though not focused on generics, also argues for a formative role of language.

I think that the evidence most strongly favors the concept-first view, but that generic language also modifies and updates children's generic concepts. Consistent with the concept-first view, there does seem to exist a prelinguistic notion of generic kind. However, once children have learned the conventions for expressing generic concepts in language, generic language then provides substantive input to generic concepts. I sketch out this argument below.

There are several pieces of evidence that kind concepts (generically construed) emerge very early in development and are likely not to require linguistic instantiation. First, the apparently universal capacity for generics, despite widely varying linguistic forms, suggests that generics are a robust form of thinking and knowing about the world (Carlson and Pelletier, 1995). Second and more directly, prelinguistic infants engage in categorizing and inductive inferences that suggest they are appealing to generic kinds. Balaban and Waxman (1997) elegantly show that infants as young as nine months of age readily extend novel words from one category instance to another. Likewise, Baldwin, Markman, and Melartin (1993) find that nine-month-old children generalize novel properties from one instance of a kind to another. For example, when shown a box that unexpectedly produces a sound, they attempt to elicit the same property in another box similar in appearance (see also Graham, Kilbreath, and Welder, 2002).

I cannot say for sure whether such generalizations are generic at this age—that is, they could consist of similarity-based generalizations from one instance to another rather than generalizations that derive from the generic class. (See also Rovee-Collier, 1993, e.g., for similarity-based inferences even much earlier in infancy.) However, we do know that by two and a half years of age such generalizations are kind-based, as information about kinds overrides outward appearances of the individual objects in consideration (as when a child treats a pterodactyl as a "dinosaur" only after hearing it named; S. Gelman and Coley, 1990). Altogether, this work suggests that children possess a prelinguistic notion of generic kind that guides their inferences and knowledge organization (also Wilcox and Baillargeon, 1998; but see Xu and Carey, 1996, for an alternative position).

Although language is not determinative of kinds, generic knowledge is not wholly independent of language, either. At the very least, generics are effective in teaching children particular category-wide generalizations, such as specific facts about the attributes of category members (S. Gelman, Star, and Flukes, 2002). A fundamental question that remains is whether generic language fosters essentialism beyond the particulars of the properties stated (see the section in chapter 7 titled "Possible Functions of Generics").

OTHER LINGUISTIC EXPRESSIONS OF ESSENTIALISM

I have focused primarily on count nouns and generics because they are frequent in the input, appear to be extremely widespread across languages (perhaps universal), and are acquired early in development. However, there are other linguistic devices that, though less common, appear to provide important information to children.

"Ser" versus "estar"

One such example that has received serious study is the contrast in Spanish between "ser" and "estar." In an investigation of Spanish verbs, Sera (1992; Sera, Reittinger, and del Castillo Pintado, 1991) found that the distinction between "ser" and "estar" maps roughly onto a distinction between inherent and accidental properties. Heyman and Diesendruck (in press) found that characterizing a person's psychological characteristics with "ser" fostered a relatively more stable conception of the traits than when the same characteristics were characterized with "estar." A sample of eighty-five children who were bilingual in Spanish and English (age range 6;4 to 10;1; mean age 8;0) were randomly assigned to one of three conditions: "ser" (Spanish), "estar" (Spanish), or "to be" (English). They heard a series of brief vignettes (e.g., in English: "I know an eight-year-old girl named Maria. Maria sits by herself at the party. Maria is shy"; in Spanish: "Conozco a una niña de ocho años que se llama Maria. Maria se sienta sola en la fiesta. Maria [es/está] penosa."). For the Spanish version, the final sentence varied whether the verb "to be" was the "ser" versus the "estar" form.

Children hearing the "ser" form rated the property as significantly more stable than children hearing the "estar" form ($Ms = 4.2$ versus 3.3 out of 6). Interestingly, the "to be" form was equivalent to that of "ser" ($M = 4.2$), suggesting that children assume stable properties as a default, but "estar" leads the Spanish speakers to overcome this default. One provocative question is whether children implicitly honor the conceptual distinction before learning its formal linguistic expression, or whether the language distinction precedes and encourages the conceptual distinction. It will be important to examine the "ser"/"estar" distinction in younger children, to examine the initial acquisition of these forms.

Explicit Linguistic Devices Do Not Convey Essentialism: The Word "Kind" and Quantifiers

Lexicalization, generics, and the "ser"/"estar" distinction all imply "kindhood" or essentialism indirectly. Languages also possess more explicit expressions of essentialism—including the word "kind" and quantifiers. Surprisingly, however, these more explicit forms do not seem to be effective means of conveying essentialism to children.

THE WORD "KIND."   Perhaps the most explicit means of expressing membership in a kind is with the word "kind" itself, as in "Robins are a *kind* of bird" (Wierzbicka, 1994). From her review of a variety of unrelated languages (including Chinese, Japanese, Thai, Ewe [a Niger-Congo language], Acehnese [an Austronesian language of Indonesia], Kalam [a Papuan language], and Kayardild [an Australian language], among others), Wierzbicka concludes not only that all languages sampled have a lexical entry for *kind*, but also that they distinguish "kind" from "like" (i.e., kinds do not reduce to similarity). For example, all the languages surveyed can express something like "These trees are the same *kind*, not two different *kinds*," as well as "This flower is *like* a rose, but it is not a rose." This result suggests the possibility of a universal conceptual distinction between kinds and other sorts of groupings.

Wierzbicka did not speculate about the mechanisms by which a concept of "kind" is expressed to young children, although she implies that having a word for a concept plays an important role:

> In human communication it is not enough to "have" a concept, it is also important to have means to convey it to other people (even assuming that one COULD "have" a concept without being able to communicate it to other people). For some concepts, this can be done by means of some circumlocution or paraphrase; for others, however, it is necessary to have a direct lexical exponent. (1994, p. 348)

However, although the word "kind" provides a window onto adult concepts, one cannot necessarily infer that it will be an important mechanism for conveying kind concepts to children. At least in English, the word "kind" can refer to one narrow sense of kind, that of a nested subtype (e.g., "What kind of cereal do you like best?"). This meaning is distinct from the notion of "kind" that is relevant to essentialism: not all subtypes are richly structured and inference-promoting (e.g., argyle socks are a kind of sock), and not all kinds are subtypes within a class-inclusion hierarchy (e.g., gold, water).

Several studies of lexical development have employed the phrase "This is a kind of Y" to express inclusion relations to young children. Notably, this phrase is equally appropriate to use for artifacts (such as clothing or furniture) and natural kinds (such as categories of animals and plants). Artifacts are not richly structured natural kinds, but they permit class-inclusion relations and allow for sentences like "Sneakers are a kind of shoe." The experimental studies employing the "X is a kind of Y" construction generally find that children between the ages of two to five years understand that it implies inclusion (Callanan, 1989; Diesendruck and Shatz, 1997; Diesendruck and Shatz, 2001; Gottfried and Tonks, 1996). This finding suggests that the "subtype" construal of the word "kind" is salient in children's early speech.

Michelle Hollander and I conducted a small-scale study of parents' and children's spontaneous speech, to determine the usage of the word "kind" in parent-child conversations, for children between the ages of two and five. Data were obtained from the CHILDES database, discussed earlier in the chapter (see MacWhinney and Snow, 1985, 1990), again focusing on the eight children studied earlier with regard to generics.

We coded three aspects of each use of the word "kind":

1. *Scope.* Does the word refer to a generic kind (e.g., "What kind of flowers do you like?," "the kind of balloon people used to fly inside of"), or does it refer to an individual or set of individuals (e.g., "What kind of game were you playing?" "What kind of basket is this?")? Uses were coded as referring to a generic kind if they made reference to the category as a whole, in a manner not tied to a specific individual or set of individuals. Uses were coded as referring to an individual or individuals if they were tied to past events, or requests for labels or modifying information (e.g., often in the form "What kind of X is this?") and did not make reference to the entire category in any way.

2. *Category level.* Does the word refer to a basic-level category (e.g., "a kind of animal"), or does it refer to a subordinate-level category (e.g., "a kind of dog")?

3. *Domain.* Does the word refer to an animate entity (e.g., person, dog), an artifact (e.g., airplane), or other (e.g., food)?

If the word "kind" is to be a useful source of information to children about inference-promoting categories, then it should be used primarily to refer to categories that are generic (not just individuals), basic level, and animate. These sorts of categories are more richly structured on a variety of tasks (generics: S. Gelman, Coley, Rosengren, et al., 1998; basic-level categories: Rosch et al., 1976; Atran, Estin, et al., 1997; animates: Keil, 1989; S. Gelman, 1988).

We conducted an in-depth analysis of one mother-child pair (Roger Brown's Adam and his mother; R. Brown, 1973), which was then bolstered by a sampling of the speech of others in the CHILDES database. Adam was selected as being representative of children's language on a variety of other measures (e.g., P. Bloom, 1990; Marcus et al., 1992), and because his data are plentiful and cover a lengthy developmental range (from 2;3 to 5;2). Adam was taped on fifty-five occasions, producing over 46,000 child utterances and over 20,000 maternal utterances. Each instance of the word "kind" was first identified as a target meaning or not (e.g., "You are a kind boy" and "He is kind of silly" would be excluded from further consideration). Nontarget uses accounted for only 3% of Adam's uses and 5% of his mother's uses. Of the remaining 365 instances of "kind" (161 for Adam, 204 for his mother), each was coded independently along each of the three dimensions described above. A second coder coded 25% of the utterances, achieving reliability of 85–96% on each of the dimensions.

As can be seen in Table 8.18, the word "kind" was rarely used to refer to generic kinds, basic-level categories, or animate entities. Less than one-third of Adam's mother's uses at any age referred to a generic kind. When we focus specifically on those utterances in which "kind" did refer to a generic kind, we find neither an animacy bias nor a basic-level bias. Uses of the word "kind" to refer to a generic kind were in fact most frequent for artifacts and subordinate-level categories. When one takes the intersection of all three factors ("kind" referring to an animate, basic-level, generic kind), we found only one such use by Adam and only four such uses by his mother.

In order to examine the generality of these findings with Adam, we analyzed a sampling of the speech from additional children in the CHILDES database. We focused on those parent-child pairs for whom data were available at age four (the age at which Adam's mother's use of "kind" was most focused on basic-level generic kinds): Abe (Kuczaj, 1976), Mark (MacWhinney, 1991), Naomi (Sachs, 1983), Ross (MacWhinney, 1991), and Sarah (R. Brown, 1973). We selected 20% or more of the transcripts for each child at age four, centering on the middle of the age range as being most representative of the input at that age. As can be seen in Table 8.19, the results from this sampling of five additional children support the

Table 8.18. Uses of the word "kind" in the speech of Adam and his mother (as percentages of total target uses at each age)

	Adam			Adam's mother		
	2 yrs.	3 yrs.	4 yrs.	2 yrs.	3 yrs.	4 yrs.
(1) Scope						
Kind-referring	**0%**	**3%**	**15%**	**7%**	**23%**	**28%**
Individual-referring	100	97	75	93	77	72
(2) Level						
Basic-level reference	**0**	**5**	**12**	**9**	**32**	**36**
Subordinate reference	100	95	78	91	68	64
(3) Domain						
Animate reference	**14**	**12**	**14**	**15**	**35**	**32**
Artifact reference	73	70	52	50	32	40
Other	14	18	34	35	32	28
(4) No. of target uses	22	66	73	68	111	25
(5) % of total utterances	0.13	0.35	0.64	0.89	1.22	0.73

Note: Within each section of scope, level, and domain, the columns add up to 100% at each age level.

Source: S. Gelman, Hollander, et al. (2000). Reprinted with the permission of Academic Press.

Table 8.19. Uses of the word "kind" in parental speech directed toward Abe, Mark, Naomi, Ross, and Sarah at age 4½ (as mean percentages of total target uses at each age)

	Mean	Range
(1) Scope*		
Kind	**34%**	**0–73%**
Individual	66%	27–100%
(2) Level*		
Basic-level	**32%**	**0–45%**
Subordinate	68%	55–100%
(3) Domain*		
Animate	**18%**	**0–45%**
Artifact	42%	27–50%
Other	39%	27–50%
(4) Mean no. of target uses	4.6	0–10
(5) % of utterances sampled	0.21%	0.00–0.65%

Note: For each child, these data are from the one parent [mother or father] who provided the most data: the mother of Naomi and Sarah, and the father of Abe, Mark, and Ross.

*For these calculations, we excluded those parents ($N = 2$) who did not produce "kind" at all within these transcripts.

Source: S. Gelman, Hollander, et al. (2000). Reprinted with the permission of Academic Press.

patterns obtained from the in-depth analysis of Adam and his mother. Once again, the word "kind" was rarely used to refer to generic kinds, basic-level categories, or animate entities. In the entire sample of over 8,000 parental utterances, only three instances referred to animate, basic-level kinds.

To summarize: the word "kind" is most often used to label an individual member of a category subtype (e.g., hypothetically, "What kind of hat did you buy?"), and only rarely to label a broader kind (e.g., hypothetically, "Chipmunks are a kind of animal that lives in trees"). We conclude that explicit use of the word "kind" is unlikely to be a source of much information to children regarding essentialism.

LOGICAL QUANTIFIERS.   A final way in which children might learn that a category is a kind is by hearing properties predicated explicitly of all members of a category. For example, the statement "All bats sleep during the day" directly conveys that bats constitute a coherent category with inductive potential. Words that refer to the entire category (universal quantifiers) include "all," "each," "every," and "any" (Vendler, 1967).

A large body of research has examined children's understanding of logical quantifiers such as "all," "each," and "some" (e.g., P. Brooks and Braine, 1996; Macnamara, 1986). Although initially Piagetian analyses suggested that children below age six or seven were incapable of understanding these constructions due to intractable cognitive limitations (Inhelder and Piaget, 1964), studies that posed fewer information-processing demands suggested that even four-year-olds can distinguish "all" and "some" (C. Smith, 1979, 1980). Children have relatively few difficulties with uses in simple declarative sentences that involve property predication (e.g., "All xs have ys"; C. Smith, 1979, 1980). Most of children's difficulties with uses of "all" and "some" involve additional processing demands, such as class inclusion (e.g., "All xs are ys"), complex syntactic constructions (e.g., "A boat is being built by all the men"; P. Brooks and Braine, 1996), or contexts with competing irrelevant cues (Donaldson and McGarrigle, 1974). Children's relatively mature performance in simple contexts suggests that logical quantifiers might be an important source of information.

Although the logical quantifier "all" can convey important and precise information regarding category properties, it is rarely used in speech to young children (see chapter 7). Recall that in the S. Gelman, Coley, Rosengren, et al. (1998) picture-book-reading task, less than 2% of uses of "all" were as a universal quantifier—or less than 0.03% of all maternal utterances.

The analyses in the S. Gelman, Coley, Rosengren, et al. (1998) studies focused exclusively on the word "all," which is just one of several universal quantifiers found in English. Michelle Hollander and I analyzed the full set of universal quantifiers in English: "all," "each," "every," and "any." We first examined overall frequency of all instances of these forms in the CHILDES database. We searched the CHILDES database for all instances of these four words, as well as all instances of longer words beginning with these strings (e.g., "everything," "anybody"). We focused on eight of the English-speaking children who had the most extensive longitudinal data, and restricted the age range to two to four years. As can be seen in Table 8.20, these quantifiers are considerably more frequent than the word "kind," and more frequent in natural speech than in the picture-book-reading context studied by S. Gelman, Coley, Rosengren, et al. (1998).

It therefore becomes particularly critical to examine the nature of these uses. We predicted that, if parents are using these terms to teach children that categories are inference-promoting kinds, then these words should function frequently as universal quantifiers (referring to entire kinds), and particularly for animate categories. Again we focused on the speech of Adam and his mother, supplemented with data sampled from a subset of the other children in the CHILDES database. We first searched the CHILDES database for Adam and his mother for all instances of these four words, as well as all instances of longer words beginning with these strings (e.g., "everything," "anybody"). Each use was classified according to function (universal quantifier, specified context, or other) and domain (animate, artifact, or other). A second coder coded a subset of the utterances and obtained agreement of over 90% on both scope and domain for both speakers.

As can be seen in Table 8.21, these words rarely functioned as universal quantifiers. Over 90% of the time, when one of these words was used, it was to refer to a specific context (e.g., "clean up all your toys") or in other ways (e.g., "all gone"). Universal-quantifier uses of these words occurred in less than 0.3% of Adam's utterances at any age, and less than 0.4% of his mother's utterances at any age.

In order to examine the generality of these findings with Adam, we analyzed a sampling of the speech from additional children in the CHILDES database. As with the analysis of "kind," we focused on Abe, Mark, Naomi, Ross, and Sarah, selecting the same 20% of the transcripts produced at age four. As can be seen in Table 8.22, the results from this sampling of five additional children support the patterns obtained from the in-depth analysis of Adam and his mother. Once again, the quantifiers "all," "any," "each," and "every" were rarely used to refer to generic kinds or animate entities.

Table 8.20.   Relative frequency of the quantifiers "all," "any," "each," and "every" in the naturally occurring speech of children and parents in the CHILDES data base, as percentage of total utterances

	Children (N = 8)	Parents* (N = 8)
Mean % of utterances containing "all," "any," "each," or "every"	2.55%	3.58%
Range (in %) across parent-child dyads	1.11–5.70%	2.68–4.54%
Total no. of instances	4,056	4,502

* Parent who contributed the most utterances

Source: S. Gelman, Hollander, et al. (2000). Reprinted with the permission of Academic Press.

Table 8.21.   Uses of the words "all," "each," "every," and "any" in the speech of Adam and his mother

	Adam			Adam's mother		
	2 yrs.	3 yrs.	4 yrs.	2 yrs.	3 yrs.	4 yrs.
(1) Function (as percentages of total uses at each age)						
Universal quantifier	**2%**	**6%**	**15%**	**9%**	**4%**	**10%**
Specified context	26	54	52	61	65	64
Other	72	40	33	30	31	27
(2) Domain (as percentages of total target uses at each age)						
Animate	**54%**	**34%**	**20%**	**25%**	**25%**	**23%**
Artifact	21	16	23	37	22	26
Other	25	50	57	39	53	51
(3) Total no. of uses	86	209	221	163	254	124
(4) % of total utterances	0.53	1.12	1.93	2.13	2.79	3.62

Source: S. Gelman, Hollander, et al. (2000). Reprinted with the permission of Academic Press.

Table 8.22.   Uses of the words "all," "any," "each," and "every" in parental speech directed toward Abe, Mark, Naomi, Ross, and Sarah at age $4\frac{1}{2}$ (as mean percentages of total target uses at each age)

	Mean	Range
(1) Function		
Universal quantifier	**12%**	**5–19%**
Specified context	50	47–54
Other	38	29–47
(2) Domain		
Animate	**24%**	**12–39%**
Artifact	21	11–28
Other	54	41–60
(3) Mean no. of target uses	62.4	13–140
(4) % of utterances sampled	3.87%	3.57–4.35%

Note: These data are from the parent who provided the most data: the mother of Naomi and Sarah, and the father of Abe, Mark, and Ross.

Source: S. Gelman, Hollander, et al. (2000). Reprinted with the permission of Academic Press.

To summarize: the words "all," "any," "each," and "every" are common in parental speech, but rarely used to refer to generic kinds. I suggest that it is therefore unlikely that these explicit forms of language play a vital role in the acquisition of essentialized concepts in children.

Summary

A logical or semantic analysis would suggest that several forms of language are kind-referring expressions that could potentially help shape children's concepts.

However, the results of the studies I have reviewed indicate a divide among these devices. As opposed to lexicalization and generics, the word "kind" and universal quantifiers map less consistently onto basic-level kinds. This finding again supports the argument made in chapter 7, that input (in this case, input language) does not explicitly instruct children about essentialism. Rather, language includes implicit cues that children can use.

CONCLUSIONS

Human languages provide a compact and unequivocal way of conveying two central points of information: membership in a kind (expressed with words) and category scope (expressed with generics). Both reflect a fundamental conceptual distinction between kinds and individuals. These two properties indirectly inform essentialism. Take words. A word by itself does not tell us that something should be essentialized. "Paperweight" is a word, but it does not imply fixed category membership, nonobvious properties, innate potential, and the like. What words do is communicate category membership, including nonobvious category membership. Children's beliefs about the category being named are what give the word its power. Likewise for generics: they emphasize kinds (as opposed to individuals) and relatively stable and inherent properties (as opposed to transient or changeable ones; Prasada, 2000).

How Fundamental a Role Does Language Play?

Can we characterize more precisely the effects of language on children's kind concepts? One fundamental question that arises is whether common nouns and generics reflect preexisting conceptual structures or play a more formative role. Scholars have proposed numerous possibilities, ranging from the argument that words do nothing at all or at best simply highlight preexisting categories to the possibility that language teaches children essentialism.

Most would agree that preexisting kind concepts are in place by the time children are learning words and generics (but see Xu, in press). Certainly the assumption that categories serve as a basis of induction is prelinguistic, and probably untaught (Baldwin, Markman, and Melartin, 1993; Hayne, Rovee-Collier, and Perris, 1987). The finding that children without exposure to a conventional language spontaneously create their own communicative system, complete with nouns and the capacity to do displaced reference (Goldin-Meadow and Mylander, 1990; Morford and Goldin-Meadow, 1997), would also suggest that a rich conceptual system is in place prior to the cultural transmission of a conventional language. Furthermore, the linguistic devices we are talking about are at best oblique and sketchy. Common nouns and generics only implicitly refer to kinds and inductive potential, and are in fact far less explicit in this way than either the word "kind" or universal quantifiers. I infer from this characterization that children must be filling in gaps based on their own extralinguistic understanding.

Nonetheless, language seem to be doing more than simply reflecting children's preexisting concepts. Language has direct effects on children's inductive inferences, as has been found in experimental scenarios that contrasted different forms of input (e.g., S. Gelman and Heyman, 1999; S. Gelman, Star, and Flukes, 2002). Words guide the structure of novel categories (e.g., Graham, Kilbreath, and Welder, 2001) and help restructure existing categories (e.g., S. Gelman and Markman, 1986). Therefore, if we grant that generics and lexicalization do affect thought, at what level do they exert an effect? Do certain forms of language allow new conceptual understandings to arise, or do they modify existing concepts? To present a somewhat simplified view of the range of possibilities, I propose three potential levels of effects, from narrowest to broadest:

1. *Content* of kinds. On this view, language helps fill in the details of the kinds that children have already established through nonlinguistic means. For example, generics may tell children which properties are true of "dogs" (as a kind), naming may tell a child which animals are (and are not) birds, and lexicalization may increase a child's confidence that a particular trait is stable over time.

2. *Which categories* are kinds. On this view, language helps children sort out which categories are relatively impermanent or arbitrary, and which categories are more stable and inference-rich. For example, lexicalization may encourage children to treat "carrot eaters" as a stable kind, and generics may imply that "robbers" are not simply a group of individuals who engaged in a particular behavior on occasion.

3. *That* there are kinds. On this view, language can exaggerate any essentializing tendencies that are already present. For example, an individual—or a culture— that engages in an extensive amount of essentializing talk may foster a higher degree of essentializing.

In this chapter I have focused on the first two sorts of effects: how language conveys to children the content of kinds, and which categories are kinds. I have argued that it is unlikely that language encourages children to construct an essentialist understanding to begin with. However, this issue has not yet been adequately tested.

Domain Issues Redux

In this chapter I have argued for the importance of language (particularly nouns and generic noun phrases) in expressing and even fostering essentialist reasoning. At first this position may appear to conflict with the arguments put forth in part I that essentialism finds domain-specific expression, primarily attaching to natural kinds and social kinds. After all, both nouns and generic noun phrases are domain-general in scope, and are well formed whether applied to animals ("*Dogs* bark"), artifacts ("*Spoons* are handy for eating ice cream"), inanimate substances ("*Salt* is a food preservative"), or social kinds ("*Firefighters* are brave").

This apparent conflict can be reconciled in two ways:

1. Language is not the source of essentialism, but rather one informative, probabilistic cue that, combined with other cues, helps contribute to a child's construal of a category. Consider common nouns, for example. Hearing a label makes one somewhat more likely to construe the category in essentialist ways, compared to hearing a verb or adjective to refer to the same grouping (see S. Gelman and Heyman, 1999). However, this information would be weighed along with other considerations, including domain, richness of property clusters, stability over transformations, and degree of overlap with other property-rich groupings. For example, Diesendruck (in press) suggests that categories in different domains differ in their "conceptual autonomy," or how much their structure is provided by a priori conceptual biases and independent of language effects. Social categories may be more susceptible to language effects than animal kinds, which have more salient perceptual similarities (Rosch et al., 1976). Accordingly, many uses of nouns will be nonessentialized. Nouns "invite" children (Waxman and Markow, 1995) to look for commonalities and, potentially, essences. They do not force these interpretations.

2. Generics are in fact more domain-specific than a grammatical analysis would suggest. Although generics can be used to refer to artifacts as well as animals, they are disproportionately used to refer to animals. (There is not yet enough information to compare how they are used for inanimate natural kinds as well as other domains, so here I focus primarily on the distinction between animals and artifacts.) I suggest that the disproportionate use of generics for animal kinds reflects the greater ease with which these categories are construed in essentialist ways. In addition to domain differences in overall frequency, there are probably domain differences in the content of generic properties that parents express. Generics that simply indicate the speaker's attitude toward the kind (e.g., "I like grapefruit") suggest little in the way of inherent features shared by category members, whereas those that indicate a behavior of the kind (e.g., "Elephants eat peanuts") carry a richer set of implications. Animate nouns are most likely to be used in the latter sort of expression, given the overall propensity for subject nouns to be animate (Slobin, 1981).

Language Differences?

Although I argue that language affects children's conceptual understanding, my position is not a Whorfian claim of radical language differences. Languages universally have the capacity to express important concepts (Au, 1988), including membership in a category and scope of quantification. The distinction between nouns and verbal predicates appears to be universal (Gentner, 1982), as is the capacity to express generics (Carlson and Pelletier, 1995). I expect that the use of these linguistic expressions to foster kind concepts is not limited to English.

Nonetheless, there is cross-linguistic variation in the expression of these concepts that could conceivably affect their acquisition and use. Regarding lexicalization, languages vary regarding the relative primacy of nouns versus verbs (S. Choi and Gopnik, 1995; Tardif, 1996; Tardif, Gelman, and Xu, 1999; but see Au, Dapretto, and Song, 1994), and there may be cognitive consequences of these differences (Gopnik and Choi, 1990). The variations in generic expression are particularly thought provoking. Recall that Twila Tardif and I found that generic noun phrases were more frequent in mothers speaking English than mothers speaking Mandarin, despite identical contexts and despite the lack of differences between the languages in the production of nongeneric noun phrases.

Tardif and I speculate that formal properties of the language may prompt speakers to notice and use generics relatively more (as with English) or less (as with Mandarin). Although the generic/nongeneric distinction itself is not obligatorily marked in either language, English conveys the contrast by means of obligatory cues (including number and determiners). The use of obligatory markers for conveying generics in English may make generic expressions more salient, more readily noticed, and so more frequently used. If so, then frequency effects should also appear in other languages that are structurally similar to Mandarin, and there should be measurable cognitive consequences on nonlinguistic tasks.

Conclusions

Language is just one of many cues available regarding category structure. There are numerous sources of information for children to consider, including but not limited to: language, perceptual similarity, functions and behaviors, similarity of context, feature correlations, feature entrenchment, and other factual knowledge. Children's use of multiple cues allows us to reconcile the domain-specificity of essentialism with the domain-generality of lexicalization and generics. As noted earlier, count nouns and generics apply to all domains (e.g., "*Cats* are good at hunting"; "I like *argyle socks*"), although generics are more frequent for animal than artifact kinds. What lexicalization and generics may do is highlight the relative coherence and stability of a set of entities. The extent to which one treats this set as essentialized will in large part be a function of domain-specific beliefs (about, for example, natural kinds versus artifacts).

At the same time, language is not simply one cue among many. Words have a privileged status, relative to any other single property.[11] This can be seen in the greater power of labels compared to other properties (reviewed in chapter 6) as well as in the special nature of words relative to other attention-drawing devices, such as auditory tones or nonreferential emotional expressions (e.g., Waxman, 1999; Xu, in press). Words have unique functions and do not simply serve to capture the child's attention and forge associative links among items.

One challenging set of issues concerns how people coordinate among these cues, as well as the degree of concord versus competition among these cues in the input to children. Some of these cues may have different strengths at different points in development. For example, the role of language may be particularly strong early in development, when children have relatively less world knowledge and information regarding specific features to guide their reasoning. These issues remain unresolved and in need of study.

Chapter 9

Theory Theories and DAM Theories

> Young children's naming of objects is principally a matter of mapping words to selected perceptual properties.
>> Linda B. Smith, Susan S. Jones, and Barbara Landau,
>> "Naming in Young Children"

In this chapter I step back to consider the implications of childhood essentialism for theories of cognitive development. In the preceding chapters, I presented wide-ranging evidence for what may be called "early competence." Preschool children appear to be surprisingly skilled: they attend to nonobvious properties, search for underlying causes, draw systematic category-based inferences, and so forth. The capacities detailed in the preceding chapters all argue against a traditional Piagetian stage theory of development, in which preschool children are incapable of constructing "true" concepts. Instead we see striking commonalities between the concepts of preschoolers and those of adults.

The focus of this chapter is why and how children show this early competence. I approach the question in two ways. First I attempt to reconcile these findings with the seemingly contradictory results from other tasks. And second, I consider which of two radically different accounts best explains why children show this early competence: the theory theory view or the "dumb attentional mechanisms" (L. Smith, Jones, and Landau, 1996) view. But first, I briefly summarize my position of theory-laden essentialism, as a launching point from which to consider alternative views.

THEORY-LADEN ESSENTIALISM

The portrait of psychological essentialism that I provide is a framework theory and importantly developmental in nature. A varied set of essentialist-like beliefs emerge early in development (by three to five years of age): certain categories promote rich inferences, are stable over transformations, have innate potential and nonobvious core features, and incorporate causal features. However, these beliefs are not the expression of a detailed knowledge base, but rather a skeletal framework for organizing new information. For example, the expectation that different birds are alike in nonobvious ways is an open-ended anticipation, not the expression of a well-informed biology. Likewise, when children privilege internal and innate features for living kinds, they are not recounting biological facts but rather are expressing an abstract expectation about the immutability of these categories.

The fact that essentialist-like beliefs emerge so early in development yet receive so little explicit instruction from parents suggests that essentialism may be a developmental constant. Yet alongside this constant, developmental changes also occur. Essentialism may start out as an assumption about kinds, only later incorporating the idea of a causal essence. This tentative conclusion receives support from the fact that evidence for kinds has been found in children about two to three years younger than those showing evidence for essences. Moreover, with age children are increasingly able to incorporate nonessentialized models of concepts (Heyman and Gelman, 2000a; Hirschfeld, 1996; Taylor, 1996), detailed biological knowledge (Gottfried, Gelman, and Schultz, 1999), and statistical information about category structure (G. Gutheil and Gelman, 1997; López et al., 1992).

Early essentialism might appear to pose a challenge to more traditional theories of children's concepts (e.g., Inhelder and Piaget, 1964), which emphasized the instability of children's concepts and their focus on superficial, accidental, or perceptual features. Yet essentialism also grants an important role to perceptual features in early concepts. That is, children seem to assume that categories have a double-layered structure: a layer of outward appearances *and* an underlying layer that supports and causes the outward layer. The studies reported in this book attempt to uncover young children's assumptions concerning the hidden layer of concepts— without denying children's fascination with the level of observable reality.

RECONCILING EARLY COMPETENCE WITH
TRADITIONAL RESULTS

Why do children do so well on tests of essentialism, compared with their difficulties in many other tasks? In other words, how can we reconcile early essentialism with more standard views of children's early concepts? To be concrete: why do three-year-old children seem to have trouble forming a coherent category grouping, so that for example a single category might consist of a red square, a red circle, and a blue circle (e.g., Inhelder and Piaget, 1964; Vygotsky, 1962), yet at the same time infer that categories share rich clusters of important similarities (S. Gelman and Markman, 1986)? Why do they at times grant special status to internal or nonobvious properties (Diesendruck, Gelman, and Lebowitz, 1998), yet at other times treat superficial shape or color cues as paramount (L. Smith and Heise, 1992)?

One possible response is to reject the essentialist findings presented in this book. After all, if children do not *truly* treat categories as having rich inductive potential, or do not *truly* grant special status to internal or nonobvious properties, then there is no contradiction to reconcile, no puzzle to be explained. Jones and

Smith (1993), in a critique of the S. Gelman and Markman induction tasks, suggested that children's seeming adherence to essentialism is an artifact of the stimuli used in the research. They argue that the line drawings used are impoverished, distorted, and misleading, and fail to present a realistic depiction of the objects of interest. For example, a picture of a snake that looks like a worm is "a very poor" depiction of any animal in the real world. Given depictions "with little surface similarity to real objects," children's use of other information (such as category labels) tells us little about children's construals of natural kinds. Children are using labels on these tasks only because the perceptual information provided is "deliberately distorted to be misleading." The implication is that if more-realistic stimuli (such as photographs) were used, then children would rely more heavily on perceptual information.

There are several problems with this line of argument. The pictures criticized by Jones and Smith are not distortions of real-world objects.[1] In all of our work on category-based induction, my collaborators and I have taken great care to ensure that the category anomalies presented are accurate. The Brahminy blind snake truly does look like an earthworm, as does the western blind snake, as well as legless lizards of the family Amphisbaenidae (see Figure 9.1). (To illustrate just how confusing the appearance of these animals is: in searching for a picture of a wormlike snake on the Web, I came across a posting titled "Snake/worm?" in which someone on a bulletin board asked whether the "baby snake worm things" she dug up in her backyard were worms or snakes.) Indeed, anomalies abound in the biological world. Whales resemble fish; flying bats look like flying birds; stick insects are dead ringers for sticks; and pyrite fooled a number of gold prospectors. Although I agree with the point that usually appearances are an excellent guide to category membership, these sorts of anomalies demonstrate that human categories cannot be reduced to surface appearances. There are sound biological reasons to expect appearances and naming to diverge at times (including homologies, camouflage, evolved deceptions, mimicry, and sexual dimorphism, among others). But more to the point, nonbiologists—adults and children alike—recognize that appearances can be misleading. Adult naming systems are rooted in the assumption that outward perception is not everything. The suggestion that appearances will not mislead reflects a serious misunderstanding of categorization and its link to biological variation.

In any case, essentialist claims do not rest on tasks that use line drawings. S. Gelman (1988) and S. Gelman and O'Reilly (1988), using photographs, found that children draw inferences to dissimilar category members. When a direct comparison of line drawings and actual three-dimensional objects was made, children drew even more category-based inductive inferences from 3-D objects than drawings (Deák and Bauer, 1996). A range of other tasks that used photographs or realistic detailed drawings also found essentialism (e.g., Diesendruck, 2001), including many of the switched-at-birth studies reviewed in chapter 4 (e.g., S. Gelman and Wellman, 1991). Keil (1989) and Rosengren et al. (1991) used photographs and re-

Figure 9.1.   Brahminy blind snake. Source: Reprinted with the permission of Kenneth Krysko at the Florida Museum of Natural History.

alistic color drawings, and found that children assumed that identity remains constant over growth, even with color change or metamorphosis. It cannot be the case, therefore, that essentialist beliefs reflect "deeply impoverished" line drawings used in the studies.

If we assume that the findings here do represent something fundamental and revealing about children's concepts, then we return to the need for an explanation to resolve the seeming contradiction with traditional results. The usual early-competence explanation might go something like this: children really are much more sophisticated than we used to think, but old methods were flawed. When we use better methods, we get much better performance. This account is compelling in many areas, including for example perspective-taking, numerical understanding, or spatial reasoning (see Siegler, 1998, for review). For example, Piaget's famous "three mountains" perspective-taking task was highly demanding from an information-processing standpoint, requiring children to imagine and recreate a complex scene from unseen perspectives. This task seriously underestimated young children's capacity to reason nonegocentrically. When simpler, more streamlined tasks are used, then children show far superior performance (Flavell and Miller, 1998). For example, even two-year-olds turn a picture so that the person they are showing it to can see it, thereby showing nonegocentrism.

For categorization, too, an information-processing overload can lead to markedly worse performance compared to tasks that ease the processing burden for children. An elegant example comes from Markman, Cox, and Machida's (1981) work showing that children sort objects into superordinate categories more often and with greater accuracy when the sorts are done into plastic baggies rather than out on a tabletop. This simple change in procedure blocks an attractive alternative strategy (forming pictures or scenes with the items).

This explanation borrows (implicitly) from the Chomskian distinction between competence and performance. On this view, there is an underlying capacity that children possess, a capacity that can be masked (by demanding procedures) or revealed (by sensitive procedures). The better performance is truer, in the sense that it more directly reflects the capacities of interest. Of course no one would deny that the gap between competence and performance is also meaningful—some speak of the greater fragility of knowledge in younger children, as seen in the greater scaffolding required for good performance. Nonetheless, the position assumes a single competence that is seen more or less clearly, depending on the task at hand.

My view of children's concepts is somewhat different. I endorse an early-competence explanation, but with a twist. I think the standard methods are not simply overloading children (though certainly at times that is also an issue) so much as they are looking at a different piece of the picture. My departure from framing children's abilities in terms of competence versus performance is rooted in the belief that categorization is not all just one thing. There is not a single competence, and there is enormous diversity in the sorts of categories we do and can use. Categories are the link between us and all the messy complexity out there in the world. If the world were a simple place, we could simply be born with all the categories we need. But instead, we need to be able to construct them, and to use them flexibly for different tasks. So whether we find children using superficial cues or being essentialists will depend on the situation—including what the task is and what the category is. In other words, children exhibit great flexibility in what information they use when classifying (Deák and Bauer, 1995, 1996; see also Rosengren and Braswell, 2001, for a broader discussion of variability in children's reasoning). By at least three years of age, children's categories sensitively reflect factors that include task and category variation. An unresolved question of great theoretical significance is when such flexibility emerges: is it built into the cognitive system, or is it a developmental outcome?

Task Variation

We have already seen in chapter 2 that the task matters: similarity judgments, categorization, inductive inferences, and word extension all reflect different sorts of knowledge (Carey, 1985; Deák and Bauer, 1995, 1996; S. Gelman, Collman, and Maccoby, 1986; Rips, 1989; Taylor and Gelman, 1993). For example: show a two-year-old a pterodactyl, and she will say that it is a bird and lives in a nest. The two-year-old has very little knowledge about how to classify the item. But tell her it is a dinosaur, and she will accept the label and report that it does not live in a nest. Her expectations fall in line with the name. Before children have the knowledge they need to form certain categories, they are firm in their beliefs about how those categories are structured.

Task variation matters for adults as well (e.g., E. Smith, Patalano, and Jonides, 1998; Yamauchi and Markman, 1998). For example, if I were to show you a picture of a yellow-footed antechinus, you would say it is a mouse and draw certain inferences about how it bears young. But once I tell you it is a marsupial (which indeed it is), some of your inferences would shift. Doug Medin and I have noted that the kinds of conceptual functions available include "rapid identification . . . , organizing information efficiently in memory, problem-solving, analogizing, drawing inductive inferences that extend knowledge beyond what is known, embodying and imparting ideological beliefs, [and] conveying aesthetic materials (e.g., metaphor, poetry)" (S. Gelman and Markman, 1993, p. 158).

There is a general pattern here, that tasks reflecting the accumulation of expertise and deeper analysis are the tasks for which subjects more consistently use information that can be characterized as nonobvious. Roughly, there seems to be a distinction between rough-and-ready information, used when we need to be quick, and more time-consuming, less obvious information, used when we need to be accurate. The "quick" information is what we find salient; the "accurate" information is what we believe the world is like. Although the two are highly correlated, nonobvious properties are privileged on tasks requiring expertise and lexicalization. Under time pressure, subjects are more likely to use global similarity than dimensional similarity (Ward, 1983), more likely to use perceptual salience than formal category structure (Lamberts, 1995), and more likely to use overall appearance than function (Kemler Nelson, Frankenfield, et al., 2000).

It is appropriate that different tasks yield use of different sorts of information. For example, if I am in the forest and worried about the possibility of a poisonous snake biting me, then even just a glimpse of a long, wriggly, legless creature will be enough to cause me to flee. Yet when accurate induction is needed, then the features available in a quick glimpse may not be enough. For example, if (while still out in the forest) I am picking mushrooms in preparation for dinner, then I would be prudent to inspect my yield more closely, to try to determine just what sorts of mushrooms I have found.

Importantly, however, perceptual information is not developmentally prior to theoretical information (Bruner, 1973). There is no perceptual-to-conceptual shift in ontogenesis (S. Gelman, 1996; Jones and Smith, 1993; Simons and Keil, 1995). Young children are sensitive to the task effects described above. Given an induction task, for instance, children as young as age two give essentialist responses (S. Gelman and Coley, 1990; Jaswal and Markman, 2002). Even on quick identification tasks, detection and use of subtle ontological information may be quite immediate, allowing children to identify an instance as a real animal versus a statue, for example (Massey and Gelman, 1988), or to overlook color, form, and substance when classifying an item into a superordinate class (Sigel, 1953, 1978). Similarly, three-year-olds attend more to tiny self-initiated movements than to large other-initiated movements when explaining animal movement (S. Gelman and Gottfried, 1996), and four-year-olds attend to subtle details of a drawing to detect the category membership of an item (e.g., the antennae on a leaf insect; S. Gelman and Markman, 1987). L. Smith and Heise (1992) have suggested that these sorts of subtle perceptual cues are what make perception smart, and argue against the need to posit theories or essentialism; I suggest instead that these provide evidence that perception is constrained by and imbued with theories.

Category Variation

Concepts are highly varied, even for young children. They range from simple dimensions of immediate perceptual experience (red, cold) to internal emotional states (happy, mad) to natural kinds (animal, bear, oak tree). Researchers often choose to focus on a select subset, for simplicity's sake—but do so at a cost, as different concepts appear to be best understood in terms of different cognitive models (e.g., Mervis and Rosch, 1981). It is probably not a coincidence that papers arguing for the centrality of perceptual information in children's concepts have used simple, nonfunctional artifacts. A category of simple geometric shapes that vary only on the dimensions of size, shape, and texture, orthogonally varied, is going to yield attention to perceptual features (see Figure 9.2). By definition, such stimuli cannot reveal attention to function, intentions, or nonobvious properties. The kinds of assumptions a child brings to bear on a category of irregular shapes made out of chicken wire are very different from the kinds of assumptions a child brings to bear on a species of mammal. None of the phenomena I discussed earlier—causality, inductive potential, and nonobvious properties—would apply to the shapes

Consider a concept that is encoded in a word, that is passed down from parent to child, and that refers to a richly structured, basic-level animal kind. Now compare this to a concept that has been invented by an experimenter, that lacks a name, and that was introduced during an experiment. How can we possibly expect that there will be no substantive differences between the two? I submit that one cannot construct a general theory of concepts from studying just one kind of concept.

Sensitivity to distinctions among categories promises to bring order to the messy inconsistency that appears when one tries to characterize conceptual structure in a way that encompasses the full variety of all forms of human categorization. The question is not "are all categories essentialized?" but rather "which categories are essentialized, if any?" For example, does the concept "things to take from a burning house" differ from the concept "dogs," or are they indistinguishable in structure? Common sense tells us that, at the very least, they differ in the perceptual similarity among instances, richness of stored knowledge, inferences that can

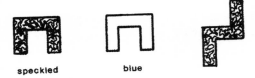

speckled   blue

Figure 9.2.   Geometric shapes. *Source*: Smith, Jones and Landau (1992). Reprinted with the permission of the American Psychological Association and Linda B. Smith.

be made, stability over time, and position in a hierarchy. Although Medin (1989) allowed for the possibility that all natural language concepts (including, e.g., waste-basket) are essentialized (see also Carey, 1995; Lakoff, 1987), I maintain that different categories have fundamentally different kinds of structure, for children and adults. At least three factors are relevant: category domain, category level, and linguistic expression.

DOMAIN DIFFERENCES.   Particularly between natural kinds and artifacts, domain differences have consequences for a variety of tasks that tap essentialist reasoning. Transformations that radically change the appearance of an object result in judgments of category change for artifacts but stability for animals (Keil, 1989), implying that animals—but not artifacts—retain some essential qualities that persist despite external appearance changes. Information about internal parts is used when extending novel labels for animals but not for artifacts (Diesendruck, Gelman, and Lebowitz, 1998), suggesting that the relevance of nonobvious internal parts—a close stand-in for essences—is domain-specific. Inductive inferences are more powerful for animal, plant, and natural-substance categories than for artifact categories (S. Gelman, 1988). Children are also more likely to attribute immanent (inherent) causes for animals than for artifacts (S. Gelman and Gottfried, 1996). In categorization, adults also distinguish between the two domains. They believe membership in animal categories is more "absolute" than membership in artifact categories (Diesendruck and Gelman, 1999), and that animal categories have defining features to a larger extent than artifact categories do (Malt, 1990). In general, these findings support the notion that children and adults hold essentialist beliefs about animals but not about artifacts. (Most studies have not included plants and natural substance kinds, leaving it unclear whether the contrast is animate/inanimate, living/nonliving, or natural/artificial.) Explanations for the domain differences vary: they may reflect an innate domain-specific module for reasoning about living kinds (Atran, 1995), a teleological/essentialist construal that finds a better match with particular domains in the world (Keil, 1995), or an assumption that entities without external similarities (i.e., natural kinds) must have internal essential causal properties (S. Gelman, Coley, and Gottfried, 1994). I return to these issues in chapters 10 and 11.

CATEGORY LEVEL.   At this point, very little is known regarding how category level intersects with judgments of essentialism, though some evidence is suggestive. The distinction between basic-level categories (e.g., dog) and superordinate-level categories (e.g., animal) may be particularly relevant, with the former essentialized more than the latter. Hunn (1998, p. 576) suggested, based on ethnobiological evidence, that higher-level taxa "are a motley crew of categories grounded in whatever association is handy, which may be morphological similarity, ecological contiguity, common utility, or some other symbolic linkage." If higher-level taxa are based on more haphazard criteria, then they should be less likely to be essentialized. Atran, Estin, et al. (1997) found that the "generic-species" level (e.g., oak, robin) is favored over other hierarchical levels for drawing inductive inferences, both for people raised in Michigan and for the Itzaj Maya people of Guatemala. Similarly, although H_2O is not the essence of "water" when the word is used at a superordinate level (including pond water, polluted water, and other exotic varieties), H_2O does seem to be the essence of "water" when the word is used at a more subordinate level ("pure water") (Malt, 1994; however, she interprets these data differently).

LINGUISTIC EXPRESSION.   Language form also predicts category structure: languages of the world do not honor every passing concept with a word (Greenberg, 1966; Rosch, 1978). As discussed in chapter 8, essentializing seems more likely to occur when a concept is encoded in language than when it is not. Certainly hearing a familiar name can foster essentializing (S. Gelman and Markman, 1986), though not every word carries with it essentialist assumptions (Davidson and Gelman, 1990).

Essentialism appears most often for basic-level living kinds that are referred to by common nouns, at least among adults (see Carey, 1995, on the need to examine these issues developmentally). A major source of confusion in the literature is that the dimensions of domain, level, and linguistic expression have generally been ignored in discussions of the validity of psychological essentialism. The scope of essentialism can be exaggerated when derived from a database focused on natural kind categories, especially basic-level animal categories with familiar common nouns as names. Conversely, the role of perception can be misleading when focused on nonlexicalized categories for which essences or theories are barely possible. For example, Landau, Smith, and Jones (1988) found that children had a strong tendency to extend labels on the basis of perceptual features such as shape—a finding that is not surprising, given that the stimuli in that study were simple novel objects (e.g., a U-shaped piece of plywood), of which it is implausible that children had much prior knowledge. Similarly, Mervis, Johnson, and Scott (1993) report a study in which participants sorted items on the basis of shape—yet the task was a silhouette identification task (Rosch et al., 1976), in which shape and size were the only dimensions available. The information a child uses will be limited by the information supplied. If the only information children receive concerns shape, texture, and size, then frequent use of shape is unsurprising. In contrast, when children are reasoning about real-world living kinds, then issues of ontology, essence, and kind become important.

Summary

In this section I have considered two divergent views of preschool children's concepts. On the one hand, we are told that preschool children are perceptually bound, mired in the concrete here and now, and incapable of forming "true concepts" (which I term the "traditional view"). On the other hand, psychological essentialism depicts preschool children as searching for causes, looking beyond the obvious, and treating concepts as stable, even immutable.

I resolve the discrepancy by noting that children use different kinds of information, depending on the concept and the task under consideration. Returning to the traditional studies finding that children below six or seven years of age have difficulty forming categories, we see that the tasks and concepts were especially unsuited to revealing essentialism. For example, Inhelder and Piaget (1964) presented children with a large array of blocks of varying shapes and colors, and asked them to put together the ones that go together. This activity required children to construct a grouping rather than reason about a category that had already been established. It involves non-basic-level categories and nonnatural kinds. It allowed for no opportunity to consider the role of causation, or origins, of innate potential. Such a task tells us little, if anything, about children's inferences and assumptions about basic-level biological kinds, or their attentiveness to properties such as causal force.

In other words, what we see depends on what questions we ask. If we ask preschool children to apply a rigid, deterministic rule to a novel array of items for which multiple sorts of classifications are possible, then they will look inconsistent, immature, and "captured" by appearances. It will seem that categories are shifting, ephemeral things for them. On such tasks, preschool children truly do look qualitatively different from U.S. college sophomores. But if we ask preschool children what it means to be a member of a lexicalized natural kind ("boy," "cat"), a wealth of expectations and assumptions pour forth. These expectations and assumptions are startlingly similar to what we hear from adults. Children's essentialism is there for all to see—but only when we ask the right questions.

THEORY THEORIES VERSUS DAM THEORIES

Essentialism has implications for an ongoing debate about the nature of cognitive development. I contrast "theory theories" with "DAM [dumb attentional mechanism] theories" (see Table 9.1). On the one side is the idea that concepts are built out of what L. Smith, Jones, and Landau (1996) call "dumb attentional mechanisms." The argument here is that children learn concepts by simple association:

Table 9.1. Comparison of major differences between theory theory and DAM theory

DAM theory	Theory theory
No stability in concepts	At least stable ontology and assumption of essence
Importance of shape and other perceptual features	Shape is only a marker; importance of nonobvious features
Tallying of *specific* contextual features and *specific* linguistic cues	Importance of generic (nonspecific) concepts
General-purpose learning mechanisms	Domain-specific theory building
Development from specific to abstract	Abstract, skeletal framework guides development
Associative, statistical learning mechanism	Importance of inferences and conceptual knowledge; theories override statistics
Nonreflective, involuntary, automatic	Strategic, deliberative (?)

Children repeatedly experience *specific* linguistic contexts (e.g., "This is a _____" or "This is some _____") with attention to *specific* object properties and clusters of properties (e.g., shape or color plus texture). Thus, by this view, these linguistic contexts come to serve as cues that automatically control attention. . . . Dumb forces on selective attention—that is, associative connections and direct stimulus pulls—underlie the seeming smartness of children's novel word interpretations. (pp. 145–146, emphasis added)

The process as described here is bottom-up, starting with concrete features in the environment that get linked to concrete linguistic features of the input. Children are said to use domain-general processes to build up deceptively "complex" concepts from simple building blocks. Simple perceptual features (such as shape) are crucial to category membership. Young children's naming is initially immune to more-conceptual information, such as function.

On the other side is the suggestion that children are naïve theorists, as Carey, Gopnik, Wellman, Murphy and Medin, P. Bloom, and others have argued. Young children form categories that include information about properties that are not directly observable, such as ontology, causation, function, and intentions. They use their categories to form inferences and explanations that go beyond the available evidence. In some cases, concepts are embedded in an identifiable, articulable theory (e.g., "beliefs" and "desires" in a theory of mind). In other cases, such a theory has not yet been identified, but the components of a theory (ontology, causation, nonobvious features) are present from an early age.

The DAM theory has numerous appeals. Most notably, it *purports to explain a wide range of data*, including children's attention to perceptual features and the context-sensitivity of concepts; it *relies on well-known and well-studied cognitive principles* (such as implicit learning of statistical regularities); and it *is a developmental account* (attempting to account for developmental change, placing few demands on children, and not assuming that knowledge is built in). Nonetheless, each of its appeals is deceptive: children rarely attend just to perceptual features; the simple, well-studied cognitive principles are limited in explanatory potential; and the theory theory provides a more compelling account. I address each of these issues in turn, devoting attention primarily to the first, as it forms the core of the empirical argument.

Attention to Perceptual Features, Especially Shape

One central dispute concerns the role of perceptual features, especially shape, in children's early concepts. The debate centers on whether perceptual features are the basis of children's concepts (the DAM theory), or instead are useful cues but secondary to other, more critical information, such as function or ontology (the theory theory).

On the DAM view, children have a general shape bias in their interpretations of novel count nouns, such that a new word (e.g., "a dax") is assumed to refer to a set of objects that share a common shape (Baldwin, 1992; Gentner and Imai, 1994; Golinkoff, Shuff-Bailey, et al., 1995; Imai, Gentner, and Uchida, 1994; Landau, Jones, and Smith, 1992; Landau, Smith, and Jones, 1988). For example, Imai et al. (1994) presented three- and five-year-olds with item sets consisting of a standard picture (e.g., a birthday cake), a thematic match (e.g., a birthday present), a taxonomic match (e.g., a pie), and a shape match (e.g., a hat). For half the children, the experimenter labeled the standard item with a novel label (e.g., "mef") and then asked children to pick another referent of the novel label from the three alternative items. They found that the most common choice by children was the shape match.

A DAM theorist would also draw up a list of some additional points: preschoolers resist incorporating nonshape information, such as function, into their categories (L. Smith, Jones, and Landau, 1996); toddlers' overextensions in language are shape-based (e.g., "ball" for any round object; Clark, 1973); even older children extend words according to shape when naming toys (e.g., a toy bear is a "bear"; Jones and Smith, 1993). Conclusion: shape overrides theory-based information. Q.E.D.

The theory theory posits that children attend to shape not because it is the basis on which words are extended, but rather because it is an indirect indicator of category membership; it correlates with and "is often . . . a good source of information about" what kind of thing an object is (Soja, Carey, and Spelke, 1992). More generally, the power of perceptual features often derives from their status as markers of theory-relevant information.

The crux of the debate can be seen in a study by Jones, Smith, and Landau (1991), who found that adding eyes to a set of U-shaped objects substantially affected three-year-old children's sorting of those objects, specifically leading to a decrease in the use of shape and an increase in the use of texture cues (e.g., a reluctance to extend a word from an object made of sponge to one made of wood). Jones, Smith, and Landau (1991; L. Smith and Heise, 1992) interpret these data as evidence for children's use of perceptual (not conceptual) features—namely, that children have learned an abstract association between the presence of eyes and object texture. However, are eyes a perceptual feature or a conceptual one? On the theory theory, eyes provide information regarding the ontological status of these objects: they are (representations of) animals rather than inanimate pieces of wood or sponge. I therefore interpret this result as supporting the theory theory: the information children received about theoretical kind (via the feature of eyes, signaling animacy) influenced which features they used.

Recent evidence by Booth and Waxman (2002) supports the theory theory interpretation directly. In two experiments, three-year-old children received a word-extension task with simple abstract objects, in which the objects were described as having either animal-relevant properties (e.g., "This dax has a mommy and daddy who love it very much. . . . When this dax goes to sleep at night, they give it lots of hugs and kisses") or artifact-relevant properties (e.g., "This dax was made by an astronaut to do a very special job on her spaceship"). Children sorted the objects differently, depending on the conceptual information provided in the story. When hearing the animate story, children relied less heavily on shape and more on texture. Conceptual information alone was sufficient to alter children's patterns of word extension. In a second study, children were confronted with a conflict between a perceptual cue (presence of eyes, strongly signaling animacy) and conceptual information describing the items as artifacts. Even in this strong test, the conceptual information guided children's word extensions: they treated the items just as they did the no-eyes artifacts in study 1. As Booth and Waxman point out, the data strongly argue against the idea that children automatically activate purely perceptually based associations between the presence of eyes and the dimension of shape.

In the remainder of this section, I lay out explicitly why each of the kinds of evidence for shape-based categorization is found wanting. In each case, what first appears to be clean evidence for a shape bias turns out to be a more complicated story in which children as young as age two seek and use theory-based information.

Nonshape Categories in Early Childhood

Shape cannot be the sole determinant of preschool children's classifications. There are striking counterexamples to the use of shape, even when children are reasoning about perceptually rich stimuli (realistic color photographs or actual objects). In a variety of cases, fundamental conceptual distinctions appear to be more predictive than shape.

Ten-month-olds classify together containers differing in shape and distinguish between same-shaped objects that differ in their capacity to contain (Kolstad and Baillargeon, 1996). Early word learners extend some labels based on function more than shape, such as using "ball" to refer to things that can be thrown (Nelson,

1974). By age two years, children weight substance more heavily than shape on a match-to-sample task in which the items are nonsolid masses (Soja, Carey, and Spelke, 1991). By two and a half years of age, children appropriately provide the same label for objects of different shapes (e.g., round cookie, windmill cookie) and different labels for objects of the same shape (e.g., round plate, round cookie). By three and four years of age, children treat plants and animals as belonging to a single category (living things), despite the extreme differences in shape between, say, a cow and a tree (Backscheider, Shatz, and Gelman, 1993; Hickling and Gelman, 1995). Conversely, children treat humans and apes as belonging to distinctly different categories, despite their shape similarity. For example, when given triads consisting of a human, a nonhuman primate, and a nonprimate animal, elementary-school children are more likely than adults to group together the primate and the animal, isolating the human (K. Johnson, Mervis, and Boster, 1992). This pattern is also found among preschoolers, even when the primate and animal differ radically in shape (such as chimpanzee and centipede; Coley, 1993).

A classic and insightful example of how children's categories reflect animacy is found in a study by Massey and R. Gelman (1988). Children three and four years of age were asked to say which of a series of unfamiliar entities could go up a hill by itself. Children were remarkably accurate, especially considering that the items were unfamiliar and that superficial cues were potentially misleading. For example, one of the inanimate entities was a statue with a face and legs, yet children appropriately judged that it could not go up a hill by itself. Conversely, one of the animate entities was an echidna, without a clearly identifiable animal shape, yet children appropriately judged that it could go up a hill by itself. Clearly, perceptual information was key here—children had only perceptual information to guide their choices. Nonetheless, what they found relevant was not "similarity" in some overall sense, but rather those subtle perceptual cues that revealed the animacy of the object.

Preschool children also judge that outer appearances do not determine what an animal is. Shipley (2000, study 1) found that three- and four-year-olds judged certain behaviors (such as what an animal eats, how it moves, and what sound it makes) as more important for determining what it is, compared to outward appearance. An animal that looks like a camel (humps on back, long neck, long eyelashes) but behaves like a tiger (eats meat, roars, climbs tree) was more often judged to be a tiger.

Shape and Function

The heart of the evidence for DAM theories comes from a series of experiments with three-year-olds, focusing on their use of perceptual salience instead of function. L. Smith, Jones, and Landau (1996) argued that three-year-old children selectively ignore functional information when extending new labels. Their evidence included a series of four experiments in which three-year-olds failed to use function when extending novel labels to novel objects. Each trial was structured as follows: participants were introduced to a target object and asked either to find more objects like the target (similarity task) or to find more objects with the same name (naming task). The test objects differed from the target in similarity and function. In some conditions, children were explicitly shown different functions that target objects had. Although children used function to answer Similarity questions, they did not use function to answer Naming questions. Their name extensions seemed influenced by changes in the relative perceptual salience of the items.

Landau, Smith, and Jones (1998) extended this line of work using a greater range of both novel and familiar objects. Across three studies of similar design, two-, three-, and five-year-olds and adults were asked to extend labels (naming task) or to infer novel functions (function task; e.g., "Could you carry water with this one?"). In general, children selected based on function on the function task and selected based on shape on the naming task, regardless of whether or not they were presented with explicit demonstrations of function.

If these provocative results are interpreted as the authors suggest, it would be damaging to the concepts-in-theories position that I am arguing for in this chapter. Yet children can and do use functional information while naming, as long as appropriate items and tasks are used. When care is taken to design tasks and items that reflect functions that are salient, sensible, and nonarbitrary, then young children incorporate function into their naming from as early as two years of age. This latter argument has been pursued vigorously in the past few years, and I briefly review some of the evidence that supports it.

Kemler Nelson, Frankenfield, et al. (2000) point out that children cannot be expected to appreciate just any type of function they encounter, any more than would an adult. They suggest that, for a fair test, it is critical to examine function/structure relations that are "compelling and nonarbitrary in a way that young children can make sense of (and may expect)" (p. 1272). Specifically, Kemler Nelson posits that the functionally relevant aspects of an object's design should be easily perceptible, that structure/function relations should be based on principles of causality that are familiar to young children, and that function/structure relations should be "convincing." For example, Kemler Nelson et al. (1995) introduced three-, four-, and five-year-old children to a novel artifact that could function in two distinct and novel ways, either to paint parallel lines or to make music. Certain features were contingent on one function whereas other features were contingent on the other (e.g., brushes for painting; wires for the music). Each child encountered only one of these functions, in either a painter or an instrument condition, when the target artifact was named. When asked to extend the novel name to test objects that varied from the target in similarity and function, children tended to extend the name in accordance with the function they saw demonstrated (though similarity relations were also taken into account).

Similarly, Diesendruck and Markson (1999) argue that young children can appreciate function when it is a permanent, exclusive property of an object (as opposed to just something that the object "does," as in L. Smith, Jones, and Landau, 1996) and when it is made readily available (e.g., through explicit demonstration and explanation, such as "This was made for X"). When these conditions are met, even three-year-olds appreciate function and use it as the basis of classification.

Kemler Nelson (1999) went on to examine the effect that direct experience with object function may have on toddlers' novel label extensions. Some children were given direct prior experience manipulating test objects before a naming session, whereas other children were not given this opportunity. Toddlers successfully generalized novel names based on function, but only if they had had previous direct experience with the objects. These results demonstrate that function can guide naming decisions in children as young as two years of age. However, toddlers' understanding of function may be less robust than that of older children.

In other cases, even minimal direct experience with test objects is sufficient for toddlers to use functional properties in their naming decisions (Kemler Nelson, Russell, et al., 2000). In experiment 2 in Kemler Nelson, Russell, et al. (2000), two-year-olds' naming decisions reflected object functions, even though the functions were never demonstrated by an experimenter but instead were discovered by the children during the course of the experiment.

What is it that makes a function more compelling to children? Kemler Nelson, Frankenfield, et al. (2000) found that four-year-old children were more likely to generalize novel names for artifacts when functions "made sense" and were more reasonably related to structure and as such, the functions intended by a designer. For example, a "sensible" (plausible) function for an object with a horizontal and vertical tube might be "when you put balls in here, it drops them one at a time," whereas an implausible function for the same object might be "a toy snake can wriggle in it." That is, although the object could readily carry out either of these functions, only the first is likely to be a function designed by the creator of the object.

Similarly, P. Bloom (2000) proposed that function is used to the extent that it is perceived as intentional—specifically, intended by the designer of the object under consideration. Children relied on function when it was highly specific and unlikely to be an accidental function (e.g., painting parallel lines; Kemler Nelson et al., 1995) but did not rely on function when it was a simple and general function that depended only on the substance that the object was made of and so potentially accidental (e.g., wiping up water; Landau, Smith, and Jones, 1998). When two objects have clearly different intended functions, children do not consistently extend a novel word from one to the other, even when the objects are identical in shape (e.g., an object and its same-shaped container; P. Bloom, Markson, and Diesendruck, 1998, cited in P. Bloom, 2000).

Shape and Representations

If, as I suggest, shape is not the core of children's naming, then why is a toy bear called a "bear" (Jones and Smith, 1993)? After all, a toy bear shares no property with real bears other than shape. Toy bears are small, cuddly, inanimate, filled with stuffing, unable to move on their own. Why are ontological distinctions commonly ignored in ordinary language use?

Soja, Carey, and Spelke (1992) suggest that it is not shape per se that children (or adults) are naming; rather, children are attempting to name that which the shape represents. A toy bear is called a "bear" because it represents a bear, not because it is shaped like a bear (see also Mandler, 1993). Indirect support for this argument comes from the observation that objects not designed to represent another kind of thing are rarely mislabeled (e.g., footballs are rarely called "eggs").

More direct evidence also supports this interpretation. P. Bloom and Markson (1998) asked children to draw a balloon and a lollipop, and several minutes later asked them to describe each picture. Although the resulting drawings were indistinguishable by shape, children consistently labeled them in accordance with their original intentions, as "balloon" and "lollipop," respectively.

Karen Ebeling and I designed a study to test this hypothesis further (S. Gelman and Ebeling, 1998). The participants were forty-seven preschool children (ranging in age from 2;5 to 3;11) and thirty-two adults. They saw a series of eight line drawings roughly shaped like various nameable objects, such as a man (see Figure 9.3). Each participant was randomly assigned to one of two conditions. For about half the participants, we described each line drawing as depicting a shape that was created intentionally—for example, someone painted the picture. For the remaining subjects, we described the same drawing as depicting a shape that was created accidentally—for example, someone spilled some paint. For each item, participants first heard the brief story, then were shown the corresponding line drawing and asked, "What is this?" Open-ended responses were coded as naming the shape (e.g., "a man"), naming the actual materials (e.g., "paint"), or other (e.g., "looks like a man," "I don't know").

We hypothesized that participants' use of shape as the basis of naming would be influenced by the representational status of the pictures, as conveyed by the verbal

Figure 9.3. Examples of the line drawings used in S. Gelman and Ebeling (1998). *Source*: S. Gelman and Ebeling (1998). Reprinted with the permission of Elsevier Science.

information: when the drawings were intended, participants should name the shapes; when the drawings were unintended, participants should refer to the pictures in some other way (e.g., describing the literal materials). In other words, when children name in accordance with shape, it is not because shape is paramount, but rather because shape is a representation (much as we may refer to a photograph of Ben as "This is Ben" rather than having to specify "This is a photograph of Ben"; no cooperative speaker would infer that Ben is a two-dimensional image). When the shape does not stand for a kind—as with accidental paint spills—then shape is no longer relevant. The findings fit the predictions: preschool children and adults named on the basis of shape (e.g., referring to the bear-shaped drawing as a "bear") significantly more often when the shape was intended than when it was not (see Table 9.2). This pattern was true for both the older group of children (mean age 3;8) and the younger group of children (mean age 2;11).

In fact, intentions are important for more than just representations: we find this effect for real objects, too. Paul Bloom and I collaborated on a study using the same paradigm, but this time we looked not just at representations (such as drawings or paintings) but also actual objects (such as a hat or a knife; S. Gelman and Bloom, 2000). So, some the items were representations, as in the earlier work, and the remainder were functional objects (see Figure 9.4). As in the earlier work, each participant was randomly assigned to one of two conditions. For example, the intentional story for the newspaper "hat" was: "Jane went and got a newspaper. Then she carefully bent it and folded it until it was just right. Then she was done. This is what it looked like." The accidental story for the newspaper "hat" was: "Jane was holding a newspaper. Then she dropped it by accident, and it fell under a car. She ran to get it and picked it up. This is what it looked like."

Three-year-olds (2;9 to 3;11, mean age 3;6), five-year-olds (4;2 to 6;0, mean age 5;3), and adults participated. As in the earlier work, we found that children and adults were more likely to name the object if it was described as intentionally created than if it was described as accidentally created (see Table 9.3). In both studies, what determined naming was not just the perceptual attributes in the immediate context, but also children's construal of the item. The finding was particularly striking in this study, because the child was viewing an actual three-dimensional object that highly resembled a familiar real-world entity (such as a hat or a knife). Yet despite the immediacy and richness of the perceptual information, children as young as three years of age refrained from labeling the immediate percept on those occasions when they believed the origins to be accidental. Although the Plexiglas knife looked very knifelike in shape and substance, three- and five-year-olds were more likely to call it "a knife" when it was the result of an intentional creation process than when it was the accidental result of an unintentional process.

Karen Ebeling and I designed a follow-up study with the following issue in mind. We wanted to know whether children were using intentionality information only because it was so transparent and explicit in the stories provided, or whether they would use intentionality even if they had to infer it from oblique hints. Malt

Figure 9.4.   Sample items from S. Gelman and Bloom (2000): newspaper "hat," Plexiglas "knife"

and Johnson (1998) point out that an intention-based account has only limited capacity if intentions must be conveyed by means of explicit information. Instead of telling children explicitly that items were intentionally or accidentally made, we tested to see if children could extract this information spontaneously, from cues available by watching the creation process. For each of seven items, children watched a brief videotape of the object being made (see Table 9.4 for the full list of items). We never said whether or not the outcome was intended, but there were

Table 9.2. Mean percentage of trials including naming and literal responses, by condition and age; S. Gelman and Ebeling (1998)

	Naming	Literal
Children		
Intentional	85%	10%
Accidental	55	41
Adults		
Intentional	90	2
Accidental	69	28

Table 9.3. Mean adjusted difference score (naming minus literal responses) as a function of item type, condition, and age; S. Gelman and Bloom (2000). (Standard deviations in parentheses.)

	Art items		Artifact items	
	Intentional	Accidental	Intentional	Accidental
3-year-olds	−1.00*	−2.20*	1.10**	−1.75**
	(1.65)	(2.11)	(2.18)	(2.35)
5-year-olds	2.20**	−1.67**	1.12*	−0.69*
	(1.81)	(3.00)	(1.71)	(2.73)
Adults	2.00**	−3.87**	2.22**	−2.81**
	(2.55)	(0.99)	(4.23)	(2.81)

** significant condition difference by t-test, $p < .02$.

* significant condition difference by t-test, $p < .05$, one-tailed.

Source: S. Gelman and Bloom (2000). Reprinted with the permission of Elsevier Science.

Table 9.4. Items from S. Gelman and Ebeling, video enactment study

Appearance	Materials
Sun	Yellow paint on paper
Ice cream cone	Two pieces of felt
Smiley face	Peas on a plate
Fish	Cooked spaghetti on a plate
House	Blocks
Flower	Playdough
Person	Crayons

cues in the facial expressions, actions, and exclamations (e.g., "Oh, no!" for an accidental event, or "Yes!" for an intentional event). Each object had both an accidental
and intentional videotape, with each child randomly assigned to one of the two
conditions. After viewing the videotape, the child saw the actual finished item.

For example, one item was a splotch of yellow paint on a piece of paper, somewhat in the shape of the sun (see Figure 9.5). In the accidental condition, a young
woman was seated at an easel (with the front angled away from the camera). Using
her finger, she dabbed paint onto the paper mounted on the easel. She had a look
of concentration on her face. She dipped her index finger into a cup to get more
paint on her finger. She then applied a few strokes to the paper. She then started to
put her finger into the cup again, when she looked into the cup and stopped. She
picked up a yellow squirt bottle and squeezed it into the cup with a frustrated expression on her face. She squeezed the bottle again, only this time closer to the
easel. She then suddenly looked at the easel with a very surprised expression on her
face, saying, "Oh, no!" (It looks like she accidentally squirted paint onto the paper.)

In the intentional condition, the same young woman was seated at the same
easel (again, with the front angled away from the camera), and was faintly smiling.
She held a cup in her hand. She applied paint to the paper mounted on the easel,
using her index finger. She carefully stroked and dotted the paint with her finger.
She put her finger into the cup to put more paint on it, and then added a few more

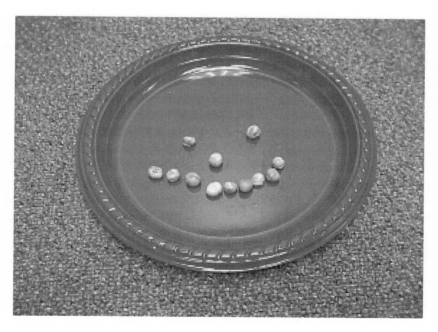

Figure 9.5.   Sample item from S. Gelman and Ebeling (video enactment study)

Table 9.5.   Mean percentage naming and literal responses as a function of condition; S. Gelman and Ebeling, video enactment study

	Naming	*Literal*
Age 2		
Intentional	53%	38%
Accidental	40	48
Age 4		
Intentional	90	7
Accidental	62	38

strokes to the paper. She then stopped, looked at the paper on the easel, and said "Good," while smiling. (It looks like she intentionally created a painting.)

Another notable aspect of this study was that we lowered the age range of participants. In addition to four- and five-year-olds (4;0 to 6;0, mean age 4;10; $N = 32$), we included a group of young two-year-olds (2;2 to 2;6, mean age 2;4; $N = 30$).

The results are shown in Table 9.5. Within each age group considered separately, we conducted a 2 (condition: intentional, accidental) × 2 (response type: naming, literal) ANOVA. We predicted an interaction between the two variables, such that naming responses would be relatively higher in the intentional condition, and literal responses would be relatively higher in the accidental condition. We found precisely the predicted pattern. Both two-year-olds and four-year-olds used the intentionality information to influence their naming. Two-year-olds displayed a significant condition × response type interaction, $F(1,28) = 4.38, p < .05$, as did four-year-olds, $F(1,30) = 14.59, p < .001$. This is sophisticated reasoning and demonstrates that young children were capable of using information that goes well beyond simple perceptual features when making a naming decision.

These findings upend the observation that started this section. Landau, Smith, and Jones (1988) asked: why is a toy bear "a bear"? They were struck by the (apparent) use of shape as a guiding principle in children's naming. Instead, I am struck by children's capacity to go beyond shape. Given how often we *do* call a toy bear "a bear," it is all the more remarkable how two-, three-, and four-year-olds distinguish between accidental and intentional processes of creation. Despite exposure to input that encourages children to treat shape as fundamental, children nonetheless insist that not all bear-shapes are alike.

Shape and Overextensions

Below age two and a half, children make many overextension errors (e.g., calling a round ball "moon"), and these errors are often described as being shape-based (Clark, 1973). But, as many researchers have been careful to point out, there are

several problems with concluding that children's concepts or semantic representations are shape-based at this age. First, previous analyses rarely attempted to tease
apart shape from taxonomic relatedness as the basis of children's overextension errors. For example, in Clark's (1973) classic paper, a child's use of "cat" to refer to
dogs, cows, and sheep was characterized as shape-based, even though the word
matches the referents on both shape and taxonomic relatedness. Second, children
may extend words for communicative effect, without believing that the word literally refers to the item so named (L. Bloom, 1973). For a child who has a limited vocabulary of less than a few hundred words, for a child who does not have the syntactic skills to differentiate "This is a cat" from "This looks like a cat" or "This
reminds me of a cat," or for a child who simply cannot come up with the right
name at the right time in the course of a conversation, overextensions may serve
pragmatic functions rather than reflect semantic representations in any precise
way. And third, children may at times treat same-shaped objects as representations
of real objects (e.g., a round candle may look like a representation of an apple), resulting in shape-based naming as we have seen above.

Marilyn Shatz offers an insightful discussion of shape, in her case study of a
child, Ricky, at twenty-one to twenty-two months of age. She noticed that Ricky
often overextended words to objects related in shape, such as "hammer" for a telephone pole with a cross-bar at the top, "ball" for a hard-boiled egg yolk, or "pig"
for a piece of cheese in the shape of a pig's head. I will quote at length from Shatz's
discussion, as the examples and discussion are particularly relevant here:

> Was Ricky creating overly general categories based on shape or just using his simple
> language to draw attention to similarities of shape? His use of language in other cir-
> cumstances supports the inference that Ricky's utterances should be glossed as "that
> *looks like* a hammer," "that *looks like* a ball," and "that *looks like* a pig" [emphases
> added] rather than "that *is* a hammer, a pig, a ball." When Ricky wanted cheese, he al-
> ways asked for it by name, never with "pig." And he had a large vocabulary of *ball*
> words, including *football*, that he always used appropriately, suggesting that he knew
> that spherical shape was not a necessary feature of *ball*. He also used the word *ham-
> mer* (although as a verb) in appropriate circumstances. (Shatz 1994, pp. 70–71)

How to demonstrate this knowledge in a systematic experimental way is potentially quite difficult. It would first appear that comprehension studies would solve
the problems posed by production studies. And there are a number of excellent
comprehension studies in the literature (e.g., Kuczaj, 1982, 1986; Thomson and
Chapman, 1977; see S. Gelman, Croft, et al., 1998, for review). These studies give insight regarding the conditions under which children are most likely to overextend.

But comprehension studies introduce other problems of their own. Specifically,
task demands can either underestimate or overestimate performance. For example,
suppose a child is asked for "a dog," and the choices are a dog and a horse. A child
might select the dog not because she knows that a horse is not a dog, but rather because she thinks the dog is a more typical instance. In other words, seemingly cor-

rect performance does not necessarily demonstrate correct extension of the word. Task demands can also underestimate performance. For example, suppose a child is asked for "a dog," and this time is shown a horse and a book. A child might select the horse because it is the closest match—even if she knows that neither the horse nor the book is a dog.

Other studies use preferential looking, where the child hears a word and coders record how often the child looks at one of two possible screens (Behrend, 1988; Naigles and Gelman, 1995). This task has the advantage of placing no explicit task demands on the child to look at one picture more than another. However, children's responses are still hard to interpret. We still do not know why a child who hears "dog" looks at a cow—is it because she thinks the cow is a dog, or because she is simply reminded of a dog?

What is needed is a task in which children report the boundaries of word meanings. Specifically, we need a task in which children can tell us not only which things are dogs (the so-called positive instances), but also which things are not dogs (the negative instances). In the examples above, we would want to know whether the child excludes cow from the referents of "dog." Dromi argues precisely this point (1987, p. 42).

Bill Croft, Panfang Fu, Tim Clausner, Gail Gottfried, and I conducted a study to assess word-meaning boundaries (S. Gelman, Croft, et al., 1998). The method was originally developed by Jean Hutchinson to study word learning (Hutchinson and Herman, 1991; Hutchinson, Inn, and Strapp, 1993). With minor modifications, the procedure is suitable for overextensions, too. The gist of the task is as follows. For each trial of the study, the child sees two pictures at a time. One of the two pictures is visible, and the other is hidden behind a cardboard "door." Children hear a word and have to decide whether or not the visible picture matches the word. For example, the visible picture in the pair might be a cow, and the child is asked to find the dog. The correct answer, of course, it to choose the covered picture. If the child chooses the cow instead, we would count it as an overextension. With this method, we asked whether children preferentially overextend by shape when given a comprehension task in which they can tell us what does not get named by a word.

Participants were two, two and a half, and four years of age. For the production task, they were simply asked to name a series of photographs. For the comprehension task, they received a series of experimental trials testing two words ("apple" and "dog"). These words were chosen because they are commonly overextended (e.g., Clark, 1973; Rescorla, 1980). The experimental trials included photographs of actual instances (e.g., a typical and an atypical apple), distractors of the same shape and same superordinate category (orange and pomegranate), distractors of the same shape but different superordinate category (baseball and round candle), and distractors of the same superordinate category but different shape (banana and star fruit).

The results argue in three ways against a shape bias in overextensions. See Tables 9.6 and 9.7. First, children were typically correct in comprehension. Even

Table 9.6. Mean percentage of overextensions on the production task as a function of age group and error type; S. Gelman, Croft, et al. (1998)

	Error type		
	Shape[a]	Taxonomic[b]	Both[c]
Age group			
Group I (younger 2-year-olds)	4%	2%	19%
Group II (older 2-year-olds)	4	1	17
Group III (4-year-olds)	2	0	10

[a]Overextension based on shape only (e.g., "moon" for whiffle ball)

[b]Overextension based on taxonomic relatedness only (e.g., "bird" for poodle)

[c]Overextension based on both shape and taxonomic relatedness (e.g., "apple" for orange)

Table 9.7. Comprehension task, percentage correct (i.e., percentage of trials on which children avoided the visible foil and selected the screened alternative instead); S. Gelman, Croft, et al. (1998)

	High familiar	Low familiar
Visible foil matches "dog" on:		
Shape only (chair, sawhorse)*	93%	81%
Taxonomic category only (chicken, whooping crane)*	89	85
Both taxonomic category and shape (cow, hippo)*	86	81
Visible foil matches "apple" on:		
Shape only (ball, candle)*	87	16
Taxonomic category only (banana, star fruit)*	79	55
Both taxonomic category and shape (orange, pomegranate)*	62	29

* Descriptions of visible foils, with familiar picture listed first, followed by unfamiliar picture.

Source: S. Gelman, Croft, et al. (1998). Reprinted with the permission of Cambridge University Press.

when presented with objects of the same shape and same taxonomic kind, most children refrained from extending a word erroneously. Second, in both comprehension and production, children typically overextended to items that matched the target word in both shape and taxonomic relatedness. Third, in comprehension children were as likely to overextend based on taxonomic relatedness alone as on shape alone. For example, when asked for an "apple," children picked a banana as often as they picked a baseball. All of these findings suggest that shape has no special priority in young children's semantic representations. Both superordinate-level taxonomic relatedness and shape are salient in children's early word meanings.

Shape and Taxonomic Level

Most prior studies examining the shape bias have pitted shape against superordinate category membership (e.g., clothing, food). Yet it is well known that children's earliest words typically name basic-level object categories (e.g., hat, apple), and that children have relative difficulty reasoning with superordinate-level categories (Markman and Callanan, 1983). Thus, pitting shape against superordinate-level categories provides a particularly stringent test of whether shape "wins out" over taxonomic kind in children's word learning. If children are searching for a basic-level match but cannot find one (because there is no basic-level match in the experimental array provided), they may rely on shape because it typically is a strong predictor of basic-level category membership.

A more sensitive test would involve pitting shape against basic-level category membership. Golinkoff, Shuff-Bailey, et al. (1995) conducted a set of experiments examining children's extensions of novel words, in which the taxonomic choices were of the same basic-level category as the targets (for instance, if the target was a high-heeled shoe, the taxonomic match was a boot). The other choices matched in perceptual similarity or thematic relatedness. Corresponding to our predictions, two-year-olds in their studies generalized novel nouns to members of the same basic-level category, overriding perceptual similarity. However, that work pitted taxonomic kind against overall perceptual similarity rather than specifically against shape. The results do not speak directly to the issue of whether children have a preference for extending words based on taxonomic relatedness versus shape.

Masha Kirzhner and I conducted a study in which shape and basic-level category membership were placed into direct conflict. This study was conducted entirely in Russian with Russian-speaking children living in the United States. Thirty-seven children between the ages of three and five years participated. They saw nine item sets, in which a target item was presented along with three choices: taxonomic, shape, and thematic. All items were color photographs of real objects. A sample set was a round cookie (target) presented with a gingerbread-man cookie (taxonomic match), a round coin (shape match), and a glass of milk (thematic match). Children in the word condition learned a new word for the target and were asked which of the choices the word also applied to. Children in the no-word (goes-with) condition saw the target and were asked which of the choices went with it. Taxonomic choices were higher than shape choices, in both the word (63% versus 33%) and no-word (28% versus 19%) conditions. Use of the word drew children's attention away from thematic choices (5% thematic choices in the word condition; 53% in the no-word condition).

Summary

Shape is not the sole or even primary factor in children's naming and classification. On tasks that provide information only about perceptual dimensions (e.g., sorting of simple, novel artifacts that vary only in shape, texture, and color), shape is an especially salient dimension. However, its salience derives largely from its value as an index or predictor of other, theory-relevant information (Medin, 1989; Soja, Carey, and Spelke, 1992; Waxman and Braig, 1996). When ontological knowledge and theoretical beliefs are available, and when they conflict with shape, children often sort and name on the basis of these other factors.

As mentioned earlier, the theory view does not aim to replace similarity in accounts of categorization; instead, it argues for the insufficiency of accounts that rely only on similarity to explain categorization. Typically, theories and attention to perceptual features go hand in hand (Medin, 1989). Essences are often correlated with and predictive of perceptual features (e.g., according to a somewhat oversimplified folk portrayal, XY chromosomes cause the observable properties of a male). However, given that typically we do not have direct access to the essence, the correlated and observable properties become crucial on many tasks (Keil, 1989). This link between observable properties and the assumption of underlying causal (essential) properties can provide an account of why perceptual prototypes, though insufficient for characterizing many categorization decisions (see Keil, 1989; Rips, 1989), are so prevalent in on-line processing of concepts.

Context Sensitivity of Concepts

One fundamental challenge to essentialism argues against the very notion that concepts have mentally stable represented cores. Instead, concepts are said to be constructions in working memory, shifting and unstable as the surrounding context. On this view, concepts are highly flexible, variable depending on the task, and influenced by perceptually immediate (on-line) properties (Barsalou, 1993a, 1993b; Jones and Smith, 1993). For example, the weight of a piano is more salient in some contexts, such as furniture moving; the sound of a piano is more salient in other contexts (M. McCloskey and Glucksberg, 1978). When asked to define a concept, people generate variable responses from one occasion to the next (Barsalou, 1993a). Category prototypes move around depending on one's perspective (e.g., telling people to rate the typicality of birds from the viewpoint of the average American citizen versus the viewpoint of the average Chinese citizen; Barsalou, 1991). Hierarchies are not fully transitive (Hampton, 1982), suggesting inconsistency across uses. Adjective meanings are contextually sensitive (Bierwisch and Lang, 1987; Coley and Gelman, 1989; Maloney and Gelman, 1987).

Similarly, L. Smith and Jones (1993; Jones and Smith, 1993) argue that categorization and labeling are best predicted by on-line, context-specific considerations. That is, cognitive acts are a result of dynamic processes, and not of structural representations. In their view, "concepts are not represented entities that exist as a unit . . . there is no set intension (definition in the head) or extension (category in the world). Both are transient and emergent in the task at hand" (Jones and Smith, 1993, p. 136).

There seems to be a contradiction between the essentialist claim that essences are at the core of concepts and the DAM claim that concepts have no core. Accordingly, a number of scholars have suggested that essentialism is incompatible with context-sensitivity (Braisby, Franks, and Hampton, 1996; Malt, 1994; L. Smith and Heise, 1992). Gil Diesendruck and I have argued that the contradiction is only apparent: Psychological essentialism is compatible with the context-sensitivity often discussed by cognitive scientists (see S. Gelman and Diesendruck, 1999, for more extended discussion). I argue for a resolution that can account for both the importance of essences and the variability in performance. The resolution rests on two main points. First, essentialism is a skeletal framework rather than a fixed definition and is therefore compatible with flexible, open-ended concepts. Second, variability in the information people use is patterned, predictable, and consistent with the notion of a theory-based core.

PSYCHOLOGICAL ESSENTIALISM: A CLARIFICATION.   Resolving the paradox between the essences-are-core and the concepts-have-no-core positions first requires a clarification of what is meant by psychological essentialism.

At first blush, essentialism may sound like a return to the defining-features view of categories (as discussed in Smith and Medin, 1981, for example). It is not. To explain why, I must remind the reader what essentialism does *not* entail. Essentialism does not entail that people know (consciously or unconsciously) what the essence is (see chapter 1). Medin and Ortony (1989) refer to this unknown-yet-believed-in entity as an essence placeholder. A child might assume that boys and girls differ in a deep, nonobvious way, without being able to identify any feature or trait as the boy or girl essence. Even when people do appeal to a particular essence (such as chromosomes for classification of someone as male or female), people rarely access the relevant information when identifying instances of the category (for example, relying on hairstyle and clothing rather than chromosomes).

The perceived essence also need not conform to what science tells us is the essence. The folk essence may include notions that have no scientific counterpart (e.g., "soul" in Western philosophy and *kunam* among the Tamil; Daniel, 1984; see chapter 4). Atran (1990) argues that essences are presumed to exist even among those living in cultures with no scientific tradition. Some even suggest that essentialism and current biological theory are incompatible (Hirschfeld, 1996; Mayr, 1991; Sober, 1994).

In sum, contrary to common depictions, essentialism is a skeletal framework (Medin, 1989; see also R. Gelman, 1990; Wellman and Gelman, 1988, for discussion of skeletal frameworks) rather than a detailed set of beliefs, scientific or otherwise. It is a guiding assumption in the mind of the cognizer (a "stance," "construal," or "heuristic"; Keil, 1995), rather than a fixed set of features contained within the concept. In this sense, I am sympathetic to the portrayal of essentialism as a meta-conceptual belief about conceptual structure (Barsalou, 1993b; Malt, 1990). However, metaconceptual does not mean epiphenomenal or divorced from conceptual structure; essentialism is a metaconceptual construal with extended conceptual implications. Although essentialism does not specify particular conceptual content, it constrains and generates such properties (to use Medin's [1989] terminology) and guides further knowledge acquisition.

Some important consequences follow from the skeletal nature of essentialism. When the essence is unknown, it may serve as a motivator and source for conceptual change (see also Waxman and Braig, 1996). I suggest that, armed with a heuristic notion that a category has a causal essence, people will search for evidence of the essence, for consequences of the essence, and for the essence itself. Because it is the (unknown) essence and not any particular set of features that is regarded as necessary, essentialized categories can incorporate anomalies and better account for conceptual change than models of concepts that presume the existence of fixed features. Because essentialism is a placeholder notion, it provides stability in the face of conceptual change and context sensitivity: what is stored is not *what* the essence is (at least not in any precise way), but *that* it exists.

STABILITY IN CONCEPTUAL REPRESENTATION.   What is stable in the representation of concepts? Barsalou (1993b) has argued that stability is in the long-term knowledge, rather than in the concepts that draw on such knowledge. Jones and Smith propose the even more extreme position that nothing is stable: "concepts have no constant structure, but are instead continually created. There is, in brief, a dynamic conceptual space of which the dynamic similarity space is part" (1993, p. 130). There are at least two problems, however, with arguing that concepts are not stable. First, at the very least there is stability in what gets linked to a word. Phonetic representations are surely stored in long-term memory, and we have at least an intuitive sense that some meanings linked to these representations are importantly the same (e.g., brown flying bat and gray flying bat), whereas others are mere homonyns and so are not (e.g., brown flying bat and baseball bat). Importantly, children as young as three years of age share these intuitions (Backscheider and Gelman, 1995; Backscheider, Gelman, et al., 2000).

Second, there appear to be constraints on which kinds of information get stored with a word or concept (Markman, 1989). Even the dynamic conceptual space referred to by Jones and Smith obeys certain constraints. For example, their use of a spatial metaphor ("conceptual space") suggests a finite, contiguous region. It seems unlikely that all such constraints could be provided by the perceptual system. How would, say, mutual exclusivity be perceptually represented? It is a logical, not a perceptual, relation.

The no-core view, though important for reminding us of the variability in concepts, seems particularly ill suited to provide a portrait of stability, since it denies its very existence. Although I do not propose to solve the problem of stability, a couple of points are worth noting. First, the nature of conceptual stability may be quite abstract, at the level of ontological commitments ("X is an animal") rather than particular features. Ontological status appears to be remarkably stable and unchanging across uses of a word or variations of a concept (Keil, 1989). Ontologies are implicitly built into our grammar (e.g., with classifier systems; see Silverstein, 1986). Even when concepts are variable, ontological commitments tend not to change. For example, although prototypes change with context (Barsalou, 1991), such changes typically leave ontological kind unaffected (e.g., although typicality ratings of birds vary depending on whether one adopts an "American" versus "Chinese" point of view, across both contexts birds are presumed to be animate, egg-laying creatures). Psychological essentialism may be one kind of ontological commitment.

The other point is that there is more stability when a task is kept constant than when averaging across tasks. Task effects are systematic and nonrandom. Conceptual stability can be masked by task differences, but it exists.

SUMMARY.   Concepts are context sensitive, leading some to question what (if anything) is stable in their representation. The skeptic might insist that nothing is stable and so nothing is represented. I have been arguing that much is represented, but it is a skeletal framework and varies depending on the kind of concept and kind of conceptual task under consideration. The argument for skeletal frameworks is akin to Wellman's (1990) suggestion regarding framework theories of mind (also Wellman and Gelman, 1988), and R. Gelman's (1990) suggestion regarding skeletal principles underlying children's acquisition of fundamental concepts such as number and animacy. It differs, however, in that skeletal principles and framework theories are domain-specific, contentful proto-theories that are extended in domain-specific ways, whereas my notion of essentialized concept does not lie fully within any particular naïve theory (Carey, 1995; Hirschfeld, 1996; Wellman and Gelman, 1998). Concepts are not atomic structures built up out of perceptual primitives and conjoining to form larger theories; rather, both levels of analysis (concepts and theories) are represented simultaneously. This conclusion should not be surprising, however, when we consider that one of the primary functions of concepts is to work with our theory-rich understandings of the world.

Reliance on Well-Established Cognitive Principles

As mentioned earlier, one appeal of the DAM theory is that it makes use of well-established cognitive principles, such as associative learning mechanisms. In contrast, terms such as "theory" can seem fuzzy or imprecise. However, the apparent gain in precision and predictiveness that comes from invoking similarity, attention, salience, and feature distinctiveness is only illusory. Problems with the construct of "similarity" were at the heart of the Murphy and Medin (1985) critique of standard approaches to concepts. The tools proposed by the DAM account do not explain the phenomena discussed in this book. Simple induction, abstraction, and salience no doubt guide human reasoning. But they fail to explain why children employ the unobservable causal constructs documented throughout the chapter, and seem to propose under-specified mechanisms of conceptual change. (See Keil, Smith, et al., 1998, for further explication.)

For instance, consider associative learning mechanisms. The DAM theory asserts that associative mechanisms explain word learning. On this view, a shape bias builds up gradually over time, based on statistical regularities in the input (L. Smith, 2000). Evidence includes the developmental course of attention to shape: the bias is not innate, but emerges at about age two years, after some initial words have been learned, and increases till about thirty-six months of age (L. Smith, 2000). Because the words children learn early on tend to refer to shape-based categories, attention to shape could derive from exposure to statistical regularities in the input—in this case, between count nouns in English and shape-based categories (L. Smith, 2000). (See also Saffran, Aslin, and Newport, 1996, for evidence of powerful statistical learning mechanisms in infancy.)

However, children are amazingly active word-learners, making use of subtle information in a manner that belies simple associative learning mechanisms. Tomasello and Akhtar (2000, p. 181) list several ways that young children override spatio-temporal contiguity and perceptual salience when learning words, including the following:

- They learn words for intentional actions more readily than for accidental actions, even if the novel word is immediately followed by the accidental action and only later followed by the intentional action.
- They learn a word for an aspect of the context that is novel for the adult, even though it is not novel for the child.
- They learn new action words for actions that they anticipate an adult will do, even when the adult has not actually performed the action.
- They use adult gaze direction rather than perceptual salience to determine reference.

Tomasello and Akhtar (2000) go on to point out that children are using well-known developmental mechanisms to acquire words (including speech processing, imitation, concept formation, and theory of mind)—but these mechanisms cannot reduce to associationism. (See also Golinkoff and Hirsh-Pasek [2000] and Woodward [2000] for further arguments that associationism cannot be the sole mechanism of word learning.)

The seeming bedrocks of information processing (e.g., memory, attention, and similarity judgments) are themselves influenced by theories. Memory is notorious for conforming to theory (rather than memory being a neutral source of information). For example, Keil (1989) pointed out that children at times had difficulty learning about animals for which origins and featural information conflicted (e.g., an animal that looked like a horse but had cow parents), erroneously remembering one piece of information as conforming to the other (e.g., that the parents were horses). Similarly, Gopnik and Sobel (2000) documented that children's memory for causal information was more often misremembered when it conflicted with perceptual similarity than when it matched perceptual similarity. See also Flavell, Flavell, Green, and Moses (1990), Heyman and Gelman (1999), and Signorella (1987) for other examples of this phenomenon. Likewise, attention is certainly guided by prior knowledge, interests, and expectations (Gopnik and Wellman, 1994).

Attention to perceptual information, too, can derive from theory (Medin and Shoben, 1988; Murphy and Medin, 1985; Wisniewski and Medin, 1994). Learning that two things are of the same kind leads to a search for similarities. I recently experienced a striking example of this phenomenon myself. Coincidentally, the husband of my husband's new colleague at work turned out to be one of my second cousins. I had never met him before and only discovered our familial relationship serendipitously. It was only after I learned of our blood tie that I began to notice how much he resembled my father's side of the family. A more common example of this phenomenon is when people remark on how much an infant resembles one or the other parent—even when, unbeknownst to the admirer, the parents had adopted the child (see Bressan and Dal Martello, 2002, for related evidence). Even when perceptual similarity and essences correlate, perceptual similarity need not be the starting point. More generally, top-down influences on cognitive processes have been recognized and studied for many years (Barsalou, 1992; Nisbett and Ross, 1980). Theories influence human concepts at multiple levels.

Developmental Issues

Some argue that the theory theory pays too little attention to important developmental changes that take place in categorization during the childhood years. This concern is undoubtedly rooted in the fact that the theory view proposes greater developmental continuity than traditional views, such as Piaget's (e.g., Inhelder and Piaget, 1964). In contrast to a perceptual-to-conceptual shift, the theory view argues that more-sophisticated concepts are present from very early on (S. Gelman, 1996). However, nearly all the work reviewed in this book (and cited as evidence for theory-based categorization) examines children who are at least three or four years old. Certainly a large gap in present knowledge concerns how these understandings develop and what understanding precede the accomplishments of preschool-aged children. I therefore stress that it will be crucial to examine these issues in younger children, including infants.

The developmental question is theoretically significant for at least two reasons. First, it raises the possibility that there may indeed be a "perceptual-to-conceptual shift"—but one that occurs at an earlier point in development than previously believed. For example, perhaps the shift from perceptual to conceptual categories occurs when comparing one-year-olds to two-year-olds, rather than when comparing five-year-olds to seven-year-olds. This possibility can be posed in slightly different terms: is there ever a point in development when children's concepts are "pretheoretic"? And if so, how do theories "switch on"? Ongoing research (e.g., by Mandler, 1988, 1992; Quinn and Eimas, 1997; Rakison and Cohen, 1999; Rakison and Poulin-Dubois, 2001) provides intriguing forays into these difficult issues. I remain agnostic on this point, though I lean toward the assumption that children's concepts are never entirely pretheoretic. For example, P. Bloom (2000) provides some very detailed arguments that rich social cognition (theory of mind) and conceptual structure are required even for the learning of very first words. See also Keil, Smith, et al. (1998) and Macnamara (1982).

A second reason that a comparison with prelinguistic infants is important is the possibility that language may have an important role in children's concepts. Prelinguistically, infants use categories to make inductive inferences, even concerning nonobvious properties (Baldwin, Markman, and Melartin, 1993). A key question that remains is how the acquisition of language modifies this inductive capacity, if at all. Language may be crucial for anchoring kinds, and for conveying culturally sanctioned categories (S. Gelman and Heyman, 1999; S. Gelman, Hollander, et al., 2000). For example, language readily conveys that a whale is a not a fish, but such information may be difficult if not impossible to convey in the absence of language. Language labels are one of the most efficient ways of passing down to future generations the hard-won knowledge of those who came before. (See chapter 8.)

I agree that developmental issues have not been sufficiently explored in research to date. Yet it is misleading to characterize the theory view as nondevelopmental. Theories are assumed to change over time, perhaps entailing fundamental reorganizations, and such changes yield important parallels to standard developmental theories (Carey, 1985; Gopnik and Meltzoff, 1997; Gopnik and Wellman, 1994; Wellman and Gelman, 1998). Melissa Koenig and I suggest that a theory view has greater power to explain causes of conceptual change, by articulating the relation between theories and evidence (S. Gelman and Koenig, in press). Whether or not a single piece of evidence suffices to verify or falsify a hypothesis may depend on how "valued" and powerful the hypothesis is. If it explains and predicts little (such as my daughter's stated belief in reincarnation, when her younger brother was born the day after our cat died), then it can be dropped or replaced when encountering alternative theories. But if it explains and predicts a great deal (such as the early-developing belief that people act according to goals), then we are loath to abandon it and are likely to retain it even in light of falsifying data (e.g., irrational behavior).

Can't a Simpler Explanation Be Found?

As I have been careful to point out, theory-based categorization does not supplant perceptual information; instead, perceptual information is typically intertwined with information about functions, ontologies, and other nonobvious properties (see discussion by S. Gelman and Medin, 1993; Jones and Smith, 1993). Functions can be inferred from salient parts (McCarrell and Callanan, 1995). Ontological status can be inferred from object contours and material substance (Massey and R. Gelman, 1988; L. Smith and Heise, 1992) as well as movement patterns (Bertenthal, 1996; Johannsen, 1973). Michotte's classic work on the perception of causality (1963) is an excellent example of how dynamic perceptual cues invoke a causal interpretation in the viewer. Perception is also an important (though fallible) source of information for identifying instances of basic-level kinds, even in infancy (Eimas and Quinn, 1994; Quinn and Eimas, 1996; Rakison and Butterworth, 1998). For all of these reasons, theories should not be misinterpreted as standing in opposition to a perceptual account.

The intermingling of perception and theory raises the challenging question of whether theories are superfluous. Can we recast the developmental findings reviewed above, as showing that children attend to perceptual information, albeit highly sophisticated perceptual information? This position is favored by some who argue that early categories are based primarily on nonstrategic attentional processes (L. Smith, Jones, and Landau, 1996). For example, instead of saying that children attend to ontological information, why not say that they attend to particular perceptual features, such as eyes (Landau, Smith, and Jones, 1988) or legs (Rakison and Butterworth, 1998)? In support of such an approach, researchers have found that eighteen-month-olds distinguish toy animals (with legs) from toy vehicles (with wheels; Mandler, Bauer, and McDonough, 1991), and by fourteen months of age will even violate the animal-vehicle distinction when toy animals are portrayed as having wheels rather than legs and toy vehicles are portrayed as having legs rather than wheels (Rakison and Butterworth, 1998). However, identifying the perceptual features of conceptual categories can be a circular exercise. For example, consider the argument that animates can be identified by the perceptual feature of legs. This argument runs into trouble when we consider that only some legs are animate. Legs of a table or chair are inanimate, yet infants do not treat animals and furniture as a single group. One could say that table legs are not really legs—that language is misleading in this respect. Table legs do not have feet and toes, for example. But this argument runs into problems, too, as some inanimate legs do have feet and toes (e.g., the legs on a bathtub or statue).

Alternatively, perhaps the perceptually relevant features exist but are subtler—features such as texture, contour, or material kind (e.g., see L. Smith and Heise, 1992, for an intriguing study that contour differentiates animates from inanimates). On this view, legs per se may not be definitive, but perhaps texture is. Yet even this retreat is problematic, because, although a cluster of features are relevant for identifying entities as animate, none are decisive. S. Johnson, Slaughter, and Carey (1998) found that twelve-month-old infants treated a novel, fur-covered object as if it were animate (namely, by looking in the direction the entity was pointed, as if following its "gaze"), if it either possessed facial features or responded contingently to the child's movements by moving and making sounds.

The difficulty of "reducing" ontology to perception is further underscored when one considers how subtle, context sensitive, and flexible are the perceptual features that correspond to the distinction between intentional and nonintentional beings. The very same movement can be interpreted as either intentional or accidental, depending on the background knowledge of the observer (Bargh, 1990). Psychological "readings" of an event are also culturally sensitive. For example, how people interpret the movement of cartoon fish in a dynamic display varies notably as a function of the cultural background of the research participants (M. Morris, Nisbett, and Peng, 1995). I doubt that any straightforward algorithm can be devised to allow a reading of intentionality to emerge from perceptual considerations alone (but see Baldwin and Baird, 2001, for a thoughtful discussion). Any attempt to do so would necessarily entail sneaking in concepts such as knowledge, causal understanding, or belief in order to make the perceptual redescription work. In so doing, the notion of "perceptual" would be extended so broadly as to lose much of its power and meaning (S. Gelman and Medin, 1993).

In brief, I argue that any alternative (nontheory) account of children's concepts still needs to incorporate domain-specific knowledge, ontological distinctions, causal understanding, and other nonobvious properties. Therefore, it seems crucial to invoke commonsense theories in an explanatory account of children's concepts.

SUMMARY AND CONCLUSIONS

In this chapter, I have argued that, by preschool age, children's categories are theory-based: they incorporate information beyond the obvious, including ontology, causality, intentions, and functions, and they foster novel inferences. However, the position remains controversial, owing to at least three considerations: debates concerning the phenomena (the role of shape and the context-sensitivity of concepts); a desire for explicit formulations rooted in well-established cognitive principles (such as associative learning); and a desire for a developmental account that can explain reorganizations with age. In reviewing each of these issues, I have argued that a domain-general, similarity-based approach is insufficient to account for the wealth of evidence, and that a theory-based approach provides theoretical parsimony. Among the many fruitful areas that remain for future research, perhaps most crucial is to discover what sorts of precursors of essentialism are found in infancy and early toddlerhood, and the extent to which there is continuity versus discontinuity over development.

PART III

IMPLICATIONS AND SPECULATIONS

Chapter 10

Unfinished Business

> The notion that there is no one quality genuinely, absolutely, and exclusively essential to anything is almost unthinkable. . . . We are so stuck in our prejudices, so petrified intellectually, that to our vulgarest names . . . we ascribe an eternal and exclusive worth.
>
> William James, *The Principles of Psychology*

> Psychological essentialism is bad metaphysics, . . . [but] may prove to be good epistemology.
>
> Douglas Medin, "Concepts and Conceptual Structure"

Essentialism is a vast, untidy topic, and my treatment here—a report on the acquisition of psychological essentialism in children—leaves many loose ends. Loose ends are appropriate, given the complexity of the issues and the rudimentary state of our knowledge, and I hope that others will pick up where I have left off. In this chapter I discuss three sets of unresolved issues: skeptical responses to psychological essentialism (is the essentialist framework necessary? what would disconfirm essentialism?), the scope of essentialism in different populations (different cultures, different species, over development, and individual differences), and broader implications for theories of concepts and of cognitive development (what can children tell us about the nature of concepts, and what can concepts tell us about the nature of children? do we ever transcend essentialist thinking?).

SKEPTICAL RESPONSES TO PSYCHOLOGICAL ESSENTIALISM

Is the Essentialist Framework Necessary?

In the introduction to this book, I suggested that essentialism has three main components: a belief that certain categories are natural kinds, a belief that some unobservable property causes observable similarities shared by members of a category, and a belief that everyday words reflect the real-world structure of categories. The many experiments reviewed in chapters 2 through 6 suggest that some of young children's categories have all three components. Certain categories are assumed to have rich inductive potential and innate potential, and to be stable across transformations; they are thought to share nonobvious properties, and both nonobvious properties and causal features are given special weight in determining category identity; and finally, children tacitly accept a division of linguistic labor in which they appear to accept adult labels even when they conflict with their own (though more work is needed to explore this phenomenon).

Although the data reviewed in this book are consistent with essentialism, they fall short of providing direct evidence for essentialism in children. Children do not explicitly articulate an essentialist perspective on the world, and the word "essence" probably does not emerge until well into the school-age years. Nor can we say with any precision what the essence of, say, a dog or a tree or an American is to a child. Perhaps, then, essentialism is unnecessary—overkill for what can be explained in more theoretically modest ways. Should we instead refer to the component phenomena discussed earlier (categories have inductive potential, categories are stable over transformations, causal features are central to categories, nonobvious features are important, and categories exhibit important domain differences in their structures), without positing an overarching essentialist construal?

There are two main reasons to go beyond the component phenomena and frame these results in terms of essentialism. First, parsimony. A range of phenomena that co-occur, developmentally and cross-culturally, seem instantiations of a single broader principle. Certainly these phenomena are distinct, but if one considered each phenomenon exclusively as distinct and unrelated to the others, one would then miss whatever broader generalizations can be reached by addressing their commonalities. The parsimony argument, though, requires a closer empirical foundation. More fine-grained analysis will be needed to discover how tightly linked these various phenomena are, both in adult cognition and in development (see Haslam, 1998, for an important start).

Second, explicit essence formulations are found in many cultures and they seem continuous with the implicit, skeletal formulations examined in these studies. Examples include the notion of a "soul" in Western philosophy, *kunam* among the Tamil (Daniel, 1984), "spirit" among some organ-transplant recipients (Sylvia and Novak, 1997), and word magic in Western and other cultures (Benveniste, 1971; Piaget, 1929). People freely bandy about the word "essence" in folk accounts in the United States. A kiosk at our local mall in Ann Arbor recently displayed a gadget that promised to reveal one's "essence"—for a fee. Here I am referring not to the loose sense of "essence" as meaning, roughly, "key point," but rather a literal construal of essence as some physical or spiritual entity that reveals who you are. Children's cartoons also often have the explicitly essentialist premise that massive transformations leave identity unchanged. The Transformers are probably the most well known of these (but see also He-Man, Superman, Go-Bots, and Power Rangers, among others). Interestingly, the Transformers are also said to have a "spark" or "life essence" and are powered by internal "energon cubes" (reminiscent of an inner vital force).[1] It also appears that laypersons' construals of "genes" and

"DNA" can be deeply essentialist (e.g., Mahalingam, Philip, and Akiyama, 2001). By treating people's implicit construals as essentialist, a common framework covers both the explicit and the implicit phenomena.

ESSENTIALISM, OR JUST AN APPEAL TO KINDS?   Although I argued above that essentialist phenomena can reasonably be construed as related to one another, this argument does not mean that the concept is indivisible. Indeed, psychological essentialism of the sort with which we are concerned appears to have two related though separable assumptions: a "kind" assumption, that people treat certain categories as richly structured "kinds," with clusters of correlated properties, and an "essence" assumption, that people believe a category has an underlying property (essence) that cannot be observed directly but that causes the observable qualities that category members share.

The major difference between kind and essence is that the latter incorporates the former and adds to it the idea that some part, substance, or quality (i.e., the essence) causes the properties shared by the kind. In the literature, the two notions have often been conflated. However, categories can be bound together in crucial ways without considering the causal basis of the kind. Strevens (2000) suggested that the empirical data taken as evidence for psychological essentialism could instead be accounted for if people simply assume that there are causal laws connecting kind membership with observable properties. He termed such causal laws "K-laws" (kind laws), and his alternative formulation the "minimal hypothesis."

Strevens and I are in agreement that people treat surface features as caused and constrained by deeper features of concepts. I am also prepared to believe that developmentally, a notion of kind may precede a notion of essence. Evidence for use of kinds is present by age two (in children's inductive inferences and generic noun phrases), but evidence for appeal to an essence (e.g., with the switched-at-birth method) has so far not appeared below age four years. An instructive line for future research would be to use converging methods to try to distinguish "kind" from "essence" at different points in development.

Nonetheless, I also believe that something more than the Minimal Hypothesis is required to account for essentialist-like behavior in children ages four years on up. (The arguments here are drawn from Ahn, Kalish, Gelman, et al., 2001; see that piece for more extended discussion.) Even very young children appear to have some consistent beliefs about what an animal's essence is like (internal, not external [see chapter 3]; biological, not transmitted by upbringing [see chapter 4]). The minimal hypothesis also makes no commitment concerning the causal structure of features, whereas essentialism implies a one-to-many "common cause" mapping from an essence to surface features (see (a) in Figure 10.1, below). In other words, a single essence is presumed to be responsible for a cluster of other properties. People seem to prefer common-cause structures to alternatives, such as (b), (c), (d), and (e) presented in Figure 10.1 (Ahn, 1999; L. Brooks and Wood, 1997; Medin,

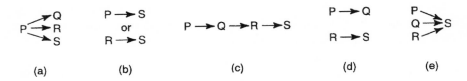

Figure 10.1.   Possible causal structures in a category. *Source:* Ahn et al. (2001). Reprinted with the permission of Elsevier Science.

Wattenmaker, and Hampson, 1987). For example, people tend not to presume that each feature has a different cause (d), or that each feature causes the next in a causal chain (c). These various beliefs cannot be explained by K-laws alone.

What Would Disconfirm Essentialism?

Essentialism would be disconfirmed if children turn out to be "externalists"— more concerned with the outward appearances of things than other sorts of properties, expecting no commonalities underlying surface variation, or drawing no distinction between surface and underlying characteristics. So, for example, any of the following would constitute evidence against essentialism: if young children privilege shape over ontological relatedness in deciding what something is, treat spatiotemporal regularities as more central to object identity than causal relations, attend to surface properties rather than internal features when making novel inferences, or attend to the spatiotemporal properties of movement rather than domain to explain actions.

Essentialism would also be disconfirmed if the different empirical phenomena described earlier fail to converge in a coherent way. For example, if beliefs about inductive potential, internal causes, and innate potential are statistically independent of one another, then "essentialism" may be too broad a construct, unable to capture people's intuitive beliefs.

I repeat, however, that essentialism does not require that people be able to state an essence explicitly, or to provide an exceptionless definition. (See also the discussion of sortal versus causal essentialism in chapter 1.) Failing to supply an essence does not constitute evidence against essentialism. Essentialism remains a placeholder notion with the details often left unstated, and it concerns causal explanations for category membership (causal essentialism) rather than rules for inclusion in a category (sortal essentialism). Accordingly, although various lines of evidence argue against essences as determining word use, the findings speak only against the attribution of sortal, not causal, essences. That is, the evidence demonstrates that people do not determine word use by means of a list of defining features, but it fails to address whether people treat certain categories as richly structured kinds with nonobvious causal features.

For example, Malt (1994) demonstrates that speakers of English use the word "water" to refer to liquids that are not pure H_2O. Because the most plausible account available for a metaphysical essence for water has been H_2O, Malt interprets the evidence as damaging to an essentialist theory. Specifically, she has shown that people do not endorse H_2O as either necessary or sufficient for "water" when the word is used at a superordinate level (including pond water, polluted water, and so forth; although her own data suggest that there is a subordinate-level usage, "pure water," which is more or less equivalent to H_2O). Critically, H_2O represents a sortal, not causal, essence, and accordingly her study argues only against the classical view of category meaning—not against essentialism in the sense I am considering.

Braisby, Franks, and Hampton similarly question whether the empirical evidence supports essentialist predictions. The essentialist predictions they consider all target sortal essences, as can be seen in how they characterize the essentialist view: "essentialism's proposal [is] that actual essences alone determine a word's reference" (1996, p. 249), and "classification of entities as members or non-members of the kind category will be determined according to their possession of the essence" (1996, p. 251). They examine subjects' intuitions about the application of various category names (cat, water, tiger, gold, bronze, lemon, and oak) following a set of counterfactual demonstrations. For example, in one scenario subjects hear, "You have a female pet cat named Tibby who has been rather unwell of late. Although cats are known to be mammals, the vet, on examining Tibby carefully, finds that she is, in fact, a robot controlled from Mars." Subjects are asked to judge the truth or falsehood of statements such as "Cats do exist" or "Tibby is a cat, though we were wrong about her being a mammal."

The results did conform to the essentialist predictions the majority of the time—despite ambiguity in the questions (e.g., does the statement "Cats do exist" refer to the robotic cats or the mammal cats?) and despite heavy information-processing demands of the task (e.g., essentialist responses required subjects to apply double negatives—judging a negative statement ["Tibby is not a cat..."] as false). However, the less-than-perfect responses led Braisby, Franks, and Hampton to conclude that "words and concepts are not used in accordance with essentialism" (1996, p. 247). On a causal essentialist view, the essence need not provide necessary and sufficient clues for determining reference (see also Medin, 1989), and accordingly the experiments are relevant to a sortal (not causal) essentialist view.

FIGURING OUT THE SCOPE OF ESSENTIALISM

Essentialism across Cultures

There are hints here and there that essentialism can be found quite broadly around the world (Astuti, 1995, 2000; Atran, Medin, et al., 2001; Bloch, Solomon, and Carey, 2001; Boyer, 1994b; Diesendruck, 2001; Stoler, 1995; Gil-White, 2001). How to interpret this recurrence, however, is a matter of some controversy.

On one view, essentialism is universally expressed, in cultures varying widely in language, environment, technology, scientific knowledge, and economy. Indirect support for universality comes from how people organize their knowledge of plants and animals into classification systems. Atran (1990) discusses two distinct aspects of systems of folk biological classification: a taxonomic principle and a causal principle. People classify animals and plants into shallow and ranked taxonomies that exhaustively partition any local environment (Berlin, 1978). These classifications are based in large part on morphological similarities—as opposed to utilitarian or symbolic associations—between category members. Such taxonomies pull together diverse instances under a single label, thereby treating them as if the same—even though other logical systems are possible (i.e., the universality is not required by logical constraints). Essentialism is universally applied to thinking about the creatures sorted into these taxonomies. According to this schema, members of each taxon share an essence or "nature" or underlying propensity to develop the appearance, behaviors, and ecological proclivities typical of that category.

Atran (1995, 1999) suggests that the taxonomic and essentialist principles are related, and that the taxonomic principle may derive from the essentialist one.[2] The categories or taxa of folk taxonomies are generally good predictors of underlying shared properties. Furthermore, the essentialist presumption that living kinds develop in a species-typical way, could explain why seemingly well bounded folk taxonomies include anomalous instances (such as three-legged, albino tigers). The anomalies are included on the basis of how they normally, typically, or naturally would have been expected to develop, rather than on the basis of whatever outward features they actually display. However, although the evidence for universal taxonomic sortings is vast, the evidence for a universal essentialist presumption in folk biology is relatively sparse.

Other sources suggest that, despite a universal impulse to essentialize, instantiations of essentialism may be culture specific. For example, Diesendruck proposes that "culture provides the content of the beliefs, and the mind provides the form in which the beliefs are represented" (2001, p. 58). Detailed ethnographies suggest distinct systems of essentialist beliefs in different cultures. For example, the Tamil *kunam* are transmitted via contact with the land rather than inheritance; the *bope* component, which Crocker (1979) describes for the Bororo, are treated as common to all animals rather than distinctive to each species; and witches among the Fang of Cameroon, West Africa, are said to possess an invisible organ (*evur*) with special causal powers, yet those possessing an *evur* do not constitute a natural kind (Boyer, 1994b). In all these examples, people appeal to nonvisible, causally efficacious inner qualities. Yet they do so in distinct ways.

In contrast to universalist claims, relativist accounts posit that essentialism is culturally specific. One set of arguments attempts to demonstrate that essentialism emerged only at particular historical moments, often emphasizing the role that systems of essentialist belief play in supporting and furthering the political and economic aims of specific groups. (Fuss's 1989 discussion of gender essentialism is a good example.) Other scholars propose broad cultural variation in cognitive processing (e.g., Nisbett, Peng, et al., 2001), variation that could potentially find its way into differences in essentializing. For example, Nisbett, Peng, et al. (2001) suggest that there is a broad and general distinction between the thought processes of East Asians versus Westerners, including differences in causal attributions (with Westerners more likely to attribute causes to dispositions that an object possesses, and Easterners more likely to attribute causes to the context) and categorization (with Westerners more focused on rule-based categories and Easterners more focused on functional relationships and part-whole relationships). Similarly, I. Choi, Nisbett, and Smith (1997) suggest that Koreans are less likely to make category-based inductive inferences than Americans.

At the moment the question remains understudied and unresolved. If I had to place my bets, I would side with Diesendruck on this issue, hypothesizing that essentialism is a species-general, universal, inevitable mode of thought—but that the form that it takes varies specifically according to the culture at hand, with the basic notion of essentialism becoming elaborated in each culture's complex theories of nature and society. In chapter 11, my suggestions regarding why we essentialize would also argue for universal underpinnings. Yet we are desperately in need of more research. (See also Coley, 2000, and Lillard, 1999, for thoughtful analyses of the importance of comparative data in understanding cognitive developmental patterns.) Astuti (1995, 2000), Atran, Medin, et al. (2001), Bloch, Solomon, and Carey (2001), Diesendruck (2001), and Walker (1992) provide exemplary models of the sorts of empirical research programs that will help us make progress on this difficult issue.

Essentialism in Other Species?

At this point we know virtually nothing about whether essentialism extends to other species. An argument could be made that other organisms, like humans, recognize the importance of nonobvious properties. Certainly nonhuman animals are capable of subtle distinctions and discriminations, including kinship recognition by voles and salamanders (e.g., Holmes and Sherman, 1983), and classification of the natural world by pigeons (Herrnstein, Loveland, and Cable, 1976). However, these skills do not imply a belief in unobservable essences. Subtle categorization judgments such as kinship recognition could simply mean that animals have highly sophisticated perceptual abilities, including some that humans lack (e.g., sonar or heightened sense of smell). Pigeons' ability to classify fish or trees also ultimately boils down to some sort of perceptual classification. Again, these data provide no evidence that pigeons assume that category members share underlying, nonobvious similarities.

Based on recent findings by Povinelli (2000) and Tomasello (1999), I speculate that essentialism may be a uniquely human construct. In Tomasello's experiments, young children—but not chimpanzees—are able to reason about intervening causal mechanisms when shown simple problems that require tools to solve. For example, when shown that a rakelike tool held a certain way will enable one to drag a treat out from a cage, a young child will track the correct way to hold the tool and successfully obtain the treat, whereas the chimp will show increased use of the tool but just as likely hold it the wrong way and fail to get the treat (but see Hauser, 1997, for more sophisticated tool use in nonhuman primates). Povinelli more generally suggests that humans and chimps differ in their capacity to reason about unobservable phenomena (2000, pp. 107, 298).

If chimpanzees were incapable of reasoning about unobservable phenomena, then what would their categories be like? In several important respects they would be no different from ours: category members would be identified initially from observable features (e.g., recognizing a mushroom by its shape, location, and texture). Perceptibly distinct objects would be treated as equivalent in certain respects—for instance, a white mushroom and a red, speckled mushroom would be treated as importantly the same, and as both edible. The chimp should also be capable of making category-based inferences of a limited sort: upon discovering that one red, speckled mushroom is tasty, he should readily extend this new property to other red, speckled mushrooms.

Where the categories of chimpanzees would differ from the categories of humans is that only the latter would possess the various capacities detailed in this book. Chimps would not be able to restructure their categories on the basis of language input (e.g., discovering that a bat is not actually a bird, but a dodo is). This would be trivially true in the case of chimps without language, but there are also two nontrivial ways in which it could be true: if language-trained chimps (e.g., Premack, 1986; Savage-Rumbaugh, Shanker, and Taylor, 1998) also fail to incorporate new instances on the basis of language, an issue that to my knowledge has yet to be tested; and also if, for non-language-trained chimps, there is no alternative way to convey the same information that young children acquire readily from language input. Chimps would also have no intuitions about the internal, hidden aspects of things (e.g., the insides of animals versus those of machines), nor would they privilege internal parts in deciding what something is.

If chimps are nonessentialist, then they will not reason about causes in the same manner as children. Their judgments about what something is would also be uninfluenced by information about properties found at birth (nature-versus-nurture issues), or by information about the origins of an object (intentional versus accidental). Perceptible features and feature correlations would form the basis of category judgments, not beliefs concerning causal structure. In short, the categories of chimps might at first glance appear fairly similar to those of humans, but a more detailed look would reveal many differences below the surface. These speculations could turn out to be wrong; we need empirical evidence on the issue.

Developmental Changes in Essentialism?

Throughout the book, I have stressed that essentialism appears early in childhood. Contrary to suggestions that essentialism is a sophisticated cognitive achievement, or one that grows out of far-reaching political aims, I have detailed a precocious essentializing bent. How can essentialism emerge so early, when children lack the scientific understanding of DNA or molecular structure? Because essentialism does not grow out of biology or scientific knowledge. Rather, the reverse is true: biology is interpreted (and, more precisely, misinterpreted) within an essentialist framework.

I have focused primarily on one period in development: the preschool years. The reasons for my interest in this age group are both theoretical (preschool children are young enough to be relatively untouched by formal schooling, thereby providing a glimpse of children's untutored beliefs) and practical (preschool children are sufficiently verbal to engage in the experimental tasks we provide). The finding of essentialism in such young children demonstrates the primacy and robustness of essentialist reasoning. However, it leaves open central developmental issues: what are the developmental origins of essentialism, and to what extent does essentialism undergo change over time? Little is known of essentialism below age four, and almost nothing is known of essentialism below age two, so I will engage in admittedly rank speculation.

I view essentialism as inhering in several very basic assumptions or tendencies, sketched out in chapter 11: appearance/reality distinctions, induction from property clusters, causal determinism, tracking identity over time, and deference to experts. To the extent that these underlying assumptions are present in early infancy, then something like essentialism may be found at that age, too. To the extent that these assumptions change over development, essentialism should change as well.

I posit that the seeds of essentialism can be found preverbally. Induction from property clusters takes place by at least nine months, when infants expect that things that are alike in obvious ways will be alike in nonobvious ways as well. Recall Baldwin, Markman, and Melartin's (1993) experiment demonstrating that nine-month-olds readily generalize novel properties from one object to other, similar objects. For example, upon learning that a can turned upside down makes an animal sound, they start turning other, similar cans upside down. Elsewhere I have argued that this inductive capacity is one of the two basic functions of categories, enabling generalization of old knowledge to new situations regarding food, danger, and other critical conditions, and thus ultimately required for survival (S. Gelman, 1996). In this sense, nine-month-olds have constructed a rudimentary notion of "kind."

A nascent (though tacit) deference to experts appears to emerge by about twelve months of age, when children begin to accept adult labels and use them to modify their category boundaries and inductive potential (Graham, Kilbreath, and Welder,

2001, 2002). Deference to experts also entails a crude understanding that reality (in the form of the adult label) and appearance can diverge. However, at this very early stage, there is no reason to suspect that children invoke invisible properties or search for mediating causal underpinnings, despite their sensitivity to causal relations in simple physical events (e.g., Leslie and Keeble, 1987). Then, between two and three years of age, children show a burst of generics (see chapter 8). It is also at about this age when children begin to consider underlying causes on the Gopnik and Sobel (2000) blicket-detector task.

I suggest that the initial assumption held by infants that the world contains property clusters (or kinds) develops in at least two further ways between nine months and two and a half years of age: (a) symbolic communication (words) can convey category membership, thereby vastly increasing the inductive power of categories and allowing for use of nonobvious information, and (b) children search for causal underpinnings of category similarities. I suspect that (a) and (b) are cognitive universals, but the precise mapping between inductive capacity and words cannot be innate, given that languages differ in how such mappings are expressed. Thus, presumably there is important developmental change in the first two years of life, regarding which classes of words in one's language map onto kinds (e.g., L. Smith, 2000; Waxman, 1999).

What developmental changes take place in essentialist reasoning, once the naming system is firmly in place (by about two and a half years)? I hypothesize that there are two marked additional changes that take place during childhood: refinement of scope, and integration with a more extensive (scientific and cultural) knowledge base. Younger children appear at first to be more blatantly and crudely essentialist, extending essentialism too broadly. Marianne Taylor's (1996) finding that children are more strongly essentialist about gender than are adults, Larry Hirschfeld's and my finding (1997) that children essentialize language in a way that adults do not, and Gail Heyman's and my findings (2000a) that children are more prone to nativist accounts of psychological traits, all suggest that children are over-ready to apply essentialism to categories that adults view in more nuanced terms.

During middle childhood, essentialism becomes integrated with scientific and cultural knowledge as well. Essentialism is at first a "placeholder" notion (S. Gelman and Diesendruck, 1999; Medin, 1989): sketchy in details and only gradually connected to developing notions of biology. Children honor an initial causal link between abstract properties (e.g., energy, ontology) and observable features of a kind. Children make use of skeletal (also known as abstract, global, or framework) principles to guide development and construct increasingly specific essentialist beliefs (R. Gelman, 1990; Mandler, Bauer, and McDonough, 1991; Simons and Keil, 1995; Wellman, 1990; Wellman and Gelman, 1988).

In sum, I expect important conceptual changes in essentialist reasoning within the first four years. If my speculations are correct, then essentialism starts out strictly as a belief that many categories are richly structured kinds, then additionally becomes a search for underlying inherent properties. It is at first a preverbal assumption about categories, later becoming an assumption linked to language (in particular, names). Over time, children refine the categories to which an essentialist framework applies and correspondingly gain an increasingly specified notion of what essences might be (often in culture-specific ways). Eventually, as adults, we may come to restructure our concepts away from essentialism altogether, with the recognition that variability and population-level characteristics are more central than commonalities shared by each individual in a category. However, I suspect that this last level of conceptual change—away from essentialism—is much rarer than is usually recognized (see the section later in this chapter titled "Broader Implications").

Individual Differences?

Up to this point I have been discussing essentialism as if it were relatively equivalent across members of a given culture. Yet intuition suggests that this picture may be too simple. Take categories of sexual orientation. Certainly there is impassioned debate within the United States, from the essentialist view that sexual orientation is innately determined and immutable to the antiessentialist view that sexual orientation is a matter of choice.

In a study of essentialist beliefs of a range of traits, Gail Heyman and I are finding empirical evidence of vast individual variation. Specifically, we asked 101 undergraduate students at the University of Michigan to judge the extent to which twelve different traits (see Table 10.1) are essentialist, using a variety of specific questions. We deliberately selected some traits that are known to have a biological basis (e.g., schizophrenic), some that are known to have strong environmental underpinnings (e.g., politically conservative), as well as others that seemed intermediate (e.g., nurturing; conscientious). The nine essentialist questions were (using X in place of the trait):

- Are some people born with a predisposition to be X?
- Will a baby who is adopted at birth grow up to be as X as the birth parents, or as X as the adoptive parents?
- Do you think scientists will ever be able to tell which babies will grow up to be X?
- In the future, will scientists be able to determine which people are X by analyzing samples of their blood?
- Do you think that there are consistent differences between the brains of people who are X and the brains of people who are not X?
- Do people who are X at age twenty tend to be X at age forty-five?
- When comparing across different countries, how do the percentages of people who are X compare across the world?
- How much does the environment a person grows up in, affect whether or not he or she will become X? (reverse-coded)
- To what extent can people change whether they are X, if they want to? (reverse-coded)

We also included three control questions (e.g., whether those with the trait would have many friends), which will not be discussed here.

All questions were presented on a scale of 1 (low) to 6 (high). For the purposes of this discussion, we averaged the nine essentialist questions (reverse-coding the two questions regarding environmental influences and capacity to change), resulting in a composite score that could range from 1 (least essentialist) to 6 (most essentialist).

I list the mean score and range for each trait in Table 10.1. Certain traits (e.g., schizophrenic, intelligent) consistently received more essentialist composite ratings than others (e.g., lazy, politically conservative). For the most part, participants favored nonessentialist accounts—not surprisingly, given which traits we selected. Had we included traits such as gender, race, athleticism, or mathematical ability, for example, I suspect the scores would have been much more essentialist. Nonetheless, we were struck by the wide variation in participants' beliefs, both within each trait and across traits. When scores were collapsed across all twelve traits, the composite essentialist score ranged dramatically: from a low of 2.00 to a high of 4.29.

Another example of stark individual variation in essentialist reasoning comes from Dweck's work on children's beliefs regarding intelligence (Dweck, 1999). Dweck finds stable individual differences in this regard, with some children consistently endorsing an "entity" theory (that intelligence is fixed and immutable—in other words, an essentialist theory) and other children consistently endorsing an "incremental" theory (that intelligence is flexible and can be improved with practice and experience—in other words, a nonessentialist theory). These differences

Table 10.1.   Essentialist scores of 12 traits, on a scale of 1 (low) to 6 (high); S. Gelman and Heyman

Trait	Composite essentialist score	Range*
Schizophrenic	4.44	2.44–6.00
Intelligent	3.83	2.00–5.56
Homosexual	3.79	1.67–5.78
Musically skilled	3.67	2.11–5.22
Anxious	3.21	1.78–5.44
Curious	3.13	1.78–4.11
Shy	2.99	1.89–4.67
Nurturing	2.96	1.56–4.22
Conscientious	2.90	1.44–4.33
Superstitious	2.61	1.44–4.11
Lazy	2.51	1.33–4.00
Politically conservative	2.37	1.33–3.78

* One participant had a mean score of 5.22 or above for all 12 traits. In order not to inflate the range artificially because of one outlier, these ranges exclude the data from that one participant.

can be seen in children as young as first grade, and have powerful implications for children's persistence in the face of failure by fifth grade (Cain and Dweck, 1995). When entity theorists fail on a task, they more or less tell themselves, "I'm no good, so there's no point in my trying any more." When incremental theorists fail they tell themselves, in effect, "I need to improve, so I'd better try harder next time."

Even below first grade, children showed individual differences in their beliefs about the stability of antisocial behavior (Giles and Heyman, 2001; Heyman, Dweck, and Cain, 1992). Among kindergartners, the belief that someone who misbehaves at the present time will always misbehave was associated with "motivational vulnerability" (feeling as if one mistake means you are not smart, and difficulty generating strategies to solve academic difficulties; Heyman, Dweck, and Cain, 1992). And among three- to five-year-olds, the belief that antisocial behavior is stable was associated with the tendency to agree that hitting someone is an appropriate means to solve problems, and with lower teacher ratings of children's social competence (Giles and Heyman, 2001). Although judgments of stability are not equivalent to essentialism, they are one important component.

We also found tremendous variation in essentialist talk, that is, in people's tendency to produce generics. In the CHILDES data reported in chapter 8, for example, the rate at which children produced generics at age two ranged from under 0.2% of all utterances in one child to nearly 3% in another child; at age three, the rates varied from a low of 0.3% in one child to over 6% in another. Individual differences are even more noticeable in semi-structured book-reading tasks. Tina Pappas and I found that, in a controlled book-reading context where each mother-child dyad was talking about the very same book, the rate of maternal generics ranged from those who produced no generics whatsoever to one mother who produced generics on an average of 41% of all utterances (Pappas and Gelman, 1998). Likewise, in an ongoing project examining parent-child conversations about gender in a naturalistic book-reading context, the rate of maternal generics ranged from those who produced none whatsoever to one mother who produced generics on 67% of all on-task utterances (S. Gelman, Nguyen, and Taylor, 2001). Even more remarkably, in the same study, children ranged from producing no generics to one child who produced generics on 92% of all on-task utterances.

Documenting these individual differences just opens up more questions. We do not yet know enough about the domain-specificity versus domain-generality of these individual differences. Are individual differences in essentializing largely limited to particular categories or domains, or are there stable differences that extend fairly broadly across categories? I presume that everyone essentializes to some extent, but there may be stable differences in people's penchant for an essentialist sort of explanation. For example, perhaps Dweck's entity theorists are also more likely to essentialize other social kinds. We also know very little about what predicts variation in essentializing. To what extent are they driven by cognitive factors (including, for example, knowledge about a domain), and to what extent by other issues altogether? Answers to these questions await future research.

BROADER IMPLICATIONS

What Can Children Tell Us about the Nature of Concepts?

Children have provided an important test case for essentialism. The findings with children show us that essentialism is a fundamental cognitive bias that emerges with remarkably little input. It does not require scientific sophistication, formal schooling, or direct instruction. It is "easy to think" or "good to think," to borrow Lévi-Strauss's (1963, p. 89) phrase. It is a habit of the mind.

The implications for theories of concepts are far-reaching. There is an idealized model of categorization that has formed the basis for much work in psychology. Standard theories of concepts have been based on considering which known properties are most privileged, and in what form. Much ink has been spilled on questions such as: Which properties define category membership? Do prototypes or exemplars more accurately form the basis of human categories? What is the precise mathematical formula for calculating prototypes? Which features are tallied, which features are correlated? In other words, the question has been what organization of known properties give rise to judgments of category membership. In contrast, essentialism tells us that known properties do not constitute the full meaning of concepts. Concepts are also open-ended. They are in part placeholders for unknown properties. They are corrigible (Putnam, 1973).

Even if we turn our attention just to those properties that are known, the usual focus has been on readily named properties such as parts, size, or texture—thereby missing the important point that the most central features may be the unstated ones that people implicitly assume but do not even think to mention (see also Murphy, 2002; Tversky and Hemenway, 1984). For example, in Rosch's classic experiments of the 1970s, people listed properties such as "have feathers" and "can fly" for birds—they did not bother to mention (though surely knew) that birds are alive, have hearts and bones, have offspring of the same species, and so forth. These latter properties have greater theoretical relevance and turn out to be at least as central to category membership. But they typically have been left aside in controlled experiments with invented categories and in studies of natural concepts.

Another important implication is that different concepts require different sorts of models and structures. As already discussed in chapter 9, people will make use of different sorts of information, depending on whether the category consists of U-shaped objects made out of wood and chicken wire, about which they have only perceptual information, or instead is a real-world natural kind. Studies of decontextualized artifacts or dot patterns will, by necessity, tell us about how people organize patterns of perceptible qualities. Such studies are important, but not the whole story. This point is not surprising; what is surprising is how often it is overlooked in theoretical accounts of what categorization entails.

Implicit here, too, is the importance of domain. Essencelike construals emerge broadly across many different kinds of categories. The creator's intent is critical in labeling artwork and simple artifacts (Bloom and Markson, 1998; S. Gelman and Bloom, 2000; S. Gelman and Ebeling, 1998), and personal history determines whether a work of art is authentic (see chapter 11). Nonetheless, essentialist construals are found most often and most emphatically with natural kinds and certain social kinds. Categories such as "penguin," "apple tree," and "male" imply inherent nonobvious properties, rich inductive potential, and innate potential in ways not found with categories such as "window," "crayon," and "sidewalk."

In addition to category differences, different tasks tap into different ways of thinking. Historically, it has often been assumed that there is a single, unitary process of categorization (Bruner, Goodnow, and Austin, 1956; Estes, 1994; Hull, 1920; Nosofsky, 1992; see E. Smith, Patalano, and Jonides, 1998, for review). Yet essentialism makes clear that categorization is not a single, unitary process. As discussed in chapters 2 and 9, categorization serves many different functions, and we recruit different sorts of information depending on the task at hand. Rapid identification calls for one kind of process; reasoning about genealogy calls for another. (However, as Keil, Smith, et al. [1998] point out, even rapid processing could recruit theory-relevant information. One might identify a stick insect as an animal after only a quick glance, if one happens to focus on its head and eyes, or if one happens to see it moving on its own.) Rips (1989) provides an elegant demonstration that task differences yield different categorization processes. For example, when adults are told to think about an object three inches in diameter (with no additional information), they judge it to be more similar to a quarter than a pizza, but more likely to be a pizza than a quarter.

Even when the task is restricted to object identification, people make use of different sorts of information depending on the task instructions (Yamauchi and Markman, 1998)—at times even in parallel on the same trial (Allen and Brooks, 1991). E. Smith, Patalano, and Jonides (1998) show that two separate categorization procedures, rule application and judging similarity to an exemplar, can readily apply to the same categories. These procedures seem qualitatively distinct, in that they activate different neural regions in the adult brain.

Essentialism also argues for the interdependence of categorization and other cognitive processes, such as causal reasoning, or reading of intentionality. Certainly no one would argue that categorization is a wholly separate entity unto itself (consider, for example, the well-appreciated links between categorization and processes of perception and memory). Theory-based approaches to concepts have powerfully made the point that categorization is intertwined with knowledge and belief systems (e.g., Murphy and Medin, 1985). However, the extent of this interdependence has not yet been sufficiently plumbed. It would be intriguing to know, for example, how categorization changes (if at all) for those people with impairments that affect other higher-level reasoning processes. We need more fine-grained studies of categorization in autism (which devastates theory of mind; see Baron-Cohen, Tager-Flusberg, and Cohen, 1993) or Williams syndrome (which seems to undercut theory construction; see S. Johnson and Carey, 1998). For an intriguing example, see P. Bloom, Abell, et al. (under review), who find deficits in naming of representations, in a sample of people with autism.

Because essentialism is found early in childhood, all these points must be operating in quite basic and fundamental ways. In other words, we cannot simply assume that they are frills added on top of basic or standard categorization. Instead, the following are important from very early in life: placeholder notions, theory-based properties, category and task variability, and interdependence of categorization and other cognitive processes. More generally, childhood essentialism overturns assumptions about what is simple or basic and what is complex. Abstract is not always hard, and concrete is not always the starting point. (See Keil, Smith, et al., 1998, for further discussion of this point.)

What Can Concepts Tell Us about the Nature of Children?

Childhood essentialism poses a challenge to more traditional theories of children's concepts (e.g., Inhelder and Piaget, 1964), which emphasized the instability of children's concepts and their focus on superficial, accidental, or perceptual features. In the extreme, Piaget and his colleagues suggested that children are incapable of forming "true" concepts. Likewise, many scholars have proposed one or another developmental dichotomy: from concrete to abstract, from surface to deep, or from perceptual to conceptual (see Bruner, Olver, and Greenfield, 1966; Inhelder and Piaget, 1964; Vygotsky, 1962; Werner and Kaplan, 1963). To the contrary, I have argued for remarkable commonalities between the concepts of children and those of adults. I acknowledge that developmental dichotomies may still exist earlier in development (e.g., from one to two years, instead of from five to seven years). However, we have seen no evidence for such a shift in the studies reported in this book, which included participants as young as age two years and (in some cases) even below.

As discussed at length in chapter 9, childhood essentialism also argues strongly in favor of a theory view of cognitive development, and against a DAM (dumb attentional mechanisms) view. Children's categories incorporate information beyond the obvious, including ontology, intentions, and functions. Associations and correlations of outward features are insufficient. Children are not simply stringing together observed properties, but rather are searching for underlying causes and explanations. In the absence of concrete theories, more-abstract framework theories serve as placeholders (Wellman, 1990).

However, essentialism does not posit that perceptual features or similarity are unimportant to early concepts. Even within an essentialist framework appearances provide crucial cues regarding an underlying essence (S. Gelman and Medin, 1993). Similarity appears to play an important role in fostering comparisons of representations and hence discovery of new abstractions and regularities (Gentner and Medina, 1998). Rather than suggesting that we overturn perception or similarity, essentialism carries with it the assumption that a category has two distinct though interrelated levels: the level of observable reality and the level of explanation and cause.

It is this two-tier structure that may in fact serve to motivate further development, leading children to develop deeper, more thoughtful understandings (Waxman and Braig, 1996; Wellman and Gelman, 1998). Most developmental accounts of cognitive change include something like this structure, such as equilibration (Inhelder and Piaget, 1958), competition (MacWhinney, 1987), theory change (Carey, 1985), analogy (Goswami, 1996), and cognitive variability (Siegler, 1994). In all these cases—as with essentialism—children consider contrasting representations. Perhaps not surprisingly, then, children look beyond observable features when trying to understand the categories of their world. If we think that what we see is what we get, then there is no real motivation for cognitive advance. But once we posit that there is a reality beyond appearances, the search is on for more information, deeper causes, and alternative construals. Theory change, in other words.

It is worth asking why the DAM view and developmental dichotomies are so persistent. Keil, Smith, et al. (1998) point out that these dichotomies are appealing for the same reasons that the empiricist tradition is appealing (see also Pinker, 2002, for discussion of the intuitive appeals—and perils—of a "blank slate" empiricist doctrine). According to empiricism, knowledge derives from our senses. To many, this doctrine has the powerful allure of common sense. It also seems to account for knowledge acquisition with a minimum of machinery. Although a stark empiricist position is clearly insufficient, the tradition persists. I also suspect that the DAM position is a backlash against the early-competence view. Indeed, I suspect that there has been a pendulum endlessly swinging, back and forth, between early-competence views and their opposite, throughout the historical literature on childhood. This instability most likely reflects a tension between two realities: children master so much so quickly, yet at the same time a young child still has so far to go before achieving adult competence. This tension can be seen in the competing metaphors of children (e.g., children as aliens versus children as little adults; Wellman and Gelman, 1998). This ambivalence is reminiscent of the uneasy relationship that adult humans have with nonhuman animals—humans both are and are not animals.

I do not argue a simple early-competence view, because the reasoning bias that is essentialism provides a decidedly mixed picture of young children. Children are competent, yes, in many surprising respects, but as we have seen throughout this volume, they are also incompetent, fixed, and wrongheaded in other respects. Rather than simply saying, "Children are competent, but also incompetent"— which is neither conceptually helpful nor a testable theory—we need to characterize in what respects children are competent and in what respects they are not. Relatedly, we need to decide which incompetencies are general cognitive limitations of people at all ages, including adults, as opposed to those that are specific to reasoning in early childhood. In other words, developmental research needs to move beyond the competence debate, toward a full characterization of children's knowledge and acquisitional processes.

A final implication of childhood essentialism is that language may play a greater role in the development of basic cognitive processes than is generally acknowledged. I do not mean to suggest that language is the source of essentializing (though whether nonlinguistic or prelinguistic humans essentialize concepts remains an intriguing untested question). Nonetheless, from the beginnings of language children seem to assume that language directly reflects essentialist structure in the world, and they seem to make use of words to bootstrap essentialism to new categories and to new category instances, seemingly without effort. This view fits in with the now growing evidence that language may shape concepts from infancy onward (e.g., Balaban and Waxman, 1997; Carey and Xu, 1999; S. Gelman and Coley, 1990; Graham, Kilbreath, and Welder, 2001; Jaswal and Markman, 2002; Waxman and Markow, 1995; Xu, 1999, in press).

To this point I was considering universal properties of human language (in particular, of lexical semantics). But it remains intriguingly possible that cross-linguistic differences in language organization might also have subtle effects on essentialist reasoning. For example, does construal of kinds vary between languages that distinguish mass from count and languages that do not? Do languages that have either more or less explicit marking of generic noun phrases give rise to developmental differences in the salience and frequency of such kind talk, and of the underlying kind concepts? These questions remain largely unexplored.

Is It Possible to Transcend Essentialism?

I started this book by admitting that I was a child essentialist. What about adults? Can adults ever escape or transcend essentialist tendencies? We no longer suffer from the most egregious essentialist errors found in children: nominal realism, overgeneralization of properties (such as when my daughter at age three soberly informed me that "Mommies wear dresses," even though I was wearing jeans at the time), overly rigid adherence to category boundaries, and belief that categories remain fixed and unchanging over historical time (Evans, 2000). But do we remain essentialists deep down?

One possible answer is that we have replaced essentialism with a radically different conceptual framework, of the sort espoused by evolutionary biology. Evolutionary theory would seem to be a triumph of reason over naïve heuristics (Mayr, 1991). The problem is, as I have mentioned several times, that it appears to be exceedingly difficult for most nonbiologists (even adults) to grasp the basic ideas of evolutionary theory. What appears to be difficult is not just the complexity of the concepts, nor the scientific methods underlying the evidence, nor even the technical underpinnings of the work. Rather, even nontechnical concepts such as the following seem almost insurmountable: within-species variability, the lack of any single feature (either morphological or genetic) that is shared by all members of a species, and the lack of biological reality to "racial" groupings of people. These conceptual difficulties call into question whether true conceptual reorganization takes place, or whether instead we are looking at the coexistence of multiple frameworks.

This issue requires more intensive research into adult reasoning (see E. Anderson and Jayaratne, 1998; Haslam and Ernst, 2002; Haslam, Rothschild, and Ernst, 2002; and Mahalingam, 1998 for highly promising examples of such ongoing work). At present, based on the anecdotal evidence, I would suggest that adults remain susceptible to less obvious but still potent essentialist assumptions. In other words, essentialism is not strictly a childhood construction. It is a framework for organizing our knowledge of the world, a framework that persists throughout life.

Chapter 11

Why Do We Essentialize?

> Are there real kinds in nature, or are kinds, instead, merely imposed upon
> nature by the human mind?
>
> Hilary Kornblith, *Inductive Inference and Its Natural Ground*

The question "Why do we essentialize?" is really several questions. Where is essentialism located (for example, how much is it a cognitive construction versus a discovery about the world, as Kornblith framed the issue)? What properties of the
mind give rise to essentialism? What are the proximate causes or triggers for essentialism, as children perceive the world? I begin by considering briefly a somewhat
different version of the question: what purpose does essentializing serve?

There are unmistakable benefits to essentialism. It provides a framework for
making valuable category-based inferences. It encourages a "scientific" mindset in
thinking about the natural world, a belief that intensive study of a natural domain
will yield ever more underlying properties.[1] The many ways in which children essentialize the natural world reveal precocious abilities to categorize and benefit
from categories.

Yet essentialism also carries with it serious costs. Most troubling, it encourages
and justifies stereotyping of social categories (including race, gender, and sexual
orientation; Haslam, Rothschild, and Ernst, 2002). It perpetuates the assumption
that artificial distinctions (such as caste or class) are natural, inevitable, and fixed.
Relatedly, it poses obstacles to a complete grasp of evolutionary biology, as it implies that each species is fixed and immutable, not allowing for the possibility of
evolutionary change over time. As Ernst Mayr noted, "It took more than two thousand years for biology, under the influence of Darwin, to escape the paralyzing grip
of essentialism" (1982, p. 87).

So the question of why we essentialize is thorny. Do we do it because of its benefits? For example, perhaps it has helped us in our ancestral past and continues to
the present day, and so is an evolved capacity. Or do we do it in order to impose
harm on others? For example, perhaps essentialism as a doctrine is a means of
maintaining power differences between the haves and the have-nots, discouraging
people from attempting to alter extant social systems. These questions are bound

up with some complex issues. For which categories do we essentialize? Is it a universal tendency? Is it correct (in a metaphysical sense)? I cannot promise a complete solution, but this chapter will present some initial ideas and boundary conditions. I will argue that essentialism is rooted neither in its costs nor its benefits, but falls out as a consequence of children being very good at a number of other skills: distinguishing appearance from reality, searching for causes, noting correlational clusters, and understanding how labeling works.

IS ESSENTIALISM A CHILDHOOD CONSTRUCTION?

To oversimplify this very complex issue, there are four major possibilities concerning the source(s) of essentialism: essentialism could be rooted in the world, in the mind, in language, or in culture. Of course, essentialism could result from an interaction of two or more factors (as with the evolutionary account that the mind is adapted so as to identify regularities in the natural world; see more on this view below), and I suspect that any reasonable person is to some degree an interactionist. Nonetheless, even within an interactionist perspective there is considerable room for disagreement. The claim that essentialism is a childhood construction is a claim that essentialism is rooted in the human mind, and not solely due to aspects of the world, language, or culture.

I start with the three primary arguments against considering essentialism to be a childhood construction. Although the arguments are intuitively plausible, they fit poorly with the available data. Children are not passive recipients of essentializing—they construct essentialism largely on their own.

Misconception 1: Children Do Not Essentialize

Fodor has put forth the view that children do not essentialize: "Natural kind concepts . . . [are] self-conscious and cultivated intellectual achievements. . . . In the history of science, and in ontogeny, and, for all I know, in phylogeny too, concepts of natural kinds as such only come late. Homer, and children, and animals, have few or them or none" (1998, pp. 154, 155). Likewise, see Jones and Smith (1993). However, the available data strongly suggest that by four years of age children treat certain categories as having rich inductive potential; privilege causes over other sorts of properties in determining category membership; invoke nonobvious, internal, or invisible qualities, and consider them more tightly linked to identity than outward properties; treat membership in a kind as stable over outward transformations; appeal to innate potential; and so forth. For more details, I refer the reader to the preceding chapters.

Misconception 2: Essentialism Is Provided by the Structure of the Input

We know surprisingly little about this issue, as most work on essentialism has focused on people's beliefs, rather than on the contexts that permit or encourage such beliefs. However, as far as we can tell, remarkably little of the input children hear provides explicit information about essentialism, even among a sample of highly educated, middle-class parents in a highly technological culture (see chapter 7 for extended discussion). Although essentialism seemingly lurks around every corner in middle-class adult causal explanations (including, for example, scientific attempts to map out the genetic contribution to a vast array of human traits, media accounts of gender differences, legal wrangles such as the Baby M. and Jessica DeBoer adoption cases, and fictional accounts of blood ties [e.g., *The Bad Seed*]), parental input to preschool children refers to essentialism indirectly at best. It is not that the input is irrelevant. I have already suggested in chapter 8 that language helps children figure out which categories are essentialized kinds. But if the available data provide a representative glimpse into this issue, then the basic essentializing impulse is not the outcome of parental instruction.

Misconception 3: Essentialism Is Provided by the Structure of the World

This possibility has been argued forcefully by Kornblith: "It is precisely because the world has the causal structure required for the existence of natural kinds that inductive knowledge is even possible" (1993, p. 35). His argument depends in part on the successes of science. The sciences (including chemistry, physics, biology, and psychology) impute unobservable structure and thereby make accurate predictions, explanations, and technological advances (p. 41). Paul Bloom likewise suggests: "Essentialism is an adaptive way of looking at the world; it is adaptive because it is true" (2000, p. 153). He acknowledges that a strict version of essentialism is wrong in positing immutable categories with sharp boundaries, but suggests that a less strict version of essentialism is importantly true: that superficial properties are caused by deeper, underlying properties. For example, in biology embryonic features and genetic structure (underlying causal features) are more important than outward appearances. This is why, for example, a hummingbird and a falcon are classified together but a bat is a different kind.

I agree with Kornblith (1993), P. Bloom (2000), and Pinker (1994) that essentialism fits with aspects of real-world structure. In particular, the commonsense assumption that nonobvious features cause outward similarities is importantly accurate in numerous domains, including biology (chromosomes and DNA have observable effects), chemistry (atomic number determines structure of the elements), and physics (quarks, electrons, and electromagnetism are all theorized and not directly observable, yet have profound effects on the world). In short, essentialism exploits certain real-world regularities. Nonetheless, essentialism is not simply "out there" in the world, waiting for children to pick up on it. Consequently, an explanatory account must invoke additional mechanisms. This is a tricky point, so I will consider it at some length here.

Socially Constructed Categories

One major argument against the view that essences are real is the rampant essentializing of categories that are socially constructed (including race, caste, at times even occupation; Allport, 1954; Banton, 1987; Goldberg, 1993; Guillaumin, 1980; Hirschfeld, 1996; Stoler, 1995). Adults—and children—readily apply essentialism to categories that demonstrably have no underlying inherent essences. Treating caste as inborn, impervious to environmental influence, immutable, and predictive of inherent nonobvious properties is sensible within an essentialist framework, but it is a metaphysical error.

Although race is essentialized, anthropologists and biologists widely agree that race has no essence (see Brace, 1964; Hirschfeld, 1996; and Templeton, 1998, for arguments against the biological reality of race). The superficial physical dimensions along which people vary (such as skin color or hair texture) do not map neatly onto racial groupings. Observable human differences also do not form correlated feature clusters. Skin color is not predictive of "deep" causal features (such as gene frequencies for anything other than skin color). There is no gene for race as it is commonly understood.

Nonetheless, the average person commonly assumes that race is the expression of a biological essence. Jayaratne (2001) find that most adults in her national sample believe that any two people of the same race are more genetically similar than any two people of different races. Over 56% of her sample of 1,186 adults either somewhat or strongly agreed to the statement, "TWO PEOPLE from the SAME RACE will always be more genetically similar to each other than TWO PEOPLE from DIFFERENT RACES." Seventy-four percent of her sample either somewhat or strongly agreed with the statement "Our genes tell us which race we belong to." Even those who are otherwise highly knowledgeable display similar misconceptions. For example, a reviewer of one of my papers (who will remain anonymous) wrote: "I agree with you that race is very often a socio-political concept, but I still say that in genetics it has an objective definition in terms of gene frequencies." These seemingly reasonable statements are simply wrong, and reveal the extent to which essentialism seeps into the reasoning of even educated adults.

Biological Species

How about with biological species? At first blush it seems as if essentialism is compatible with scientific descriptions of the world, and even paves the way for scientific advances. Doesn't science—like essentialism—tell us that categories have nonobvious causal properties? Isn't the biological structure of tigers (DNA) the scientific equivalent of an essence? If so, then it would seem reasonable to propose that people's essentialist views may derive from real-world properties. And yet, however tempting it may be to suppose that the world provides us with real essences, studies of essentialist construals and of biological species strongly suggest that essentialism does not reside in biological species.

First, the strongest version of essentialism (in which species are immutable categories) is incompatible with evolutionary theory, which posits that species change over time (Mayr, 1991). This critique is not altogether convincing, since one can be essentialist without believing that essentialized categories are unchanging (Sober, 1994). However, Sober rejects a metaphysical reality to essentialism for another reason: essentialism assumes that the essence resides in each individual organism—that it is a property of each organism. In contrast, according to evolutionary theory, species cannot be characterized in terms of properties of individual members but rather in terms of properties of the population. To use familiar Kuhnian terminology, there was a paradigm shift in how biologists think about species, and essentialism revealed itself to be dependent on the old paradigm.

I quote at length from Sober to make this point clear. He argues that "the essentialist requires that a *species* be defined in terms of the characteristics of the *organisms* which belong to it. We might call this kind of definition a *constituent definition*. . . . Constituent definitions are *reductionistic*, in that concepts at higher levels of organization (e.g., species) are legitimate only if they are definable in terms of concepts applying at lower levels of organization (e.g., organisms)" (1994, p. 205). He then contrasts essentialism with population thinking: "population thinking emancipated biology from the need for constituent definitions of species. . . . No phenotypic characteristic can be postulated as a species essence; . . . no genotypic characteristic can be postulated as a species essence" (p. 225). He also points out that

> the essentialist searched for a property *of individual organisms* which is invariant across the organisms in a species. The Hardy-Weinberg law and other more interesting population laws, on the other hand, identify properties of *populations* which are invariant across all populations of a certain kind. In this sense, essentialism pursued an individualistic (organismic) methodology, which population thinking supplants by specifying laws governing objects at a higher level of organization. . . . Essentialism lost its grip when populations came to be thought of as real. (1994, p. 227)

Sober suggests there is no essence for biological species—let alone groupings of people, such as races—at a surface level or even at a genetic level. Wilson explains the difficulty as follows:

> The chief problem with either suggestion [morphological or genetic essentialism] is empirical. . . . There simply is no set of phenotypes that all and only members of a given species share. . . . Precisely the same is true of genetic properties. The inherent biological variability or *heterogeneity* of species with respect to both morphology and genetic composition is, after all, a cornerstone of the idea of evolution by natural selection. (1999, p. 190)

At this point the reader may object that the arguments against biological essences are directed against sortal essences, not causal essences. Recall that in chapter 1, I distinguished between the two, arguing that my interest is in causal, not sortal essences. Whereas sortal essences are defining features used to identify all and only members of a category, causal essences are underlying features believed to cause clusters of observable properties. Sobel argues that there are no properties shared by all and only members of a biological species, at either a surface level (morphology) or an underlying causal level. He does not deny that underlying features have surface effects; for example, he accepts that genes are responsible for important category-typical behaviors. Rather, he maintains that there is no biological essence that is both causal and sortal. A critic may wish to argue on behalf of biological essentialism by noting that causal essences do exist, they just are not sortal.

My problem with this argument on behalf of species essentialism rests on my original motivations for distinguishing sortal from causal essences. The first reason for my interest in causal essences is that sortal essences alone are not essential enough. A sortal essence could be a trivial feature or set of features. I could define the invented category of "fep" such that it has a clear sortal essence (feps are all and only those objects that are smaller than three cubic inches), but it fails to adhere to essentialism in the sense discussed in this volume. (There is no rich inductive potential, no boundary intensification, no stability over transformations, no inductive potential.) The second reason is that essences are rarely used to determine reference in everyday thought. In part the disconnect between essences and reference-determination exists because the essence is often unknown (in Medin's terms, there is an essence placeholder rather than a fully articulated and known essence), and in part this disconnect exists because even if the essence is known, it is inaccessible and rarely available for consultation. I may firmly believe that the essence of water is H_2O, but I do not have the time or resources to check out the chemical structure of what I am drinking before I name it.

Taken together, these reasons suggest the following: the problem with sortal essentialism as a psychological claim is not that it posits that all members of a kind share a set of features, but rather that it is simultaneously too weak (failing to distinguish surface from underlying causal features, thus allowing for a trivial version of essentialism) and too strong (positing that placeholder notions will be used to determine reference). However, once these concerns are addressed, then I do maintain that causal essentialism presumes a kind of sortal essentialism—with two caveats: (1) on causal essentialism, the causal features are the defining (sortal) features, and (2) the causal essence is typically unknown, and even when known is rarely consulted to determine reference. Another way of phrasing the psychological claim is that people implicitly believe that the causal essence is shared by all and only members of the category, but this metabelief rarely has direct implications for determining word reference.

The point here is that Sober's and Wilson's arguments against the biological reality of essences are pertinent to claims about psychological essentialism. Sober and Wilson are arguing against a version of essentialism that is simultaneously causal and sortal. As I have argued so far, causal psychological essentialism is also sortal (in theory), even when the causal essence is not used to determine reference in everyday thought.

Taking a somewhat different (and perhaps more controversial) approach, Dupré (1993) suggests that species are real, just not in the sense we usually assume. He argues that each organism belongs to numerous natural kinds, each with its own essence (a view he calls "promiscuous realism"), a position that undermines the notion of a single real category (or single real essence) for each organism.

The problems with biological essentialism are surprisingly difficult for non-biologists to grasp. For example, an otherwise brilliant paper by Kamp and Partee reveals an essentialist misconstrual of species: "The vast majority of natural kind terms are sharp in the strict sense of being determinately true or false of everything that is found in the real world. For instance, to belong to a particular biological species an individual must have the DNA of that species; and almost without exception this is a property which an individual organism either definitely has or else definitely lacks" (1995, p. 175).

Further Points Regarding Essentialism as a Mental Construct

The one domain that seems most promising for an essentialist framework is that of chemistry (see Sober, 1994). The elements in the periodic table each seem to have a clearly identified, underlying causal essence that is responsible for clusters of important properties that members of each chemical kind share. All samples of gold have certain surface properties that can be traced to their microscopic structure. If one wished to argue that essentialism derives from real-world structure, that might be the domain to use as a case in point.

Outside the domain of chemistry, essences are misleading. At the same time, for biological species, essences are heuristically useful much of the time. The basic idea that underlying features cause clusters of surface features seems to be quite right with respect to animal and plant kinds. In this sense, essentialism is akin to statistical reasoning biases (Kahneman, Slovic, and Tversky, 1982; Nisbett and Ross, 1980) or folk physics (M. McCloskey, 1983): generally useful but not fully right. Essentialism allows us to navigate the world pretty well, but it is not 100% accurate. In fact, there are fundamental ontological misconceptions there.

Even if the world were composed of real essences, this is a far cry from demonstrating that such essences are available to young children. The world does seem to provide natural perceptual discontinuities that humans are predisposed to notice (Berlin, 1978). However, natural discontinuities fall far short of an essence—an invisible causal mechanism that accounts for such discontinuities. The child looking at and interacting with the natural world will never see, hear, or touch an essence directly. Essentialism is a childhood construction.

The human tendency to essentialize is unquestionably a psychological fact, regardless of whether essences are real. It is a psychological fact because our categories are not logically constrained to capture deep similarities (Quine, 1977). One clear alternative, for example, would be to group things based on shape, color, and size. Instead, we deliberately shape and reshape our concepts with the goal of capturing nonobvious properties.

Given the problems with these commonsense proposals, I am left with the conclusion that *children's own constructions are critical. In other words, there are important properties of the mind that give rise to essentialism.* Input and world structure, no matter how significant, are not enough. Hirschfeld (1996) provides an extended analysis of racial essentializing that powerfully illustrates this point. Children essentialize race before they can reliably categorize or sort people on the basis of perceptible surface features (such as skin color); parents rarely talk about race with their young children; and parental input about race does not predict individual children's racial beliefs and attitudes (see Hirschfeld, 1996, for discussion and citations). All of these points argue that children construct racial categories; they are not simply imparted by adults or "read off" the world.

The question then becomes: what properties of the mind give rise to essentialism? There are two radically different sorts of proposals regarding how the mind creates essentialism: modularity and general cognitive processing. On the modularity view, essentialism is initially specific to folk biology and later spreads by analogy to other domains. On a general cognitive processing view, essentialism is at first a domain-general assumption which only later gets refined to those domains that best support it. These accounts lead to two competing developmental predictions: either essentialism should start out domain-specific and get broader over time, or essentialism should start out domain-general and get more specific over time. In contrast, I will put forth a third position: that essentialism involves several domain-general assumptions that are invoked differently in different domains.

Is Essentialism a Folk-Biology Module?

Atran (1998), Gil-White (2001), and Pinker (1994) suggest that essentialism is a part of a folk-biology module.[2] In other words, humans have evolved an innate, domain-specific, automatic, highly constrained means of processing the biological world (including plants and animals). This module is hypothesized to include, in addition to essentialism, a distinctive means of organizing categories of living things into a folk taxonomy. Pinker (1994) also suggests that a folk-biology module would account for infants' intuitions about the implications of animacy for causal reasoning (e.g., that only animates engage in self-generated movement), and adults' detailed attention to and knowledge of the behavior and implications of the plant and animal world. The modular position assumes that essentialism is domain-specific in that it is tied to folk biology, universal, acquired early in development, and not dependent on cultural input for its emergence. A corollary is that essentialism is a reasonably accurate reflection of the world and has adaptive benefits (hence its evolutionary basis).

One of the toughest challenges for modularity theory is to account for the essentialism of nonbiological kinds. If essentialism is a component of a folk biology, then why do people essentialize ethnic groups (Jews, Irish, Italians, WASPs) and personality types (shy people, smart people), for example? The general solution that has been proposed is that people analogize from biology outward to other domains. Without a clear account of how such analogizing takes place, however, the modular position lacks explanatory appeal. It cannot simply be that people assume that all human groups (or even all out-groups) are biological kinds, since people are selective in which outgroups they essentialize. As Gil-White (2001) notes, we have ethnic hatred and warfare but not occupational warfare or inter-university hatred (at least not to the same degree!).

Gil-White (2001) articulates an intriguing (and testable) position. He proposes that "categories that *look* like a species . . . will tend to be essentialized." Our biology module readily essentializes folk species, but also is tricked into essentializing categories that resemble folk species in important respects. For example, ethnic groupings are not species, but they resemble species in that members are born into a particular ethnic group, "inheriting" group membership from their parents, and (in some parts of the world) members tend to marry within their ethnic group—much as a cat is born a cat, from cat parents, and breeds only with other cats. Specifically, Gil-White suggests, people are sensitive to two priming conditions: endogamous groups and descent-based groups. For example, Gil-White's respondents essentialize ethnic groups much more than clans—because, he argues, ethnic groups but not clans are endogamous and descent-based.

Gil-White's endogamy account is problematic, however. Children essentialize at a young age, but they are unlikely to have much knowledge of endogamy, especially when it comes to other people (as opposed to animal kinds). When children first essentialize human groups, do they know who may marry whom? And do their beliefs predict which groups they essentialize? These are open empirical questions, but I am doubtful. A more serious objection is that, among the social groups examined by Gil-White, endogamy is confounded with several other factors, including immutability of group membership, sharpness of group boundaries, inductive potential, possession of numerous obvious similarities, and (belief in) possession of numerous nonobvious similarities. These need to be deconfounded before we can conclude that endogamy per se primes essentialism.

This account is most convincingly undermined by the fact that adults essentialize categories to which endogamy and descent cannot apply, including natural substances (such as gold), gender, and traits. In fact, adults essentialize nonliving natural kinds even more than they essentialize living kind categories (S. Gelman and Markman, 1986). The counterargument might go something like this: endogamy and descent are relevant only for species essences; gold clearly does not have a species essence (as it is not a living kind), and so the same reasoning process does not apply. Yet if one can have a natural kind essence that does not reduce to species, it would seem more parsimonious to look for an account that can cover all the cases.

Another problematic example is caste essentialism in India. As mentioned in chapter 4, Mahalingam (1998) finds that upper-caste adults essentialize caste differences but lower-caste adults do not. Lower-caste adults tend instead toward social constructivist sorts of accounts, despite the presumed descent-based membership and endogamy of caste. Why is gender consistently essentialized (e.g., Taylor, 1996), whereas caste is essentialized only inconsistently? Although the answer is not yet known, at the least we need to look for an explanation outside of normative endogamy or descent-based membership. (The social-psychological literature provides a wealth of data and theory regarding contextual factors that might contribute to essentialism; Rothbart and Park, in press.) And if we need to look elsewhere to explain gender and caste, then it becomes plausible that we need to look elsewhere for essentializing of other ethnic groups as well.

In sum, although Gil-White's proposal for when and how essentialism extends from biology outward to other domains is intriguing and admirably precise, it seems not to fit the available evidence. We are back to not having a clear account of how analogizing from biological kinds to human kinds takes place, and how such analogizing is constrained.

For modularity to be a plausible account, it also must apply in developmental time. In other words, we should find that children at first essentialize animal and plant kinds, and only later extend out to other domains. The main proponents of modularity (Atran, 1998; Gil-White, 2001) present no developmental evidence on this issue, focusing instead on cross-cultural work with adults. But a closer look at the child data suggests that biology is not a uniquely privileged domain. By age four, children draw category-based inferences that extend beyond appearances for nonliving natural kinds as much as for living kinds (S. Gelman and Markman, 1986). Young children appear more likely to essentialize social categories (e.g., gender, personality traits) than older children or adults are. And when examining children's spontaneous generic statements (plausibly a stand-in for essentialized categories; see chapter 8; Prasada, 2000), children apply them to nonbiological natural kinds (e.g., clowns, farmers, Germans) as well as to biological species. More detailed developmental data are needed on this question, but the available evidence certainly raises problems for the modularity position.

Rothbart and Taylor (2001) also question the putative adaptive benefits of essentializing human kinds (one of the prime arguments for an evolved, essentializing cognitive module). They persuasively argue that intergroup cooperation is at least as beneficial as intergroup conflict, noting that social interactions outside one's own group can lead to innovations and more creative thinking. They stress instead the importance of social beliefs and social context for fostering essentialism—in particular, perceived unalterability and perceived inductive potential.

Altogether, modularity remains a problematic account. I turn next to a closer consideration of the scope of essentialism, as a starting point for considering what sort of nonmodular mental structure(s) might give rise to essentialism.

BROADENING THE NOTION OF ESSENCE

> The main attraction these days is a three-strand faux-pearl necklace that once belonged to Jackie Kennedy. Franklin Mint Vice Chairman Lynda Resnick bought the necklace at auction for $211,500 (pre-auction estimated value: $700). . . . As Resnick said in a prepared statement just after the pearls were purchased, "The people of the world adored Jackie, and now we can make part of Camelot accessible to all who visit our museum."
>
> —www.roadsideamerica.com, "Your online guide to off-beat attractions"

The paradigm example of essentialism, particularly in the psychological literature, is that of a biological species: tigers have in common an essence that causes a rich set of properties (both observable and unknown) to be shared among members of the kind. However, at least for adults, essentialism also appears outside the realm of biological species, to play a role in our understanding of what it means to be kin-folk and what it means to be an individual. As I have already discussed above, kinship essences and individual essences call into question the notion that essentialism is specific to folk biology.

Perhaps even more challenging to the notion of essence as a biologically specific notion is the observation that essentialism appears to fall squarely within a larger class of related phenomena. Consider first some of the central properties that essences share:

1. There is a nonvisible part, substance, or quality in each individual (as an individual or as a member of a category).
2. This part, substance, or quality is inherent and very difficult to remove.
3. The part, substance, or quality has the property of transferability—it is passed along from parent or host to offspring or client, typically at a specific moment or brief period.
4. This transfer from parentor host to offspring or client does not diminish the amount of essence or its consequences for identity in the parent or host.
5. This nonvisible part, substance, or quality has vast, diffuse, unknown causal implications.
6. The implications include authenticity and identity.

It is striking that, as a package, this causal account[3] differs markedly from those in most physical domains such as naïve mechanics (e.g., energy can be transferred from one object to another, but the amount of energy in that case is diminished). These are not properties of the world at large.

At the same time, these properties are shared by a set of other phenomena quite distinct from the realm of biology, including contamination, fetishes, and blessings (see Table 11.1). To illustrate, I compare contagion by germs to contamination.

Table 11.1. Essentialism compared to related phenomena

Phenomenon	Invisible agent	Embodied in	Transfer process	Causal implications
Essentialism	Kind essence	Tigers	Inheritance	Morphology, behavior,
Essentialism	Indiv. essence	Tim	Body-part transplant, sharing of blood	Behavior, preferences
Witchcraft	Indiv. essence	Hair, fingernail clippings	Embodiment (part for whole)	Harm to original
Contagion	Germs	Sick person	Coughing	Illness
Contamination	Value	Hitler's sweater	Wearing	?
Fetish	Value	Jackie O.'s pearls; autographs	Owning	?
Blessing	Value	Pope	Touching	?

Note: Thanks to Janet McIntosh for some of these examples.

Germs, like essences, are nonvisible (see Au, Sidle, and Rollins [1993]; Kalish [1996]), are very difficult to remove (Rozin and Nemeroff, 1990), are transferrable to others, and have broad, diffuse, unknown effects (including effects on identity, especially for serious illness such as AIDS). Although one could consider germs themselves to be biological entities, one finds precisely the same set of properties when considering nonbiological contamination. Rozin and Nemeroff (1990) provide the example of people feeling uncomfortable with the idea of wearing Hitler's sweater. There is some quality in the sweater (let's call it "negative value"—intriguingly, Rozin and Nemeroff call it "essence") that is nonvisible, very difficult to remove (e.g., the sweater is still noxious even after being sterilized in boiling water or gashed with scissors), transferable to others (e.g., by wearing the sweater; although note that the transfer process does not remove the negative value from the sweater nor even from the previous wearer), and having broad, diffuse, unknown causal implications (e.g., vaguely, that something bad may happen). Finally, the invisible quality is central to the identity of the item. One does not *become* Hitler by wearing his sweater; one does not *become* Jackie O. by wearing her pearls. Rather, you possess a bit of their being. (Perhaps this is like using a person's hair or fingernail clippings in witchcraft [Douglas, 1966], or keeping fragments of the bones of saints.)[4]

I am not suggesting that essentialism is the only way to account for such evaluation. Certainly there are simpler possibilities. With respect to Jacqueline Onassis's faux pearls that recently fetched a small fortune at auction: you might like Onassis and therefore assume that you will like her faux pearls, you might think that she had extraordinary taste, or you might observe that lots of people held Onassis in high regard and imagine that a well-motivated market strategy is to buy her things in anticipation of being able to sell them for a profit later. I acknowledge that essentializing her pearls is only one explanation for wanting to own them. Importantly, however, these alternative accounts are insufficient, particularly to explain the peculiar significance of direct physical contact with the objects in question.

I return once again to the pope's robe or Hitler's sweater. The value of these objects is contingent on touching them, not simply owning them (Rozin and Nemeroff, 1990). Touching them is more valuable (or more negatively valuable in the case of Hitler's sweater) than just seeing them or standing next to them. Consider, for example, Gloria Steinem's (1964) interview with John Lennon, where she reports that a girl waiting outside the Beatles' hotel, on discovering that Steinem had seen and touched the Beatles, asked for her (Steinem's) autograph! (And this was before Steinem was famous in her own right.) The importance of physical contact makes sense only on an essentialist account; it is wholly unpredicted by accounts that involve common liking, confidence in another's judgment, or principles of market speculation.

How Are These Phenomena Related?

There are at least three possibilities for explaining how these diverse phenomena converge: (1) they may be wholly distinct entities that are only coincidentally similar; (2) one of these phenomena may be conceptually prior, with the others being similar because they borrow or analogize from the central example; or (3) they may all be instantiations of a single framework for causal interpretation—either within the biological domain, or spanning across domains.

COINCIDENTALLY SIMILAR ENTITIES ACROSS DOMAINS?   In favor of the first possibility, there are certainly differences among the phenomena. They differ in whether they involve a category (species essence), an individual (contagion), or something intermediate (kinship essence). They also differ in their gradedness: species essence is presumably nongraded (but see debate between Kalish [1995] and Diesendruck and Gelman [1999]), whereas kinship essence and fetishizing admit of degrees (e.g., seeing versus touching versus owning the Pope's robe). And they differ in terms of which domains are implicated (e.g., species essences seem relevant for living or natural things, not artifacts, whereas contamination, fetishizing, blessing, and contagion may all involve artifacts somewhere along the causal chain). These phenomena are therefore not identical.

However, for reasons of parsimony, it is troubling to suggest that essentialism emerges in these several varied respects more or less independently. The appeal of this interpretation is limited if too many distinct kinds of domains are implicated. If the proposal here is correct—that essentialist reasoning about biological species, gender, race, kinship, contagion, contamination, fetishization, and the like cannot in structure or development be clearly distinguished—this concern is well grounded. A further argument against treating the phenomena as distinct is that none of these examples is independently motivated from evidence in the world. Given the lack of an external source, it is plausible to hypothesize some sort of common cognitive motivation.

ANALOGIZING FROM A BASE DOMAIN?   As discussed earlier, a common cognitive motivation might involve analogies from a base to more peripheral domains. Indeed, a frequently encountered explanation for the recurrence of essentialist reasoning across content areas in adult cognition is analogical transfer. On this interpretation, essentialism is a domain-specific assumption that is then "borrowed" by other domains (Allport, 1954; Atran, 1990; Boyer, 1990; Rothbart and Taylor, 1990).

Atran (1990) proposes that analogical transfer also takes place over development: essentialism begins (ontogenetically) as a domain-specific biological assumption and then is adopted by other domains. For example, differences between human groups can be (though are not necessarily) construed along the lines that we consider differences between animal species. In this way, essentialist principles initially limited to folk biology transfer to social cognition. This explanation works only if essentialism in fact develops first in folk biology and subsequently emerges in other domains.

Although no one has yet done the sorts of careful studies needed to examine children's reasoning across domains, the available evidence strongly argues against the transfer-by-analogy account. Children appear to construe several phenomena in essentialist-like ways quite early. Au, Sidle, and Rollins (1993) showed that by three years of age, children appeal to invisible particles in explaining how a substance can continue to exist despite visual disappearance (e.g., when explaining why water in which sugar has been dissolved still tastes sweet). Fetishizing also emerges early with many children's attachment to transitional objects (e.g., a particular soft blanket; Litt, 1986; Passman, 1987). Although the meaning children associate with such attachments is unclear, the traditional interpretation is that children conceive of the object as taking the place of the mother, in a sense invested with the mother's essence (Winnicott, 1969). While such a claim clearly speculates about the child's conceptualization far beyond the evidence, intriguingly, a major cultural determinant of children's attachments to transitional objects is when the young child and the mother sleep in separate beds (Wolf and Lozoff, 1989).

Similarly, evidence supports the idea that essentialist beliefs about contamination and contagion emerge early in the preschool years, at much the same age as essentialism in biology, race, and gender. For example, Siegal and Share (1990) found that three-year-olds discriminate contaminated from safe substances, even when the outward appearances of the two substances are identical (e.g., moldy bread with jam concealing the mold versus unmoldy bread with jam spread on it). In a study examining children's explanations for disease, Springer and Ruckel (1992) found that most children, even those who appear to be relying on a notion of immanent justice, attribute illness to germs and other unseen agents (see also Kalish, 1996). Springer and Ruckel (1992, pp. 440–441) suggest that the similarities between disease and inheritance explanations may reflect a single underlying belief system.

INSTANTIATIONS OF A SINGLE BIOLOGICAL FRAMEWORK? Together, these data suggest a close developmental convergence in essentialist reasoning across several independent content areas. By three to four years of age, children appeal to essentialism or essentialist-like notions in reasoning about biological species, race, gender, and kinship, on the one hand, and contamination, contagion, and (perhaps) fetishes, on the other. This pattern is more likely to reflect the multiple instantiations of a single essentialist framework, rather than either coincidental similarities across diverging phenomena or the penetration of biological reasoning into other conceptual systems.

If these phenomena are all part of a single framework, that still leaves open at least two possibilities: that there is a single, biological framework, or that there is a domain-general framework that applies across domains. It could be that essentialism is biological, not in the scientific sense (which would exclude race, fetishes, and cooties, for example), but rather in a folk sense. For example, perhaps race is mistakenly presumed to be a biological category, and contagion is mistakenly presumed to be a biological process. In favor of this possibility is Rozin and Nemeroff's (1990) observation that the source of contagion is usually a living thing (plant, nonhuman animal, or person), especially a person. On the other hand, inanimate objects may also be sources of contagion (Rozin and Nemeroff, 1990, p. 206), so an absolute line is not drawn here between living and nonliving things.

What about the process of passing along essential properties? Inheritance is not the only mechanism that people invoke for transmitting essences from one individual to another. Jacques Guillemeau, a seventeenth-century French physician, noted: "It is an accepted thing that milk . . . has the power to make children resemble their nurses in mind and body, just as the seed makes them resemble their mother and father" (quoted in Fairchild, 1984, p. 195). Similarly, the Dutch colonial administration in the nineteenth century seemed convinced (or worried) that too long an exposure to Javanese culture and climate would cause Dutch settlers to become Javanese in some sense (Stoler, 1995). Even educated adults seem to adhere to an implicit belief that "you are what you eat," judging people of a hypothetical culture to take on the personality traits of the animals they eat (e.g., phlegmatic versus excitable, for eating marine turtle versus boar; Nemeroff and Rozin, 1989). (This belief was taken to a literal extreme by James McConnell, a psychologist who fed ground-up mealworms to other mealworms in an attempt to see if learning from one organism could be transferred to another organism by ingestion (McConnell, 1962).) Although these essentialist transmissions are clearly outside the framework of (scientific) biological reproduction, Hirschfeld (1996) has argued that they are not outside the framework of natural reproduction. Perhaps, then, natural reproduction of biological entities falls within the folk-biological domain.

If we treat contagion as biological, and so applicable to all biological beings, it is puzzling that we do not act as if biological entities constantly leave traces, in all their interactions with the world. Rozin and Nemeroff (1990) suggest that thoughts or actions against contagion are limited or contained by disregarding all but the most salient examples, by reducing the salience of examples by other means (such as shrink-wrapping food as if it were artificially processed), and by adhering to strict rules (e.g., among Hindus in India, using only the left hand for toilet functions and the right hand for cooking and serving food). In other words, there may be an underlying belief in the constant "shedding of self and the permeability of the person" (p. 213), yet the belief is kept in check by other means so as not to be overpowering.

Despite these arguments in favor of treating essentialism as a broadly biological notion (within the folk-biological realm), there are other problems with this position. I present them below, arguing for a domain-general essentialist framework that is manifested in distinct ways in different domains.

INSTANTIATIONS OF A SINGLE DOMAIN-GENERAL FRAMEWORK?   Perhaps most directly damaging to the position that essentialism, contagion, contamination, and so forth are instances of biology writ large, is the previously discussed point that undeniably nonbiological natural kinds (such as gold or water) are also essentialized by young children. There seems to be no coherent account according to which gold or water are accepted into the biological domain by young children. Another problem is that contagion appears to involve entities that are both physical (e.g., passed by physical contact) and immaterial (e.g., the persistence of contamination despite washing; conversely, the effectiveness of purification rituals that involve no physical washing away of substance; see Rozin and Nemeroff, 1990). The assumption of nonphysical, immaterial essences would seem to contradict a biological ontology.

It also seems difficult to find any properties that would identify all essencelike events as biological. We cannot simply say that all events involving biological entities are biological; the laws of gravity as they apply to my cat are still physical (not biological) laws. Moreover, the very same action could be construed as contamination or physics, depending on the outcome. For example, if a disliked child pushed Rudy, and Rudy fell to the floor, that would clearly not be a biological event—it would be an instance of physics. Yet if a disliked child pushed Rudy, and Rudy believed that he got cooties, that would count as a contamination event. The problem here is the potential circularity in positing that the latter event is biological simply *because* it involves contamination.

Something like an essentialist impulse arguably extends to artifacts as well—albeit in a different form. Here I am thinking of works of art, and the twin notions of authenticity and forgeries. An authentic Picasso is staggeringly valuable. I suspect that even Picasso's childhood scribbles would be valuable, despite having little aesthetic interest. Yet a forgery of a Picasso will never have the same value as the real thing—even if it looks identical (P. Bloom, 2000). In fact, an exquisite forgery of Picasso's best work (e.g., *Guérnica*) may (perhaps) even be less valuable than the authentic copy of Picasso's most childish scribble. What is crucial is the process by which the work of art was created: by a particular person in a particular time and place. Once a painting (or autograph, or book manuscript, or musical recording) is discovered to be created not by the purported artist but instead by some imposter, it plunges in value. In this respect, works of art would seem to possess something essencelike. Benjamin goes so far as to use the language of essentialism in describing this phenomenon: "The authenticity of a thing is the essence of all that is transmissible from its beginning, ranging from its substantive duration to its testimony to the history which it has experienced" (1955, p. 221).

I stop short of calling authenticity "essentialism," because there is no evidence that people believe there is some nonvisible underlying quality to be found in the original work of art. Nonetheless, whatever it is that makes us care about authenticity for artwork may stem from the same impulse that leads to species essentialism (which privileges the parentage, and therefore the historical origins, of an organism) as well as to contagion (which privileges the historical path an item undertakes; Rozin and Nemeroff, 1990). In all of these cases, the history of an item is more crucial than its appearances.

One might even say that the notion of object constancy partakes of some of the same logic. After all, if a particular Bic pen is my pen, then I will still recognize that it was *my* pen, even if my daughter swaps it with a seemingly identical pen, and even if I do not care (in any material way) that the pens were exchanged. Preschool children, too, track identity in terms of historical continuity (see Gutheil, 1993). They also judge that Mr. Rogers's *actual* sweater is more appropriate for display in a museum than an identical sweater that is brand new (C. Johnson and Jacobs, 2001). Likewise, the capacity to track the individual identity of people crucially rests on personal history, not feature listings (see also Kripke, 1972). Our cognitive systems are structured to invoke personal history—rather than observable features—as constituting identity.

Essentialism as Domain-General Yet Invoked Differently in Different Domains

The above considerations suggest that essentialism is a domain-general assumption that is invoked differently in different domains depending on the causal structure of each domain (S. Gelman, Coley, and Gottfried, 1994). Although speculative, this account is most compelling in part because it predicts a broad yet not promiscuous application of essentialism.

Sperber (1994), Leslie (1994), and Keil (1994) provide a view of cognitive architecture that is consistent with this suggestion. On their view, many domain differences lie with neither the perceptual structure nor the conceptual organization of the domain itself, but at the level of more abstract mechanisms or modes of understanding that come to be incorporated in different domains. To date, a relatively small number of modes of understanding (or modes of construal) have been proposed: an intentional mode, a mechanical mode, a teleological mode, an essentialist mode, perhaps a vitalistic mode (Inagaki and Hatano, 1993; S. Morris, Taplin, and Gelman, 2000), and a deontological mode (Atran, 1996).

Modes of construal are not uniquely assigned to particular domains. For example, an essentialist mode would fit well with domains in which categories seem to capture clusters of information in the face of outward variation (such as living kinds), but would not be exclusively biological in any fixed sense. In several publications, Keil suggests that the linkage between mode of construal and domain occurs as children and adults search for resonances between modes of construal and "real world structure" (1994, p. 252). Elsewhere he elaborates, proposing that "much of our adult intellectual adventures involve trying to see which mode of construal best fits a phenomenon, sometimes trying several different ones, such as thinking of a computer in anthropomorphic "folk-psychology" terms, in fluid dynamic terms, or in physical-mechanical terms" (Keil 1995, p. 260).

Although this approach is promising, it raises two difficulties. First, it is unmotivated, failing to explain why should we have such tendencies. Is an essentialist mode of construal a capacity unto itself, or can we instead build essentialism out of pieces we already have good reason to believe are part of children's mental structure? Second, it does not fully address the domain-specificity issue. Although it seems plausible that resonance with "real world structure" provides the motivation to link the biological domain with an essentialist mode of construal (e.g., for animals, clusters of outward properties predict underlying shared properties), it is much less clear how "real world structure" would motivate an essentialist interpretation of contaminants, disease, or fetishes.

Where I depart from Keil's sort of proposal is in suggesting that essentialism is not a single mode of construal but is instead the result of several converging psychological capacities or tendencies. What follows is a tentative listing of these abilities, somewhat arbitrary in number and organization. I have attempted to include tendencies that children might reasonably develop early in life, for purposes that extend beyond essentialism per se. I have tried to exclude capacities that simply restate essentialism. For example, categorical realism—though highly relevant to essentialism—was excluded because categorical realism is a large part of what I am trying to explain. (It would again be like saying that children have an essentialist mode of construal.) I have also excluded capacities that, though prerequisite to developing essentialism, are fundamental to any sort of conceptual system. These would include, for example, the capacity to form categories, or the capacity to detect similarity.

Table 11.2 summarizes the framework I am proposing, in which several independent capacities individually and jointly lead to essentialist effects. As can be seen, each root capacity has a related essentialist instantiation (e.g., the basic capacity to distinguish appearance from reality is the root cause of children treating nonobvious properties as core to the identity of a natural kind category). In addition, the root capacities together yield effects that none alone would be sufficient to

Table 11.2. Root capacities underlying essentialism

Root capacities		Essentialist instantiations
Appearance/reality distinction	→	Nonobvious properties as core
Induction from property clusters	→	Inferences about the unknown
Causal determinism	→	Causal properties as core
Tracking identity over time	→	Importance of origins
Deference to experts	→	Acceptance of category anomalies
Above, collectively	→	Realist assumption about categories and names
		Boundary intensification
		Immutability; stability over transformations
		Importance of nature over nurture

provoke. For example, category realism grows out of none of the causes considered individually but rather the full set of capacities considered together.

Each of these capacities is one that is useful as children make their way through the world. For example, recognizing an appearance/reality distinction allows children to make more-accurate predictions about the world around them, and causal determinism motivates children to understand intervening mechanisms and so reach a more comprehensive understanding of events. In other words, each of the root causes has its own independent motivation. In this respect, essentialism is a consequence of other capacities—but reducible to no single one of them.

APPEARANCE/REALITY DISTINCTION. A prerequisite to essentialist understanding is a distinction between appearance and reality. Specifically, an appearance/reality distinction seems necessary for thinking about nonobvious properties, for accepting category anomalies (e.g., that a bat is not a bird), and for distinguishing what something "is" from what it "is like." Although it is not until about four years of age that children can reflect on the appearance/reality distinction in a metacognitive way (Flavell, Flavell, and Green, 1983), a basic appreciation seems well in place much earlier. The two-year-old's capacity to accept her mother's word that a pterodactyl is a dinosaur, not a bird, is evidence of this core understanding.

Paul Bloom (2000) suggests that an appearance/reality distinction is all that is needed for essentialism to develop. His account does not explain domain differences, because Bloom suggests that essentialism is fundamentally domain-general, underlying the categorization of even artifacts. For example, when deciding whether something is a sculpture or a paperweight, appearance is not important; the intent of the creator is decisive. I am wholly sympathetic to Bloom's analysis of artifact concepts. The data are compelling that creator's intent is given special weight in people's (including young children's) classifications of artifacts, and there is no question that such intent is "nonobvious," "underlying," and "beyond appearances." This view is in rough strokes consistent with the point I am trying to make, that essentialist-like impulses are found broadly in human cognition.

But surely there are differences between the intuition that an artifact is categorized by the intentions of its creator versus the intuition that natural kinds have underlying inherent commonalities. The rich property clusters, significance of internal properties, transmission from parent to offspring, and fixedness of category membership are all unique to living kinds. What artifacts and living kinds share can perhaps be generated by an appreciation of an appearance/reality distinction; their differences suggest that more is required for reasoning about natural kinds.

Carey provides a related, though distinct, take on this issue. She suggests that essentialism grows out of the logical requirements of using count nouns: "biological essentialism is the theoretical elaboration of the logical/linguistic concept, substance sortal" (1996, p. 194). Count nouns are "substance sortals" (Hall and Waxman, 1993; Macnamara, 1986): they refer to kinds, and supply a "principle of application" for their use. As long as the principle of application is met, other properties can freely vary. An important implication is that "the application of every count noun carries with it the idea that the identity of the entity picked out by the noun is unchanged in the face of surface changes" (Carey, 1996, p. 193). This implication leads to the universal contrast between "kind" (A poodle is a kind of dog) and "like" (A cat is like a dog; Wierzbicka, 1994).

Here we have, then, the roots of an appearance/reality distinction. Although Carey does not supply details, reading between the lines would suggest that the core starting point is the same for her as for Bloom: an appreciation for a distinction between what something "is" and what something "is like." Carey does not dwell on where this logical insight comes from, though she suggests it is innate (a "default assumption" regarding count nouns).[5] Then, as children attempt to understand this distinction more fully for living kinds, it develops into full-fledged essentialism in the biological domain. The linking of the appearance/reality distinction to the logic of sortals is ingenious. This position seems correct as far as it goes, but more needs to be said regarding what is involved in developing essentialism beyond the appearance/reality distinction.

Carey's position is not simply that having the same word for diverse things leads to essentialism (as suggested by Hallett, 1991; Mayr, 1991). On the latter position, language input is the misleading basis. Yet Carey seems to be saying that the logical capacity to use nouns requires a key conceptual contrast ("is" versus "is like"; appearance versus reality), and that it is this conceptual contrast that eventually finds expression in essentialism. The accounts also appear to differ in how they would treat nonsortal words. The words-promote-essentialism position (to be consistent) should argue that we essentialize even property terms, such as "red." After all, there are many different "reds" and we call them all by the same word. The essentializing-based-on-sortals position would not make such a claim, since "red" is not a sortal but a predicate.

INDUCTION FROM PROPERTY CLUSTERS.   I speculate that people assume (implicitly, not explicitly) that property clusters attract other properties. The more commonalities you have learned about a category in the past, the stronger your inferences about that category are in the future. Metaphorically, property clusters are magnets: the more mass they accumulate, the more strongly they pull in new properties. Inductive success is rewarded with more induction. Conversely, a category that lacks such property clusters (e.g., the category of red things) will not be expected to attract new properties. It is this core assumption that could grow into a sort of categorical realism: the belief that the world consists of natural kinds. This assumption would favor essentialism for categories that have demonstrated inductive potential (e.g., basic-level object kinds) but not for, say, superordinate categories (tools, living things), or single properties with little to no inductive potential (big things, striped things). This assumption might also contribute to domain differences, given the richer property clusters for natural kinds versus simple artifacts (e.g., S. Gelman, 1988; see also Boyd, 1999, Keil, 1989, and Kornblith, 1993, on the greater homeostatic property clusters for living kinds).

To be clear: the suggestion here is not simply that categories permit induction (although they do). Instead, we generate the second-order inference that categories will continue to permit even more inductions into the future. A first-order inference would be something like this: after tasting three red, speckled mushrooms and getting sick from each one, Joe sees a fourth red, speckled mushroom and decides not even to taste it, because he infers that it will make him sick. I assume that all organisms have some capacity for category-based induction of this sort. A second-order inference would be the assumption that the new mushroom not only is poisonous, but also shares as-yet-unknown properties with others of the same kind.

Importantly, the property clusters that give rise to such inferences are not restricted to properties directly encountered or experienced, but also include properties that are conveyed secondhand, through language. Simply being told that members of a category look a certain way or behave a certain way will be sufficient to trigger these inferences. So, if I tell you that Martians are small and green, make squeaky sounds, and are cunning (formally, let us say that they share properties A, B, C, and D), the principle of induction from property clusters would kick in and encourage you to assume that Martians will share even more properties (E, F, G, H, and so on). Note the importance of such a process for essentializing social groups. Reputation and social practice can both intensify property clusters that are not "natural" or built in. I believe that this is what Rothbart and Taylor (2001) mean when they say that "inductive potential is itself a complex function of social reality and social perception."

Initially, relevant property clusters may be identified by something as simple as overall similarity in appearance. Eventually, more peripheral and indirect cues may also be useful, including labels (S. Gelman and Heyman, 1999) and Shipley's (1993) "over-hypotheses."

CAUSAL DETERMINISM.   Causal determinism is the assumption that properties and events are caused (A. Brown, 1990; Bullock, Gelman, and Baillargeon, 1982; S.

Gelman and Kalish, 1993; Shultz, 1982). In the case of natural events, causal determinism comes to mean that events without external cause demand some sort of mediating, inherent cause. I discussed this possibility in chapter 5, as well as the possibility that humans may be the only species that attends to causal mechanisms. A search for underlying causes can be seen as the engine to theory construction, though more is required for full-fledged theories (e.g., domain-specific ontologies, coherence; see Carey, 1985; Gopnik and Meltzoff, 1997; Gopnik and Wellman, 1994). The power of causal determinism for essentialism is in generating a search for hidden, nonobvious, as-yet-unknown properties.

Causal determinism could also yield domain-specificity in the application of essentialism. Gail Gottfried, John Coley, and I proposed that children would notice that animals are self-moving and have no apparent external cause, and so infer that animals have some "inner, inherent nature" that causes their movement (S. Gelman, Coley, and Gottfried, 1994, pp. 358–359). In contrast, simple artifacts (e.g., wastebaskets) have the properties they do because of the people who made and use them; there is no need to appeal to inherent properties or essences. The claim here is not that essentialism emerges whenever children lack a causal understanding of an event. More must be involved; otherwise, essentialist accounts would emerge wherever knowledge is sparse (e.g., to explain garage-door openers, television remote-control devices, and light switches).

One way that children might determine when to apply essentialism is by means of general framework theories that (provisionally) type an event, to determine what sort of causal explanatory account will be required. Natural events call for inherent, essential properties; nonnatural events do not. In the case of remote-control devices (for example), children could promptly determine that humans are ultimately responsible for the outcome (after all, the television goes on only after a person pushes the button), so that therefore the television's going on is not an inherent property of the television. (See Gopnik and Sobel, 2000, for evidence that even two-year-olds are sensitive to the actions of humans as implying that an event is either human-caused or inherent to an object.)

There is no single rule that marks an event as "natural" and so open for essentialist explanations, but rather a variety of information and heuristics. Agentive entities with self-initiated movements (such as animals and people) may be particularly susceptible to essentialist accounts, because what "makes them tick" seems (intuitively) intrinsic to these entities. An essentialist mode of construal is also likely to be recruited when the entities of a domain undergo regular and radical transformations, inexplicable with reference to any other causal mode. Living kinds undergo regular transformations in outward appearance and behavior during the growth process. They exist in immature and mature forms. They flower and bear fruit (if plants); they grow fur and bear young (if mammals). Inanimate natural substances (such as water, gold, or quartz) undergo regular and radical transformations as they encounter fire, intense cold, or striking blows. In all these examples, lawlike, powerful transformations call out for explanations of an essentialist sort.

This suggestion may seem at first surprising, since rather the opposite sort of argument can also be made, namely, that essentialism arises as a result of rich within-category similarity. (See, for example, the arguments above about category-based induction.) Yet sameness or homogeneity per se does not call for essentialism (e.g., similarity among Dixie cups does not demand or provoke an essentialist account). Likewise, change per se does not require essentialism (e.g., the capacity of a Dixie cup to burn to a crisp tells us nothing essential about cups per se, though it does tell us something important about woody material). Rather, the crucial conditions include the regularity of the transformation, the lack of an alternative explanatory account, and the continued sameness of identity.[6]

TRACKING IDENTITY OVER TIME.   By including this capacity, I am in danger of violating one of the criteria I set earlier: that this list should exclude abilities (such as categorization) that are required for any cognitive system. Surely the ability to recognize that an item is the same over spatial and temporal transformations is critical to many animals, not just humans, and does not by itself implicate an essentialist stance. Recognizing offspring, tracking relative position in a social hierarchy, even thinking about ownership all require that one recognize the same object over time. Nonetheless, the centrality of this concept for essentialism is potentially so profound, I would be remiss to say nothing about it.

Tracking an individual over time requires some hefty insights: that a thing can retain identity despite outward changes in appearance (the appearance/reality distinction again), and that personal history is central to identity. For example, the changes in an animal or plant wrought by growth are enormous, and mean that tracking identity is not a matter of tallying outward features, but rather involves learning the historical path that an individual has taken over time (see also Kripke, 1971). I do not mean to imply that these insights are metacognitive or the result of an explicit reasoning process. Instead, these insights are contained within the cognitive act of deciding that an entity is the same thing at time T as it is at time T + 1.

Consider, for example, the following situation. While my son Adam was playing at a friend's house last year, his socks got muddy and his friend's mother lent him a pair of socks. I took both pairs of socks home, washed them, and a few days later returned one pair of socks to Adam's friend's mother. The next time I saw her, she returned them to me, explaining that the socks I had returned were not actually her son's socks, but Adam's. Although both pairs of socks were identical in size, cleanliness, and amount of wear, and although the socks were nearly identical in appearance, there were minor differences in the design of the heels that had escaped my notice. What I find interesting about this exchange is the importance of individual identity even for something so trivial as a pair of socks. Although materially there was no good reason for the other mother to return the socks (after all, the design differences would not even show up when the child was wearing shoes), as a matter of principle she felt it was important to return that which was not rightly hers. Of course, we do not always care to track individual identity. Coins, unopened pop bottles, blades of grass—in all of these cases, the identity of individual tokens tends not to matter. However, in principle we remain capable of applying the concept of individual identity to anything.

There is now solid evidence that infants can track the identity of individual objects (Spelke et al., 1995; Xu and Carey, 1996), and that by preschool age children can track the identity of individuals when applying proper names (Gutheil and Rosengren, 1996; Hall, 1996; Liitschwager and Markman, 1993, cited in Sorrentino, 2001; Sorrentino, 2001). For example, if a doll wearing a distinctive green cloth cape is named "daxy," and the doll is then moved to a new location and the distinctive cape is removed while a new doll is placed in the old location with the distinctive cape added, three-year-olds report that the original doll—not the new doll—is daxy. What is crucial to determining individual identity (as marked by the name) is historical path, not the location and appearance present at the original naming.

This capacity seems implicated both in reasoning about kind essentialism, and in reasoning about contagion and fetishes. Indeed, kind essentialism seems in some ways an extension of the insights about individual identity (see also Kripke, 1972; Schwartz, 1979). Just as an individual remains the same over outward variations, so too are members of a kind the same as one another despite outward variations. Just as the identity of an individual is decided by consulting the historical record, so too is the identity of a living kind decided by consulting its origins (namely, parentage).

There may be a link between tracking individual identity and kind essentialism in another way as well. That is, the sorts of objects for which we prefer to track individual identity (e.g., people, not paper clips) seem by and large to be the same sorts of objects that we tend to essentialize. Perhaps the value placed on certain entities initiates a process of individual identity-tracking, which then leads to hypothesizing that this sort of thing has unique and essential qualities.

DEFERENCE TO EXPERTS.   I also suggest that children honor a tacit division of linguistic labor, in which the child defers to others as the ultimate arbiters of correct naming. Children can consult experts (parents and other adults or even older children) to find out what something *truly* should be called (see Putnam, 1973, for extensive discussion). This principle dovetails with the appearance/reality distinction (the assumption that what something looks like to me may not be what it really is). It entails a willingness to suspend the evidence of our own eyes: "That looks like a bird to me, but you say it's a dinosaur—so it must be a dinosaur."

At least in our culture, deference to experts can be extreme. While I was chatting with a couple that I know, the subject of eye colors came up. The mother informed me that her doctor explained that eyes that look gray or green are in fact truly blue, but just have more pigment in them. She went on to say that her son's eyes were blue, according to the doctor. I gazed into the boy's eyes: a beautiful shade of green. Yet the expert had said they were "really" blue!

We have seen in chapter 3 that adults defer to experts in matters of naming natural kinds (Malt, 1990; but see Kalish, 1995), and that children do so even more strongly (Kalish, 1998). Children readily accept experimenter-provided labels, even when such labels are surprising and counterintuitive (S. Gelman and Coley, 1990; S. Gelman and Markman, 1986, 1987; Graham, Kilbreath, and Welder, 2001, 2002; Jaswal and Markman, 2002). A two-year-old in one study we conducted even articulated this principle to his mother afterwards: "I thought it was a stick, but the man [i.e., the experimenter] said it was a snake." Children also distinguish names made up on the spot from conventional names (Sabbagh and Baldwin, 2001). It would be interesting to know the depths of children's deference to experts. Does it extend across the board in all knowledge domains, perhaps as a result of children's genuine ignorance about most things, or is it particularly strong in the case of naming? Do children defer to adult naming in all realms (including attribute terms and simple artifacts), or only for natural kinds? What is the developmental course of this willingness to incorporate others' knowledge? Are young children most open to expert knowledge because they are least knowledgeable and most in need of adult input? Or does deference to expert knowledge grow as children become more metacognitively aware of their own limitations?

Deference to experts in the matter of naming also implies a sort of nominal realism: the assumption that there is a correct name. In other words, according to nominal realism, a word is an objective and true indication of what something is. If we call a creature "a lizard," then that is what it is—not as a matter of convention or convenience, but as a matter of fact. Such a belief would bolster, and be bolstered by, the essentialist presumption that categories are real. Each natural kind is assumed to have a unique name (and the reverse is often though not always true: the name for a thing may indicate the natural kind to which it belongs).

Nominal realism is typically portrayed as a childhood weakness that we eventually overcome—much like chicken pox or egocentrism. And to be sure, the more blatant forms of nominal realism seem not to survive early childhood. For example, it is only quite young children who mistakenly judge that the form of a word is nonarbitrary (so that cats could not be called "dogs," even if all English speakers agreed to the switch; see Rosenblum and Pinker, 1983) or mistakenly judge that a name is interchangeable with the object to which it refers (e.g., that one can buy a piece of candy with the *word* "nickel"; see Markman, 1976). However, I suggest that more subtle forms of nominal realism are retained throughout the lifespan, just as egocentrism is (see Flavell, 1985, p. 125). We are not bound to it, but it remains a tempting way to think about the relation between words and world.

It seems likely that a child could essentialize without a division of linguistic labor or nominal realism (consider, for example, the deaf children of hearing parents studied by Goldin-Meadow and colleagues, who display rich conceptual systems with little to no conventional language; Goldin-Meadow and Mylander, 1990). But leaving off this component would miss the important point that essentialist assumptions are readily linked to language. Logically, there is no need for language and essentialism to go together. Children could believe, for example, that there is a proper way to divide the world into categories with essences, but that natural language is too flawed to reveal such categories. Yet language and essentialism do fit together, securely and seamlessly, in everyday thought.

I think this linkage is neither coincidence nor simply a matter of convenience. Instead, by linking essentialism to language, children can most readily take advantage of cultural knowledge. Language helps children solve the problem of which categories to essentialize. It helps children figure out which instances belong to a kind. And it reinforces appearance/reality contrasts, when labels conflict with children's a priori expectations.

I suggest that each of these tendencies can contribute to essentialism, though none are unique to it. So essentialism is a by-product of other things that we do that are very useful. It is not a single cognitive predisposition, but the convergence of several fruitful capacities or tendencies. It is domain-general, and it develops to the extent that these underlying capacities develop. My position here is similar to that of Kornblith (1993, p. 95), who suggests we have "a set of dispositions which incline us in the right direction" (though I am not so sure the direction they incline toward is "right" in a metaphysical sense). Two of his "innate dispositions" correspond to ones that I have proposed: "a tendency to carve the world into kinds in ways which presuppose a certain causal structure" (induction from property clusters; causal determinism), and "a tendency to look beyond the superficial characteristics of objects in classifying them into kinds" (appearance/reality distinction).

My position is also consistent with the notion that essentialism is not one single thing. This view has been argued by Haslam (1998; Haslam, Rothschild, and Ernst, 2000). In one study adults were asked to rate a set of twenty social categories on a set of nine essentialist factors: discreteness, naturalness, immutability, stability, necessity, uniformity, informativeness, inherence, and exclusivity. Two distinct dimensions emerged, which Haslam, Rothschild, and Ernst refer to as "naturalness" (encompassing discreteness, naturalness, immutability, stability, and necessity), and "entitativity" (encompassing uniformity, informativeness, inherence, and exclusivity). For example, being "male" is highly natural but not very entitative, whereas being "Republican" is highly entitative but not especially natural. Leaving aside for the moment whether these two dimensions might typically converge in the case of nonsocial categories, I propose that the naturalness dimension may follow more from causal determinism, and the entitativity dimension may follow more from induction from property clusters.

Although the proposed principles are domain-general, essentializing is not. We do not essentialize wastebaskets or gumballs (but see P. Bloom, 2000). Domain-specificity emerges because of properties of the world (as we perceive it). For example, we only try to come up with causal stories when there is no ready-made causal account already available. Such ready-made causal accounts might include

the effects of human construction, which are clearly well grasped by the time children are four years of age (S. Gelman, 1988; S. Gelman and Kremer, 1991).

How would the present model work for those difficult cases discussed earlier,
including germs, Jackie Onassis's pearls, Hitler's sweater, or witchcraft? Although
this question is far from resolved in the present framework, I suggest that a subset
of the underpinnings of essentialism would contribute to these phenomena. For
example, a distinction between appearance and reality could give rise to the idea of
some invisible something attached to seemingly ordinary objects (a sneezed-upon
toothbrush, a celebrity's faux pearls, or a madman's sweater). Likewise, tracking
identity over time could highlight the importance of the historical path that an object takes (e.g., that the faux pearls used to be owned by Jackie O.). Other underpinnings of essentialism would be irrelevant to these phenomena (including induction from property clusters, or division of linguistic labor). Conversely, some
aspects of contagion may have nothing whatsoever to do with essentialism (including the intense feelings of desire or revulsion that get attached to things associated with objects of desire or revulsion).

Let me try to make the link a bit clearer. Essentialism implies that identity is
vested in invisible qualities; that an entity is imbued with essence through and
through; and that the essence is permanent, fixed, and cannot be removed. I also
suspect that our tendency to evoke these qualities is directly proportional to how
closely we track someone or something as an individual. So, for example, I might
posit an essence to myself, to other people, or to my pets—but I am unlikely to
posit an essence to my pencil sharpener. All these beliefs about identity emerge in
witchcraft, where portions of one's body (fingernail, hair clippings, or transplanted
heart) retain some essential quality of the person. In the cases of contagion and
fetishes, an individual essence is also perceived as transferring to some other object, not by means of inheritance (as with parent-to-child essence transfer of living
kinds), but by means of touch.

To the extent that essence is seen to permeate one's being, then it is perhaps not
surprising that it can transfer (at least a little) to other objects. Jackie O.'s essence
ran throughout her, from her inner core through to her fingertips and skin. And so
her jewelry (literally) touched her essence. But the problem is that transfer of
essence does not ordinarily take place via touch (e.g., pigness does not "rub off" on
a calf raised with pigs). The difference between contagion and biological essences
may lie in part in the powerful emotional associations in the former case. On an
intuitive, purely associationist level, we wish to make contact with things linked
with beloved people, and we wish to avoid things linked with detested people. It is
our essentializing tendencies that help reify and extend this intuitive response in
predictable ways.

This discussion is all highly speculative, and I in no way suggest that people's intuitive beliefs about these matters approach anything resembling an explicit or
stateable form. However, a cluster of domain-general capacities could work together to contribute to full-fledged essentialism (in the case of biological kinds and

many social categories), or essencelike beliefs (in the case of contagion, fetishes, witchcraft).

DISCUSSION

I begin the discussion by summarizing the main points of this chapter. My claim is twofold.

1. Essentialism fundamentally reflects human cognitive capacities. I do grant some role for input (see arguments about role of language in directing essentialism; chapter 8) and for world structure (see Keil's argument regarding the ways in which human tendencies fit with world structure). But essentialism could not emerge without powerful cognitive predispositions. An obvious but nontrivial point here is that other species arguably do not develop essentialism, even though they live in our world.

2. The cognitive capacities that give rise to essentialism are a varied assortment of abilities that emerged for other purposes but inevitably converge in essentialism. In that sense, essentialism is something we do neither because it is "good" for survival, nor because it is "bad" for people who are manipulated by essentialist rhetoric. Essentialism is something that we as humans cannot help but do.

This proposal implies several conclusions about what essentialism is not. I argue that it is not a dedicated, hardwired unit that responds specifically to biological input ("biology module")—there is no evidence that biology per se is a privileged domain for children, and it is too problematic to account for the many ways that essentialism extends beyond biology. I also argue that it cannot emerge from simple, wholly general processes of similarity, generalization, and categorization—the "dumb attentional mechanisms" discussed in chapter 9. As discussed already, such accounts gravely underdetermine the phenomena of interest. Finally, I argue that we cannot simply say that people possess a single, undifferentiated essentializing tendency or essentialist mode of construal. Such a proposal fails to explain where such a tendency or mode of construal comes from, and why it would be instantiated in such different respects when it comes to the peripheral phenomena discussed in this chapter (including contagion, fetishes, and witchcraft).

To return to the crude distinction made at the beginning of the chapter: is essentialism in the world, the mind, language, or culture? My answer is that essentialism is a product of all of these forces. I have stressed most emphatically in this chapter that the mind has an essentializing bent, the outcome of several fundamental processes. This way of thinking has ready convergence with much of the world, including the homeostatic property clusters of living kinds (Boyd, 1999) and the regular and radical transformations found in the growth of organisms, human and nonhuman alike. Nonetheless, the fit is not perfect, as discussed in chapter 10. For some categories (such as race), the fit is downright awful, and once you look closely enough (e.g., how genes really work, or evolution across time— the sorts of issues that were inaccessible to our hominid ancestors), the framework falters badly even for biological kinds. Essentialism is a reasoning heuristic that allows us to make fairly good predictions much of the time, but it should not be confused with the structure of reality. As the aphorism goes, it is close enough for government work.

Language is implicated in two sorts of ways. First, labels and generics tell children *when* (which kinds) to essentialize. For example, we are more likely to essentialize a social category when it is lexicalized. Second, some of the capacities required for language learning appear also to serve essentializing functions: namely, the logic of sortals (this is Carey's [1995, 1996] idea) and the logic of proper nouns (Kripke, 1971). Questions for the future include: can people essentialize without language? and can organisms without a language capacity essentialize?

At this point we know too little about the effects of culture on essentialism. I am suggesting that children's essentializing is not a historical or cultural aberration but a universal consequence of how children organize their knowledge about the world (see also Hirschfeld, 1996). Yet this suggestion does not mean that cultural and historical forces have no effect. Ethnographies and available experimental data suggest essencelike constructs in remarkably varying cultures, as well as cross-cultural variation in the content and workings of such constructs. The data available suggest that people in different cultures essentialize different sorts of things (e.g., caste essentialism and occupation essentialism can be found in some cultures, but neither is universal). There are also cultural differences in the sorts of explanatory stories people provide for how essentialism is passed along (e.g., via inheritance versus breast milk versus growing up on the land). Cultural differences may also contribute to variation in how much people essentialize, though that possibility is still almost wholly unknown at this point. We really do not yet know enough about cultural sameness and variability.

Cultural and historical forces may serve to heighten (or dampen) what is an essentializing tendency (see also Bem, 1981). For example, gender-typed practices in a culture may serve as a mechanism for fostering gender essentialism in children. Children are not born knowing which categories to essentialize. I have suggested that they look for categories with many converging, correlated cues—if a category already has a cluster of correlated properties, children will expect it to have even more correlated properties. Stereotyping and gender-typed practices in the culture serve to magnify and highlight correlational cues. For example, hair length, clothing design, clothing color, accessories—all of these magnify and highlight differences between male and female and encourage children to consider gender an essentialized kind. In support of this view, Bigler (1995) finds that use of gender as a functional category in the classroom (i.e., making use of physical or spatial dichotomies and verbal categorizations based on gender) leads to increased gender stereotyping, especially among children with less advanced categorization skills.

Where do the components of essentialism come from? Here is where the Hydra-like nature of these issues comes forth. Unless the components are innate (a possibility that cannot yet be dismissed), then we may have simply pushed the question of "Why do we essentialize?" back one more level. In other words, now instead the question has become multiple: "Why do we adhere to causal determinism?" "Why do we construct an appearance/reality distinction?" and so forth. However, I hope that these questions are somewhat more precise and so can be pursued more fruitfully.

I conclude by considering why we essentialize in the teleological sense—in plain terms, what it buys us. There are, I think, two sorts of answers. First, each of the underpinnings of essentialism is useful for making sense of the world, each in its own distinct way. We track identity over time in order to recognize individuals. We adhere to a division of linguistic labor in order to benefit from cultural knowledge. We draw inductive inferences from property clusters and distinguish appearance from reality, in order to make (generally) accurate predictions. We search for causes in order to create more useful tools and technologies. And so forth. In other words, each of the underpinnings of essentialism is motivated for independent purposes—not for essentialism per se. There is a second answer as well. Essentialism is a by-product, with unintended and unpredictable consequences. Each strand that underpins essentialism is beneficial in our interactions with the world. Yet the cumulative effect of these tendencies is more mixed, presenting deep problems alongside the benefits.

Notes

CHAPTER 1

1. "Natural kind" is an ambiguous term. As used here, I mean "kind found in nature." However, "natural kind" can also be used to refer to a kind embedded in a theory. On the latter usage, money is a natural kind within a theory of economics, though not within a theory of physics—even though money is both an economic and a physical entity (Fodor, 1975; Kalish, 2002). The reason is that money enters into causal laws for economics, but has no theoretical standing within physics.

2. This third component is not a *necessary* element of psychological essentialism. Someone who lacked language but still held the first two beliefs would still qualify as essentialist, on my reckoning. Likewise, a scientist who viewed ordinary language as misleading could nonetheless be essentialist about the realm she studies. However, I include the third component here because it captures an important empirical phenomenon in childhood essentialism.

3. The picture is more complicated than this initial statement would suggest, in that artifact concepts have some essentialist qualities (including moderate inductive potential and a basis in nonobvious properties, notably the creator's intent). However, full-fledged essentialism appears to be restricted to natural and social kinds. See chapters 6 and 11 for more discussion.

CHAPTER 2

1. Ahn and Kalish (2000) refer to this as induction in the "broad sense." This usage contrasts with induction in the "narrow sense," which refers strictly to reasoning from particulars to a general conclusion (e.g., Josephson and Josephson, 1994). See Holland et al. (1986) and Skyrms (1966) for defense and discussion of the usage employed here.

2. The no-label condition also measures whether children treat categories as the basis of induction. However, because inferences in the no-label condition could be governed by similarity alone, the label condition is more directly relevant to claims of essentialism.

3. Florian's data with adults showed no effects of labeling or properties on property inferences, and only counterintuitive effects of labeling on label inferences. One reading of this result is that adults have no expectations concerning novel labels and properties. However, another reading of this result is that the stimuli were designed in such a way that adults did not find these to be coherent natural kinds. I favor the latter interpretation. In experiment 3, the categories had a complete confounding of perceptual and verbal information. In experiment 4, although the confounding was lessened, the data from the L → L condition suggested that the adults disagreed with the experimenter-supplied labels.

4. Though not always—see Lakoff, 1987, and Medin, 1989, who proposed that artifacts can be construed as having essences.

5. In Waxman et al.'s data, one item set out of three (fish) permitted a test of whether children preferred the basic level (fish) or the generic species level (e.g., parrotfish). Overall children's responses were consistent with a basic level preference, not a generic species level preference. It is not clear whether this reflects a developmental difference compared to Coley, Medin, et al.'s (1999) data, or a methodological difference based on the tasks the two sets of researchers used.

6. Mandler, Bauer, and McDonough (1991) refer to these as "global" categories rather than "superordinate" categories because they do not represent the upper level in a hierarchy. Furthermore, they may be broader in scope than typical superordinates (e.g., the distinction between animal and vehicle is broader than the distinction between vehicle and furniture, or between animal and plant). However, Mandler and McDonough argue that global categories are not as broad as ontological categories (see Keil, 1979).

CHAPTER 3

1. An important point is that Sylvia's example concerns essentializing of individuals (e.g., the essence of Tim), rather than of kinds (e.g., the essence of men). In chapter 6 I take up the question of whether and how individual essentialism differs from kind essentialism. For now, the example serves simply to illustrate that people readily articulate the notion of an essence, and do so by reference to invisible qualities.

2. Boundary intensification may also contribute to the in-group favoritism so often found in laboratory studies of person perception (e.g., Robinson, 1996; Tajfel, 1970). Children or adults who are asked to reason about "minimal groups" (i.e., social categories invented for the purpose of the experiment, such as "overestimaters" versus "underestimaters," so called because of their purported estimation of line length on a perceptual task) strongly favor in-group members and judge them as smarter and more attractive. These findings do not measure boundary intensification directly, but they do seem to imply at least a heightened attention to boundaries for arbitrary social groups.

3. There is some disagreement in the literature as to whether all categories admit of a dissociation between category membership and typicality (Osherson and Smith, 1997) or whether concepts can be divided into those for which the prototype determines category membership and those for which prototypes and category membership are independent (Kamp and Partee, 1995). In any case, even if one concedes that all concepts allow for a dissociation, this does not tell us whether or to what degree domains differ in the extent of this dissociation.

CHAPTER 5

1. This is not to suggest that classical views and prototype views are equivalent. See E. Smith and Medin (1981) for discussion. Prototype views include at least the following insights not found in the classical view: (1) concepts are not arbitrary inventions (Rosch and Mervis, 1975), (2) not all concepts are alike (compare arbitrary concepts invented in the laboratory with those embedded in natural language), and (3) identifying category boundaries is not the most important task of categorization (compare the stability of prototypes with the instability of category boundaries).

2. Interestingly, there may be a more subtle form of childhood artificialism that persists throughout early elementary school. Kelemen (1999a, 1999b) finds that until about fourth grade, children apply teleological explanations to all kinds of objects, including natural kinds. For example, young children report that tigers exist for a purpose, and rocks are pointy for a reason (in contrast to the adult intuition; see Keil and Richardson, 1999; see also Keil, 1994, for domain-specific teleological reasoning in children). This research has important theoretical implications regarding the scope of a teleological stance. For the current discussion, however, what is most relevant to essentialism is children's early understanding that natural kinds undergo causal processes that are outside the realm of human control.

3. Preschoolers also attribute goal-directed action more to animals than plants. It is not until fifth grade that children consistently treat plants as goal directed in the same way as animals (Opfer and Gelman, 2001).

4. Children were also asked about a set of three plants, though the results of those items will not be discussed here as the predictions were less clear.

CHAPTER 6

1. A qualification here is in order: I assume that children will focus on category membership only when it is conceptually salient and available. If the category in question is one children have difficulty accessing, such as a superordinate category, then they should fail either to use coverage or to focus on category membership.

2. The results do not indicate a pervasive difficulty making consistent judgments on this sort of task, since even the youngest children made use of the typicality of the premise category, and of the similarity between premise and conclusion categories.

3. Heit and Hahn (2001) suggest that children's difficulty in past work may have been due to the use of hidden properties that were not displayed in the pictures. They present one study (experiment 4) showing much worse performance on items regarding nonvisible properties (e.g., predicting what picture a book would have inside, what texture a hat would have, or what sound a stuffed toy would make). However, I think there is a more straightforward explanation for this result: the items for which Heit and Hahn failed to find diversity were ones about which people (at least adults, and maybe children) have strong a priori beliefs regarding the causes of variability. For example, on one item, children learned that a set of books with red covers had pictures of Teletubbies inside, whereas a set of books with different-color covers (green, blue, and purple) had pictures of the Spice Girls inside. Children were then asked what picture a yellow book would have inside. Children presumably have ample experience that the color of a book cover does not predict the contents of the pictures inside of it. All the items were of this sort. Thus, it seems likely that children's failure to use

diversity for these properties reflects their prior knowledge about the content of these properties, rather than anything about hidden properties per se. Based on this analysis, I suspect
that adults, too, would use diversity rarely if at all on such items.

4. Lo et al. present an intriguing new model, the premise probability principle (PPP), to
account for their data. This model departs from the diversity principle in important ways,
and the authors argue that PPP has a stronger normative basis. For now I will focus on diversity in order to make more direct comparisons with prior work. However, see Lo et al. (2002)
for discussion of the distinction.

5. Naming patterns are more complicated than this, in that we can introduce name
changes at certain crucial junctures, for example at marriage for many women, or with sex-
change operations. However, the fact that continuity of naming is typical and expected un-
derscores the centrality of historical paths.

CHAPTER 7

1. It is also interesting how frequently generics were found in the commercially available
texts. It would be interesting to examine generics in children's literature (both fiction and
nonfiction) more broadly, to discover the generality of this phenomenon. At the very least,
this result raises a host of questions, as yet unexplored, concerning how generics are distributed in written versus spoken language, and what role literacy plays in the use and distribution of generic knowledge.

CHAPTER 8

1. Proper names (e.g., Noah, Jamie) may encourage essentializing of a different sort,
namely, essentializing of individual identity rather than category identity. Recall children's
tendencies toward nominal realism—the idea that a name is nonarbitrarily linked to its category. A triceratops is called a triceratops because it *is* a triceratops. I speculate that there may
be a parallel sort of nominal realism with proper names: the idea is that a person's name reveals his or her identity, and that losing one's name is akin to losing one's identity.

In contrast to kind essentialism, in which the name fosters inductive inferences to others
with the same name, proper-name essentialism might be something like: there is a name that
indicates your *uniqueness*. Certainly names have enormous emotional and social significance
in many (if not all) cultures. As Hall (1999) points out, having a proper name is considered a
basic human right, and in some countries the government has authority to regulate the
names that parents give their children (though not, as far as I know, the names they give their
boats or pets). Great significance is also placed on giving one's child the *right* name. Hall
gives the example of a Swedish court that ruled "Brfxxcxxmnpcccclllmmnprxvclmncks-
sqlbb1116" (pronounced "Albin") to be an unacceptable name. Loss of individuality also
tends to be accompanied by loss of names (note the substitution of numbers for names in
prisons and concentration camps).

In the extreme, naming decisions can take on monumental significance. I know of one
family in which the mother still could not bring herself to decide on names for her second
and third children after several years, and referred to them as "Sissy" (for the second-born,
short for "sister") and "Baby" (for the youngest) when they were five and a half and two and
a half years old. (This case is also interesting for the amount of distress and arguments the
mother's indecision evoked in members of the immediate and extended family.) Admittedly,

it is a leap from these observations to the interpretation that proper names are linked to essences. I leave it as an unresolved puzzle how one might operationalize and test this idea.

2. Whether or not these generic-sounding utterances are actually generics can only be addressed by means of more in-depth analysis. See later in this chapter for evidence that young children do interpret utterances of this type to be generic.

3. I am most grateful to Twila Tardif for her collaborations on both the empirical work and the linguistic and conceptual foundation.

4. To maintain consistency, we present this and all Mandarin examples in Hanyu *pinyin* form (with tone markings designated by numerals at the end of each syllable), although it should be noted that A. Bloom (1981) used a different system of transcription.

5. Nongenerics were coded in the second data set only, as there was too little information about context to permit coding the domain of nongenerics in the first dataset.

6. Further evidence for the importance of formal cues comes from an analysis of the four utterances (out of sixteen) that yielded the largest differences in interpretation between Mandarin and English speakers (S. Gelman and Tardif, 1998, study 3). In each of these four cases, the formal cues in English were potentially at odds with the world-knowledge cues. In interpreting the sentences, English-speakers typically went with the formal cues that were not available to Mandarin-speakers. For example, "The tractor doesn't have a nose" (nongeneric in form, but generically true of tractors) was interpreted as nongeneric by 91% of English-speakers but only 22% of Mandarin-speakers. Conversely, "Do you like buttons?" (generic in form, but content applicable to an individual) was interpreted as generic by 91% of English-speakers, but only 41% of Mandarin-speakers.

7. I am extremely grateful to Simone Nguyen and Melissa Koenig for help with coding the data.

8. Although a singular noun preceded by "the" can be generic ("The lion is a ferocious beast"), this construction is more formal and rarely used in parental speech to children (S. Gelman, Coley, et al., 1998; see also Karmiloff-Smith, 1979, for discussion of why generics using the definite article should be late acquired). By excluding such utterances we are providing a conservative estimate of generic usage in children's speech.

9. Waxman, Lynch, et al. (1997) found no effect of "generalizable" versus "non-generalizable" predicates in an induction task with three-year-olds. Their generalizable statements were generic (e.g., "We call this kind Noocs. They help us pull sleds"), whereas their nongeneralizable statements appeared to be a mixture of generic and nongeneric information (e.g., "We call this kind Noocs. They just took a bubble bath"). The ambiguity of the nongeneralizable statements derives from combining "this kind" (which implies reference to the generic kind) with "just took a bubble bath" (which is decidedly nongeneric). It would be interesting in future work to determine whether three-year-olds draw a distinction when the verbal information is more distinct (e.g., generic: "These are Noocs. Noocs help us pull sleds"; nongeneric: "These are Noocs. These Noocs just took a bubble bath"). Waxman, Lynch, et al. also discuss other procedural details that might have contributed to lack of sensitivity on this task.

10. The claim here is not that people never change their generic beliefs in the face of contradictory evidence, but rather that generic knowledge can never be certain on the basis of empirical evidence alone.

11. My argument here concerns the role of language in promoting kind concepts. There is a separate set of issues regarding whether or not words are special and distinctive in other respects, such as speed of acquisition (see Behrend, Scofield, and Kleinknecht, 2001;

P. Bloom and Markson, 2001; Markson and Bloom, 1997; and Waxman and Booth, 2000, 2001, for debate).

CHAPTER 9

1. I agree, however, that invented stimuli do show distortions; e.g., Davidson and Gelman, 1990; Farrar, Raney, and Boyer, 1992. I discuss the implications of such distortions in chapter 2.

CHAPTER 10

1. I thank John Rauschenberg for these examples.

2. Carey (1995) has pointed out that one problem with this position is that taxonomies are found broadly across domains (e.g., Rosch, 1978). However, there is some disagreement as to whether biological and nonbiological taxonomies are equivalent in structure. For example, there may be more violations of mutual exclusivity in nonbiological domains (e.g., a piano can be both furniture and a musical instrument, whereas a bat cannot be both a bird and a mammal).

CHAPTER 11

I thank Larry Hirschfeld for allowing me to adapt much of the material from S. Gelman and Hirschfeld (1999) in this chapter.

1. To be clear, this is not a claim that essentialism encourages scientific reasoning per se. For example, the scientific ideal of objectively and systematically evaluating evidence takes years to develop for children in literate, technological societies, and never emerged in many cultures and historical contexts. Rather, the claim is that essentialism encourages the perspective that closer examination of the world will pay off.

2. "Module" here does not necessarily mean the same thing as "module" in grammar (Chomsky, 1988) or vision (Marr, 1982).

3. One question that arises is whether all these examples should be considered causal. Certainly in all the examples listed, the causal mechanism is unknown: we do not know exactly how essences result in morphology and behaviors, why eating dirt leads to illness, or precisely what happens after we kiss the hem of the pope's robe. These phenomena are more similar to what Au and Romo (1999) call "input-output relations" than articulated causal mechanisms. Why, then, call these causal, as opposed to stimulus-response pairings of the sort that lead to "superstitious" behavior in pigeons (as Skinner has shown)? Whereas the pigeons' "superstitions" were based on observable stimulus-response pairings, the causal links discussed here are theorized even in the absence of evidence. Moreover, people start building stories to fill in the gaps: they attribute theorized causal agents (essences, germs, personality, gods) to do the work. These theorized components are neither observed nor known (e.g., we do not know what the essence is, and we do not know what happens if we own Jackie O.'s necklace). That people appeal to these causal chains nonetheless suggests that we may have a propensity to invoke unobservable causal constructs.

4. There is little evidence to date about children's beliefs about transfer of essence of this sort. An intriguing example is C. N. Johnson and Jacobs's (2001) study of children's and adults' beliefs about the causal effects of wearing Mr. Rogers's sweater. They found that most

adults and some six- to eight-year-old children endorse the possibility that wearing Mr. Rogers's sweater will lead to behavior changes (the child will act friendlier), emotional changes (the child will feel more special), and even transfer of essence (the sweater will pass "something of Mr. Rogers" to its wearer). In this example, adults endorsed magical contagion more than children. However, more research is needed to determine the generality of this developmental pattern.

5. It is possible that the appearance/reality distinction emerges for other reasons—for example, in the attempt to reconcile expectations with conflicting outcomes.

6. In S. Gelman and Hirschfeld (1999), we also suggested a second condition that might trigger essentialism: when an event is unpredicted or causally anomalous with respect to other events in the same domain. For example, the hypervaluation of Jackie O.'s pearls is causally anomalous in that it cannot be explained in terms of more typical determinants of value, such as the materials or their aesthetic value. The pearls might *initially* be attractive for associationist reasons (as found in classical conditioning). "However, vague associations do not provide satisfying causal accounts, so the story does not end there: The associative preference then calls out for a causal explanation (in this case, an essentialist one), which then leads to even greater valuation, in an increasing spiral. This search for a causal account may be further heightened by Onassis's prominence in the public sphere. . . . As this value became more recognized, it *demanded* a causal explanation. The 'best' one available, we further suggest, is essentialist" (pp. 436–437). In other words, what starts out as a causally anomalous preference then gets recruited to an essentialist explanation.

However, one problem with this account is that such a preference need not be viewed as anomalous in principle; it could be incorporated into a theory of mind account (I want the faux pearls because I like them) or an aesthetic account (the faux pearls are much more chic because they are endorsed by someone whose aesthetic judgments I trust). Further, we have all sorts of preferences that have no clearer causal account than Jackie O.'s pearls (e.g., my favorite color) yet that are not essentialized. I therefore now think it is more plausible and parsimonious to assume that essentialist assumptions precede and give rise to the hypervaluation of Jackie O.'s pearls.

References

Aarsleff, H. (1983). Language and Victorian ideology. *American Scholar, 52*, 365–372.

Abelson, R. P., and Kanouse, D. E. (1966). The subjective acceptance of verbal generalizations. In S. Feldman (Ed.), *Cognitive consistency: Motivational antecedents and behavioral consequents* (pp. 171–197). New York: Academic Press.

Aboud, F. E. (1988). *Children and prejudice*. Cambridge, MA: Basil Blackwell.

Adams, A. K., and Bullock, D. (1986). Apprenticeship in word use: Social convergence processes in learning categorically related nouns. In S. A. Kuczaj and M. D. Barrett (Eds.), *The development of word meaning* (pp. 155–197). New York: Springer-Verlag.

Ahn, W. (1998). The role of causal status in determining feature centrality. *Cognition, 69*, 135–178.

Ahn, W. (1999). Effect of causal structure on category construction. *Memory and Cognition, 27*, 1008–1023.

Ahn, W., Gelman, S. A., Amsterlaw, J. A., Hohenstein, J., and Kalish, C. W. (2000). Causal status effect in children's categorization. *Cognition, 76*, B35–B43.

Ahn, W., and Kalish, C. W. (2000). The role of mechanism beliefs in causal reasoning. In F. C. Keil and R. A. Wilson (Eds.), *Explanation and cognition* (pp. 199–225). Cambridge, MA: MIT Press.

Ahn, W., Kalish, C., Gelman, S. A., Medin, D. L., Luhmann, C., Atran, S., Coley, D. J., and Shafto, P. (2001). Why essences are essential in the psychology of concepts. *Cognition, 82*, 59–69.

Ahn, W., Kalish, C., Medin, D. L., and Gelman, S. A. (1995). The role of covariation versus mechanism information in causal attribution. *Cognition, 54*, 299–352.

Ahn, W., Kim, N. S., Lassaline, M. E., and Dennis, M. J. (2000). Causal status as a determinant of feature centrality. *Cognitive Psychology, 41*, 361–416.

Ahn, W., and Lassaline, M. E. (1995). Causal structure in categorization. *Proceedings of the Seventeenth Annual Conference of the Cognitive Science Society*, Pittsburgh, PA, pp. 521–526.

Allen, S. W., and Brooks, L. R. (1991). Specializing the operation of an explicit rule. *Journal of Experimental Psychology: General, 120*, 3–19.

Allport, G. (1954). *The nature of prejudice.* Addison-Wesley.

Aloise, P. A. (1993). Trait confirmation and disconfirmation: The development of attribution biases. *Journal of Experimental Child Psychology, 55,* 177–193.

Anderson, E., and Jayaratne, T. (1998). *Genetic explanations of group differences: Old or new racism, sexism, and classism?* Unpublished ms., University of Michigan.

Anderson, J. R. (1990). *The adaptive character of thought.* Hillsdale, NJ: Erlbaum.

Antill, J. K. (1987). Parents' beliefs and values about sex roles, sex differences, and sexuality: Their sources and implications. In P. Shaver and C. Hendrick (Eds.), *Review of personality and social psychology (Vol. 7), Sex and gender* (pp. 294–328). Newbury Park, CA: Sage.

Aristotle. (1924). *Metaphysics.* Oxford: Clarendon Press.

Armstrong, S. L., Gleitman, L. R., and Gleitman, H. G. (1983). On what some concepts might not be. *Cognition, 13,* 263–308.

Aslin, R. N., Saffran, J. R., and Newport, E. L. (1998). Computation of conditional probability statistics by 8-month-old infants. *Psychological Science, 9,* 321–324.

Astuti, R. (1995). "The Vezo are not a kind of people": Identity, difference, and "ethnicity" among a fishing people of western Madagascar. *American Ethnologist, 22,* 464–482.

Astuti, R. (2000). *Are we all natural dualists? A cognitive developmental approach.* The Malinowski Memorial Lecture.

Atran, S. (1990). *Cognitive foundations of natural history.* New York: Cambridge University Press.

Atran, S. (1995). Causal constraints on categories and categorical constraints on biological reasoning across cultures. In D. Sperber, D. Premack, and A. Premack (Eds.), *Causal cognition: A multidisciplinary debate* (pp. 205–233). Oxford: Oxford University Press.

Atran, S. (1996). Modes of thinking about living kinds: Science, symbolism, and common sense. In D. Olson and N. Torrance (Eds.), *Modes of thought: Explorations in culture and cognition.* Cambridge: Cambridge University Press.

Atran, S. (1998). Folk biology and the anthropology of science: Cognitive universals and cultural particulars. *Behavioral and Brain Sciences, 21,* 547–609.

Atran, S. (1999). Itzaj Maya folk-biological taxonomy. In D. Medin and S. Atran (Eds.), *Folk biology.* Cambridge, MA: MIT Press.

Atran, S., Estin, P., Coley, J. D., and Medin, D. L. (1997). Generic species and basic levels: Essence and appearance in folk biology. *Journal of Ethnobiology, 17,* 22–45.

Atran, S., Medin, D., Lynch, E., Vapnarsky, V., Ek', E. U., and Sousa, P. (2001). Folkbiology doesn't come from folkpsychology: Evidence from Yukatek Maya in cross-cultural perspective. *Journal of Cognition and Culture, 1,* 3–42.

Au, T. K. (1988). Language and cognition. In L. Lloyd and R. Schiefelbusch (Eds.). *Language Perspectives II* (pp. 125–146). Austin: Pro-Ed.

Au, T. K., Dapretto, M., and Song, Y-K. (1994). Input versus constraints: Early word acquisition in Korean and English. *Journal of Memory and Language, 33,* 567–582.

Au, T. K., and Romo, L. F. (1999). Mechanical causality in children's "folkbiology." In D. L. Medin and S. Atran (Eds.), *Folkbiology.* Cambridge, MA: MIT Press.

Au, T. K., Sidle, A. L., and Rollins, K. B. (1993). Developing an intuitive understanding of conservation and contamination: Invisible particles as a plausible mechanism. *Developmental Psychology, 29,* 286–299.

Backscheider, A. G., and Gelman, S. A. (1995). Children's understanding of homonyms. *Journal of Child Language, 22,* 107–127.

Backscheider, A. G., Gelman, S. A., Martinez, I., and Kowieski, J. (2000). Children's use of different information types when learning homophones and nonce words. *Cognitive Development, 14,* 515–530.

Backscheider, A. G., Shatz, M., and Gelman, S. A. (1993). Preschoolers' ability to distinguish living kinds as a function of self-healing. *Child Development, 64,* 1242–1257.

Baillargeon, R. (1993). The object concept revisited: New direction in the investigation of infants' physical knowledge. In C. Granrud (Ed.), *Visual perception and cognition in infancy* (265–315). Hillsdale, NJ: Erlbaum.

Balaban, M. T., and Waxman, S. R. (1997). Do words facilitate object categorization in 9-month-old infants? *Journal of Experimental Child Psychology, 64,* 3–26.

Baldwin, D. A. (1992). Clarifying the role of shape in children's taxonomic assumption. *Journal of Experimental Child Psychology, 54,* 392–416.

Baldwin, D. A., and Baird, J. A. (2001). Discerning intentions in dynamic human action. *Trends in Cognitive Sciences, 5,* 171–178.

Baldwin, D. A., Markman, E. M., and Melartin, R. L. (1993). Infants' ability to draw inferences about nonobvious object properties: Evidence from exploratory play. *Cognitive Development, 64,* 711–728.

Banton, M. (1987). *Racial theories.* New York: Cambridge University Press.

Bargh, J. A. (1990). Goal ≠ intent: Goal-directed thought and behavior are often unintentional. *Psychological Inquiry, 1,* 248–277.

Baron-Cohen, S., Tager-Flusberg, H., and Cohen, D. J. (Eds.). (1993). *Understanding other minds: Perspectives from autism.* New York: Oxford University Press.

Barrett, S. E., Abdi, H., Murphy, G. L., and Gallagher, J. M. (1993). Theory–based correlations and their role in children's concepts. *Child Development, 64,* 1595–1616.

Barsalou, L. W. (1985). Ideals, central tendency, and frequency of instantiation as determinants of graded structure in categories. *Journal of Experimental Psychology: Learning, Memory, and Cognition, 11,* 629–654.

Barsalou, L. W. (1991). Deriving categories to achieve goals. In G. H. Bower (Ed.), *The psychology of learning and motivation* (pp. 1–64). New York: Academic Press.

Barsalou, L. W. (1992). *Cognitive psychology: An overview for cognitive scientists.* Hillsdale, NJ: Erlbaum.

Barsalou, L. W. (1993a). Flexibility, structure, and linguistic vagary in concepts: Manifestations of a compositional system of perceptual symbols. In A. C. Collins, S. E. Gathercole, and P. E. M. Morris (Eds.), *Theories of memory.* Hillsdale, NJ: Erlbaum.

Barsalou, L. W. (1993b). Challenging assumptions about concepts. *Cognitive Development, 8,* 169–180.

Bartsch, K., and Wellman, H. M. (1995). *Children talk about the mind.* New York: Oxford University Press.

Bedard, J., and Chi, M. T. (1992). Expertise. *Current Directions in Psychological Science, 1,* 135–139.

Behrend, D. A. (1988). Overextensions in early language comprehension: Evidence from a signal detection approach. *Journal of Child Language, 15,* 63–75.

Behrend, D. A., Scofield, J., and Kleinknecht, E. E. (2001). Beyond fast mapping: Young children's extensions of novel words and novel facts. *Developmental Psychology, 37,* 698–705.

Bem, S. (1981). Gender schema theory: A cognitive account of sex-typing. *Psychological Review, 88,* 354–364.

Bem, S. (1989). Genital knowledge and gender constancy in preschool children. *Child Development, 60,* 649–620.

Benjamin, W. (1955). The work of art in the age of mechanical reproduction. In H. Arendt (Ed.), *Illuminations* (pp. 217–251). New York: Schocken Books.

Benveniste, E. (1971). *Problems in general linguistics.* Coral Gables, FL: University of Miami Press.

Berlin, B. (1978). Ethnobiological classification. In E. Rosch and B. Lloyd (Eds.), *Cognition and categorization.* Hillsdale, NJ: Erlbaum.

Berlin, B. (1992). *Ethnobiological classification: Principles of categorization of plants and animals in traditional societies.* Princeton, NJ: Princeton University Press.

Berlin, B., Breedlove, D., and Raven, P. (1973). General principles of classification and nomenclature in folk biology. *American Anthropologist, 74,* 214–242.

Berndt, T., and Heller, K. (1986). Gender stereotypes and social inferences: A developmental study. *Journal of Personality and Social Psychology, 50,* 889–898.

Bertenthal, B. I. (1996). Origins and early development of perception, action, and representation. *Annual Review of Psychology, 47,* 431–459.

Bhat, D. N. S. (1979). *The referents of noun phrases.* Pune, India: Deccan College Postgraduate and Research Institute.

Bierwisch, M., and Lang, E. (Eds.) (1987). *Dimensional adjectives: Grammatical structure and conceptual interpretation.* Berlin: Springer-Verlag.

Bigler, R. S. (1995). The role of classification skill in moderating environmental influences on children's gender stereotyping: A study of the functional use of gender in the classroom. *Child Development, 66,* 1072–1087.

Bigler, R. S., Brown, C. S., and Markell, M. (2001). When groups are not created equal: Effects of group status on the formation of intergroup attitudes in children. *Child Development, 72,* 1151–1162.

Blewitt, P. (1983). Dog versus collie: Vocabulary in speech to young children. *Developmental Psychology, 19,* 602–609.

Bloch, M. (1993). Zafimaniry birth and kinship theory. *Social Anthropology, 1,* 119–132.

Bloch, M., Solomon, G. E. A., and Carey, S. (2001). Zafimaniry: An understanding of what is passed on from parents to children: A cross-cultural investigation. *Journal of Cognition and Culture, 1,* 43–68.

Bloom, A. H. (1981). *The linguistic shaping of thought.* Hillsdale, NJ: Erlbaum.

Bloom, L. (1970). *Language development; form and function in emerging grammars.* Cambridge, MA: MIT Press.

Bloom, L. (1973). *One word at a time.* The Hague: Mouton.

Bloom, P. (1990). Syntactic distinctions in child language. *Journal of Child Language, 17,* 343–355.

Bloom, P. (1996). Intention, history, and artifact concepts. *Cognition, 60,* 1–29.

Bloom, P. (2000). *How children learn the meanings of words.* Cambridge, MA: MIT Press.

Bloom, P., Abell, F., Happé, F., and Frith, U. (under review). *Picture naming in children with autism.*

Bloom, P., and Markson, L. (1998). Intention and analogy in children's naming of pictorial representations. *Psychological Science, 9,* 200–204.

Bloom, P., and Markson, L. (2001). Are there principles that apply only to the acquisition of words? A reply to Waxman and Booth. *Cognition, 78,* 89–90.

Bloom, P., Markson, L., and Diesendruck, G. (1998). *Origins of the shape bias.* Unpublished ms., University of Arizona.

Booth, A. E., and Waxman, S. R. (2002). Word learning is "smart": Evidence that conceptual information affects preschoolers' extension of novel words. *Cognition, 84,* B11–B22.

Bowerman, M. (1996). Learning how to structure space for language: A crosslinguistic perspective. In P. Bloom, M. Peterson, L. Nadel, and M. Garrett (Eds.), *Language and space* (pp. 385–436). Cambridge, MA: MIT Press.

Bowerman, M. (2000). Where do children's word meanings come from? Rethinking the role of cognition in early semantic development. In L. P. Nucci, G. B. Saxe, and E. Turiel (Eds.), *Culture, thought, and development* (pp. 199–230). Mahwah, NJ: Erlbaum.

Boyd, R. (1999). Homeostasis, species, and higher taxa. In R. A. Wilson (Ed.), *Species: New interdisciplinary essays* (pp. 141–185). Cambridge, MA: MIT Press.

Boyer, P. (1990). *Tradition as truth and communication: A cognitive description of traditional discourse.* Cambridge: Cambridge University Press.

Boyer, P. (1994a). *The naturalness of religious ideas: A cognitive theory of religion.* Berkeley, CA: University of California Press.

Boyer, P. (1994b). Cognitive constraints on cultural representations: Natural ontologies and religious ideas. In L. A. Hirschfeld and S. A. Gelman (Eds.), *Mapping the mind: Domain specificity in cognition and culture* (pp. 391–411). New York: Cambridge University Press.

Brace, C. L. (1964). A nonracial approach towards the understanding of human diversity. In A. Montagu (Ed.), *The concept of race.* New York: The Free Press.

Braisby, N., Franks, B., and Hampton, J. (1996). Essentialism, word use, and concepts. *Cognition, 59,* 247–274.

Bressan, P., and Dal Martello, M. F. (2002). Talis pater, talis filius: Perceived resemblance and the belief in genetic relatedness. *Psychological Science, 13,* 213–218.

Brooks, L. R., and Wood, T. (1997). Identification in service of use: Characteristic of everyday concept learning. *Paper presented at the 38th annual meeting of the Psychonomic Society.*

Brooks, P. J., and Braine, M. D. S. (1996). What do children know about the universal quantifiers *all* and *each? Cognition 60,* 235–268.

Brown, A. L. (1990). Domain-specific principles affect learning and transfer in children. *Cognitive Science, 14,* 107–133.

Brown, A., and Kane, M. (1988). Preschool children can learn to transfer: Learning to learn and learning from example. *Cognitive Psychology, 20,* 493–523.

Brown, R. (1957). Linguistic determinism and the part of speech. *Journal of Abnormal and Social Psychology, 55,* 1–5.

Brown, R. (1976). Reference: In memorial tribute to Eric Lenneberg. *Cognition, 4,* 125–153.

Brown, R. W. (1973). *A first language: The early stages.* Cambridge, MA: Harvard University Press.

Bruner, J. S. (1973). *Beyond the information given.* New York: Norton.

Bruner, J. S., Goodnow, J. J., and Austin, G. A. (Eds.). (1956). *A study of thinking.* New York: Wiley.

Bruner, J. S., Olver, R. R., Greenfield, P. M., et al. (1966). *Studies in cognitive growth.* New York: John Wiley.

Bullock, M., Gelman, R., and Baillargeon, R. (1982). The development of causal reasoning.

In W. J. Friedman (Ed.), *The developmental psychology of time* (pp. 209–254). New York: Academic Press.

Cain, K. M., and Dweck, C. S. (1995). The relation between motivational patterns and achievement cognitions through the elementary school years. *Merrill-Palmer Quarterly, 41*, 25–52.

Cain, K. M., Heyman, G. D., and Walker, M. E. (1997). Preschoolers' ability to make dispositional predictions within and across domains. *Social Development, 6*, 53–75.

Callanan, M. A. (1985). How parents label objects for young children: The role of input in the acquisition of category hierarchies. *Child Development, 56*, 508–523.

Callanan, M. A. (1989). Development of object categories and inclusion relations: Preschoolers' hypotheses about word meanings. *Developmental Psychology, 25*, 207–216.

Callanan, M. A. (1990). Parents' descriptions of objects: Potential data for children's inferences about category principles. *Cognitive Development, 5*, 101–122.

Callanan, M. A., and Oakes, L. M. (1992). Preschoolers' questions and parents' explanations: Causal thinking in everyday activity. *Cognitive Development, 7*, 213–233.

Cannon, J. (1993). *Stellaluna.* New York: Harcourt, Inc.

Carey, S. (1985). *Conceptual development in childhood.* Cambridge, MA: MIT Press.

Carey, S. (1995). On the origins of causal understanding. In D. Sperber, D. Premack, and A. J. Premack (Eds.), *Causal cognition: A multi-disciplinary approach* (pp. 268–308). Oxford: Clarendon Press.

Carey, S. (1996). Cognitive domains as modes of thought. In D. R. Olson and N. Torrance (Eds.), *Modes of thought: Explorations in culture and cognition* (pp. 187–215). New York: Cambridge University Press.

Carey, S., and Spelke, E. (1994). Domain-specific knowledge and conceptual change. In L. A. Hirschfeld and S. A. Gelman (Eds.), *Mapping the mind: Domain specificity in cognition and culture* (pp. 169–200). New York: Cambridge University Press

Carey, S., and Xu, F. (1999). Sortals and kinds: An appreciation of John Macnamara. In R. Jackendoff, P. Bloom, and K. Wynn (Eds.), *Language, logic, and concepts: Essays in memory of John Macnamara.* Cambridge, MA: MIT Press.

Carlson, G. N. (1977). A unified analysis of the English bare plural. *Linguistics and Philosophy, 1*, 413–456.

Carlson, G. N., and Pelletier, F. J. (Eds.) (1995). *The generic book.* Chicago: University of Chicago Press.

Chandler, M. J., and Lalonde, C. E. (1994). Surprising, magical and miraculous turns of events: Children's reactions to violations of their early theories of mind and matter. *British Journal of Developmental Psychology, 12*, 83–95.

Chi, M. T. H., Hutchinson, J. E., and Robin, A. F. (1989). How inferences about novel domain-related concepts can be constrained by structured knowledge. *Merrill-Palmer Quarterly, 35*, 27–62.

Chi, M. T. H., and Koeske, R. (1983). Network representation of a child's dinosaur knowledge. *Developmental Psychology, 19*, 29–39.

Choi, I., Nisbett, R. E., and Smith, E. E. (1997). Culture, categorization, and inductive reasoning. *Cognition, 65*, 15–32.

Choi, S. (2000). Caregiver input in English and Korean: Use of nouns and verbs in book-reading and toy-play contexts. *Journal of Child Language, 27*, 69–96.

Choi, S., and Gopnik, A. (1995). Early acquisition of verbs in Korean: A crosslinguistic study. *Journal of Child Language, 22*, 497–529.

Chomsky, N. (1988). *Language and problems of knowledge.* Cambridge, MA: MIT Press.

Christiansen, M. H., Allen, J., and Seidenberg, M. S. (1998). Learning to segment speech using multiple cues: A connectionist model. *Language and Cognitive Processes, 13,* 221–268.

Clark, E. V. (1973). What's in a word? On the child's acquisition of semantics in his first language. In T. E. Moore (Ed.), *Cognitive development and the acquisition of language.* New York: Academic Press.

Clark, E. V. (1987). The principle of contrast: A constraint on language acquisition. In B. MacWhinney (Ed.), *Mechanisms of language acquisition* (pp. 1–33). Hillsdale, NJ: Erlbaum.

Clark, E. V., Gelman, S. A., and Lane, N. (1985). Noun compounds and category structure in young children. *Child Development, 56,* 84–94.

Cohen, L. B., and Oakes, L. M. (1993). How infants perceive a simple causal event. *Developmental Psychology, 29,* 421–433.

Coley, J. D. (1993). *Emerging differentiation of folkbiology and folkpsychology: Similarity judgments and property attributions.* Ph.D. dissertation, University of Michigan, Ann Arbor.

Coley, J. D. (2000). On the importance of comparative research: The case of folkbiology. *Child Development, 71,* 82–90.

Coley, J. D., and Gelman, S. A. (1989). The effects of object orientation and object type on children's interpretation of the word "big." *Child Development, 60,* 372–380.

Coley, J. D., and Luhmann, C. C. (2001). *Domain specific relations between typicality and absolute category membership.* Unpublished ms., Northeastern University.

Coley, J. D., Medin, D. L, and Atran, S. (1997). Does rank have its privilege? Inductive inferences within folkbiological taxonomies. *Cognition, 64,* 73–112.

Coley, J. D., Medin, D. L., Proffitt, J. B., Lynch, E., and Atran, S. (1999). Inductive reasoning in folkbiological thought. In D. L. Medin and S. Atran (Eds.), *Folkbiology* (pp. 205–232). Cambridge, MA: MIT Press.

Crocker, J. C. (1979). Selves and alters among the Eastern Bororo. In D. Maybury-Lewis (Ed.), *Dialectical societies: The Ge and Bororo of Central Brazil* (pp. 249–300). Cambridge, MA: Harvard University Press.

Croft, W. (1990). *Typology and universals.* New York: Cambridge University Press.

Cunningham, C. J. (1999). *Illnesses as labels: The influence of linguistic form class.* Undergraduate honors thesis, University of Michigan.

Dahl, O. (1975). On generics. In E. L. Keenan (Ed.), *Formal semantics of natural language* (pp. 99–111). Cambridge University Press.

Daniel, E. V. (1984). *Fluid signs: Being a person the Tamil way.* Berkeley, CA: University of California Press.

Danziger, E. (2001). *Relatively speaking: Language, thought, and kinship among the Mopan Maya.* New York: Oxford University Press.

Darley, J. M., and Fazio, R. H. (1980). Expectancy-confirmation processes arising in the social interaction sequence. *American Psychologist, 35,* 867–881.

Davidson, N. S., and Gelman, S. A. (1990). Inductions from novel categories: The role of language and conceptual structure. *Cognitive Development, 5,* 151–176.

Deák, G., and Bauer, P. J. (1995). The effects of task comprehension on preschoolers' and adults' categorization choices. *Journal of Experimental Child Psychology, 60,* 393–427.

Deák, G., and Bauer, P. J. (1996). The dynamics of preschoolers' categorization choices. *Child Development, 67,* 140–168.

DeLoache, J. S. (1991). Symbolic functioning in very young children: Understanding of pictures and models. *Child Development, 62,* 736–752.

DeLoache, J. S., and DeMendoza, O. A. P. (1987). Joint picturebook interactions of mothers and 1-year-old children. *British Journal of Developmental Psychology, 5,* 111–123.

Dennett, D. C. (1995). *Darwin's dangerous idea: Evolution and the meanings of life.* New York: Simon and Schuster.

DeVries, R. (1969). Constancy of generic identity in the years three to six. *Society for Research in Child Development Monographs, 34* (Whole No. 127).

Diesendruck, G. (2001). Essentialism in Brazilian children's extensions of animal names. *Developmental Psychology, 37,* 49–60.

Diesendruck, G. (in press). Categories for names or names for categories? The interplay between domain-specific conceptual structure and language. *Language and Cognitive Processes.*

Diesendruck, G., and Gelman, S. A. (1999). Domain differences in absolute judgments of category membership: Evidence for an essentialist account of categorization. *Psychonomic Bulletin and Review, 6,* 338–346.

Diesendruck, G., Gelman, S. A., and Lebowitz, K. (1998). Conceptual and linguistic biases in children's word learning. *Developmental Psychology, 34,* 823–839.

Diesendruck, G., and Markson, L. (1999, April). *Function as a criterion in children's object naming.* Poster presented at the Biennial Meeting of the Society for Research in Child Development, Albuquerque, NM.

Diesendruck, G., and Shatz, M. (1997). The effect of perceptual similarity and linguistic input on children's acquisition of object labels. *Journal of Child Language, 24,* 695–717.

Diesendruck, G., and Shatz, M. (2001). Two-year-olds' recognition of hierarchies: Evidence from their interpretation of the semantic relation between object labels. *Cognitive Development, 16,* 577–594.

Disney, W. (1977). *Lambert the sheepish lion.* New York: Random House.

Donaldson, M., and McGarrigle, J. (1974). Some clues to the nature of semantic development. *Journal of Child Language, 1,* 185–194.

Douglas, M. (1966). *Purity and danger: An analysis of concepts of pollution and taboo.* New York: Praeger.

Dozier, M. (1991). Functional measurement assessment of young children's ability to predict future behavior. *Child Development, 62,* 1091–1099.

Droege, K. L., and Stipek, D. J. (1993). Children's use of dispositions to predict classmates' behavior. *Developmental Psychology, 29,* 646–654.

Dromi, E. (1987). *Early lexical development.* Cambridge University Press.

Dupré, J. (1993). *The disorder of things: Metaphysical foundations of the disunity of science.* Cambridge, MA: Harvard University Press.

Dweck, C. S. (1999). *Self-theories: Their role in motivation, personality, and development.* Philadelphia: Psychology Press.

Eakin, E. (2001, February 24). Screwdriver scholars and pencil punditry. *New York Times.*

Eder, R. A. (1989). The emergent personologist: The structure and content of 3?-, 5?-, and 7?-year-olds' concepts of themselves and other persons. *Child Development, 60,* 1218–1228.

Eimas, P. D., and Quinn, P. C. (1994). Studies on the formation of perceptually based basic-level categories in young infants. *Child Development, 65,* 903–917.

Ellis, B. D. (2001). *Scientific essentialism*. New York: Cambridge University Press.

Ellis, L. (1998). The evolution of attitudes about social stratification: Why many people (including social scientists) are morally outraged by *The Bell Curve*. *Personality and Individual Differences, 24*, 207–216.

Emmerich, W., Goldman, K. S., and Kirsh, B. (1977). Evidence for a transitional phase in the development of gender constancy. *Child Development, 48*, 930–936.

Errington, S. (1989). *Meaning and power in a Southeast Asian realm*. Princeton, NJ: Princeton University Press.

Estes, W. K. (1994). *Classification and cognition*. New York: Oxford University Press.

Evans, E. M. (2000). Beyond Scopes: Why creationism is here to stay. In K. S. Rosengren, C. N. Johnson, and P. L. Harris (Eds.), *Imagining the impossible* (pp. 305–333). New York: Cambridge University Press.

Evans, E. M. (2001). Cognitive and contextual factors in the emergence of diverse belief systems: Creation versus evolution. *Cognitive Psychology, 42*, 217–266.

Fairchild, C. (1984). *Domestic enemies: Servants and their masters in old regime France*. Baltimore: Johns Hopkins Press.

Farrar, M. J., Raney, G. E., and Boyer, M. E. (1992). Knowledge, concepts, and inferences in childhood. *Child Development, 63*, 673–691.

Flavell, J. H. (1963). *The developmental psychology of Jean Piaget*. Princeton, NJ: Van Nostrand.

Flavell, J. H. (1977). *Cognitive Development*. Englewood Cliffs, NJ: Prentice-Hall.

Flavell, J. H. (1985). *Cognitive development*, 2nd ed. Englewood Cliffs, NJ: Prentice-Hall.

Flavell, J. H., Flavell, E. R., Green, F. L. (1983). Development of the appearance-reality distinction. *Cognitive Psychology, 15*, 95–120.

Flavell, J. H., Flavell, E. R., Green, F. L., and Moses, L. J. (1990). Young children's understanding of fact beliefs versus value beliefs. *Child Development, 61*, 915–928.

Flavell, J. H., and Miller, P. H. (1998). Social cognition. In D. Kuhn and R. Siegler (Eds.), *Handbook of child psychology*, 4th ed., *Cognitive development* (pp. 851–898). New York: Wiley.

Florian, J. E. (1994). Stripes do not a zebra make, or do they? Conceptual and perceptual information in inductive inference. *Developmental Psychology, 30*, 88–101.

Fodor, J. (1975). *The language of thought*. Cambridge, MA: MIT Press.

Fodor, J. (1998). *Concepts: Where cognitive science went wrong*. Oxford: Oxford University Press.

Fugelsang, J. A., and Thompson, V. A. (2000). Strategy selection in causal reasoning: When beliefs and covariation collide. *Canadian Journal of Experimental Psychology, 54*, 15–32.

Fuss, D. (1989). *Essentially speaking: Feminism, nature, and difference*. New York: Routledge.

Gelman, R. (1978). Cognitive development. *Annual Review of Psychology, 29*, 297–332.

Gelman, R. (1987, August). *Cognitive development: Principles guide learning and contribute to conceptual coherence*. Paper presented at the meetings of the American Psychological Association, Division I, New York.

Gelman, R. (1990). First principles organize attention to and learning about relevant data: Number and the animate-inanimate distinction as examples. *Cognitive Science, 14*, 79–106.

Gelman, R., Durgin, F., and Kaufman, L. (1995). Distinguishing between animates and inanimates: Not by motion alone. In D. Sperber, D. Premack, and A. J. Premack

(Eds.), *Causal cognition: A multidisciplinary debate* (pp. 150–184). Oxford: Clarendon Press.

Gelman, S. A. (1988). The development of induction within natural kind and artifact categories. *Cognitive Psychology, 20,* 65–96.

Gelman, S. A. (1992). Children's conception of personality traits—commentary. *Human Development, 35,* 280–285.

Gelman, S. A. (1993). Children's conceptions of biological growth. In J. Montangero and A. Tryphon (Eds.), *Conceptions of change over time* (pp. 197–208). Cahiers de la Foundation Archives Jean Piaget No. 13.

Gelman, S. A. (1996). Concepts and theories. In R. Gelman and T. Au (Eds.), *Handbook of perception and cognition volume 13: Perceptual and cognitive development.*

Gelman, S. A. (2000). The role of essentialism in children's concepts. In H. W. Reese (Ed.), *Advances in child development and behavior, Vol. 27* (pp. 55–98). San Diego: Academic Press.

Gelman, S. A. (in press). Learning words for kinds: Generic noun phrases in acquisition. To appear in D. G. Hall and S. R. Waxman (Eds.), *Weaving a lexicon.* Cambridge, MA: MIT Press.

Gelman, S. A., and Bloom, P. (2000). Young children are sensitive to how an object was created when deciding what to name it. *Cognition, 76,* 91–103.

Gelman, S. A., and Coley, J. D. (1990). The importance of knowing a dodo is a bird: Categories and inferences in 2-year-old children. *Developmental Psychology, 26,* 796–804.

Gelman, S. A., and Coley, J. D. (1991). Language and categorization: The acquisition of natural kind terms. In S. A. Gelman and J. P. Byrnes (Eds.), *Perspectives on language and thought: Interrelations in development* (pp. 146–196). Cambridge: Cambridge University Press.

Gelman, S. A., Coley, J. D., and Gottfried, G. M. (1994). Essentialist beliefs in children: The acquisition of concepts and theories. In L. A. Hirschfeld and S. A. Gelman (Eds.), *Mapping the mind: Domain specificity in cognition and culture* (pp. 341–365). Cambridge University Press.

Gelman, S. A., Coley, J. D., Rosengren, K., Hartman, E., and Pappas, T. (1998). Beyond labeling: The role of parental input in the acquisition of richly structured categories. *Monographs of the Society for Research in Child Development.* Serial No. 253, Vol. 63, No. 1.

Gelman, S. A., Collman, P., and Maccoby, E. E. (1986). Inferring properties from categories versus inferring categories from properties: The case of gender. *Child Development, 57,* 396–404.

Gelman, S. A., Croft, W., Fu, P., Clausner, T., and Gottfried, G. (1998). Why is a pomegranate an *apple*? The role of shape, taxonomic relatedness, and prior lexical knowledge in children's overextensions of *apple* and *dog. Journal of Child Language, 25,* 267–291.

Gelman, S. A., and Diesendruck, G. (1999). What's in a concept? Context, variability, and psychological essentialism. In I. E. Sigel (Ed.), *Development of mental representation: Theories and applications* (pp. 87–111). Mahwah, NJ: Erlbaum.

Gelman, S. A., and Ebeling, K. S. (1998). Shape and representational status in children's early naming. *Cognition, 66,* B35–B47.

Gelman, S. A., and Gottfried, G. (1996). Causal explanations of animate and inanimate motion. *Child Development, 67,* 1970–1987.

Gelman, S. A., and Heyman, G. D. (1999). Carrot-eaters and creature-believers: The effects of lexicalization on children's inferences about social categories. *Psychological Science,* *10,* 489–493.

Gelman, S. A., and Hirschfeld, L. A. (1999). How biological is essentialism? In S. Atran and D. Medin (Eds.), *Folk biology.* Cambridge, MA: MIT Press.

Gelman, S. A., Hollander, M., Star, J., and Heyman, G. D. (2000). The role of language in the construction of kinds. In D. Medin (Ed.), *Psychology of learning and motivation, Vol. 39* (pp. 201–263). New York: Academic Press.

Gelman, S. A., and Kalish, C. W. (1993). Categories and causality. In R. Pasnak and M. L. Howe (Eds.), *Emerging themes in cognitive development, Vol. II: Competencies* (pp. 3–32). New York: Springer-Verlag.

Gelman, S. A., and Koenig, M. A. (in press). Theory-based categorization in early childhood. In D. H. Rakison and L. M. Oakes (Eds.), *Early category and concept development: Making sense of the blooming, buzzing confusion.* New York: Oxford University Press.

Gelman, S. A., and Kremer, K. E. (1991). Understanding natural cause: Children's explanations of how objects and their properties originate. *Child Development, 62,* 396–414.

Gelman, S. A., and Markman, E. M. (1985). Implicit contrast in adjectives versus nouns: Implications for word-learning in preschoolers. *Journal of Child Language, 12,* 125–143.

Gelman, S. A., and Markman, E. M. (1986). Categories and induction in young children. *Cognition, 23,* 183–209.

Gelman, S. A., and Markman, E. M. (1987). Young children's inductions from natural kinds: The role of categories and appearances. *Child Development, 58,* 1532–1541.

Gelman, S. A., and Medin, D. L. (1993). What's so essential about essentialism? A different perspective on the interaction of perception, language, and conceptual knowledge. *Cognitive Development, 8,* 157–167.

Gelman, S. A., Nguyen, S. P., and Taylor, M. G. (2001). *Maternal talk about gender to 2-, 4-, and 6-year-old children.* Unpublished data, University of Michigan, Ann Arbor.

Gelman, S. A., and O'Reilly, A. W. (1988). Children's inductive inferences within superordinate categories: The role of language and category structure. *Child Development, 59,* 876–887.

Gelman, S. A., and Opfer, J. (2002). Development of the animate-inanimate distinction. In U. Goswami, *Handbook of Cognitive Development* (pp. 151–166). Oxford, UK: Blackwell.

Gelman, S. A., and Raman, L. (in press). Preschool children use linguistic form class and pragmatic cues to interpret generics. *Child Development.*

Gelman, S. A., Star, J., and Flukes, J. (2002). Children's use of generics in inductive inferences. *Journal of Cognition and Development, 3,* 179–199.

Gelman, S. A., and Tardif, T. Z. (1998). Generic noun phrases in English and Mandarin: An examination of child-directed speech. *Cognition, 66,* 215–248.

Gelman, S. A., and Taylor, M. (1984). How 2-year-old children interpret proper and common names for unfamiliar objects. *Child Development, 55,* 1535–1540.

Gelman, S. A., and Taylor, M. G. (2000). Gender essentialism in cognitive development. In P. H. Miller and E. K. Scholnick (Eds.), *Toward a feminist developmental psychology* (pp. 169–190). New York: Routledge.

Gelman, S. A., and Wellman, H. M. (1991). Insides and essences: Early understandings of the nonobvious. *Cognition, 38,* 213–244.

Gelman, S. A., Wilcox, S. A., and Clark, E. V. (1989). Conceptual and linguistic hierarchies in young children. *Cognitive Development, 4,* 309–326.

Gentner, D. (1982). Why nouns are learned before verbs: Linguistic relativity versus natural partitioning. In S. A. Kuczaj II (Ed.), *Language development: Syntax and semantics.* Hillsdale, NJ: Erlbaum.

Gentner, D., and Imai, M. (1994). A further examination of the shape bias in early word learning. *Proceedings of the Child Language Research Forum.* Stanford, CA.

Gentner, D., and Medina, J. (1998). Similarity and the development of rules. *Cognition, 65,* 263–297.

Giles, J. W., and Heyman, G. D. (2001, April). *Preschoolers' social beliefs as predictors of their social competence.* Paper presented at the Biennial Meeting of the Society for Research in Child Development, Minneapolis, MN.

Gil-White, F. J. (2001). Are ethnic groups biological "species" to the human brain? *Current Anthropology, 42,* 515–554.

Glucksberg, S. (2001). Understanding figurative language: From metaphors to idioms. New York: Oxford University Press.

Gobbo, C., and Chi, M. (1986). How knowledge is structured and used by expert and novice children. *Cognitive Development, 1,* 221–237.

Goldberg, T. (1993). *Racist culture: Philosophy and the politics of meaning.* Blackwell.

Goldin-Meadow, S., and Mylander, C. (1990). Beyond the input given: The child's role in the acquisition of language. *Language, 66,* 323–355.

Golinkoff, R. M., and Hirsh-Pasek, K. (2000). Word learning: Icon, index, or symbol? In *Becoming a word learner: A debate on lexical acquisition* (pp. 3–18). New York: Oxford University Press.

Golinkoff, R. M., Mervis, C. B., and Hirsh-Pasek, K. (1994). Early object labels: The case for a developmental lexical principles framework. *Journal of Child Language, 21,* 125–155.

Golinkoff, R. M., Shuff-Bailey, M., Olguin, R., and Ruan, W. (1995). Young children extend novel words at the basic-level: Evidence for the principle of categorical scope. *Developmental Psychology, 31,* 494–507.

Gomez, R. L., and Gerken, L. (1999). Artificial grammar learning by 1-year-olds leads to specific and abstract knowledge. *Cognition, 70,* 109–135.

Goodman, N. (1972). Seven strictures on similarity. In N. Goodman (Ed.), *Problems and project.* Bobbs-Merrill.

Goodman, N. (1973). *Fact, fiction, and forecast* (3rd ed.). Indianapolis: Bobbs-Merrill.

Gopnik, A. (2000). Explanation as orgasm and the drive for causal knowledge: The function, evolution, and phenomenology of the theory formation system. In F. C. Keil and R. A. Wilson (Eds.), *Explanation and cognition.* Cambridge, MA: MIT Press.

Gopnik, A., and Choi, S. (1990). Do linguistic differences lead to cognitive differences? A cross-linguistic study of semantic and cognitive development. *First Language, 10,* 199–215.

Gopnik, A., Choi, S., and Baumberger, T. (1996). Cross-linguistic differences in early semantic and cognitive development. *Cognitive Development, 11,* 197–227.

Gopnik, A., and Meltzoff, A. N. (1997). *Words, thoughts, and theories.* Cambridge, MA: Bradford Books/MIT Press.

Gopnik, A., and Sobel, D. M. (2000). Detecting blickets: How young children use information about novel causal powers in categorization and induction. *Child Development, 71,* 1205–1222.

Gopnik, A., and Wellman, H. (1994). The theory theory. In L. A. Hirschfeld and S. A. Gelman

(Eds.), *Mapping the mind: Domain specificity in cognition and culture.* NY: Cambridge University Press.

Goswami, U. (1996). Analogical reasoning and cognitive development. In H. W. Reese (Ed.), *Advances in Child Development and Behavior, Vol. 26* (pp. 92–138). San Diego: Academic Press.

Gottfried, G. M., Gelman, S. A., and Shultz, J. (1999). Children's understanding of the brain: From early essentialism to biological theory. *Cognitive Development, 14,* 147–174.

Gottfried, G. M., and Tonks, S. J. M. (1996). Specifying the relation between novel and known: Input affects the acquisition of novel color terms. *Child Development, 67,* 850–866.

Gould, S. J. (1989). *Wonderful life.* New York: W. W. Norton and Co.

Graham, S. A., Kilbreath, C. S., and Welder, A. N. (2001). Words and shape similarity guide 13-month-olds' inferences about nonobvious object properties. In J. D. Moore and K. Stenning (Eds.), *Proceedings of the Twenty-Third Annual Conference of the Cognitive Science Society* (pp. 352–357). Hillsdale, NJ: Erlbaum.

Graham, S. A., Kilbreath, C. S., and Welder, A. N. (2002). *The importance of being a FLUM: 12-month-olds rely on shared labels and shape similarity for inductive inferences.* Paper presented at the Thirteenth Biennial International Conference on Infant Studies, Toronto, Canada.

Green, M. (1978). Structure and sequence in children's concepts of chance and probability: A replication study of Piaget and Inhelder. *Child Development, 49,* 1045–1053.

Greenberg, J. H. (1966). *Language universals.* The Hague: Mouton.

Guillaumin, C. (1980). The idea of race and its elevation to autonomous scientific and legal status. In *Sociological theories: Race and colonialism* (pp. 37–68). Paris: UNESCO.

Gumperz, J. J., and Levinson, S. C. (Eds.). (1996). *Rethinking linguistic relativity.* New York: Cambridge University Press.

Gunnar-von Gnechten, M. R. (1978). Changing a frightening toy into a pleasant toy by allowing the infant to control its actions. *Developmental Psychology, 14,* 157–162.

Gutheil, D. G. (1993). *Preschoolers' understanding of individual identity stability in simple objects.* Unpublished Ph.D. dissertation, University of Michigan.

Gutheil, G., and Gelman, S. A. (1997). Children's use of sample size and diversity information within basic-level categories. *Journal of Experimental Child Psychology, 64,* 159–174.

Gutheil, G., and Rosengren, K. S. (1996). A rose by any other name: Preschoolers' understanding of individual identity across name and appearance changes. *British Journal of Developmental Psychology, 14,* 477–498.

Hall, D. G. (1993). Basic-level individuals. *Cognition, 48,* 199–221.

Hall, D. G. (1994). How mothers teach basic-level and situation-restricted count nouns. *Journal of Child Language, 21,* 391–414.

Hall, D. G. (1996). Preschoolers' default assumptions about word meaning: Proper names designate unique individuals. *Developmental Psychology, 32,* 177–186.

Hall, D. G. (1999). Semantics and the acquisition of proper names. In R. Jackendoff, P. Bloom, and K. Wynn (Eds.), *Language, logic, and concepts: Essays in memory of John Macnamara.* Cambridge, MA: MIT Press.

Hall, D. G., and Moore, C. E. (1997). Red bluebirds and black greenflies: Preschoolers' understanding of the semantics of adjectives and count nouns. *Journal of Experimental Child Psychology, 67,* 236–267.

Hall, D. G., and Waxman, S. R. (1993). Assumptions about word meaning: Individuation and basic-level kinds. *Child Development, 64,* 1550–1570.

Hall, D. G., Waxman, S. R., and Hurwitz, W. R. (1993). How 2- and 4-year-old children interpret adjectives and count nouns. *Child Development, 64,* 1661–1664.

Hallett, G. L. (1991). *Essentialism: A Wittgensteinian critique.* Albany, NY: SUNY Press.

Hamilton, D. L., and Sherman, S. J. (1996). Perceiving persons and groups. *Psychological Review, 103,* 336–355.

Hamilton, D. L., Sherman, S. J., and Lickel, B. (1998). Perceiving social groups: The importance of the entitativity continuum. In C. Sedikides, J. Schopler, and C. A. Insko (Eds.), *Intergroup cognition and intergroup behavior.* Mahwah, NJ: Erlbaum.

Hampton, J. A. (1982). A demonstration of intransitivity in natural categories. *Cognition, 12,* 151–164.

Hampton, J. A. (1998). Similarity-based categorization and fuzziness of natural categories. *Cognition, 65,* 137–165.

Harnad, S. (1987). *Categorical perception: The groundwork of cognition.* New York: Cambridge University Press.

Harre, R., and Madden, E. H. (1975). Causal powers: A theory of natural necessity. Oxford: Blackwell.

Haslam, N. (1998). Natural kinds, human kinds, and essentialism. *Social Research, 65,* 291–314.

Haslam, N., and Ernst, D. (2002). Essentialist beliefs about mental disorders. *Journal of Social and Clinical Psychology, 21.*

Haslam, N., Rothschild, L., and Ernst, D. (2000). Essentialist beliefs about social categories. *British Journal of Social Psychology, 39,* 113–127.

Haslam, N., Rothschild, L., and Ernst, D. (2002). Are essentialist beliefs associated with prejudice? *British Journal of Social Psychology, 41,* 87–100.

Hatano, G., and Inagaki, K. (1999). A developmental perspective on informal biology. In D. L. Medin and S. Atran (Eds.), *Folkbiology* (pp. 321–354). Cambridge, MA: MIT Press.

Hauser, M. D. (1997). Artifactual kinds and functional design features: What a primate understands without language. *Cognition, 64,* 285–308.

Hayne, H., Rovee-Collier, C., and Perris, E. E. (1987). Categorization and memory retrieval by three-month-olds. *Child Development, 58,* 750–767.

Heath, S. B. (1983). *Ways with words.* Cambridge University Press.

Heit, E., and Hahn, U. (2001). Diversity-based reasoning in children. *Cognitive Psychology, 43,* 243–273.

Heit, E., and Rubinstein, J. (1994). Similarity and property effects in inductive reasoning. *Journal of Experimental Psychology: Learning, Memory, and Cognition, 20,* 411–422.

Heller, K. A., and Berndt, T. J. (1981). Developmental changes in the formation and organization of personality attributions. *Child Development, 52,* 683–691.

Helweg, H. (1978). *Farm animals.* New York: Random House.

Herey, G. (1985). Generic descriptions, default reasoning, and typicality. *Theoretical Linguistics, 12,* 33–72.

Herrnstein, R. J., and de Villiers, P. A. (1980). Fish as a natural category for people and pigeons. In G. H. Bower (Ed.), *The psychology of learning and motivation, 14,* 59–95. New York: Academic Press.

Herrnstein, R. J., Loveland, D. H., and Cable, C. (1976). Natural concepts in pigeons. *Journal of Experimental Psychology: Animal Behavior Processes, 2,* 285–302.

Heyman, G. D., and Diesendruck, G. (in press). The Spanish ser/estar distinction in bilingual children's reasoning about human psychological characteristics. *Developmental Psychology*.

Heyman, G. D., Dweck, C. S., and Cain, K. M. (1992). Young children's vulnerability to self-blame and helplessness: Relationship to beliefs about goodness. *Child Development, 63*, 401–415.

Heyman, G. D., and Gelman, S. A. (1998). Young children use motive information to make trait inferences. *Developmental Psychology, 34*, 310–321.

Heyman, G., and Gelman, S. A. (1999). The use of trait labels in making psychological inferences. *Child Development, 70*, 604–619.

Heyman, G. D., and Gelman, S. A. (2000a). Beliefs about the origins of human psychological traits. *Developmental Psychology, 36*, 665–678.

Heyman, G. D. and Gelman, S. A. (2000b). Preschool children's use of novel predicates to make inductive inferences about people. *Cognitive Development, 15*, 263–280.

Heyman, G. D., and Gelman, S. A. (2000c). Preschool children's use of trait labels to make inductive inferences. *Journal of Experimental Child Psychology, 77*, 1–19.

Hickling, A. K., and Gelman, S. A. (1995). How does your garden grow? Evidence of an early conception of plants as biological kinds. *Child Development, 66*, 856–876.

Hickling, A. K., and Wellman, H. M. (2001). The emergence of children's causal explanations and theories: Evidence from everyday conversation. *Developmental Psychology, 37*, 668–683.

Hill, J., and Mannheim, B. (1992). Language and world view. *Annual Review of Anthropology, 21*, 381–406.

Hird, M. J., and Germon, J. (2001). The intersexual body and the medical regulation of gender. In K. Backett-Milburn and L. McKie (Eds.), *Constructing gendered bodies*. New York: Palgrave.

Hirschfeld, L. A. (1995). Do children have a theory of race? *Cognition, 54*, 209–252.

Hirschfeld, L. A. (1996). *Race in the making: Cognition, culture, and the child's construction of human kinds*. Cambridge: MIT Press.

Hirschfeld, L. A. (2002). Why don't anthropologists like children? *American Anthropologist, 104*.

Hirschfeld, L. A., and Gelman, S. A. (1997). What young children think about the relation between language variation and social difference. *Cognitive Development, 12*, 213–238.

Hoffner, C., and Cantor, J. (1985). Developmental differences in responses to a television character's appearance and behavior. *Developmental Psychology, 21*, 1065–1074.

Holland, J. H., Holyoak, K. J., Nisbett, R. E., and Thagard, P. R. (1986). *Induction: Processes of inference, learning, and discovery*. Cambridge, MA: MIT Press.

Hollander, M. A., Gelman, S. A., and Star, J. (in press). Children's interpretation of generic noun phrases. *Developmental Psychology*.

Holmes, W. G., and Sherman, P. W. (1983). Kin recognition in animals. *American Scientist, 71*, 46–55.

Hull, C. L. (1920). *Quantitative aspects of the evolution of concepts, an experimental study*. Princeton, NJ: Psychological Review Company.

Hunn, E. S. (1998). Atran's biodiversity parser: Doubts about hierarchy and autonomy. *Behavioral and Brain Sciences, 21*, 576–577.

Hutchinson, J. E., and Herman, J. P. (1991). *The development of word-learning strategies in delayed children.* Paper presented at the Boston University Conference on Language Development.

Hutchinson, J., Inn, D., and Strapp, C. (1993). *A longitudinal study of one year-olds' acquisition of the mutual exclusivity and lexical gap assumptions.* Paper presented at the Stanford Child Language Research Forum.

Imai, M. (1995). Asymmetry in the taxonomic assumption: Word learning versus property induction. In E. V. Clark (Ed.), *The proceedings of the 27th annual Child Language Research Forum.* Chicago, IL: Center for the Study of Language and Information.

Imai, M., and Gentner, D. (1997). A cross-linguistic study of early word meaning: Universal ontology and linguistic influence. *Cognition, 62,* 169–200.

Imai, M., Gentner, D., and Uchida, N. (1994). Children's theories of word meaning: The role of shape similarity in early acquisition. *Cognitive Development, 9,* 45–75.

Inagaki, K., and Hatano, G. (1993). Young children's understanding of the mind-body distinction. *Child Development, 64,* 1534–1549.

Inagaki, K., and Hatano, G. (1996). Young children's recognition of commonalities between animals and plants. *Child Development, 67,* 2823–2840.

Inagaki, K., and Hatano, G. (2002). *Young children's naïve thinking about the biological world.* New York: Psychology Press.

Inhelder, B., and Piaget, J. (1958). *The growth of logical thinking from childhood to adolescence.* New York: Basic Books.

Inhelder, B., and Piaget, J. (1964). *The early growth of logic in the child.* New York: Norton.

Jackendoff, R. (1983). *Semantics and cognition.* Cambridge, MA: MIT Press.

James, W. (1890/1983). *The principles of psychology.* Cambridge, MA: Harvard University Press.

Jaswal, V. K., and Markman, E. M. (2002). *Effects of non-intuitive labels on toddlers' inferences.* Paper presented at the annual meeting of the International Conference on Infant Studies.

Jayaratne, T. (2001). *National sample of adults' beliefs about genetic bases to race and gender.* Unpublished raw data, University of Michigan.

Johannsen, G. (1973). Visual perception of biological motion and a model for its analysis. *Perception and Psychophysics, 14,* 201–211.

Johnson, A., and Ames, E. (1994). The influence of gender labelling on preschoolers' gender constancy judgements. *British Journal of Developmental Psychology, 12,* 241–249.

Johnson, C., and Keil, F. (2000). Explanatory knowledge and conceptual combination. In F. C. Keil and R. A. Wilson (Eds.), *Explanation and cognition* (pp. 327–359). Cambridge, MA: MIT Press.

Johnson, C. N. (1990). If you had my brain, where would I be? Children's understanding of the brain and identity. *Child Development, 61,* 962–972.

Johnson, C. N., and Jacobs, M. G. (2001, April). *Enchanted objects: How positive connections transform thinking about the very nature of things.* Poster presented at the meeting of the Society for Research in Child Development, Minneapolis, MN.

Johnson, K. E., and Eilers, A. T. (1998). Effects of knowledge and development on subordinate level categorization. *Cognitive Development, 13,* 515–545.

Johnson, K., Mervis, C., and Boster, J. (1992). Developmental changes within the structure of the mammal domain. *Developmental Psychology, 28,* 74–83.

Johnson, S. C., and Carey, S. (1998). Knowledge enrichment and conceptual change in folkbiology: Evidence from Williams syndrome. *Cognitive Psychology, 37,* 156–200.

Johnson, S. C., Slaughter, V., and Carey, S. (1998). Whose gaze will infants follow? The elicitation of gaze following in 12-month-olds. *Developmental Science, 1*, 233–238.

Johnson, S. C., and Solomon, G. E. A. (1997). Why dogs have puppies and cats have kittens: The role of birth in young children's understanding of biological origins. *Child Development, 68*, 404–419.

Johnson-Laird, P. N., and Byrne, R. M. J. (1991). *Deduction.* Hillsdale, NJ: Erlbaum.

Johnson-Laird, P. N., and Wason, P. C. (Eds.). (1977). *Thinking: Readings in cognitive science.* New York: Cambridge University Press.

Jones, S., and Smith, L. (1993). The place of perception in children's concepts. *Cognitive Development, 8*, 113–39.

Jones, S. S., Smith, L. B., and Landau, B. (1991). Object properties and knowledge in early lexical learning. *Child Development, 62*, 499–516.

Josephson, J. R., and Josephson, S. G. (Eds.). (1994). *Abductive inference: Computation, philosophy, technology.* New York: Cambridge University Press.

Kahneman, D., Slovic, P., and Tversky, A. (Eds.). (1982). *Judgment under uncertainty: Heuristics and biases.* New York: Cambridge University Press.

Kaiser, M. K., McCloskey, M., and Proffitt, D. R. (1986). Development of intuitive theories of motion: Curvilinear motion in the absence of external forces. *Developmental Psychology, 22*, 67–71.

Kalish, C. W. (1995). Graded membership in animal and artifact categories. *Memory and Cognition, 23*, 335–353.

Kalish, C. W. (1996). Preschoolers' understanding of germs as invisible mechanisms. *Cognitive Development, 11*, 83–106.

Kalish, C. W. (1998). Natural and artificial kinds: Are children realists or relativists about categories? *Developmental Psychology, 34*, 376–391.

Kalish, C. W. (2001). *Children's inductive inferences about natural and intentional causal relations.* Unpublished ms., University of Wisconsin-Madison.

Kalish, C. W. (2002). Gold, jade, and emeruby: The value of naturalness for theories of concepts and categories. *Journal of Theoretical and Philosophical Psychology, 22*, 45–56.

Kalish, C. W., and Gelman, S. A. (1992). On wooden pillows: Young children's understanding of category implications. *Child Development, 63*, 1536–1557.

Kamp, H., and Partee, B. (1995). Prototype theory and compositionality. *Cognition, 57*, 129–191.

Kanouse, D. E. (1987). Language, labeling, and attribution. In E. E. Jones (Ed.), *Attribution: Perceiving the causes of behavior* (pp. 121–135). Hillsdale, NJ: Erlbaum.

Kanouse, D. E., and Abelson, R. P. (1967). Language variables affecting the persuasiveness of simple communications. *Journal of Personality and Social Psychology, 7*, 158–163.

Karmiloff-Smith, A. (1977). More about the same: Children's understanding of post-articles. *Journal of Child Language, 4*, 377–394.

Karmiloff-Smith, A. (1979). *A functional approach to child language: A study of determiners and reference.* Cambridge: Cambridge University Press.

Karmiloff-Smith, A. (1992). *Beyond modularity: A developmental perspective on cognitive science.* Cambridge, MA: MIT Press.

Karniol, R. (1980). A conceptual analysis of immanent justice responses in children. *Child Development, 51*, 118–130.

Katz, N., Baker, E., and Macnamara, J. (1974). What's in a name? A study of how children learn common and proper names. *Child Development, 45*, 469–473.

Keil, F. C. (1979). *Semantic and conceptual development: An ontological perspective.* Cambridge, MA: Harvard University Press.

Keil, F. C. (1987). Conceptual development and category structure. In U. Neisser (Ed.), *Concepts and conceptual development: Ecological and intellectual factors in categorization* (pp. 175–200). New York: Cambridge University Press.

Keil, F. (1989). *Concepts, kinds, and cognitive development.* Cambridge, MA: Bradford Book/MIT Press.

Keil, F. (1994). The birth and nurturance of concepts by domains: The origins of concepts of living things. In L. A. Hirschfeld and S. A. Gelman (Eds.), *Mapping the mind: Domain specificity in cognition and culture* (pp. 234–254). New York: Cambridge University Press.

Keil, F. C. (1995). *The growth of causal understandings of natural kinds.* In D. Sperber, D. Premack, and A. Premack (Eds.), *Causal cognition: A multidisciplinary debate* (pp. 234–262). Oxford: Oxford University Press.

Keil, F. C. (1998). Words, moms, and things: Language as a road map to reality. *Monographs of the Society for Research in Child Development, 63,* 149–157.

Keil, F. C., and Richardson, D. C. (1999). Species, stuff, and patterns of causation. In R. A. Wilson (Ed.), *Species: New interdisciplinary essays.* Cambridge, MA: MIT Press.

Keil, F. C., Smith, W. C., Simons, D. J., and Levin, D. T. (1998). Two dogmas of conceptual empiricism: Implications for hybrid models of the structure of knowledge. *Cognition, 65,* 103–135.

Kelemen, D. (1999a). The scope of teleological thinking in preschool children. *Cognition, 70,* 241–272.

Kelemen, D. (1999b). Why are rocks pointy? Children's preference for teleological explanations of the natural world. *Developmental Psychology, 35,* 1440–1452.

Kelley, H. H. (1967). Attribution theory in social psychology. *Nebraska symposium on motivation, 15,* 192–238.

Kemler Nelson, D. G. (1999). Attention to functional properties in toddlers' naming and problem-solving. *Cognitive Development, 14,* 77–100.

Kemler Nelson, D. G., and 11 Swarthmore College Students. (1995). Principle-based inferences in young children's categorization: Revisiting the impact of function on the naming of artifacts. *Cognitive Development, 10,* 347–380.

Kemler Nelson, D. G., Frankenfield, A., Morris, C., and Blair, E. (2000). Young children's use of functional information to categorize artifacts: Three factors that matter. *Cognition, 77,* 133–168.

Kemler Nelson, D. G., Russell, R., Duke, N., and Jones, K. (2000). Two-year-olds will name artifacts by their functions. *Child Development, 71,* 1271–1288.

King-Smith, D. (1983). *Babe: The gallant pig.* New York: Crown.

Kirkham, N. Z., Slemmer, J. A., and Johnson, S. P. (2002). Visual statistical learning in infancy: Evidence of a domain general learning mechanism. *Cognition, 83,* B35–B42.

Kister, M. C., and Patterson, C. J. (1980). Children's conceptions of the causes of illness: Understanding of contagion and use of immanent justice. *Child Development, 51,* 839–846.

Kohlberg, L. (1966). A cognitive-developmental analysis of children's sex-role concepts and attitudes. In E. Maccoby (Ed.), *The development of sex differences* (pp. 82–173). Palo Alto, CA: Stanford University Press.

Kolstad, V., and Baillargeon, R. (1996). *Appearance- and knowledge-based responses of 10.5-month-old infants to containers.* Unpublished ms., University of Illinois.

Kornblith, H. (1993). *Inductive inference and its natural ground: An essay in naturalistic epistemology.* Cambridge, MA: MIT Press.

Koslowski, B. (1996). *Theory and evidence: The development of scientific reasoning.* Cambridge, MA: MIT Press.

Krascum, R. M., and Andrews, S. (1998). The effects of theories on children's acquisition of family-resemblance categories. *Child Development, 69,* 333–346.

Krifka, M. (1995). Common nouns: A contrastive analysis of Chinese and English. In G. N. Carlson and F. J. Pelletier (Eds.), *The generic book* (pp. 398–411). Chicago: Chicago University Press.

Krifka, M., Pelletier, F. J., Carlson, G. N., ter Meulen, A., Link, G., and Chierchia, G. (1995). Genericity: An introduction. In G. N. Carlson and F. J. Pelletier (Eds.), *The generic book* (pp. 1–124). Chicago: Chicago University Press.

Kripke, S. (1971). Identity and necessity. In M. K. Munitz (Ed.), *Identity and individuation.* New York: New York University Press.

Kripke, S. (1972). Naming and necessity. In D. Davidson and G. Harman (Eds.), *Semantics of natural language.* Dordrecht: D. Reidel.

Kuczaj, S. (1976). *-Ing, -s and -ed: A study of the acquisition of certain verb inflections.* Ph.D. dissertation, University of Minnesota.

Kuczaj, S. A. (1982). Young children's overextensions of object words in comprehension and/or production: Support for a prototype theory of early object word meaning. *First Language, 3,* 93–105.

Kuczaj, S. A. (1986). Thoughts on the intentional basis of early object word extension: Evidence from comprehension and production. In S. A. Kuczaj and M. D. Barrett (Eds.), *The development of word meaning* (pp. 99–120). New York: Springer-Verlag.

Kuhn, D. (1989). Children and adults as intuitive scientists. *Psychological Review, 96,* 674–689.

Kuhn, D. (1995). Microgenetic study of change: What has it told us? *Psychological Science, 6,* 133–139.

Kuzmak, S. D., and Gelman, R. (1986). Young children's understanding of random phenomena. *Child Development, 57,* 559–566.

Labov, W. (1973). The boundaries of words and their meanings. In C. N. Bailey and R. W. Shy (Eds.), *New ways of analyzing variations in English* (pp. 340–373). Washington, DC: Georgetown University Press.

Lakoff, G. (1987). *Women, fire, and dangerous things.* Chicago: University of Chicago Press.

Lamberts, K. (1995). Categorization under time pressure. *Journal of Experimental Psychology: General, 124,* 161–180.

Landau, B. (1982). Will the real grandmother please stand up? The psychological reality of dual meaning representations. *Journal of Psycholinguistic Research, 11,* 47–62.

Landau, B., Jones, S. S., and Smith, L. B (1992). Perception, ontology, and naming in young children: Commentary on Soja, Carey, and Spelke. *Cognition, 43,* 85–91.

Landau, B., Smith, L. B., and Jones, S. S. (1988). The importance of shape in early lexical learning. *Cognitive Development, 3,* 299–321.

Landau, B., Smith, L. B., and Jones, S. S. (1998). Object shape, object function, and object name. *Journal of Memory and Language, 38,* 1–27.

Langer, E. J. (1975). The illusion of control. *Journal of Personality and Social Psychology, 32,* 311–328.

Langer, E., and Roth, S. (1975). Heads I win, tails it's chance: The illusion of control as a function of the sequence of outcomes in a purely chance task. *Journal of Personality and Social Psychology, 32,* 951–955.

Lawler, J. M. (1973). Tracking the generic toad. *Papers from the ninth regional meeting of the Chicago Linguistic Society* (pp. 320–331). Chicago: Chicago Linguistic Society.

Leslie, A. M. (1994). ToMM, ToBY, and Agency: Core architecture and domain specificity. In L. A. Hirschfeld and S. A. Gelman (Eds.), *Mapping the mind: Domain specificity in cognition and culture* (pp. 119–148). New York: Cambridge University Press.

Leslie, A. M., and Keeble, S. (1987). Do six-month-old infants perceive causality? *Cognition, 25,* 265–288.

Levinson, S. C. (1996). Language and space. *Annual Review of Anthropology, 25,* 353–382.

Lévi-Strauss, C. (1963). *Totemism.* Boston: Beacon Press.

Levy, G., Taylor, M. G., and Gelman, S. A. (1995). Traditional and evaluative aspects of flexibility in gender roles, social conventions, moral rules, and physical laws. *Child Development, 66,* 515–531.

Li, P., and Bowerman, M. (1998). The acquisition of lexical and grammatical aspect in Chinese. *First Language, 18,* 311–350.

Liben, L. S., and Signorella, M. L. (Eds.). (1987). *Children's gender schemata. (New Directions for Child Development,* No. 38.) San Francisco: Jossey-Bass.

Lieven, E. V. M. (1994). Crosslinguistic and crosscultural aspects of language addressed to children. In C. Gallaway and B. J. Richards (Eds.), *Input and interaction in language acquisition* (pp. 56–73). Cambridge University Press.

Liittschwager, J. C., and Markman, E. M. (1993). *Young children's understanding of proper nouns versus common nouns.* Poster presented at the biennial meeting of the Society for Research in Child Development, New Orleans, LA.

Lillard, A. (1999). Developing a cultural theory of mind: The CIAO approach. *Current Directions in Psychological Science, 8,* 57–61.

Litt, C. J. (1986). Theories of transitional object attachment: An overview. *International Journal of Behavioral Development, 9,* 383–399.

Livesley, W. J., and Bromley, B. D. (1973). *Person perception in childhood and adolescence.* New York: Basic.

Lizotte, D. J., and Gelman, S. A. (1999). *Essentialism in children's categories.* Poster presented at the Cognitive Development Society, Chapel Hill, NC.

Lo, Y., Sides, A., Rozelle, J., and Osherson, D. (2002). Evidential diversity and premise probability in young children's inductive judgment. *Cognitive Science, 26,* 181–206.

Locke, J. (1959). *An essay concerning human understanding,* vol. 2. New York: Dover. (Originally published in 1671.)

López, A., Gelman, S. A., Gutheil, G., and Smith, E. E. (1992). The development of category-based induction. *Child Development, 63,* 1070–1090.

Lucariello, J., and Nelson, K. (1986). Context effects on lexical specificity in maternal and child discourse. *Journal of Child Language, 13,* 507–522.

Lucy, J. (1992). *Language diversity and thought: A reformulation of the linguistic relativity hypothesis.* New York: Cambridge University Press.

Lucy, J. (1997). Linguistic relativity. *Annual Review of Anthropology, 26,* 291–312.

Lugaresi, E., Gambetti, P., and Rossi, P. (1966). Chronic neurogenic muscular atrophies of infancy: Their nosological relationships with Werdnig-Hoffman's disease. *Journal of Neurological Science, 3,* 399–407.

Lynch, E., Coley, J., and Medin, D. (2000). Tall is typical: Central tendency, ideal dimensions and graded category structure among tree experts and novices. *Memory and Cognition, 28,* 41–50.

Lyons, J. (1977). *Semantics, Vol. 1.* New York: Cambridge University Press.

Macario, J. F., Shipley, E. F., and Billman, D. O. (1990). Induction from a single instance: Formation of a novel category. *Journal of Experimental Child Psychology, 50,* 179–199.

Macnamara, J. (1982). *Names for things.* Cambridge, MA: MIT Press/Bradford Book.

Macnamara, J. (1986). *A border dispute.* Cambridge, MA: MIT Press.

MacWhinney, B. (1987). The competition model. In B. MacWhinney (Ed.), *Mechanisms of language acquisition* (pp. 249–308). Hillsdale, NJ: Erlbaum.

MacWhinney, B. (1991). *The CHILDES project: Tools for analyzing talk.* Hillsdale, NJ: Erlbaum.

MacWhinney, B., and Snow, C. (1985). The child language data exchange system. *Journal of Child Language, 12,* 271–296.

MacWhinney, B., and Snow, C. (1990). The child language data exchange system: An update. *Journal of Child Language, 17,* 457–472.

Mahalingam, R. (1998). *Essentialism, power, and representation of caste: A developmental study.* Ph.D. dissertation, University of Pittsburgh.

Mahalingam, R., Philip, C., and Akiyama, M. (2001, July). *Expertise, essentialism and folk theories about the genetic causes of social differences: An expert-novice study.* Paper presented at the Annual Meeting of International Society for Political Psychology, Cuernavaca, Mexico.

Maloney, L. T., and Gelman, S. A. (1987). Measuring the influence of context: The interpretation of dimensional objectives. *Language and Cognitive Processes, 2,* 205–215.

Malt, B. C. (1990). Features and beliefs in the mental representation of categories. *Journal of Memory and Language, 29,* 289–315.

Malt, B. C. (1994). Water is not H_2O. *Cognitive Psychology, 27,* 41–70.

Malt, B. C., and Johnson, E. C. (1998). Artifact category membership and the intentional-historical theory. *Cognition, 66,* 79–85.

Malt, B. C., and Smith, E. E. (1984). Correlated properties in natural categories. *Journal of Verbal Learning and Verbal Behavior, 23,* 250–269.

Mandler, J. M. (1988). How to build a baby: On the development of an accessible representational system. *Cognitive Development, 3,* 113–136.

Mandler, J. M. (1992). How to build a baby: II. Conceptual primitives. *Psychological Review, 99,* 587–604.

Mandler, J. M. (1993). On concepts. *Cognitive Development, 8,* 141–148.

Mandler, J. M., Bauer, P. J., and McDonough, L. (1991). Separating the sheep from the goats: Differentiating global categories. *Cognitive Psychology, 23,* 263–298.

Mandler, J. M., and McDonough, L. (1993). Concept formation in infancy. *Cognitive Development, 8,* 291–318.

Mandler, J. M., and McDonough, L. (1996). Drinking and driving don't mix: Inductive generalization in infancy. *Cognition, 59,* 307–335.

Mandler, J. M., and McDonough, L. (1998). Studies in inductive inference in infancy. *Cognitive Psychology, 37,* 60–96.

Mangelsdorf, S. C. (1992). Developmental changes in infant-stranger interaction. *Infant Behavior and Development, 15*, 191–208.

Maratsos, M. (1974). Preschool children's use of definite and indefinite articles. *Child Development, 45*, 446–455.

Maratsos, M. P. (1976). *The use of definite and indefinite reference in young children.* New York: Cambridge University Press.

Maratsos, M., and Chalkley, M. A. (1980). The internal language of children's syntax. In K. Nelson (Ed.), *Children's language* (Vol. 2, pp. 127–213). New York: Gardner Press.

Marcus, G. F. (2000). Pabiku and Ga Ti Ga: Two mechanisms infants use to learn about the world. *Current Directions in Psychological Science, 9*, 145–147.

Marcus, G. F., Pinker, S., Ullman, M., Hollander, M., Rosen, T. J., and Xu, F. (1992). Overgeneralization in language acquisition. *Monographs of the Society for Research in Child Development, 57* (serial no. 228), 1–182.

Markman, E. M. (1976). Children's difficulty with word-referent differentiation. *Child Development, 47*, 742–749.

Markman, E. M. (1989). *Categorization and naming in children: Problems in induction.* Cambridge: Bradford Book/MIT Press.

Markman, E. M. (1992). Constraints on word learning: Speculations about their nature, origins, and domain specificity. In M. A. Gunnar and M. Maratsos (Eds.), *Modularity and constraints in language and cognition* (pp. 59–101). Hillsdale, NJ: Erlbaum.

Markman, E. M., and Callanan, M. A. (1983). An analysis of hierarchical classification. In R. Sternberg (Ed.), *Advances in the psychology of human intelligence* (Vol. 2). Hillsdale, NJ: Erlbaum.

Markman, E. M., Cox, B., and Machida, S. (1981). The standard object sorting task as a measure of conceptual organization. *Developmental Psychology, 17*, 115–117.

Markman, E. M., and Hutchinson, J. E. (1984). Children's sensitivity to constraints on word meaning: Taxonomic versus thematic relations. *Cognitive Psychology, 16*, 1–27.

Markson, L., and Bloom, P. (1997). Evidence against a dedicated system for word learning in children. *Nature, 385*, 813–815.

Marler, P. (1991). The instinct to learn. In S. Carey and R. Gelman (Eds.), *The epigenesis of mind: Essays on biology and cognition* (pp. 37–66). Hillsdale, NJ: Erlbaum.

Marr, D. (1982). *Vision.* New York: W. H. Freeman.

Martin, C. L. (1989). Children's use of gender related information in making social judgments. *Developmental Psychology, 25*, 80–88.

Martin, C. L., and Parker, S. (1995). Folk theories about sex and race differences. *Personality and Social Psychology Bulletin, 21*, 45–57.

Martinez, I. M., and Shatz, M. (1996). Linguistic influences on categorization in preschool children: A crosslinguistic study. *Journal of Child Language, 23*, 529–545.

Massey, C., and Gelman, R. (1988). Preschoolers' ability to decide whether a photographed unfamiliar object can move itself. *Developmental Psychology, 24*, 307–317.

Mayr, E. (1982). *The growth of biological thought.* Cambridge, MA: Harvard University Press.

Mayr, E. (1988). *Toward a new philosophy of biology: Observations of an evolutionist.* Cambridge, MA: Belknap Press of Harvard University Press.

Mayr, E. (1991). *One long argument: Charles Darwin and the genesis of modern evolutionary thought.* Cambridge, MA: Harvard University Press.

McCarrell, N., and Callanan, M. (1995). Form-function correspondences in children's inference. *Child Development, 66*, 532–546.

McCawley, J. D. (1981). *Everything that linguists have always wanted to know about logic.* Chicago: University of Chicago Press.

McCloskey, D. N. (1999). *Crossing: A memoir.* Chicago, IL: University of Chicago Press.

McCloskey, M. (1983). Intuitive physics. *Scientific American, 248*, 122–130.

McCloskey, M. E., and Glucksberg, S. (1978). Natural categories: Well defined or fuzzy sets? *Memory and Cognition, 6*, 462–472.

McConnell, J. V. (1962). Memory transfer through cannibalism in planarians. *Journal of Neuropsychiatry* (Suppl.), 42–48.

McDonald, K. A. (1998, October 30). Genetically speaking, race doesn't exist. *Chronicle of Higher Education*, p. A19.

McDonough, L., and Mandler, J. M. (1998). Inductive generalization in 9- and 11-month-olds. *Developmental Science, 1*, 227–232.

McGarrigle, J., and Donaldson, M. (1974). Conservation accidents. *Cognition, 3*, 341–350.

McNamara, T. P., and Sternberg, R. J. (1983). Mental models of word meaning. *Journal of Verbal Learning and Verbal Behavior, 22*, 449–474.

McNaught, H. (1978). *The truck book.* New York: Random House

Medin, D. (1989). Concepts and conceptual structure. *American Psychologist, 44*, 1469–81.

Medin, D. L., and Ortony, A. (1989). Psychological essentialism. In S. Vosniadou and A. Ortony (Eds.), *Similarity and analogical reasoning* (pp. 179–195). Cambridge: Cambridge University Press.

Medin, D. L., and Shoben, E. J. (1988). Context and structure in conceptual combination. *Cognitive Psychology, 20*, 158–190.

Medin, D. L., Wattenmaker, W. D., and Hampson, S. E. (1987). Family resemblance, conceptual cohesiveness, and category construction. *Cognitive Psychology, 19*, 242–279.

Mehler, J., and Fox, R. (1985). *Neonate cognition: Beyond the blooming, buzzing confusion.* Hillsdale, NJ: Erlbaum Associates.

Merriman, W. E., and Bowman, L. L. (1989). The mutual exclusivity bias in children's word learning. *Monographs of the Society for Research in Child Development*, Vol. 54, No. 3–4 (Serial No. 220).

Mervis, C. B., Johnson, K. E., and Scott, P. (1993). Perceptual knowledge, conceptual knowledge, and expertise: Comment on Jones and Smith. *Cognitive Development, 8*, 149–155.

Mervis, C. B., and Mervis, C. A. (1988). Role of adult input in young children's category evolution. I. An observational study. *Journal of Child Language, 15*, 257–272.

Mervis, C. B., and Pani, J. R. (1980). Acquisition of basic object categories. *Cognitive Psychology, 12*, 496–522.

Mervis, C. B., and Rosch, E. (1981). Categorization of natural objects. In M. R. Rosenzweig and L. W. Porter (Eds.), *Annual review of psychology, vol. 32.* Palo Alto, CA: Annual Reviews.

Metz, K. E. (1998). Emergent understanding and attribution of randomness: Comparative analysis of the reasoning of primary grade children and undergraduates. *Cognition and Instruction, 16*, 285–365.

Michotte, A. (1963). *The perception of causality.* New York: Basic Books.

Mill, J. S. (1843). *A system of logic, ratiocinative and inductive.* London: Longmans.

Miller, J. L., and Bartsch, K. (1997). The development of biological explanation: Are children vitalists? *Developmental Psychology, 33*, 156–164.

Miller, P. H., and Aloise, P. A. (1989). Young children's understanding of the psychological causes of behavior: A review. *Child Development, 60*, 257–285.

Moravcsik, J. (1994). Essences, powers, and generic propositions. In T. Scaltsas, D. Charles, and M. Gill (Eds.), *Unity, identity, and explanation in Aristotle's Metaphysics* (pp. 229–244). Oxford: Blackwell.

Morford, J. P., and Goldin-Meadow, S. (1997). From here to there and now to then: The development of displaced reference in homesign and English. *Child Development, 68,* 420–435.

Morison, P., and Gardner, H. (1978). Dragons and dinosaurs: The child's capacity to differentiate fantasy from reality. *Child Development, 49,* 642–648.

Morris, M. W., Nisbett, R. E., and Peng, K. (1995). Causality across domains and cultures. In D. Sperber, D. Premack, and A. J. Premack (Eds.) *Causal cognition.* New York: Oxford University Press.

Morris, S. C., Taplin, J. E., and Gelman, S. A. (2000). Vitalism in naive biological thinking. *Developmental Psychology, 36,* 582–595.

Moser, D. J. (1996). *Abstract thinking and thought in ancient Chinese and early Greek.* Ph.D. dissertation, University of Michigan, Ann Arbor.

Murphy, G. L. (2002). *The big book of concepts.* Cambridge, MA: MIT Press.

Murphy, G. L. (1993). Theories and concept formation. In I. Van Mechelen, J. Hampton, R. Michalski, and P. Theuns (Eds.), *Categories and concepts: Theoretical views and inductive data analysis* (pp. 173–200). New York: Academic Press.

Murphy, G. L., and Medin, D. L. (1985). The role of theories in conceptual coherence. *Psychological Review, 92,* 289–316.

Naigles, L., and Gelman, S. A. (1995). Overextensions in comprehension and production revisited: Preferential-looking in a study of "dog," "cat," and "cow." *Journal of Child Language, 22,* 19–46.

Naigles, L. R., and Terrazas, P. (1998). Motion-verb generalizations in English and Spanish: Influences of language and syntax. *Psychological Science, 9,* 363–369.

Nave, A. (2000). Marriage and the maintenance of ethnic group boundaries: The case of Mauritius. *Ethnic and Racial Studies, 23,* 32952.

Neisser, U. (Ed.) (1987). *Concepts and conceptual development: Ecological and intellectual factors in categorization.* New York: Cambridge University Press.

Nelson, K. (1973). Structure and strategy in learning to talk. *Monographs of the Society for Research in Child Development, 38* (1 and 2, Serial No. 149).

Nelson, K. (1974). Concept, word, and sentence: Interrelations in acquisition and development. *Psychological Review, 81,* 267–285.

Nelson, K., Rescorla, L., Gruendel, J., and Benedict, H. (1978). Early lexicons: What do they mean? *Child Development, 49,* 960–968.

Nemeroff, C., and Rozin, P. (1989). "You are what you eat": Applying the demand-free "impressions" technique to an unacknowledged belief. *Ethos, 17,* 50–69.

Nisbett, R. E., Krantz, D. H., Jepson, C., and Kunda, Z. (1983). The use of statistical heuristics in everyday inductive reasoning. *Psychological Review, 90,* 339–363.

Nisbett, R. E., Peng, K., Choi, I., and Norenzayan, A. (2001). Culture and systems of thought: Holistic versus analytic cognition. *Psychological Review, 108,* 291–310.

Nisbett, R. E., and Ross, L. (1980). *Human inference: Strategies and shortcomings of social judgment.* Englewood Cliffs, NJ: Prentice-Hall.

Nosofsky, R. M. (1992). Exemplars, prototypes, and similarity rules. In W. K. Estes (Ed.), *From learning theory to connectionist theory: Essays in honor of William K. Estes.* Hillsdale, NJ: Erlbaum.

Nosofsky, R. M., Kruschke, J. K., and McKinley, S. C. (1992). Combining exemplar-based category representations and connectionist learning rules. *Journal of Experimental Psychology: Learning, Memory, and Cognition, 18*, 211–233.

Oakes, L. M., and Cohen, L. B. (1990). Infant perception of a causal event. *Cognitive Development, 5*, 193–207.

Opfer, J. E. (2000). *Developing a biological understanding of goal-directed action.* Ph.D. dissertation, University of Michigan, Ann Arbor.

Opfer, J. E., and Gelman, S. A. (2001). Children's and adults' models for predicting teleological action: The development of a biology-based model. *Child Development, 72,* 1367–1381.

Osherson, D., and Smith, E. E. (1997). On typicality and vagueness. *Cognition, 64,* 189–206.

Osherson, D. N., Smith, E. E., Wilkie, O., López, A., and Shafir, E. (1990). Category-based induction. *Psychological Review, 97,* 185–200.

Pappas, A., and Gelman, S. A. (1998). Generic noun phrases in mother-child conversations. *Journal of Child Language, 25,* 19–33.

Parker, D. S. (1998). *The idea of the middle class: White-collar workers and Peruvian society, 1900–1950.* University Park, PA: Pennsylvania State University Press.

Parritz, R. H., Mangelsdorf, S., and Gunnar, M. R. (1992). Control, social referencing, and the infants' appraisal of threat. In S. Feinman (Ed.), *Social referencing and the social construction of reality in infancy* (pp. 209–228). New York: Plenum.

Passman, R. H. (1987). Attachments to inanimate objects: Are children who have security blankets insecure? *Journal of Consulting and Clinical Psychology, 55,* 825–830.

Peevers, B. H., and Secord, P. F. (1973). Developmental changes in attribution of descriptive concepts to persons. *Journal of Personality and Social Psychology, 27,* 120–128.

Petrovich, O. (1999). Preschool children's understanding of the dichotomy between the natural and the artificial. *Psychological Reports, 84,* 3–27.

Piaget, J. (1929). *The child's conception of the world.* London: Routledge and Kegan Paul.

Piaget, J. (1930). *The child's conception of physical causality.* London: Kegan Paul.

Piaget, J. (1948). *The moral judgment of the child.* Glencoe, IL: Free Press.

Piaget, J. (1970). Piaget's theory. In P. H. Mussen (Ed.), *Carmichael's manual of child psychology* (Vol. 1). New York: Wiley.

Piaget, J., and Inhelder, B. (1975). *The origin of the idea of chance in children.* New York: Norton.

Pinker, S. (1994). *The language instinct.* New York: W. Morrow.

Pinker, S. (2002). *The blank slate: The denial of human nature in modern intellectual life.* New York: Viking/Penguin.

Popper, K. R., and Eccles, J. C. (1977). *The self and its brain.* New York: Springer.

Povinelli, D. J. (2000). *Folk physics for apes: The chimpanzee's theory of how the world works.* Oxford: Oxford University Press.

Prasada, S. (2000). Acquiring generic knowledge. *Trends in Cognitive Sciences, 4,* 66–72.

Premack, D. (1986). *Gavagai! Or the future history of the animal language controversy.* Cambridge, MA: MIT Press.

Putnam, H. (1970). Is semantics possible? In H. E. Kiefer and M. K. Munitz (Eds.), *Language, belief, and metaphysics.* State University of New York Press.

Putnam, H. (1973). Meaning and reference. *Journal of Philosophy, 70,* 699–711.

Putnam, H. (1975). The meaning of "meaning." In H. Putnam, *Mind, language, and reality* (pp. 215–271). Cambridge: Cambridge University Press.

Quine, W. V. (1960). *Word and object.* Cambridge, MA: MIT Press.

Quine, W. V. (1977). Natural kinds. In S. P. Schwartz (Ed.), *Naming, necessity, and natural kinds* (pp. 155–175). Ithaca, NY: Cornell University Press.

Quinn, P. C., and Eimas, P. D. (1996). Perceptual organization and categorization in young infants. In C. Rovee-Collier and L. P. Lipsitt (Eds.), *Advances in infancy research* (pp. 1–36). Norwood, NJ: Ablex.

Quinn, P. C., and Eimas, P. D. (1997). A reexamination of the perceptual-to-conceptual shift in mental representations. *Review of General Psychology, 1,* 171–187.

Rakison, D. H. (2000). When a rose is just a rose: The illusion of taxonomies in infant categorization. *Infancy, 1,* 77–90.

Rakison, D. H., and Butterworth, G. E. (1998). Infants' use of object parts in early categorization. *Developmental Psychology, 34,* 49–62.

Rakison, D. H., and Cohen, L. B. (1999). Infants' use of functional parts in basic-like categorization. *Developmental Science, 2,* 423–431.

Rakison, D. H., and Poulin-Dubois, D. (2001). The developmental origin of the animate-inanimate distinction. *Psychological Bulletin, 127,* 209–228.

Ramsey, P. (1987). Young children's thinking about ethnic differences. In J. Phinney and M. Rotheram (Eds.), *Children's ethnic socialization.* New York: Sage.

Rescorla, L. A. (1980). Overextension in early language development. *Journal of Child Language, 7,* 321–335.

Reznek, L. (1987). *The nature of disease.* New York: Routledge and Kegan Paul.

Rholes, W. S., and Ruble, D. N. (1984). Children's understanding of dispositional characteristics of others. *Child Development, 55,* 550–560.

Rips, L. J. (1975). Induction about natural categories. *Journal of Verbal Learning and Verbal Behavior, 14,* 665–681.

Rips, L. J. (1989). Similarity, typicality, and categorization. In S. Vosniadou and A. Ortony (Eds.), *Similarity and analogical reasoning.* New York: Cambridge University Press.

Rips, L. J., and Collins, A. (1993). Categories and resemblance. *Journal of Experimental Psychology: General, 122,* 468–486.

Robinson, W. P. (Ed.). (1996). *Social groups and identities: Developing the legacy of Henri Tajfel.* Boston: Butterworth-Heinemann.

Rosch, E. (1978). Principles of categorization. In E. Rosch and B. B. Lloyd (Eds.), *Cognition and categorization* (pp. 27–48). Hillsdale, NJ: Erlbaum.

Rosch, E., and Mervis, C. (1975). Family resemblances: Studies in the internal structure of natural categories. *Cognitive Psychology, 8,* 382–439.

Rosch, E., Mervis, C. B., Gray, W. D., Johnson, D. M., and Boyes-Braem, P. (1976). Basic objects in natural categories. *Cognitive Psychology, 8,* 382–439.

Rosen, A. B., and Rozin, P. (1993). Now you see it, now you don't: The preschool child's conception of invisible particles in the context of dissolving. *Developmental Psychology, 29,* 300–311.

Rosenberg, C. (1997). Banishing risk: Continuity and change in the moral management of disease. In A. Brandt and P. Rozin (Eds.), *Morality and health* (pp. 35–51). New York: Routledge.

Rosenblum, T., and Pinker, S. A. (1983). Word magic revisited: Monolingual and bilingual children's understanding of the word-object relationship. *Child Development, 54,* 773–780.

Rosengren, K. S., and Braswell, G. (2001). Variability in children's reasoning. In H. W. Reese and R. Kail (Eds.), *Advances in Child Development and Behavior, 28.* Academic Press.

Rosengren, K., Gelman, S. A., Kalish, C., and McCormick, M. (1991). As time goes by: Children's early understanding of biological growth. *Child Development, 62,* 1302–1320.

Rotenberg, K. J. (1982). Development of character constancy of self and other. *Child Development, 53,* 505–515.

Rothbart, M., and Park, B. (in press). The mental representation of social categories: Category boundaries, entitativity, and stereotype change. In V. Yzerbyt, C. M. Judd, and O. Corneille (Eds.), *The psychology of group perception: Contributions to the study of homogeneity, entitativity, and essentialism.* New York: Psychology Press.

Rothbart, M., and Taylor, M. (1990). Category labels and social reality: Do we view social categories as natural kinds? In G. Semin and K. Fiedler (Eds.), *Language and social cognition* (pp. 11–36). London: Sage.

Rothbart, M., and Taylor, M. (2001). Comment on Gil-White, "Are ethnic groups biological 'species' to the human brain?" *Current Anthropology, 42,* 544–545.

Rovee-Collier, C. K. (1993). The capacity for long-term memory in infancy. *Current Directions in Psychological Science, 2,* 130–135.

Rozin, P., and Nemeroff, C. (1990). The laws of sympathetic magic: A psychological analysis of similarity and contagion. In J. Stigler, R. Shweder, and G. Herdt (Eds.), *Cultural psychology: Essays on comparative human development.* New York: Cambridge University Press.

Sabbagh, M. A., and Baldwin, D. A. (2001). Learning words from knowledgeable versus ignorant speakers: Links between preschoolers' theory of mind and semantic development. *Child Development, 72,* 1054–1070.

Sachs, J. (1983). Talking about the there and then: The emergence of displaced reference in parent-child discourse. In K. E. Nelson (Ed.), *Children's language, Vol. 4.* Hillsdale, NJ: Erlbaum.

Saffran, J. R., Aslin, R. N., and Newport, E. L. (1996). Statistical learning by 8-month-old infants. *Science, 274,* 1926–1928.

Saint-Exupéry, A. de (1943). *Le petit prince.* New York: Reynal and Hitchcock.

Samarapungavan, A., and Wiers, R. W. (1997). Children's thoughts on the origin of species: A study of explanatory coherence. *Cognitive Science, 21,* 147–177.

Savage-Rumbaugh, S., Shanker, S. G., and Taylor, T. J. (1998). *Apes, language, and the human mind.* New York: Oxford University Press.

Schieffelin, B. B., and Ochs, E. (1986). Language socialization. *Annual Review of Anthropology, 15,* 163–191.

Schlottmann, A. (2001). Perception versus knowledge of cause and effect in children: When seeing is believing. *Current Directions in Psychological Science, 10,* 111–115.

Schor, N., and Weed, E. (Eds.). (1994). *Essential difference.* Indiana University Press.

Schwartz, S. P. (1977). (Ed.). *Naming, necessity, and natural kinds.* Ithaca: Cornell University Press.

Schwartz, S. P. (1979). Natural kind terms. *Cognition, 7,* 301–315.

Sera, M. D. (1992). To be or to be: Use and acquisition of the Spanish copulas. *Journal of Memory and Language, 31,* 408–427.

Sera, M., Rettinger, E., and Castillo-Pintado, J. (1991). Developing definitions of objects and events in English and Spanish speakers. *Cognitive Development, 6,* 119–143.

Seuss, Dr. [Theodore Geisel] (1940). *Horton hatches the egg.* New York: Random House.

Seuss, Dr. [Theodore Geisel] (1961). *The sneetches and other stories.* New York: Random House.

Shatz, M. (1991). Using cross-cultural research to inform us about the role of language in development: Comparisons of Japanese, Korean, and English, and of German, American English, and British English. In M. H. Bornstein (Ed.), *Cultural approaches to parenting* (pp. 139–153). Hillsdale, NJ: Erlbaum.

Shatz, M. (1994). *A toddler's life: Becoming a person.* New York: Oxford University Press.

Shi, R., Werker, J. F., and Morgan, J. L. (1999). Newborn infants' sensitivity to perceptual cues to lexical and grammatical words. *Cognition, 72,* B11–B21.

Shipley, E. F. (1989). Two kinds of hierarchies: Class inclusion hierarchies and kind hierarchies. *Genetic Epistemologist, 17,* 31–39.

Shipley, E. F. (1993). Categories, hierarchies, and induction. In D. Medin (Ed.), *The psychology of learning and motivation* (Vol. 30, pp. 265–301). New York: Academic Press.

Shipley, E. F. (2000). Children's categorization of objects: The relevance of behavior, surface appearance, and insides. In B. Landau, J. Sabini, J. Jonides, and E. Newport (Eds.), *Perception, cognition, and language: Essays in honor of Henry and Lila Gleitman* (pp. 69–85). Cambridge, MA: MIT Press.

Shoemaker, S. (1984). Personal identity—A materialist account. In S. Shoemaker and R. Swinburne (Eds.), *Personal identity.* Oxford: Basil Blackwell.

Shultz, T. R. (1982). Rules of causal attribution. *Monographs of the Society for Research in Child Development,* Vol. 47, No. 1 (Serial No. 194).

Siegal, M., and Robinson, J. (1987). Order effects in children's gender-constancy responses. *Developmental Psychology, 23,* 283–286.

Siegal, M., and Share, D. L. (1990). Contamination sensitivity in young children. *Developmental Psychology, 26,* 455–458.

Siegler, R. S. (1994). Cognitive variability: A key to understanding cognitive development. *Current Directions in Psychological Science, 3,* 1–5.

Siegler, R. S. (1998). *Children's thinking.* Upper Saddle River, NJ: Prentice Hall.

Siegler, R. S., and Crowley, K. (1991). The microgenetic method: A direct means for studying cognitive development. *American Psychologist, 46,* 606–620.

Siegler, R. S., and Ellis, S. (1996). Piaget on childhood. *Psychological Science, 7,* 211–215.

Sigel, I. E. (1953). Developmental trends in the abstraction ability of children. *Child Development, 24,* 131–144.

Sigel, I. E. (1978). The development of pictorial comprehension. In B. S. Randhawa and W. E. Coffman (Eds.), *Visual learning, thinking, and communication* (pp. 93–111). New York: Academic Press.

Signorella, M. L. (1987). Gender schemata: Individual differences and context effects. In L. S. Liben and M. L. Signorella (Eds.), *Children's gender schemata* (pp. 23–37). San Francisco: Jossey-Bass.

Silverstein, M. (1986). Cognitive implications of a referential hierarchy. In M. Hickmann (Ed.), *Social and functional approaches to language and thought* (pp. 125–164). New York: Academic Press.

Simons, D. J., and Keil, F. C. (1995). An abstract to concrete shift in the development of biological thought: The insides story. *Cognition, 56,* 129–163.

Skyrms, B. (1966). *Choice and chance: An introduction to inductive logic.* Belmont, CA: Dickenson.

Slobin, D. I. (1981). The origins of grammatical encoding of events. In W. Deutsch (Ed.), *The child's construction of language* (pp. 185–199). London: Academic Press.

Sloman, S. A. (1993). Feature-based induction. *Cognitive Psychology, 25,* 231–280.

Smith, C. L. (1979). Children's understanding of natural language hierarchies. *Journal of Experimental Child Psychology, 27,* 437–458.

Smith, C. L. (1980). Quantifiers and question answering in young children. *Journal of Experimental Child Psychology, 30,* 191–205.

Smith, C., Carey, S., and Wiser, M. (1985). On differentiation: A case study of the development of the concepts of size, weight, and density. *Cognition, 21,* 177–237.

Smith, E. E. (1989). Concepts and induction. In M. I. Posner (Ed.), *Foundations of cognitive science* (pp. 501–526). Cambridge, MA: MIT Press.

Smith, E. E., and Medin, D. (1981). *Categories and concepts.* Cambridge: Harvard University Press.

Smith, E. E., and Osherson, D. (1988). Compositionality and typicality. In S. Schiffer and S. Stelle (Eds.), *Cognition and representation.* Boulder, CO: Westview Press.

Smith, E. E., Patalano, A. L., and Jonides, J. (1998). Alternative strategies of categorization. *Cognition, 65,* 167–196.

Smith, J., and Russell, G. (1984). Why do males and females differ? Children's beliefs about sex differences. *Sex Roles, 11,* 1111–1120.

Smith, L. B. (1995). Self-organizing processes in learning to learn words: Development is not induction. In C. A. Nelson (Ed.), *Basic and applied perspectives on learning, cognition, and development: The Minnesota Symposia on Child Psychology, Vol. 28* (pp. 1–32).

Smith, L. B. (2000). Learning how to learn words: An associative crane. In *Becoming a word learner: A debate on lexical acquisition* (pp. 51–80). New York: Oxford University Press.

Smith, L. B., and Heise, D. (1992). Perceptual similarity and conceptual structure. In B. Burns (Ed.), *Percepts, concepts and categories* (pp. 233–272). Amsterdam: North-Holland.

Smith, L. B., and Jones, S. S. (1993). Cognition without concepts. *Cognitive Development, 8,* 181–188.

Smith, L. B., Jones, S. S., and Landau, B. (1996). Naming in young children: A dumb attentional mechanism? *Cognition, 60,* 143–171.

Sober, E. (1994). *From a biological point of view.* NY: Cambridge University Press.

Soja, N. N., Carey, S., and Spelke, E. S. (1991). Ontological categories guide young children's inductions of word meaning: Object terms and substance terms. *Cognition, 38,* 179–211.

Soja, N. N., Carey, S., and Spelke, E. S. (1992). Perception, ontology, and word meaning. *Cognition, 45,* 101–107.

Solomon, G. E. A., and Johnson, S. C. (2000). Conceptual change in the classroom: Teaching young children to understand biological inheritance. *British Journal of Developmental Psychology, 18,* 81–96.

Solomon, G. E. A., Johnson, S. C., Zaitchik, D., and Carey, S. (1996). Like father, like son: Young children's understanding of how and why offspring resemble their parents. *Child Development, 67,* 151–171.

Sorrentino, C. M. (2001). Children and adults represent proper names as referring to unique individuals. *Developmental Science, 4,* 399–407.

Spelke, E. S., Kestenbaum, R., Simons, D. J., and Wein, D. (1995). Spatio-temporal continuity, smoothness of motion, and object identity in infancy. *British Journal of Developmental Psychology, 13,* 113–142.

Sperber, D. (1975). Pourquoi les animaux parfaits, les hybrides et les monstres sont-ils bon à penser symboliquement? *L'Homme, 15*, 5–24.

Sperber, D. (1994). The modularity of thought and the epidemiology of representations. In L. A. Hirschfeld and S. A. Gelman (Eds.), *Mapping the mind: Domain specificity in cognition and culture* (pp. 39–67). New York, NY: Cambridge University Press.

Sperber, D. (1996). *Explaining culture: A naturalistic approach.* Oxford: Blackwell Publishers.

Springer, K. (1992). Children's awareness of the biological implications of kinship. *Child Development, 63*, 950–959.

Springer, K. (1995, April). *The role of factual knowledge in a naive theory of biology.* Paper presented at the meeting of the Society for Research in Child Development, Indianapolis.

Springer, K. (1996). Young children's understanding of a biological basis of parent-offspring relations. *Child Development, 67*, 2841–2856.

Springer, K., and Keil, F. C. (1989). On the development of biologically specific beliefs: The case of inheritance. *Child Development, 60*, 637–648.

Springer, K., and Keil, F. C. (1991). Early differentiation of causal mechanisms appropriate to biological and nonbiological kinds. *Child Development, 62*, 767–781.

Springer, K., and Ruckel, J. (1992). Early beliefs about the cause of illness: Evidence against immanent justice. *Cognitive Development, 7*, 429–443.

Steinem, G. (1964). Beatle with a future. *Cosmopolitan.* [reprinted in: E. Thomson and D. Gutman (Eds.). (1987). *The Lennon companion* (pp. 31–38). New York: Schirmer Books.]

Sternberg, R. J., Chawarski, M. C., and Allbritton, D. W. (1998). If you changed your name and appearance to those of Elvis Presley, who would you be? Historical features in categorization. *American Journal of Psychology, 111*, 327–351.

Stoler, A. (1995). *Race and the education of desire: Foucault's history of sexuality and the colonial order of things.* Duke University Press.

Strevens, M. (2000). The essentialist aspect of naive theories. *Cognition, 74*, 149–175.

Sylvia, C., and Novak, W. (1997). *A change of heart.* Boston: Little, Brown.

Tajfel, H. (1970). Experiments in intergroup discrimination. *Scientific American, 223*, 96–102.

Tardif, T. (1996). Nouns are not always learned before verbs: Evidence from Mandarin speakers' early vocabularies. *Developmental Psychology, 32*, 492–504.

Tardif, T. Z., Gelman, S. A., and Xu, F. (1999). Putting the "noun bias" in context: A comparison of Mandarin and English. *Child Development, 70*, 620–635.

Tardif, T., and Wellman, H. M. (2000). Acquisition of mental state language in Mandarin- and Cantonese-speaking children. *Developmental Psychology, 36*, 25–43.

Taylor, M. (1984). Seeing and believing: Children's understanding of the distinction between appearance and reality. *Child Development, 55*, 1710–1720.

Taylor, M. G. (1993). *Children's beliefs about the biological and social origins of gender differences.* Unpublished Ph.D. dissertation, University of Michigan, Ann Arbor.

Taylor, M. G. (1996). The development of children's beliefs about social and biological aspects of gender differences. *Child Development, 67*, 1555–71.

Taylor, M. G. (1997, April). *Boys will be boys, cows will be cows: Children's causal reasoning about human and animal development.* Poster presented at the biennial meeting of the Society for Research in Child Development, Washington, DC.

Taylor, M. G., and Gelman, S. A. (1993). Children's gender and age-based categorization in similarity and induction tasks. *Social Development, 2*, 104–121.

Templeton, A. R. (1998). Human races: A genetic and evolutionary perspective. *American Anthropologist, 100,* 632–650.

Thagard, P. (2000). Explaining disease: Correlations, causes, and mechanisms. In F. C. Keil and R. A. Wilson (Eds.), *Explanation and cognition* (pp. 255–276). Cambridge, MA: MIT Press.

Thomson, J. R., and Chapman, R. S. (1977). Who is "Daddy" revisited: The status of two-year-olds' over-extended words in use and comprehension. *Journal of Child Language, 4,* 359–375.

Thompson, E. P. (1963). *The making of the English working class.* New York: Pantheon Books.

Tomasello, M. (1999). *The cultural origins of human cognition.* Cambridge, MA: Harvard University Press.

Tomasello, M., and Akhtar, N. (2000). Five questions for any theory of word learning. In *Becoming a word learner: A debate on lexical acquisition* (pp. 179–186). New York: Oxford University Press.

Tversky, B., and Hemenway, K. (1984). Objects, parts, and categories. *Journal of Experimental Psychology: General, 113,* 169–193.

Ullian, D. (1976). The development of conceptions of masculinity and femininity. In B. Lloyd and J. Archer (Eds.), *Exploring sex differences.* London: Academic Press.

Vendler, Z. (1967). Each and every, any and all. In Z. Vendler, *Linguistics in philosophy.* Ithaca, NY: Cornell University Press.

Vygotsky, L. S. (1934/1962). *Thought and language.* Cambridge, MA: MIT Press.

Walker, S. J. (1992). Supernatural beliefs, natural kinds, and conceptual structure. *Memory and Cognition, 20,* 655–662.

Ward, T. B. (1983). Response tempo and separable-integral responding: Evidence for an integral-to-separable processing sequence in visual perception. *Journal of Experimental Psychology: Human Perception and Performance, 9,* 103–112.

Waxman, S. R. (1991). Convergences between semantic and conceptual organization in the preschool years. In S. A. Gelman and J. P. Byrnes (Eds.), *Perspectives on language and cognition: Interrelations in development* (pp. 107–145). New York: Cambridge University Press.

Waxman, S. R. (1999). The dubbing ceremony revisited: Object naming and categorization in infancy and early childhood. In D. L. Medin and S. Atran (Eds.), *Folkbiology* (pp. 233–284). Cambridge, MA: MIT Press.

Waxman, S. R. (in press). Links between object categorization and naming: Origins and emergence in human infants. In D. H. Rakison and L. M. Oakes (Eds.), *Early category and concept development: Making sense of the blooming, buzzing confusion.* New York: Oxford University Press.

Waxman, S. R., and Booth, A. E. (2000). Principles that are invoked in the acquisition of words, but not facts. *Cognition, 77,* B33–B43.

Waxman, S. R., and Booth, A. E. (2001). On the insufficiency of evidence for a domain-general account of word learning. *Cognition, 78,* 277–279.

Waxman, S. R., and Braig, B. (1996, April). *Stars and starfish: How far can shape take us?* Paper presented at the International Conference on Infant Studies, Providence, RI.

Waxman, S. R., and Hall, D. G. (1993). The development of a linkage between count nouns and object categories: Evidence from 16- to 21-month-old infants. *Child Development, 64,* 1224–1241.

Waxman, S. R., and Hatch, T. (1992). Beyond the basics: Preschool children label objects flexibly at multiple hierarchical levels. *Journal of Child Language, 19*, 153–166.

Waxman, S. R., Lynch, E. B., Casey, K. L., and Baer, L. (1997). Setters and samoyeds: The emergence of subordinate level categories as a basis for inductive inference. *Developmental Psychology, 33*, 1074–1090.

Waxman, S. R., and Markow, D. B. (1995). Words as invitations to form categories: Evidence from 12- to 13-month-old infants. *Cognitive Psychology, 29*, 257–302.

Waxman, S. R., Senghas, A., and Benveniste, S. (1997). A cross-linguistic examination of the noun-category bias: Its existence and specificity in French- and Spanish-speaking preschool-aged children. *Cognitive Psychology, 32*, 183–218.

Waxman, S. R., Shipley, E. F., and Shepperson, B. (1991). Establishing new subcategories: The role of category labels and existing knowledge. *Child Development, 62*, 127–138.

Weissman, M. D., and Kalish, C. W. (1999). The inheritance of desired characteristics: Children's view of the role of intention in parent-offspring resemblance. *Journal of Experimental Child Psychology, 73*, 245–265.

Welder, A. N., and Graham, S. A. (2001). The influence of shape similarity and shared labels on infants' inductive inferences about nonobvious object properties. *Child Development, 72*, 1653–1673.

Wellman, H. M. (1990). *The child's theory of mind.* Cambridge, MA: MIT Press.

Wellman, H., and Gelman, S. A. (1988). Children's understanding of the nonobvious. In R. J. Sternberg (Ed.), *Advances in the psychology of human intelligence,* Vol. 4 (pp. 99–135). Hillsdale, NJ: Erlbaum.

Wellman, H. M., and Gelman, S. A. (1992). Cognitive development: Foundational theories of core domains. *Annual Review of Psychology, 43*, 337–375.

Wellman, H. M., and Gelman, S. A. (1998). Knowledge acquisition. In D. Kuhn and R. Siegler (Eds.), *Handbook of child psychology,* 4th ed., *Cognitive development* (pp. 523–573). New York: Wiley.

Werner, H., and Kaplan, B. (1963). *Symbol formation: An organismic-developmental approach to language and the expression of thought.* New York: Wiley.

White, E., Elsom, B., and Prawat, R. (1978). Children's conceptions of death. *Child Development, 49*, 307–310.

White, E. B. (1945). *Stuart Little.* New York: Harper and Brothers.

White, P. A. (1989). A theory of causal processing. *British Journal of Psychology, 80*, 431–454.

White, P. A. (1995). *The understanding of causation and the production of action: From infancy to adulthood.* Hove, England: Erlbaum.

Whitehead, H. (1986). The varieties of fertility cults in New Guinea (Parts 1 and 2). *American Ethnologist, 13*, 80–99, 271–289.

Whorf, B. L. (1956). *Language, thought, and reality.* Cambridge, MA: MIT Press.

Wierzbicka, A. (1994). The universality of taxonomic categorization and the indispensability of the concept "kind." *Rivista di Linguistica, 6*, 347–364.

Wilcox, T., and Baillargeon, R. (1998). Object individuation in infancy: The use of featural information in reasoning about occlusion events. *Cognitive Psychology, 37*, 97–155.

Williamson, T. (1994). *Vagueness.* London: Routledge.

Wilson, R. A. (1999). Realism, essence, and kind: Resuscitating species essentialism? In R. A. Wilson (Ed.), *Species: New interdisciplinary essays* (pp. 187–207). Cambridge, MA: MIT Press.

Winnicott, D. W. (1969). *The child, the family, and the outside world.* Baltimore: Penguin Books.

Wisniewski, E. J. (1995). Prior knowledge and functionally relevant features in concept learning. *Journal of Experimental Psychology: Learning, Memory, and Cognition, 21,* 449–468.

Wisniewski, E. J., and Medin, D. L. (1994). On the interaction of theory and data in concept learning. *Cognitive Science, 18,* 221–281.

Wittgenstein, L. (1953). *Philosophical investigations.* Oxford: Basil Blackwell.

Wolf, A. W., and Lozoff, B. (1989). Object attachment, thumbsucking, and the passage to sleep. *Journal of the American Academy of Child and Adolescent Psychiatry, 28,* 287–292.

Wood, C. C. (1976). Discriminability, response bias, and phoneme categories in discrimination of voice onset time. *Journal of the Acoustical Society of America, 60,* 1381–1389.

Woodward, A. L. (2000). Constraining the problem space in early word learning. In *Becoming a word learner: A debate on lexical acquisition* (pp. 81–114). New York: Oxford University Press.

Xu, F. (1999). Object individuation and object identity in infancy: The role of spatiotemporal information, object property information, and language. *Acta Psychologica, 102,* 113–136.

Xu, F. (in press). The development of object individuation in infancy. In J. Fagen and H. Haynes (Eds.), *Progress in infancy research, Vol. 3.* Mahwah, NJ: Erlbaum.

Xu, F., and Carey, S. (1996). Infants' metaphysics: The case of numerical identity. *Cognitive Psychology, 30,* 111–153.

Yamauchi, T., and Markman, A. B. (1998). Category learning by inference and classification. *Journal of Memory and Language, 39,* 124–148.

Younger, B. (1990). Infants' detection of correlations among feature categories. *Child Development, 61,* 614–620.

Zadeh, L. A. (1982). A note on prototype theory and fuzzy sets. *Cognition, 12,* 291–297.

Author Index

Subject Index